FESTIVALS OF FREEDOM

FESTIVALS

OF FREEDOM

MEMORY AND MEANING IN
AFRICAN AMERICAN
EMANCIPATION CELEBRATIONS,
1808–1915

MITCH KACHUN

UNIVERSITY OF MASSACHUSETTS PRESS
Amherst and Boston

LC 2003002465
ISBN 1-55849-407-3

Designed by Milenda Nan Ok Lee
Set in Adobe Minion and Bodoni Poster Condensed
by Binghamton Valley Composition
Printed and bound by Thomson-Shore, Inc.

Library of Congress Cataloging-in-Publication Data

Kachun, Mitchell A. (Mitchell Alan)
    Festivals of freedom : memory and meaning in African American
emancipation celebrations, 1808–1915 / Mitch Kachun.
        p. cm.
Includes bibliographical references and index.
    ISBN 1-55849-407-3 (alk. paper)
    1. Slaves—Emancipation—United States—Anniversaries, etc. 2.
African Americans—Anniversaries, etc. 3. African Americans—Politics
and government—19th century. 4. African Americans—Politics and
government—20th century. 5. Political culture—United States—
History—19th century. 6. Political culture—United States—
History—20th century. 7. Festivals—United States—History
—19th century. 8. Festivals—United States—History—20th century.
9. Memory—Social aspects—United States—History. 10. Memory—
Political aspects—United States—History. I. Title.

E453 .K33 2003
326'.8'0973—dc21

                                                    2003002465

British Library Cataloguing in Publication data are available.

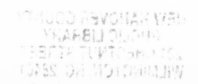

For my father
Steve Kachun
1922–1986

CONTENTS

Illustrations follow page 146.

ACKNOWLEDGMENTS

In a project that has been in progress for nearly ten years, I have of course incurred intellectual and personal debts too numerous to list. Colleagues, university administrators, library and archive personnel, students, friends, and family members have all helped make the completion of this project possible.

I would like to thank Michael Kammen, Robert L. Harris Jr., and Nick Salvatore at Cornell University for their unflagging support and patience during early stages of this project; their comments and criticisms invariably steered me toward more intellectually challenging engagements with both my sources and my interpretations. Their guidance and friendship have continued through the years since I left Ithaca. I also owe thanks to others from Cornell's History Department, especially R. Laurence Moore, David Sabean, and Margaret Washington, each of whom added immensely to my appreciation for the discipline of historical study. My cohort of graduate students at Cornell provided a collegial atmosphere for the exchange of both ideas and lamentations as we wended our way through various intellectual, personal, and bureaucratic crises.

Administrators and staff at Southeast Community College in Lincoln, Nebraska, provided support for further research and development of this project far beyond what might be expected from a teaching institution. Special thanks to Richard Ross, Sharon Hanna, and Barbara Tracy for their friendship. Also in Nebraska, members of the Nineteenth-Century Studies Group at the University of Nebraska–Lincoln, especially Benjamin Rader, Dane Kennedy, and Timothy Mahoney, provided valuable commentary and much-appreciated collegiality during my sojourn in Huskerland. While a visiting professor at Grand Valley State University, in Allendale, Michigan, I was made to feel accepted and appreciated, and I am particularly grateful for support from Frances Kelleher and Dean Donald Williams.

At Western Michigan University, fellow members of the History Department have been welcoming, supportive, and truly collegial. I am thankful for having found a place among such stimulating scholars and such warm and reasonable people. Special thanks to Robert Berkhofer, Amos Beyan, Linda Borish, Juanita De Barros, Nora Faires, Marion W. Gray, Bruce Haight, Barbara Havira, Catherine Julien, Carolyn Podruchny, John Saillant, Larry J. Simon, and Judith F. Stone. Western Michigan University also provided financial support for securing the images used in this book.

I owe a special debt of gratitude to David Blight, who read multiple versions of the manuscript, generously offered his encouragement and feedback, and introduced my work to Clark Dougan of the University of Massachusetts Press. Clark, Carol Betsch, and the rest of the Press's staff have been consistently supportive and patient in shepherding me through my first book and have helped make this a positive and relatively painless experience. Thanks also to the anonymous manuscript readers, whose comments challenged me to develop and refine the book's scope and argument. Anne R. Gibbons was a careful and efficient copy editor who prevented a number of potentially embarrassing errors and maintained her cordial manner even when I insisted on having things my way.

I have benefited greatly from friends and colleagues who graciously agreed to read portions of the manuscript, or who commented on material at conferences and colloquia. These include Richard Blackett, Dickson Bruce, James L. Conyers Jr., Roy Finkenbine, Jacqueline Goggin, Stephen G. Hall, Graham Hodges, James O. Horton, Lois E. Horton, Ellen Litwicki, David Lowenthal, Richard Newman, William Pencak, Patrick Rael, Linda Reed, John Saillant, Kirk Savage, Karen Sotiropoulos, Michael Vorenberg, David Waldstreicher, Shane White, and Julie Winch. Without question this book profited from their ideas and comments. I must also thank Paul Lee of Detroit, Michigan, independent scholar extraordinaire and director of Best Efforts, Inc., who missed a deadline because he genially acquiesced to my occupation of his favorite microfilm copier at Wayne State University's Reuther Library.

My deepest thanks go to my family for putting up with me through all of this. My entry into graduate school was virtually simultaneous with the birth of my daughter, Michelle Kachman, and the genesis of this project corresponded more closely than was comfortable with the arrival of my son, Silas Kachman. You both have lived with this book for as long as you can remember. Thank you for being there to keep my priorities in order, and also to occasionally ask, "Aren't you done with that yet?" Without my partner in life, Karen Libman, this book would never have been begun, let alone completed. Putting your own work on hold, always there with your counsel, you have sustained and nurtured me in every conceivable way. You mean everything to me. I cannot begin to thank my mother, Elsie Kachun, for her unwavering love and support through all my life's twists and turns. Even when you did not understand my choices and changes, you always let me know that you believed in me. This book is dedicated to my father, Steve Kachun, who left this life far too soon. I try to imagine what you would think of all this, and wish you were here to tell me.

INTRODUCTION

Tradition . . . cannot be inherited, and if you want it you must obtain it by great labour.

—T. S. Eliot

The white American has charged the Negro American with being without past or tradition (something which strikes the white man with a nameless horror) . . . ; and the Negro knows that both were "mammy-made" right here at home. What's more, each secretly believes that he alone knows what is valid in the American experience.

—Ralph Ellison

THE MEANING of a nation's history is always at issue, always up for grabs; and it is consistent with America's egalitarian ethos that anyone can reach for the interpretive gold ring. As the historian James M. McPherson has written, "no license is required to practice history in the United States."[1] Amateur historians, journalists, and history buffs have a long record of participation in public historical discourse. The emergence of the Internet has provided a new forum for the discussion and exegesis of historical topics open to all with the desire and the wherewithal to participate. A curious mix of academics and amateurs with a wide range of interests and levels of knowledge can be found in cyberspace discussing Lincoln's attitudes toward black suffrage, the relative bloodthirstiness of male and female potentates, and even the appropriateness of aficionados without academic credentials considering themselves "historians."

But if, at some level, everyone can be his or her own historian, factors of time, money, access to public discourse, and perceived legitimacy severely restrict the impact that the perspective of an individual can have on the rest of society. Academic historians in the 1990s expressed alarm that the Disney Corporation's proposed historic theme park, "Disney's America," would deliver its version of the American past to more people in a single business day than a college professor might reach during the course of a career. And, at the level of the individual, the survivor of an attempted lynching, without access to some public forum, cannot really communicate his or her distinctive perspective on the past beyond family and friends. Egalitarianism may apply to the *right* to interpret the past, but the *dissemination* of a given interpretation requires resources and public acceptance possessed by relatively few.[2]

Modern Americans encounter the past in a wide variety of forms: brilliantly (and poorly) conceived documentaries, Hollywood feature films, and made-for-TV movies; erudite academic texts and pulp fiction; museums, historic monuments, and amusement parks; newspapers, magazines, and Web sites of uneven credibility; and discussions among families, friends, and coworkers. Drawing upon multifarious images and opinions, we each construct (often with less conscious labor than Eliot ascribed to the poet) our own version of the American past and develop our own sense of American traditions. But the fact remains that we all must arrive at some understanding of the past in which our own existence and experience make sense. If the predominant interpretations we encounter and absorb provide a context for our lives that is unflattering or untenable, we must resign ourselves to accept the unacceptable or else go about constructing a past that has validity and provides meaning and a tolerable framework for our lives. The validity of a particular construction of the past, then, is somewhat subjective and is in large part dependent upon its usefulness to those who would accept such a construction.[3]

The creation of a "usable past," to borrow Van Wyck Brooks's exceedingly usable phrase, emanates from motives that are deeply personal and yet that also have broad implications in the realm of cultural politics. The extent to which a nation or a people can reach some consensus regarding its past and traditions defines the degree to which it can truly consider itself a coherent cultural entity. Ralph Ellison's speculation regarding white and black Americans' contestation over the meaning of their immutably linked histories reminds us that the necessity for creating a usable past is presupposed by the horrifying prospect of a people not having a past or tradition upon which to build.

Unthinkable as that notion was, in Ellison's view, for white Americans, it has been equally untenable for their black fellow citizens. For generations African American intellectuals and community leaders have expended considerable energy in refuting the assumption that blacks have no past or traditions. The recent debates over multiculturalism and Afrocentric versions of the past are not entirely new—they represent the latest incarnation of ideas with a long history among African American intellectuals. At least from the earliest years of the nineteenth century, black Americans consciously and publicly exercised their right to interpret and make use of the past. They made every effort against great odds to disseminate, among themselves and throughout the larger society, a vision of their experience in

America that captured the inherent tension between their distinctiveness as a people and their fundamental right to claim the status of American citizens. I explore the history of this discourse by focusing on African Americans' use of public commemorations to construct a firm foundation of history and tradition—a usable past—upon which to erect the edifice of African American identity between the early nineteenth and early twentieth centuries.

⋆This book presents an interpretive overview of African American freedom festivals and their place in American political culture from the first celebrations of the abolition of the Atlantic Slave Trade in 1808 through the fiftieth anniversary of U.S. emancipation in 1915.[4] One theme that suffuses this study is that African Americans' public Freedom Day commemorations were consistently used for the purposes of defining, revising, and retelling the collective history of African American people. Both the content and the context were subject to change, but celebration organizers persisted in passing the story of the people from one generation to the next, and creating commemorative traditions to be carried on. Another central theme, an important concomitant of the first, relates to the ongoing conflict and controversy public commemorations generated, not merely between blacks and the white-dominated broader society but also among black leaders and within black communities. After examining hundreds of freedom festivals over this long time period, I am struck by the complexity of the story they offer us about the African American individuals and communities who organized and argued about them. And argue they did. As much as the Freedom Day tradition illustrates the persistence of blacks' claiming the right to control their own history, it just as clearly calls our attention to the bitter antagonisms that often divided black leaders and black communities over issues of politics, activism, economics, and culture. The prominence of these themes suggests the significance of public freedom festivals for understanding African Americans' cultural and political agendas during the nineteenth century.

The study of emancipation celebrations must necessarily blur the lines of political, cultural, social, and intellectual history. This is the case partly because of the very broad functions the celebrations served for black communities, and partly because the somewhat arbitrary categories of political, social, cultural, and intellectual cannot fully reflect the complex realities experienced by individuals in their daily lives. In some respects these can be useful conventions for historians trying to make sense of the past, but at the same time these categories impose restrictions on how we view events and individuals and motives that necessarily distort the complex lived realities we seek to understand. Clearly, organizers of celebrations were acting politically, had a desire to affect blacks' cultural practices, were concerned with economic and social issues, and were operating under certain intellectual assumptions that shaped their worldview and their activism. At times in my analysis I will doubtless slip into the conventions of talking about culture, or politics, or civil rights activism as if they were separate and distinct from one another. I want to emphasize at the outset my recognition that these categories are largely conveniences and that emancipation celebrations and the activities surrounding them were complex and multilayered events not so easily reduced to simple categorization.

Indeed, one of the reasons these celebrations were so important is that they touched upon so many aspects and elements of black experiences, attitudes, priorities, and actions during the period under study. While much of my attention is directed toward issues of history, tradition, and memory, blacks' public freedom festivals also served a number of additional overlapping functions, both for local and regional African American communities and for broader-based abolitionist, civil rights, and race uplift movements across this period. Many of the functions and patterns of celebration and commemoration maintained a remarkable continuity between the early nineteenth and early twentieth centuries. However, shifting social, cultural, and political contexts, as well as increasing contestation within African American communities regarding collective memory, public conduct, political orientation, and other issues, contributed to significant transformations in the practice and meaning of these commemorative observances, especially during the half century after 1865.

Throughout the nineteenth century—and especially after the disruptions and realignments created by the Civil War and Reconstruction—both blacks and whites struggled to assess and interpret African Americans' place in the American polity. Black leaders used every forum at their disposal to demonstrate—primarily to whites—that African Americans were worthy of full inclusion as citizens, with access to education, jobs, housing, and political participation limited only by individual ability rather than racial designation. At the same time black leaders were concerned with the education and uplift of the race. They worked to expand intraracial communications among freeborn and newly freed, northerners and southerners, urban and rural orientations, and the various religious denominations, fraternal organizations, and other cultural institutions that provided the framework of African American community life.

Much of this discourse, whether internal to the black community or directed toward a wider audience, emanated from a relatively small and diffuse fellowship of ministers, educators, journalists, businessmen, fraternalists, and others who assumed the roles of national spokespersons and leaders of black America. Before the Civil War these leaders were primarily concerned with the abolition of slavery in the South and the acquisition of full citizenship rights for blacks across the nation. After emancipation the quest for nondiscriminatory inclusion in the national family consumed most of their energies. As they approached this enterprise in both the antebellum and postbellum periods, many of these leaders assumed a solicitous stance toward the cultural values that had formed under slavery. They were extremely concerned with eradicating much of slave culture and inculcating a Christian morality based on self-restraint, education, a strong work ethic, religion, and sobriety. While many of these leaders were themselves southern-born, those with institutional bases (e.g., church, newspaper, fraternal organization, women's club) were often tied more to the North than to the South. Even southern-born men like South Carolinians Henry McNeal Turner and Daniel Payne claimed to have been deeply influenced by what they considered northern values. Turner wrote disparagingly of southern "lethargical inertness" compared with "northern energy," and Payne said that his "noblest ideas" emerged from "Northern institutions, on Northern soil, under Northern influences." And while a good number were, in fact, former slaves, their cultural ideals reflected a moral vision that was often at odds with the lives of the masses of black Americans whose value systems had been largely shaped under the peculiar institution.[5]

Nationally recognized leaders like Samuel Cornish, Charles B. Ray, Daniel Payne, Benjamin T. Tanner, Frederick Douglass, Josephine St. Pierre Ruffin, Frances E. W. Harper, and others who adhered to this moral code were not simply absorbing an ideology imposed by the dominant society. They were living according to a strict standard of personal responsibility that was rooted in their identities as black men and women, as Americans, and as Christians. To a large extent their lives were organized around a sense of commitment to the advancement of themselves, of their communities, and of the entire race. The same was true of the many community activists among the black working poor and middle classes who exerted their influence more narrowly, as leaders in local church, fraternal, or benevolent activities. Their relative anonymity notwithstanding, these largely forgotten local activists lived their lives as members of the same moral community as their better-remembered colleagues. Beyond their essential personal commitments to right living, these African Americans were well aware of the tangible and intangible rewards available in American society, and they hoped to reap those rewards—for themselves and for the race—by behaving as respectable and responsible citizens.[6]

Inextricably bound up with these activists' self-definition as respectable, Christian Americans was their clear identification of themselves *as blacks.*

They were concerned with fostering, among all African Americans, a sense of themselves as a people—a worthy race with a heritage to be proud of, with heroes to be emulated, with a history of contribution to American culture, and with a significant and positive role to play in the nation's future. This complex sense of their racial and American identities was forged during the antebellum decades and had congealed into a vibrant African American culture of social activism by the eve of the Civil War. Emancipation and enfranchisement seemed for a while to promise blacks a place in the main stream of national life. But as the free-flowing hopes of the early Reconstruction era became clouded by the sediment of disfranchisement, exclusion, Jim Crowism, and racial violence, postbellum African American leaders adjusted accordingly. To be sure, they continued the tradition of activism and protest instituted during the antebellum abolitionist struggle, and for the most part, they stood by their claims to Americanness. But, like their antebellum forebears, they turned inward as well, seeking to establish and maintain a distinctive sense of history and race pride in the face of the racist caricatures proliferating in the mainstream popular culture. African American leadership was perhaps at its best when these drives toward activism and tradition building coalesced as they did in many of the public celebrations held by blacks as they traversed the ground between slavery and freedom.

Black history and black accomplishments, needless to say, were not featured in the curricula of the nation's public schools during the nineteenth century. Popular written histories and textbooks did not mention African Americans as contributors to the culture and history of the United States. Even—or perhaps especially—blacks' role in preserving the Union during the Civil War was being erased from the public memory of that conflict. As Reconstruction gave way to Redemption and white sectional reconciliation, America's popular imagery defined it more forcefully than ever as a "white man's country." To the extent that blacks' presence in the nation was acknowledged in the popular press, they were characterized as a collective "problem," and all the "solutions" involved their complete subordination to a superior white race.[7]

To counter this set of perceptions, African Americans made the most of the relatively limited resources at their disposal. At the end of the Civil War roughly 90 percent of African Americans were illiterate, and many freedpeople had little direct knowledge of the world outside their own plantations. The small minority of educated blacks who could claim some degree of experience in the world as free men and women embraced wholeheartedly the responsibilities of race leadership. Many had been active in the antebellum period and continued activities begun well before emancipation.

They helped to set up schools; they organized denominational church membership; they accelerated the activities of fraternal organizations; they founded military companies and literary societies; and they wrote. They wrote both scholarly and colloquial histories and biographies chronicling African American contributions to the nation and the world; they wrote fiction exposing the cruelties of slavery, the struggles and injustices of the postemancipation period, and the mounting violence of the age of Jim Crow; they wrote historical and social-scientific analyses for the black press. Collectively, these efforts affirmed that African Americans *deserved* the benefits of equal citizenship: they had worked and suffered and sacrificed and celebrated and lived and died in this country; they had *earned* their rights through patriotism and sacrifice; they had heroes and a history in which they could take pride.

➤ Beyond the written material produced by African Americans in this effort to create and perpetuate a usable past, blacks organized and participated in numerous public celebrations—commemorative rituals that attempted to convey a similar message of historical black activism and accomplishment. These festivals of freedom began in the early nineteenth century and became more integral to northern black communities by the 1850s, evolving into huge events that attracted many whites in a racially diverse shared public sphere. Following the Civil War the southern freedpeople were incorporated into this commemorative tradition and blacks played a large part in public celebrations across the nation: many Fourth of July observances in the South were undertaken almost exclusively by African Americans and white Republicans; Decoration Day commemorated the sacrifices of black as well as white Union soldiers. But blacks were most prominent in their own freedom festivals commemorating emancipation and other events connected with black liberation and enfranchisement.

As Reconstruction waned and the age of Jim Crow set in, public commemorations generally became more racially circumscribed events. African Americans were increasingly excluded from national public rituals, and whites withdrew from blacks' commemorations of emancipation. The latter observances were further tarnished by the realities of blatant racism, exclusion, and violence that divested them of their full meaning. After the early 1870s biracial public celebrations took place less frequently; increasingly, black commemorations were attended by more racially uniform crowds in a more racially segregated public sphere.

Nonetheless, African Americans continued to commemorate a variety of historic events and individuals they considered important components of a tradition-in-process. Significantly, however, not all blacks deemed the same individuals worthy of inclusion in the pantheon that was taking shape: was it more appropriate to erect a monument to John Brown or Nat Turner? Even the more widely accepted events were not celebrated in the same ways. Emancipation Day, for example, evoked considerable controversy and discord: Which date was most appropriate (January 1, June 19, August 1, September 22, April 3 . . .)? Were parades proud assertions of freedom and the right to use public space or disgusting and profane displays by the lower classes that opened African Americans to white mockery? Might it be wiser to discontinue emancipation celebrations altogether, since they served only as shameful reminders of the slave past? These and other questions were part of a continuous, if not always prominent, debate that I have followed in the black press during the long century between the 1808 abolition of the Atlantic slave trade and the fiftieth anniversary of U.S. emancipation in 1915.

Much of my evidence for defining the transformation of Freedom Day traditions and for assessing their shifting functions for African American communities comes from newspaper accounts of celebrations; editorials and other contemporary commentaries on the importance of commemoration, history, and memory; and texts of Freedom Day orations. I have also drawn upon the growing body of secondary literature dealing with festive culture, commemoration, and historical memory in American society, and internationally, during this period. Organizers of Freedom Day commemorations throughout the nineteenth century quite consciously and consistently argued that the identity of any people requires a history, a set of heroes, and special days set aside to fix in memory the accomplishments of their forebears. Orations at Freedom Day affairs are consistent in articulating historical interpretations rooted in blacks' experiences and priorities, emphasizing the importance of a people's establishing a commemorative tradition, and arguing for the necessity of passing on a legacy as a foundation upon which coming generations might build. Oration texts and newspaper accounts of these events provide a clear sense of the social, political, and historical roles that Freedom Day events were intended to play.

✘ But those sources also call attention to the intense disagreements that often surfaced regarding freedom festivals and their connection with blacks' political, economic, and cultural priorities. My analysis considers not only the conflicts among celebration proponents, but also the dissenting voices that argued against holding public commemorations in the first place. Especially after the 1870s, increasing numbers of black spokespersons contended that certain aspects of the black past were best forgotten, or that public displays by the black masses did more harm than good, or that financial resources would be better spent elsewhere. These questions of priorities and public presentation, and the related tensions between remembering and forgetting, became prominent themes in black Americans' attention to their history and their commemorative practices during the half century after emancipation.

Nineteenth-century black newspapers provide a remarkable window into these debates. African American editors before and after emancipation were often among the most vocal and opinionated participants in local or national discussions. Their control of a powerful written forum gave them a distinct advantage in spreading their views and in having those views recorded for posterity. Moreover, many were popular as featured orators at commemorations and other public events. Thus black journalists' voices reached large numbers of their fellows through both written and oral forms of expression—an important breadth of coverage among a people rooted in an oral culture and very concerned with the expansion of literacy. The black press, then, was central to the construction of African American commemorative rituals and festive culture, and black journalists, their ideas, and their activism feature prominently in my interpretations.

• In this first book-length historical analysis of nineteenth-century emancipation celebrations, I try to suggest the variety and complexity of these public freedom festivals that became a key part of the historical tradition African Americans were in the process of constructing. This book expands upon previous scholarship in two major ways. First, I offer a coherent interpretation of the various functions these celebrations played among free black communities in the antebellum North, and for a broader spectrum of African Americans after Lincoln's Emancipation Proclamation. Most succinctly, festivals provided opportunities for nineteenth-century blacks *to congregate,* African Americans from across a region coming together to socialize, network, and enjoy themselves with large numbers of their fellows; *to educate,* African American leaders presenting their own truths about the black past and attempting, often against considerable resistance, to instruct the black masses in "appropriate" behavior; and *to agitate,* local and national activists mobilizing their constituencies for action and making their case for equal rights before the court of American public opinion. Second, I survey Freedom Day celebrations from their inception in 1808 into the twentieth century, where I posit a turning point for their meaning in African American culture. In exploring this long span of time, I am purposely breaking away from the rigid custom that seems to make the year 1863 an impenetrable barrier to holistic interpretation. The 1863 Emancipation Proclamation was undeniably a major watershed in African Americans' lives and in their individual and collective memories.[8] But it is important to grasp the equally meaningful continuities between antebellum traditions and their postemancipation counterparts in order to understand more fully the role Freedom Day celebrations played in African American history and culture.

In chapter 1 I discuss the decline of eighteenth-century slave festivals in the northeast and the emergence of the first public commemorations organized by free black Americans in that region. The shift from a culture mired in slavery to one driven by the expanding promise and prospect of freedom is central to understanding the earliest freedom festivals. Starting with the abolition of the Atlantic slave trade in 1808, free blacks in several northern states instituted a tradition of commemoration that attempted to define the race's status within a nation founded upon the principles of liberty and equality. Black Americans recognized, of course, that those founding principles had limited meaning while the vast majority of their brethren were enslaved and the rights of the free remained severely circumscribed. Still, the abolition of the slave trade gave America's people of African descent some hope that they would eventually share fully in the nation's professed ethos. During the first decades of the nineteenth century, African American leaders set important and meaningful precedents. They established public Freedom Day commemorations as important forums for blacks' participation in American political culture. But they also found in those events a venue for airing divisions among themselves over political strategy and cultural orientation. And they met with little success in their attempts to construct a unified and coherent tradition of public commemoration.

Chapter 2 turns to the decades between the 1830s and the 1850s, when black leaders accomplished this goal through commemorations of Great Britain's August 1, 1834, act abolishing slavery in its West Indian colonies. By the 1850s a vibrant commemorative tradition centered on August 1 observances of West Indian emancipation had taken shape throughout the free states, and the freedom festivals became crucial institutions in African American political culture. Hundreds of large, biracial events were held during the antebellum decades, establishing a black presence in an expanding public sphere, articulating black-centered interpretations of history, and establishing freedom festivals as important annual opportunities for black political and social regional networking. The celebrations drew attendees from around a given region, and thus provided African Americans who did not often have opportunity to interact a crucial venue for socializing, renewing acquaintances, establishing business contacts, and strengthening regional activist networks. Freedom festivals were especially important tools for black leaders attempting to bridge the gap between their own orientation toward middle-class values and literacy, and the black masses, whose world was more rooted in face-to-face interaction and the folk culture of slavery. Partly because they occupied this cultural nexus, these events also continued to serve as lightning rods for heated debates that divided antebellum black leaders and black communities over public issues involving class, culture, activism, and conduct, as well as private conflicts over money and ego.

Chapter 3 assesses the events surrounding U.S. emancipation and black male enfranchisement, and the profound changes those events augured for African American freedom festivals. The social and political transformations of the 1860s and 1870s marked the high point of the Freedom Day tradition but also presented new circumstances requiring adaptations that ultimately served to disrupt what had been a largely unified antebellum tradition. After the Civil War, emancipation celebrations expanded in two important ways. First, new dates commemorating the recent emancipatory events worked their way into many communities' commemorative calendars. In addition, emancipation celebrations became possible in the South for the first time, and the freedpeople introduced their own distinctive cultural priorities and practices into what had been an exclusively northern tradition. In part because of this calendrical and geographic expansion, the tradition began to fragment. Disagreement over which dates or events to commemorate, debates over the memory and legacy of slavery, conflict over the proper form of celebration, and the gradual erosion of black rights in the face of white sectional reconciliation combined to disrupt a once focused and vibrant commemorative tradition.

In chapter 4 I move my discussion beyond the freedom festivals in order to examine the broader context of African Americans' attention to history, memory, and public commemoration between the 1860s and the 1910s. As was the case for other groups of Americans, for the nation as a whole, and for nations and peoples around the world, this period saw unprecedented attention to the construction of collective identities and historical memory. Like those other peoples, black Americans used monuments, historical societies, scholarly investigations, and various cultural institutions to construct histories and traditions to define and legitimate their place in the nation and in the world. But black proponents of these endeavors faced many obstacles, both from an increasingly hostile dominant society concerned more with white sectional reconciliation than with black history, and also from other blacks who showed little enthusiasm for black history. Many were ambivalent or even embarrassed about calling attention to the race's past in Africa and in American slavery; probably more were simply indifferent to historical work that seemed to have little relevance for their day to day lives; some were downright hostile to expending limited energies and financial resources on the apparently intangible benefits of monuments and other public historical displays. Attempts to construct a usable past during the late nineteenth century were therefore often frustrating, but many black leaders' attention to the race's history continued to expand.

Chapter 5 returns to the freedom festivals and examines their changing role within this context of remembering and forgetting. Freedom Day celebrations remained widespread throughout the nation during the late nineteenth century, but the functions they served had to be adapted to new cultural and political realities. To some extent black celebrations across the nation served similar needs as vehicles for the political and historical education of a black public that was still largely denied the opportunities of formal schooling. The role of annual social gathering for blacks from around a given region also helped maintain the vitality of the tradition in all sections. But there were regional differences as well. In the North and West, for example, the festivals continued to be important sites of political and civil rights agitation, but southern celebrations were far less likely to broach such controversial issues as Jim Crow tightened the vice of white dominance by the century's end.

While chapter 6 covers the same chronology as the preceding chapter, I use a more geographically focused examination of emancipation celebrations in Washington, D.C., to exemplify the details of the organization and practice of celebration during the late nineteenth century. Both the black population and the Freedom Day tradition in the nation's capital were in many respects distinctive, as were the widespread attention the celebrations generated and the fractious divisions they manifested in the black community. But the in-depth look at the disruption of a once vibrant tradition by the 1890s suggests larger patterns affecting freedom festivals around the nation. I hope this discussion of the celebrations' role in a single community will also suggest the value in using emancipation celebrations as a lens through which to examine how black communities worked with regard to managing community conflicts, negotiating class and race relations, organizing political activism, nurturing institutional development, and defining the responsibilities of local leadership.

By the early twentieth century conflicts like those in Washington, along with broader developments in American society, helped cause the dissolution of the Freedom Day commemorative tradition. Chapter 7 discusses these issues and offers an explanation of why emancipation celebrations fell out of practice among blacks in many cities and towns. Many functions that Freedom Day events had once served for black communities had been absorbed by other practices and institutions, especially as the African American population shifted toward urban areas in the North and South. The attractions of popular culture, the increasing reliance on print media, and the activities of various historical, social, and self-help organizations all contributed to the erosion of Freedom Day commemorations' usefulness and significance. After a brief resurgence of commemorative zeal surrounding the 1915 semicentennial of emancipation, the freedom festivals fell out of practice in many communities, in fact becoming rather rare outside the rural South by the 1920s.

The festivals of freedom discussed in these chapters were crucial sites for debates over the construction of African American historical consciousness and collective memory. Throughout the nineteenth century and into the twentieth, black Americans struggled to resolve tensions inherent in their collective situation. Most fundamentally, African Americans, whether or not they were active participants in commemorative activities, had to define an individual and collective identity that took into account both their incontrovertible right to claim Americanness and their singular experience as a racially distinct and oppressed people. More specific to the question of African Americans' collective memory of their unique past, blacks had to balance the need to preserve, interpret, and disseminate their heritage and history with the desire to eradicate many of the more painful and degrading aspects of that history. African Americans' thinking on these and other related issues, of course, was never monolithic. At times their grappling with issues of identity led to considerable disagreement—rooted in differences of class, region, color, and more—over who held the power to define black identity and black culture. These tensions—between Americanness and distinctiveness, between constructive memory and selective amnesia, between middle-class values and the folk culture of slavery—lay at the crux of African Americans' struggles with historical memory and collective identity. To the considerable extent that they provided a forum for these debates, African Americans' freedom festivals became important rituals of self-definition and legitimation for a people in the process of becoming.[9]

These public commemorations—indeed the very presence of such a commemorative tradition—provided important vehicles for making statements about African Americans' collective identity and history, both to themselves and to the American nation. This is important for historians to pay attention to for many reasons, one of which is to help us understand the development of African American historical thinking *before* what scholars tend to identify as the beginnings of African American historiography around 1915 with Carter G. Woodson. African American historical consciousness was expressed in various written and nonwritten forms throughout the nineteenth century, and these interpretations are important not only for understanding subsequent historiographical traditions but also for understanding how historical knowledge was disseminated among African American communities, and especially across generational lines, before written histories and school instruction were widely available. It is important and useful to recognize an overlap and complement between written approaches that historians are often more comfortable with, and perhaps more likely to recognize as legitimate, and oral or visual presentations of historical information that may have been just as effective, perhaps more so in particular times and places, in delivering history lessons to a broad-based black audience.

I also hope that the interpretations I offer and the questions I raise can provide a springboard for subsequent analyses of blacks' public commemorations. This scholarship might proceed in a variety of directions: chronologically, looking at how commemorative traditions continued to change during the twentieth century; transnationally, comparing African Americans' practices with those among blacks in other parts of the diaspora; and in the opposite direction, looking more closely at the ways black commemorations worked in particular American communities and regions. Local and community studies of Freedom Day traditions are particularly important because, ultimately, it is at the community level that we can really see how these events worked and what they meant for the people who participated in them. Our understanding of the "big picture" has to be based on our understanding of what people were doing and thinking at the local level. While I do suggest some of the local particularities relating to Washington, D.C., celebrations in chapter 6, I have not made an intensive study of any community or region. But there is a great opportunity to connect the broad-based findings I present here with the more narrowly focused research of historians working at the community and regional level. Emancipation celebrations can provide a useful window into the ways black communities operated internally, how they connected with one another across a region, and how particular local traditions fit into broader national patterns. Given the rapid growth of regional and community studies, this is one area where connections between microanalysis and macroanalysis can refine our understandings of African American history.

The fundamental underlying argument in this book, one with which the nineteenth-century African Americans it features would heartily concur, is that collective memory matters. That it matters is as clear to those who would erase the memory of the past as it is to those who would preserve that memory. Iwona Irwin-Zarecka has coined the term "memory project" to describe efforts "to give presence to the previously absent or silenced past . . . both through explicit 'editorials' and [through the] unabashed creation of new symbolic resources."[10] Though their efforts at times exhibited considerable multivocality and contention, and lacked an overarching sense of design, nineteenth-century African Americans entered upon just such a project as they struggled with the simultaneous pain and pride inherent in the race's turbulent history. They also struggled to construct a historical interpretation of their collective experience that incorporated both their uncompromising assertion of the right to enjoy the full fruits of American citizenship and their equally intense affirmation of a history and heritage that was uniquely their own. They did, in T. S. Eliot's phrase, obtain their traditions through great labor. I wish both to recognize and to critically assess the nature of those labors as African Americans laid claim not only to the past but also to the power to define that past.

CHAPTER ONE

"A DAY OF PUBLICK THANKSGIVING"

FOUNDATIONS, 1808–1834

Let the first of January, the day of the abolition of the slave trade in our country, be set apart in every year, as a day of publick thanksgiving for that mercy. Let the history of the sufferings of our brethren, and of their deliverance, descend by this means to the remotest generations; and when they shall ask, in time to come, saying, What mean the lessons, the psalms, the prayers and the praises in the worship of this day? let us answer them.

—Absalom Jones, 1808

Without meetings, without rituals, ceremonies, myths and symbols, there can be no great people. Afro-Americans, recognizing this, . . . went out into the alleys and the fields and formed their own institutions and, in the process, invented themselves.

—Lerone Bennett Jr., 1968

PHILADELPHIA CLERGYMAN Absalom Jones, when he delivered his sermon on the United States' abolition of the Atlantic slave trade on January 1, 1808, identified key elements of an incipient African American commemorative tradition that would persist for more than a century. To give thanks to heavenly and earthly benefactors was certainly of central concern to the pastor of St. Thomas's African Episcopal Church. But of at least equal importance was Jones's explicit exhortation that the ongoing public observance of the occasion should serve as an opportunity to explain the lessons of history and the meaning inherent in the event, especially to the youth of his day and to generations yet unborn. Jones's vision extended far into the future of his race and his nation. Between 1808 and the late 1820s public festive rituals among northern free blacks underwent important changes and were, as Jones hoped, becoming integral components of a maturing African American political culture. But African Americans' regular participation in a different sort of public ritual and celebration had been established several generations earlier. An assessment of the characteristics, functions, and meanings of nineteenth-century African American Freedom Day celebrations must begin, then, at least briefly, with their precursors in the slave festivals of the pre-Revolutionary period.

By the middle of the eighteenth century, enslaved Africans in the North American colonies had begun to use public space in ways that established important precedents for their cultural descendants in the nineteenth. In certain respects, the eighteenth century provided more open access to black participation in public life than was later the case. Notwithstanding the entrenchment of racial slavery in the colonies by the early eighteenth century, the hierarchical social order of colonial society still offered opportunities for regular and ongoing social relations among blacks and whites, at least among the lower orders of society. The size and intimacy of northern cities provided particularly fertile environments for interracial contact, and crowd actions, work relationships, social interactions, and sexual liaisons across race lines were far from uncommon. As the case of Crispus Attucks testifies, black political action in mixed-race groups extended at least into the Revolutionary era.[1] Within this matrix of public activity, no form of colonial African American public life had more direct bearing on later commemorative traditions than blacks' activities during the so-called slave festivals in the Northeast.

Well before the abolition of the Atlantic slave trade, and continuing sporadically into the early nineteenth century, enslaved African Americans made use of public spaces in annual Negro Election Day, Militia Training Day, and Pinkster festivals throughout much of New England, New York, and New Jersey. In these annual public celebratory rituals, enslaved African Americans in the Northeast fused European and African traditions of political and festive culture and adapted them to their own uses. Slave festivals presented black leaders to their own communities and to the broader society, and reinforced the legitimacy of blacks' assertive participation in the public sphere. In so doing, enslaved Africans in the eighteenth century laid the foundations for commemorative traditions that would become important components of a maturing free black culture in the antebellum North.[2]

Distinctive colonial slave festivals most likely originated in impromptu social gatherings—replete with African-influenced singing, dancing, and gaming—among slaves brought to town by their white masters on special occasions, like the early summer election week activities that were common throughout New England. Understandably wary of unregulated gatherings of their slaves, masters tried to contain their bondspeople's activities by providing financial sponsorship and sanction for what came to be known as Negro Election Day—a separate set of activities held primarily by and for blacks, but with the assurance of white supervision. By the middle of the eighteenth century, however, enslaved Africans had appropriated the festivals for their own social uses and instilled in them their own cultural and political meanings. Alongside the music, dancing, and general conviviality at these events, one of the central features of New England Negro Election Day festivals was the annual election of a black king or governor who would often wield considerable authority within the black community, acting variously as arbitrator, judge, adviser, and liaison with whites. Contenders for office would vie for support with stump speeches and vigorous electioneering, partly serious and partly in mockery of white election practices. On the day of the festival the winner would be escorted through the streets of the city in an elaborate parade, usually on horseback and in resplendent attire. Negro Election Day festivities, held outdoors in the summer, attracted large numbers of whites and blacks who joined together in athletic competition, gambling, dancing, music, eating, and drinking, frequently to excess. Enslaved blacks took advantage of the relative freedom of activity to enjoy a break from the work routine, to dress in their finest clothes, and to socialize with other blacks from around a given region with whom they might ordinarily interact in public relatively infrequently.[3]

It is difficult to speak definitively about contemporary whites' impressions of the celebrations since most surviving white accounts of eighteenth-century slave festivals come from nineteenth-century reminiscences, laden with both nostalgia and racist condescension. Most scholars contend that, since they were sanctioned and financed by white slaveholders, the slaves' public festivals were seen by whites primarily as exotic entertainments that reinforced their view of blacks as imitative, unruly, and ultimately uncivilizable children. It seems reasonable to interpret the loosening of restrictions on blacks' uses of public space as being consistent with whites' cautious paternalism, which demanded attentive oversight of black activities. Whites' sponsorship and participation allowed them a sense of safety and control. Blacks, however, claimed extensive control over the cultural spaces provided by these events, using them both as festive social occasions for the expression of black folk culture and as serious political venues for the public assertion of black community solidarity and leadership. The slave festivals thus represent an important foundation for the legitimate free black entry into the public sphere, which did not reach its full expression until after the 1830s.

By the early nineteenth century, however, the festivals had begun to fall out of practice. I am largely in agreement with the historian Shane White's assessment of the festivals' demise as a consequence of two coincident phenomena. First, whites caught up in the era's "powerful currents of moral reform" objected to what they saw as the depraved behavior of the lower orders of both races on festival days. Cities and towns across the Northeast began legislating against such black-centered celebrations. Second, and I think more important for understanding African Americans' stake in these events, the festivals "no longer seemed as relevant" to northern blacks in transition from slavery to freedom as gradual emancipation began to take effect throughout the region. By the 1810s, White points out, "the newly freed African Americans were expending their considerable energies elsewhere."[4] Indeed, northern free blacks were immersed in the challenge of transforming their world from one defined by the reality of slavery into one defined more by the promise of freedom.

During the era of the American Revolution many enslaved blacks, North and South, were manumitted by their masters or were given the opportunity to hire themselves out in order to purchase their freedom. Some gained access to these roads to freedom in acknowledgment of military service, some simply in the spirit of liberty that had driven the colonists' rebellion, some because it was no longer profitable for their masters to hold them as slaves, and some because their masters realized that many of the enslaved would likely liberate themselves anyway. Such purely pragmatic positions notwithstanding, a spirit of antislavery activism was in the air, and the institution was disintegrating in most of the North. Within twenty years after the founding of the first antislavery society in Pennsylvania in 1775, similar organizations existed in every state of the new republic. And by 1804 all the states above the Mason-Dixon line had either initiated gradual emancipation laws or had abolished slavery outright.[5]

Between the 1780s and the prohibition of the Atlantic slave trade in 1808 the free black population in the United States increased dramatically, especially in urban centers around the Chesapeake region and in the Northeast. Blacks in the post-Revolutionary decades took advantage of the rhetoric and the emerging reality of liberty and began to found a variety of institutions—churches, fraternal organizations, schools, and mutual aid societies—that attempted to ease their communities' transition to a circumscribed freedom and to push revolutionary rhetoric to its logical conclusion. With the abolition of the slave trade—an act that gave rise to the first ongoing tradition of freedom celebrations among northern free blacks—African American leaders focused their rhetoric and activities more intently than ever on accelerating the demise of chattel slavery and preparing for the prospect of freedom and full citizenship rights.[6]

It seems obvious that the meaning of the celebrations that began in 1808 should be organized around the idea of freedom. Even during the eighteenth century it was the promise of a small taste of freedom that gave African Americans' public celebrations their central meaning. Shane White affirms that the popular Election Day and Pinkster slave festivals in the Northeast were permeated with "a sense of exhilaration at being free, if only for a few brief hours."[7] This focus on freedom is itself a significant point of continuity linking subsequent Freedom Day celebrations with the slave festivals that provided models for nineteenth-century blacks' celebratory use of public space. During those hours of relatively unrestricted use of the public arena, African Americans established a number of other practices that helped to shape the Freedom Day celebrations of the nineteenth century.

Freedom Day celebrations, however, differed from slave festivals in ways that reflect black Americans' cultural transformation in the first decades of the nineteenth century. In freedom celebrations kings and governors were no longer elected, and the African American organizers, along with most black participants, were no longer enslaved. As the black population of the early republic became overwhelmingly American born, the most obviously African cultural styles of public singing and dancing became less visible. Likewise, the melange of African languages commented on by white observers of the festivals began to fade as the importation of African-born slaves abated considerably with the proscription of the Atlantic trade. Formal sermons and orations, consistent with comparable features in white American commemorations, began to replace the more festive and performative aspects of the events that were rooted more in African oral traditions. Many black leaders in the early republic, themselves caught up in the era's "powerful currents of moral reform," consciously attempted to distance themselves from the "clouds of paganism and error"[8] they identified in the African cultural practices that were increasingly deemed by many black spokespersons to be inappropriate for a free, Christian people in a modern republic. The transition from slave festival to freedom celebration conforms with the process through which Africans in the United States, by the 1830s, had become African Americans.

A salient feature of that larger transformation involved blacks' adoption and adaptation of the Christian faith. Even as the slave festivals took shape in the mid-eighteenth century, enslaved Africans and their descendants began to merge their traditional spiritual beliefs and practices with European American Christianity.[9] Especially after the Revolution, free blacks in the urban North began founding separate congregations and denominations outside the oversight of whites. They made their churches, and their Christian faith, central to the building of community networks and the orchestration of social activism. Regardless of denomination, many black ministers, as leaders of their communities, publicly espoused what historian David Swift has termed "a liberation theology" that posited a just God who was deeply involved in directing the course of human history toward universal freedom. Defining themselves "as Christians, as unapologetic blacks, and as full-fledged Americans," northern activist clergy helped to construct the institutions and ideology that allowed black Americans to envision and work toward a legitimate identity as full and equal citizens in the land of their birth. Through organizing public meetings, preaching sermons, publishing pamphlets, and after the 1820s, founding newspapers, these spiritual, political, and intellectual leaders also were central to the dissemination of information about black history and accomplishments. "In doing so," Swift argues, "these minister journalists were pioneers in the recording of Afro-American history by Afro-Americans."[10]

The role of black journalists and editors—whether ministers or not—in disseminating information regarding black history cannot be underestimated. Throughout the nineteenth century newspaper editors such as Samuel Cornish, Thomas Hamilton, Philip A. Bell, Frederick Douglass, Benjamin Tucker Tanner, T. Thomas Fortune, Calvin Chase, and others took the lead in calling attention to blacks' historical accomplishments and contributions. By the second half of the nineteenth century, as African American literacy rose steadily, black periodical literature became increasingly important not only in mobilizing social and political activism and keeping the black public generally informed but also for articulating a historical consciousness and encouraging black participation in commemorative traditions. Even in the early national and antebellum periods black editors and pamphleteers helped to bridge the gap between the predominantly oral culture of most African Americans and the exciting potential available through literacy and education. Indeed, the interplay among oral, performative, and literate forms of public expression is vital to understanding the attempts of African American leaders to mobilize mass support for their various social, cultural, and political programs of action.[11]

During the early nineteenth century, print resources were limited and black literacy rates were relatively low. Gary Nash, for example, cites high illiteracy rates among former slaves in early national Philadelphia. The absence of common schools, low school attendance, exclusion from most private schools, and the demands of scraping together a living in a hostile racial climate all inhibited black literacy. In 1807 only 18 of 49 people signing the Bethel AME Church's articles of incorporation could sign their names. Between 1813 and 1815 only 28 percent of African American mariners could sign their names, compared to 80 percent of whites. In 1822 at Absalom Jones's elite St. Thomas Episcopal Church, 54 of 88 male members (about 61 percent) could sign their names.[12] And this was the cream of the crop. Facing this reality, many ministers and community leaders utilized important nonwritten vehicles for the implementation of an activist agenda, the promulgation of a black-centered interpretation of history, and the creation of an African American commemorative tradition. Drawing on existing black and white models for public celebration, early black leaders created a distinctly African American form in their freedom celebrations.

Though African cultural forms and African American experiences had a significant impact on the style and content of their celebrations, free black organizers attempting to make the most of their participation in American public culture had to enter that discourse using vehicles of expression that would be both recognized and respected by the broader society. The most obvious established model for politicized public celebrations in the early republic was the Fourth of July. White Americans' celebrations of the nation's natal day were themselves rooted in colonial traditions of public ritual carried from England. In their American context, however, those European traditions were complicated by new vocabularies and adapted to new functions. Especially after independence, the vocabulary of liberty and the need to move away from British associations and construct American nationalism gave rise to a peculiarly American celebratory style. One could also argue that the vocabularies and priorities articulated by enslaved Africans during slave festivals and other public gatherings of the colonial and revolutionary era added to the distinctiveness of American ritual and festive forms. Indeed, just how much of American culture is African in its origin is a subject worthy of considerable discussion, though it is beyond the focus of my present analysis. However great or small the African component of American public rituals, it is clear that by the early nineteenth century July Fourth celebrations had begun to congeal into an accepted ritual form.[13]

John Adams's frequently cited prescription for the perpetual commemoration of national independence touches on the key components of the July Fourth tradition as it took shape. "I am apt to believe," he wrote to his wife, Abigail, in 1776, "that it will be celebrated, by succeeding Generations, as the great anniversary Festival. It ought to be commemorated, as the Day of Deliverance by solemn Acts of Devotion to God Almighty. It ought to be solemnized with Pomp and Parade, with Shews, Games, Sports, Guns, Bells, Bonfires, and Illuminations, from one End of this Continent to the other from this Time forward forever more."[14]

Indeed, the firing of cannons and the ringing of bells at dawn usually initiated early national celebrations, rousing the slumbering populace and calling to mind the unusual significance of the day. Specially trained and outfitted militia companies, representing the armed populace that had helped make independence a reality, would parade, drill, and fire volleys to add to the spectacle. These companies were usually made up of fairly well-off men who could afford both the time to train and the fine uniforms and equipment needed to present the proper inspiring appearance. Often several companies from around a region would engage in a prideful competition of personal appearance, as well as of musketry and military drill.[15]

Two central public components of July Fourth celebrations were the procession, or parade, and the public oration. If organizers generally intended the latter to be the centerpiece of the day's observance, the former may have held the greater popular appeal. But parades were not mere spectacles to amuse the masses; political leaders designed them explicitly to teach the public the lessons of patriotism as well as their place in the social order. Civic processions in the early republic were controlled by those with social and political authority, and were used to make public statements reinforcing that authority, while allowing at least a pretense of popular participation. July Fourth parades almost always featured local and regional political leaders, other dignitaries, and militia companies. Somewhat less consistent, but still frequent, was the inclusion of groups of fraternal orders, students, clergy, artisans, bands of musicians, and occasionally women. Though African Americans were often interested onlookers, their infrequent appearances in the line of march were only as entertainment—marching bands or trick horseback riders—and never as true members of the national family. This racially exclusive vision of the social and political order was one of the central lessons taught at early national Independence Days.[16]

Their educative potential aside, parades, with music, ostentation, and martial display, were extremely entertaining for the many onlookers who were released from work and crowded the sidewalks along the parade route. Other amusements quickly became part of the July Fourth tradition. Prepared illuminations and fireworks displays, as well as illicit ignitions of homemade squibs, added to the sights and sounds at least as early as the 1780s. Sideshows and early museums presented special exhibitions of their fabulous attractions—two-headed creatures, shaved bears, flying men— along with more subdued paintings and wax figures. Ice cream and other treats were available from roving vendors. Alcohol was readily obtainable and, despite customary press reports asserting the peace and order of the festivities, drunkenness was not uncommon. Music was played by structured orchestras and improvisational performers throughout the day, and the evening saw both formal balls among the social elite and impromptu dancing among the lower orders.

Probably the least amusing and most frankly didactic exercises of the day involved the public July Fourth orations, which generally took place during the afternoon at the culmination of the procession. Almost always held indoors in a church or meeting hall, the principal oration would be preceded by an opening prayer, often a reading of the Declaration of Independence, and the singing of hymns and specially composed patriotic odes. Though orators generally had idiosyncratic and partisan political axes to grind, they were expected to follow a rather standardized formula. Orations were explicitly intended for the patriotic education of the populace, especially the rising generation. To reach those who could not attend the address, as well as to reinforce the message for those who had heard it, the speeches were usually published in pamphlet form so that "our youth will, by this means, be trained into the habits of thinking and speaking" suitable to the citizens of a republic.[17] Auditors and readers alike would be informed as to the causes and consequences of the Revolution, the great heroes and their exploits and sacrifices during the struggle, the benefits of republicanism, and the necessity of a virtuous and well-behaved citizenry to insure the nation's survival.

Notwithstanding the seemingly greater attraction of the parade for the masses, the oration remained the most definitive statement of the day's importance for the construction of an American collective memory and identity. Orators passed down the story of the Revolution—the nation's creation myth—a process that became especially important as the years passed and young people who had not experienced those events needed to be embraced into the fold and entrusted with the responsibility to carry on national traditions. Clearly, the educative potential of the ritualized public observance of American independence was recognized by the future French revolutionary Honore-Gabriel Riqueti Mirabeau, who was quoted in the *Independent Gazetteer* in 1786: "Let the youth, the hope of his country, grow up amidst annual festivals, commemorative of the events of the war, and sacred to the memory of your heroes. Let him learn from his father to weep over the tombs of those heroes, and bless their virtues."[18] Not only through the orations then but also through the act of commemoration itself, the past, present, and future of the republic were bound together in a national commemorative ritual that, as John Adams hoped, would be perpetuated through each rising generation.

After the oration concluded the formal public commemoration of the day, the crowd would disperse to additional public activities like fireworks displays, and other more or less private functions replete with feasting, drinking, and patriotic toasts. The range of private activities included formal gatherings among elites; somewhat less restrained dinners held by the respective militia companies and fraternal orders; and boisterous, unstructured revels among the masses in taverns, public houses, private homes, or in the streets. The overall function of the day's activities—cannons and bells calling the people out, martial displays, the ritual procession, assorted amusements, group public prayer, statements of national pride and identity, and convivial communal gatherings—served to foster American patriotism, nationalism, and political participation. But all this did not serve a simple national consensus. As Waldstreicher demonstrates, various social and political factions attached their own complex and competing meanings to the ritual festival and to the character of American nationalism, while they encouraged voter turnout to serve their respective partisan ends. Most centrally for understanding the development of African American celebrations, the early national July Fourth celebrations established the template for legitimate commemorative ritual practice in the American public sphere.[19]

African American participation in July Fourth activities is difficult to measure for the late eighteenth century, but it seems to have generated little controversy. Black involvement in crowd actions, festive occasions like Election Days, and other aspects of public life during the colonial and revolutionary eras was regular and expected in most contexts. After the 1790s, however, blacks' public activities became increasingly suspect and were discouraged in American cities North and South. There seems to be a direct correlation between the violent slave uprising and political revolution in Haiti, the subsequent influx of white French refugees into several U.S. seaports, and the growing intolerance among American whites for black participation in the public sphere. After the discovery of Gabriel's Rebellion in Virginia in 1800, the related Easter Plot of 1801–2, the Louisiana insurrections in 1811–12, and the 1822 Denmark Vesey Conspiracy in Charleston, white fears of black rebellion and white attempts to control African Americans' public activities grew to obsessive proportions.[20] On the Fourth of July in Philadelphia in 1804, black youths, obviously aware of, and inspired by, recent events in the Caribbean, roamed the streets beating and harassing whites, and threatening to "shew them San Domingo." The following year white mobs took their vengeance by forcing blacks off the streets when they attempted to take part in the Independence Day celebration. Similar rejections of blacks' right to participate were evident in other cities in the early 1800s.[21] African Americans' exclusion from white nationalist celebrations coincided approximately with the abolition of the Atlantic slave trade in 1808, which became the first event marked by a black nationalist commemorative celebration. In mounting their observances of the day, black leaders consciously modeled their commemorations on the well-established July Fourth tradition, adapting it to their own purposes.[22]

The historian Len Travers has noted that while ritual forms can be quite flexible and may be imbued with a variety of meanings, "new rites stand a better chance of acquiring legitimacy if they are initially recognizable to the people who will ultimately award them authority."[23] Legitimacy was extremely important to free black leaders, and as they developed the first observances of the abolition of the Atlantic slave trade they recognized the need to adhere to ritual forms that were part of the established public discourse of both whites and blacks in the early republic. At the same time, they had to work within the constraints of racial exclusion. Cannon firings and militia musters were not options generally available to northern free blacks. African Americans were not, as a rule, given access to heavy ordnance, and militia membership was denied blacks by most states after the passage of the federal militia law of 1792. Parades, however, remained notable—and hotly contested—components of freedom celebrations throughout the nineteenth century.

Beginning in 1808 hundreds of black males in Boston marched annually through the principal streets of the city to the African church on Belknap Street, where they would hear a sermon delivered by a sympathetic white minister. The Boston events were held on July 14, a date explained by some contemporaries as having been chosen "for convenience, merely," perhaps as a continuation from the midsummer colonial slave festivals. Historian William B. Gravely has suggested that the date may have corresponded with the abolition of slavery in Massachusetts, though I have found no specific references linking July 14 to that event. The date also corresponds with Bastille Day. Though I have found no direct evidence that black Bostonians were consciously honoring that connection with French radicalism, it seems at least plausible that black activists might associate their own cause with French revolutionaries, especially given the importance of the Haitian Revolution for African American intellectuals in the early republic.[24]

Whatever the rationale, the July 14 celebrations persisted into the 1820s despite opposition from hostile whites. Physical conflict over black parading in Boston emanated primarily from lower-class whites who followed the processions, taunting, jeering, and even threatening violence against well-organized blacks displaying their freedom. At least as early as the late 1810s black parades were targeted by young white men and boys throwing stones and dirt, along with mocking insults, at the marchers. With no protection forthcoming from the authorities, despite their advance knowledge of such attacks, blacks often tried to alter their parade route to avoid confrontations. But on at least one occasion in the 1820s, blacks apparently decided to arm and protect themselves. As related some years later by Lydia Maria Child, the outnumbered black paraders were being beaten back until one elderly, musket-wielding black Revolutionary War veteran impeded the white mob's assault long enough for elite whites from Beacon Hill to intervene and restore order.[25]

Physical attacks on black parades in Boston and other cities after the 1810s were a direct response to free African Americans' rejection of the increasingly narrow limits whites attempted to place on black public activity by the 1820s. African Americans were laying claim to their Americanness, and to all that came with it: public voice, political and civil rights, the right to pursue upward socioeconomic mobility to the best of their abilities, and in general, a recognition of their status as U.S. citizens. This whites would not abide. Physical assaults on these assertions of black equality were accompanied by, possibly preceded and inspired by, even more telling propaganda attacks in the form of broadsides and press reports lampooning black celebrations of the "Grand Bobalition, or Great Annibersary Fussible." Beginning at least as early as 1816, and continuing through the 1820s, broadsides containing grossly exaggerated racist caricatures of African American speech patterns and physical appearance were distributed around Boston, coincident with the July 14 parades. White press reports also mocked black celebrations through their use of clearly fraudulent "reports" on the events, including spurious "quotations" by black organizers saying, "After the parade we mooved to the African Meetnus were an addres was delivered for the edifigation of the herers."[26]

These physical and literary assaults on black public commemorations demonstrate whites' recognition of the seriousness and potential ramifications of blacks' appropriation of ritual commemorative forms and their claims on the use of public space. Excluded from American nationalist celebrations of independence, and increasingly marginalized in public life generally, free black leaders created their own nationalist rituals, based on acknowledged commemorative forms but imbued with an unmistakably African American substance and meaning. The degree to which these rituals should be viewed as *black* nationalist or *American* nationalist is open to debate. As with so many aspects of African American public life in the early republic, it is difficult to claim with certainty whether black public commemorations were primarily a reaction to blacks' exclusion from national rituals or an expression of an incipient black nationalist consciousness. It is entirely possible that the slave trade celebrations would not have taken on the importance they did had blacks not been excluded from full participation in national public life. The complexities of black political and cultural identity pervade debates within early national black communities as well as blacks' public challenges to white Americans. Even at this early stage in the development of black community life and political expression, the sometimes overlapping, sometimes conflicting allures of an undifferentiated Americanness on the one hand and a powerful racially defined consciousness on the other exerted considerable influence in shaping early national black public discourse.[27]

What is clear about the slave trade celebrations is that they became the foundation of a commemorative tradition that fulfilled various functions for black communities throughout the nineteenth century. Specific functions of freedom celebrations, of course, shifted over time and from place to place. But from the first slave trade celebrations in 1808, and continuing through subsequent public commemorations throughout the nineteenth century, African American organizers consistently used freedom celebrations to articulate a distinctive, black-centered historical consciousness and sense of peoplehood. No other component of the celebration was more central to this intellectual pursuit than the sermon or oration. The emergence of slave trade commemorations in 1808 marks African Americans' entrance into the public-speaking arena.[28] Held in New York and Philadelphia as well as Boston, slave trade commemorations, whether or not they included a parade, always featured somber, indoor religious ceremonies, usually at an African house of worship. The benediction, prayers of thanksgiving, the singing of hymns, the reading of the act of abolition, and a collection often accompanied the keynote of the occasion—a formal sermon or oration delivered by a prominent spokesperson, typically a clergyman. Unlike the black Bostonians, who celebrated on July 14, New Yorkers and Philadelphians held their observances on January 1, the date the law went into effect. Celebrations in these cities also differed from the Boston affairs in that the featured orators were not sympathetic whites, but were almost always black men.[29]

White and black orators at slave trade celebrations seem to have shared some common themes in the content of their speeches, but often their emphases could diverge dramatically. For example, at two of the later celebrations, in 1822 and 1823, respectively, white clergyman Thaddeus Mason Harris in Boston and black Presbyterian minister Jeremiah Gloucester in Philadelphia related a condensed history of the slave trade, and each used the identical invocation that "God hath made of one blood all nations" in order to emphasize that black and white were members of the same human family. Each also made a point of condemning the continued violation of the slave trade ban, as well as the recent Missouri Compromise, which set a disheartening precedent by extending slavery beyond the Mississippi River into the Louisiana Territory. But there, for the most part, the similarities end. In Boston, the white Reverend Harris offered a rather detached narrative of the history of the slave trade and American slavery, making a special point of embroidering his account with the exaggeration that Massachusetts slaves, unlike those farther south, "were always treated humanely; were well fed and clothed; were instructed by their masters and mistresses, particularly on the Lord's day; and were required to be present in the morning and evening, when the family were called together to hear the Bible read and to unite in prayers; their children were baptized, and, when old enough, were sent to school; and, in short, their condition was merely that of servants, not of slaves."[30]

In a bizarre effort to support his point, Harris cited the 1641 law establishing slavery in Massachusetts, with its stipulation "that 'none shall be held in bond slavery . . . unless it be lawful captives taken in just wars, such as willingly sell themselves and are sold to us.' " Rather than recognizing that the statute made Massachusetts the first mainland English colony to create a legal foundation for the institution, Harris underscored the "none shall be held" phrase in trying to persuade his black auditors that "slavery is altogether repugnant to the institutions and feelings of the people of New England," and of Massachusetts in particular. He noted with pride that no slaves were counted in the state in the 1790 census and that Massachusetts was "the only state represented in the first Congress held at New York in 1789, which had formally abolished slavery." Much of his address, then, was explicitly geared toward convincing his audience, and perhaps himself, that "[y]ou live among those who acknowledge and respect your rights and franchise, who are disposed to treat you with kindness, and from whom you are daily receiving tokens of civility and favour."[31] By the 1820s black Bostonians would not be appeased by mere "tokens." Moreover, the "Bobalition" broadsides and vicious mobs that regularly harassed black celebrants hardly lent credibility to the minister's assurances.

Similarly discrediting Harris's statement was his unbridled enthusiasm for the American Colonization Society (ACS). Like many well-meaning but uncomprehending whites who opposed slavery, Harris claimed to "look forward to the gradual emancipation of such as are yet held in bondage; and rejoice that the Colonization Society interests itself so zealously in behalf of such as obtain freedom." Founded in late 1816, the ACS promoted gradual emancipation, financial compensation for the slaveholders, and the resettling of liberated blacks to the West African colony of Liberia. Both white and black antislavery advocates initially showed interest in the organization, but by the early 1820s black support had dwindled. It became clear to many that the ACS leadership was dominated by southern slaveholders whose primary concern was not to dismantle slavery but rather to rid the nation of its free black population. The Reverend Harris's prayers—and his solicitation of contributions—that Africa "may become civilized" through the works of black Christian Americans "who are returning to those shores to found a new colony" probably were not as warmly received as he hoped. Black Bostonians probably also took exception to Harris's telling them, "you are as strangers in a foreign land."[32]

Certainly Jeremiah Gloucester, who spoke at the Philadelphia celebration a year later, would not have taken Harris's sentiments as kindly as they were apparently intended. Eldest son of the prominent black Philadelphia clergyman John Gloucester, young Jeremiah was vehement in denouncing the ACS. Not only did the Reverend Gloucester make clear his belief that the organization intended to remove free blacks in order to strengthen slaveholders' control over their human property, he specifically linked the ACS to the Missouri Compromise as corroborating evidence of the nation's intention to expand and perpetuate slavery. Gloucester also heaped praise on the "brilliant exploits" of Haitian revolutionaries, a subject few whites or blacks dared to broach. The Reverend Harris had consigned to a footnote his own jeremiadic reference to the bloody 1790s slave revolt, which led to Haitian independence in 1804. Gloucester emphasized Africans' agency in securing their own liberty and "proclaim[ing] the imprescribable rights of man" on the island. With an angle of vision distinct from that of his Boston counterpart, the youthful black minister entered forcefully into a nascent tradition of African American political, cultural, and historical analysis.[33]

Early African American slave trade celebration orators like Jeremiah Gloucester brought certain distinctive qualities to their public presentations, and in doing so they established precedents that would be built on by their intellectual inheritors throughout the nineteenth century. Gloucester himself was treading ground that had been opened a decade and a half earlier. When the Atlantic slave trade came to its legal conclusion on January 1, 1808, black orators began to use freedom events to articulate their historical visions and political agendas to black and white America, establishing general patterns of black public festive political culture that I will trace into the twentieth century.[34] Their overlapping purposes in this project were to instill a sense of pride in history, tradition, and peoplehood among their black auditors, to make clear their political and social objectives, and to articulate their distinctive historical interpretations to both blacks and whites in the expanding public sphere of the early republic.

At celebrations of the abolition of the slave trade, individual addresses concentrated variously on a related panoply of topics that would be reiterated by black orators for decades to come: the horrors of slavery, the natural right of freedom, the labors of British and American abolitionists, the grandeur of ancient Africa, the hand of Divine Providence at work in the deliverance of African peoples from bondage, the contributions blacks had made in building the American republic, and most centrally, the fundamental rightness of blacks' claims to American citizenship. The orations are replete with the Revolutionary rhetoric that pervaded public discourse during the early republic, and some explicitly include themselves in that broader discourse by addressing specific nonracial political issues of the day.[35] While not all early orators touched on all of the above themes, enough did so to create in those themes an indelible legacy for subsequent orators to emulate. What held these themes together—in the early slave trade orations as well as in those over the course of the nineteenth century—is the orators' consistent efforts to relate the history of African peoples in the United States, and the history of the nation itself, from a decidedly black perspective.[36]

The most recurrent interpretive narrative offered by these early African American historians revolved around recounting the glory of the African past and the inhumanity of the slave trade.[37] In his 1815 narrative, William Hamilton began at the beginning, suggesting that Africa's geographical location made it "an eligible situation for the growth of man in his first state of existence." Hamilton traced Africa's past from birthplace of the human race through the cradle of Egyptian civilization to "the ultimate point of degradation" inflicted by "that low, sly, wicked, cunning, peculiar to Europeans." Orators generally played up "the national greatness of our [African] progenitors," often emphasizing the artistic and scientific prowess of the ancient Egyptians.[38] William Miller was typical in asserting that "the first learned nation, was a nation of blacks." And none of these men left any doubt that "the [slave] trade was began by white men, and by Europeans." All commented to some degree on Europeans' "wicked arts, by which wars have been fomented among the different tribes of the Africans, in order to procure captives, for the purpose of selling them for slaves."[39] White "avarice" and "desire for gain" were consistently identified as the driving force behind that "horrid traffic" that "has filled this earth with more moral turpitude than any other event that has ever occurred."[40]

Black orators often mocked this "enterprising spirit of European genius," comparing it unfavorably not only with the grandeur of ancient African civilizations but also with the "simplicity, innocence and contentment" of more contemporary "harmless Africans" living in what "might truly be called paradise." A paradise that survived only "until the man-stealing crew entered."[41] "Fancy yourself," Russell Parrott invited his audience, "on the fertile plains of Africa—see, reposing beneath the luxuriant foliage of the palm, the child of her soil"—a child about to be torn "from the bosom of his family" and subjected to the coffle, the Middle Passage, and perpetual bondage, all related in gruesome detail by numerous orators.[42] In marked contrast to the detached narrative in the Reverend Harris's 1822 Boston address, black orators more often used the powerful rhetorical technique employed here by Parrott, inviting their listeners to situate themselves as eyewitnesses to the abominations inflicted on African innocents.[43] Peter Williams transported his audience to Africa, "once the garden of the world, the seat of almost paradisiacal joys," where he entreated them to "hear now the shrieks of the women; the cries of the children; the shouts of the warriors; the groans of the dying" that were the bitter fruits of the slave trade. After describing, in like manner, the torture and murder of infants, the use of thumbscrews and irons, the rending of families, and the "pound of flesh" extracted by the driver's lash, William Hamilton delivered a telling imputation of that "bloated pride" with which "the European . . . conceives himself an order of being above any other order of men." "If these are some of the marks of superiority," Hamilton implored, "may heaven in mercy always keep us inferior."[44]

This unrelenting indictment of white European and American barbarity contrasts with a more hopeful assessment of the potential for liberty in the republican United States. Often using a roll call of British and American abolitionists for a transition (Woolman, Benezet, Wilberforce, Sharp, Rush, Clarkson, and others), slave trade celebration orators exhibited a definite pride in the principles of the Revolution and an expectation that their application would culminate in "a more general extension of freedom."[45] Blacks also used the occasions to claim their identity as part of the national family. "As an American," Peter Williams proclaimed in 1808, "I glory in informing you that Columbia boasts the first men who distinguished themselves eminently in the vindication of our rights, and the improvement of our state." Five years later George Lawrence reminded his auditors that "the land in which we live gives us the opportunity rapidly to advance the prosperity of liberty. This government [was] founded on the principles of liberty and equality . . . declaring them to be the free gift of God." In 1816 Russell Parrott went beyond the ground of natural rights in claiming that American blacks had earned their citizenship rights through national service in the battles of the Revolution and in the more recent war against Britain. The black citizen-soldier had fought "with noble daring, mingling his blood, with the ungrateful soil, that refused him everything but a grave." These patriots thus demonstrated the race's possession of "all the rich materials for the formation of the good, the useful citizen."[46]

The narratives offered in slave trade orations reflect blacks' concern with presenting the history of their African and American experiences as leading ultimately to their reclamation of freedom, a right "as inherent in [the Africans], as in the Europeans."[47] George Lawrence felt the need to justify the "excruciatingly painful" recitation of African suffering, but deemed it necessary, since, "in reflecting on [the enslaved Africans'] situation, our celebration demonstrates itself to be fully sensible of ours."[48] These early race leaders recognized that a knowledge of their history was essential to black Americans' comprehension of their present and future condition in the United States.

Scrutiny of the past also provided material by which to judge the relative merits of past civilizations and the possibilities for present ones. Russell Parrott was explicit in interpreting the demise of ancient slaveholding cultures on both the African and European shores of the Mediterranean as a judgment of Divine Providence. Envisioning African and European states as equals in worldly accomplishments as well as in the eyes of a God who directed the course of history, Parrott cleverly juxtaposed polities from opposite shores, observing that neither "the wisdom and learning of Egypt and Greece" nor "the patriotism and valour of Rome and Carthage [could] save them from the indignation of the Most High." In a similar jeremiad, William Hamilton noted the "weakness and degradation" that had befallen the once-dominant Iberian nations and predicted that "they shall continue to sink . . . until they are below the African they have so debased. . . . It is fortunate for England," he counseled, "that she is making something like an atonement for her more than base treatment of the African people."[49]

That atonement, exemplified by the banning of the Atlantic slave trade, was shared by the United States. The 1787 prohibition of slavery in the Northwest Territories, gradual emancipation in the northern states, and the abolition of the slave trade appeared to give blacks a stake in the Revolutionary rhetoric they so readily imbibed and echoed. For African American leaders these acts relating to their race's liberation bore a significance not merely for their fellow Africans; they represented the universal progress of freedom, the principle by which black Americans throughout the nineteenth century ordered their interpretations of history.

For slave trade celebration orators, emancipatory acts—wherever they occurred throughout the globe—were the defining moments of the Age of Revolution, of far greater importance than the related emergence in the Western world of industrialization, capitalism, or nationalism. "The abolition of the slave trade," Russell Parrott proclaimed in 1814, "is one of the greatest events that mark the present age."[50] The act, furthermore, should not hold such high meaning only for blacks; it "should be hailed by every lover of genuine liberty, as the commencement of that happy era, in which freedom shall reign to the 'furthest verge of the green earth.'" Similarly, Jeremiah Gloucester asserted in 1823 that "[a]mong the events which frequently appear in the history of nations . . . the abolition of the slave trade must be admitted a conspicuous place."[51] Joseph Sidney spoke for many of his colleagues when he pronounced that "auspicious day" a "jubilee of freedom" from which Americans could "look forward to the period when slavery, in this land of freedom, will be unheard of and unknown."[52] The teleology of these first slave trade celebration orators left little doubt that the history they recounted would continue its inexorable march until "Freedom and Justice reign triumphant in the world, universally."[53] Just as July Fourth orators used their platforms to tell the story of the American republic's birth, black orators used their platforms to tell the story of their own people.

Moreover, they explicitly connected their story to that of the United States and broadened its significance further, characterizing it as the natural extension of the quest for universal liberty in a post-Enlightenment era defined by the onward march of freedom.

These spokespersons also took seriously their own, and their successors', responsibility to continue using freedom anniversaries to pass on a legacy. They saw the slave trade celebrations as part of a continuing tradition that would be expanded on as African Americans claimed their place in the national family. Numerous orators explicitly entreated their audiences to maintain the January 1 observances as annual events on the African American commemorative calendar. Like the organizers of July Fourth celebrations, black spokespersons hoped to establish a commemorative tradition, to articulate their historical consciousness to the American public, and to leave a legacy for coming generations. Joseph Sidney hoped that "every return of this anniversary may be accompanied with additional causes for joy and rejoicing." Henry Sipkins also spoke for continued commemoration so that the slave trade, that "most indelible blot in the history of nations," might "ever be held as a monument of contempt by rising generations." William Miller cast the day in a more positive light, suggesting that "it becomes us to set it apart as consecrated, for a day of prayer, and praises, and thanksgivings to God, and the singing of psalms to his honor." Absalom Jones, at Philadelphia's first slave trade commemoration in 1808, added to this blueprint for commemoration, underscoring the necessity of retelling the history surrounding the event in order to perpetuate its memory and its lessons: "Let the first of January, the day of the abolition of the slave trade in our country, be set apart in every year, as a day of publick thanksgiving for that mercy. Let the history of the sufferings of our brethren, and of their deliverance, descend by this means to the remotest generations; and when they shall ask, in time to come, saying, What mean the lessons, the psalms, the prayers and the praises in the worship of this day? let us answer them."[54]

Jones also indicated in his exhortation the proper method of conducting such anniversary commemorations, an issue that was to be a continuing point of contestation among African Americans throughout the nineteenth century. Consistent with the solemn activities he described, and markedly in contrast to John Adams's recommendations for July Fourth frivolity and merriment, the Episcopal priest made it clear that "the pomp of public worship, and the ceremonies of a festive day, will find no acceptance with [God]." Blacks should "conduct ourselves in a manner as to furnish no cause of regret to the deliverers of our nation. . . . [L]et us be sober-minded, humble, peaceable, temperate in our meats and drinks, frugal in our apparel."[55]

Though these last prescriptions were to apply in daily life as well as during celebrations, the contrast with the extravagances of July Fourth, and also of the slave festivals, could not have been much clearer.

The concerns of Jones and others notwithstanding, many black leaders decided that asserting their right to the public streets outweighed any anxieties regarding the behavior of the black masses or the reactions of white mobs. In New York, in 1809, the members of the Wilberforce Philanthropic Association took their chances in the streets as they made "every exertion . . . to fulfill the intentions of their constituents, to show their gratitude *in the most public manner,* for so great a blessing" as the abolition of the slave trade. Their celebration featured two processions between Liberty Hall on Broadway and "the Lyceum in Warren Street." The line of march included "the Wilberforce band of music . . . [and] the Maritime and Musical Associations, decorated with their badges, and accompanied with their appropriate banners. The novelty of the procession," the association's published report noted, "attracted the attention of an immense concourse of citizens, and presented a spectacle both grand and interesting." Though no disturbances were reported, Absalom Jones's reaction to such a display is not difficult to imagine.

New York held a total of three observances of the anniversary in 1809, the other two seemingly somewhat more solemn than the Wilberforce Association's. One, held by the New York African Society for Mutual Relief, did include a procession, but the march "from the African School to the [Universalist] Church" seems to have been a far less festive affair. The "crowded audience" at the third, held at the African Church, was remarkable for its "attentive seriousness" and "respectable appearance." Clearly, a rift among the city's African American leaders had emerged regarding the observance of the day. It is not clear if the division was created by disagreements about parading or if other factors contributed to the apparent lack of unity. Given the partisan (pro-Federalist) nature of Joseph Sidney's oration at one celebration, political affiliations may also have played a role. It seems likely, though, that questions about public processions were at least one factor, as the organizers of the Wilberforce affair were explicitly unapologetic for the "most public manner" of their celebration. They did, however, "lament that a division should exist, and indulge[d] the flattering hope, that all dissentions [would] cease."[56]

The obvious lack of unity manifested in many of the slave trade celebrations was clearly a matter of concern for black spokespersons. Jeremiah Gloucester expressed his appreciation for the show of concord at a Philadelphia slave trade celebration in 1823: "My brethren, I am highly gratified to see so many of you united together in those different societies, celebrating the anniversary of the abolition of the slave trade." The list of participating societies was an impressive one, including "the Angolian Society" and the "Rush Beneficial" as well as the "Granville, Harmony, Benezet Philanthropic, Wilberforce, Farmers, Mechanics, Warner Mifflin, and . . . the Union Sons of Africa." African Americans also marched "not only as members of the different societies, but as fathers, as men."[57]

Despite this apparent show of unity in Philadelphia, discord over when and how to celebrate, the propriety of parading, and the proper parameters of public conduct continued to mark Freedom Day celebrations—and, indeed, black social debates generally—into the twentieth century. Boston's July 14 parades, relatively staid as they appear to have been, stirred up their share of civic controversy. In fact, that was a large part of Absalom Jones's point. In their desire to be accepted as respectable members of American society, many African American leaders sought to avoid unnecessary confrontations with whites or situations that opened blacks to public ridicule. The unwanted attention from white mobs generated by public processions served only to call attention to cultural practices in speech, dress, and performance within black communities that leaders like Jones were trying to reform or eradicate. What was beginning to emerge in these celebrations was a conflict among a range of competing cultural orientations within incipient free black communities in the nineteenth-century North. Attempts to control public behavior illustrate the intertwining of the cultural and the political, since blacks' public decorum had a direct bearing on the political goals of abolition and citizenship. When freedom orators exhorted their brethren, as Russell Parrott did in 1812, to maintain "a peaceful demeanor, a respectful observance of the laws, and due reverence to the constituted authority," they were explicitly advocating "respectable" public behavior, in part to convince white society that slavery's corrosive and enervating influence could be eliminated in the free black after emancipation.[58] Free blacks in the North who adhered to a strict code of personal rectitude in their public and private conduct attempted to aid those more attuned to the folk culture of slavery in acclimating themselves to the broader, white-dominated society, largely in order to demonstrate blacks' abilities to participate as equals in that society. Such acculturation, it was thought, would help not only in uplifting individual lives but also in acquiring social acceptance and justice for the entire race. These issues of acculturation and public presentation were peculiar to African Americans and did not become matters of debate in the same way among white participants in July Fourth affairs.[59]

The issue of acculturation was vital to African Americans in the North during the half century after the Revolution as they attempted to reconcile the diverse cultural influences that swirled around them. It is crucial to recognize that acculturation was not simply a matter of some African Americans imitating "white" behavior and others maintaining a more authentically "black" cultural bearing. Both blacks and whites in antebellum American cities had access to a thriving street life that included food vendors, ragpickers, draymen, prostitutes, bootblacks, and the growing throngs of blacks, immigrants, and native-born whites who swelled the urban population after the 1820s. Much of the antebellum popular culture of the street spilled over from the saloons, brothels, oyster houses, and other venues of venality and vice that opened into public thoroughfares. In addition to the influences of this biracial demimonde, the public sphere provided access to the purveyance of news by newspaper hawkers; the evangelical messages of marching church groups; the ministrations of temperance advocates and other humanitarian reformers; and the marches of benevolent societies and fraternal organizations. Fire companies took to the streets to compete and at times do battle with one another. Workingmen's associations and political groups marched to deliver their respective social messages to the general public. As black city dwellers took in all this cultural information, they individually drew from it what was deemed useful and adaptive to their survival and progress in the cities of the antebellum North. Not surprisingly, their choices spanned a broad spectrum of belief and practice.[60]

Gary B. Nash has called specific attention to the variety of "cultural styles" practiced in an increasingly stratified northern black community in the early nineteenth century. Nash a bit too neatly bifurcates Philadelphia's blacks into two groups. On the one hand stood the "respectable" class of longtime residents who owned property, belonged to a church, schooled their children, dressed and comported themselves with decorum and modesty, and were active in fraternal organizations and other cultural institutions. In short, they "had acquired most of the accoutrements of respectability" and displayed the "cardinal virtues" of "industry, frugality, circumspection, sobriety, and religious commitment." Juxtaposed against this group at "an economic and cultural distance" was "the mass of black city dwellers, many of them recent arrivals." The competing cultural style of this much larger group exhibited "a penchant for conviviality, an unrestrained display of emotions," and a desire to establish an individualistic public "reputation" in the streets that was far more important than was the approbation either of whites or of the "respectable" classes of blacks. "Some of them spoke in southern dialect, drank and gambled, dressed flamboyantly, sometimes ran afoul of the law, and affected a body language—the sauntering gait, unrestrained singing and laughing, and exuberant dancing—that set them apart from 'respectable' black society."[61] Most black Philadelphians probably did not fit tidily into either of these cultural extremes; rather, most would likely have been influenced in their practices and attitudes by a wide assortment of white and black cultural models, all of which were superseded in import by the demands of daily survival. But the cultural styles Nash describes suggest the wide range of orientations available to free blacks in the antebellum North.

This division within the black community over public behavior was less a function of socioeconomic class, property acquisition, or even educational attainment than Nash seems to suggest. It is more constructive to consider the "cardinal virtues" valued by the "respectable" classes of blacks as the reflection of a particular moral code deeply rooted in their identity as Christian Americans and in their sense of racial destiny. Adhering to standards of morality and respectability can hardly be reduced to blacks simply assimilating to "white" cultural norms. One scholar has recently argued that an important strain of thought among antebellum black intellectuals held that blacks were in fact morally and intellectually superior to whites. It is partly in this context that David Walker wondered in his 1829 *Appeal,* "whether they are as *good by nature* as we are or not."[62] The clergy were at the forefront of the African American moral community, but they were hardly alone. Joining them were black fraternalists, members of temperance societies, laymen and -women active in their local communities, and vast numbers of unremarkable working folk who shared the belief in a just and Divine Providence that guided human affairs and the common commitment, based on that belief, to moral rectitude, right living, and the quest for justice and equality in the land of their birth and citizenship.

As they absorbed the cacophony of cultural voices on the city streets, black leaders struggled along with the rest to untangle their own conflicting motives and define the available choices regarding issues of personal responsibility and moral conduct as they related to public and private comportment. Those leaders used their addresses at slave trade and other Freedom Day celebrations to promote their various views to the rest of the African American community, many of whom did not value similar standards of conduct. Along with the historical interpretations and the construction of commemorative tradition embodied in the celebrations, an equally important aspect of the events involves the larger issue of race "elevation." Freedom Day orators delivered fairly consistent admonitions directed specifically at blacks to work hard, educate themselves, and generally make themselves worthy of inclusion as full and equal American citizens. This program involved both private and public behavior, and was not simply for the purpose of presenting an acceptable face to white society. Pursuing respectability, many black leaders believed, would result in concrete advances in blacks' educational, economic, social, and political empowerment, as well as the development of individual self-respect and race pride.[63] These sentiments were as pervasive in Freedom Day orations as they were in written vehicles of expression throughout the nineteenth, and indeed much of the twentieth, century. They help to characterize the process of contestation, interchange, and adaptation through which African American political culture—including traditions of public commemoration—took shape in the early nineteenth century.

Slave trade commemorations, and the later Freedom Day celebrations that replaced them, represent one of the most visible sites on the contested terrain of cultural discourse within northern black communities. They drew on divergent strains of black cultural life in the early republic, juxtaposing competing celebratory traditions: the festive and the serious, the outdoor and the indoor, the secular and the sacred. On the one hand were the receding slave festivals with their emphasis on good times, feasting, music, dancing, gambling, and outdoor recreation. On the other were the slave trade celebrations. New York and Bostonian parading traditions notwithstanding, these commemorations generally involved indoor religious and rhetorical exercises that represented the antithesis of the slaves' exuberant Election Day rituals. Both events drew from white cultural models as well as African traditions, and the two types of public celebration themselves served as competing models for future Freedom Day celebrations.

And it is important to recognize that the organizers of these first freedom events did have in mind their long-term continuation. The slave trade celebrations in particular, through their orations, left an intellectual legacy that became the foundation of a tradition of African American public address, historical interpretation, and commemorative practice for the next century. The orators made it clear that not only the historical consciousness manifest in their addresses but also the fact of the celebrations themselves was integral to establishing a viable heritage for their descendants. The celebrations, and the tradition they represented, needed to be maintained, and the view of history that they articulated also needed to be preserved and passed on.

The importance of the celebrations is suggested by the preponderance of slave trade orations among the scant written sources from the early nineteenth century. These seminal artifacts of African American expressive culture constitute probably the most well-represented genre of public address among African American documents dated before 1815. We have them to interrogate today primarily because they were reprinted at the time in pamphlet form, to be disseminated among the broader public. As with contemporaneous July Fourth orations, published versions of slave trade sermons and addresses were political tools of nationalism, intended to inform and educate readers—in this case to recount the historical development of slavery and abolitionism, and to tell the story of the African American people. As David Waldstreicher has noted, the published slave trade orations also filled the role of the partisan newspaper report by providing an overview of the celebrations in an era before a black press existed. Positive descriptions of slave trade commemorations in pamphlets were particularly important because white papers generally ignored them except to mock and denigrate them, and many whites knew of the celebrations primarily through the demeaning "bobalition" broadsides. Beyond the descriptions, the texts of the orations themselves provided an irrefutable tribute to African American intellect and capability. As New York orator William Hamilton explicitly pointed out in 1809, as he held up a copy of the previous year's oration, "If we continue to produce specimens like these, we shall soon put our enemies to the blush; abashed and confounded they shall quit the field, and no longer urge their superiority of souls."[64]

The distinctly black-centered historical narrative embodied in the available texts is a remarkably consistent one. The fundamental cornerstone supporting African American historical interpretations, of course, was the knowledge that Divine Providence controlled the destiny of human progress toward universal freedom and justice. Black orators emphasized the ancient greatness of African cultures and the innocence of contemporary ones, contrasting both with the avarice and cruelty of white European oppressors. But while blacks clearly identified themselves as Africans, they also attempted to claim an identity as American citizens. Blacks' contributions to American society through community and military service were emphasized in order to justify their rights in the eyes of whites. But the most profound connection blacks made between themselves and their country revolved around the ethos of liberty and equality that seemed to promise their people's own liberation.

Blacks' interpretations of history, like those of most post-Enlightenment intellectuals, were deeply imbued with the ideal of progress. But for African Americans progress was most fundamentally defined by the onward march of freedom. Freedom was the central organizing principle in their historical interpretations, and no other evaluative tool carried nearly the same weight in their assessments of the merits of past or present civilizations. Though they saw their relationship with the rhetoric of freedom as distinctive because of their own experiences with slavery, slave trade celebration orators recognized the broader implications of their devotion to the ideal of universal liberty. As they forged a tradition of historical interpretation and commemoration in the early years of the republic, African Americans consciously defined their ideals as more than those of a marginal subculture. Though of particular interest to blacks, these first freedom celebrations were presented as events that should be observed by all lovers of liberty regardless of race or condition. Black orators' ultimate goal was to universalize their historical perspective so that the principle of freedom would come to define the interpretations—and the policies—of leaders in the United States and the world.

These high hopes notwithstanding, the slave trade celebrations, like the slave festivals, had largely disappeared by the end of the 1820s. As the nation moved into a new era of technological development and political reorientation, African Americans, too, adapted to the rapidly changing social environment. By the 1820s the Africans of the eighteenth century were well on their way to becoming African Americans. The slave trade celebrations had ended by the late 1820s for a variety of reasons: slave traders' blatant disregard for the law in the continued importation of Africans; the burgeoning domestic trade that intensified with the growth of the southern Cotton Kingdom in the 1820s; the failure of civic authorities to protect black celebrants from white harassment and violence; and the absence of any indication that American government or society was about to act more forcefully against slavery. If anything, the institution seemed more firmly entrenched than ever, and the major white "antislavery" response came in the form of the colonization movement—hardly acceptable in the eyes of most black activists. Many African Americans, despairing of ever finding justice and equality in America, carefully considered emigration, and thousands did emigrate to Haiti or West Africa during the 1820s. But the white-dominated American Colonization Society was condemned by most African Americans as a proslavery group bent on ridding the nation only of its free black population.[65]

In 1829, at what must have been one of the last July 14 slave trade celebrations in Boston, white supporters of the gradualism and colonization program of the ACS got a sense of black Bostonians' anticolonizationist sentiments. As was the custom in Boston, a white "clergyman of the city" delivered the oration at Thomas Paul's African Baptist Church to the "members of the African Abolition Society" and their guests. In the course of his address, he "was endeavoring to prove, that the liberation of two millions of slaves . . . would be neither a blessing to them nor safe for the country—it was wholly out of the question. The slaves had no land to cultivate—they were degraded in mind and morals—their dependence was entire. They must receive instruction, before they could be qualified for freedom—&c. &c. &c." At this statement, "[a] very audible murmer ran round the house, which spoke a language that could not be misunderstood. The argument did not obtain." When an ACS agent in the crowd "attempted to maintain the same position with considerable ingenuity of illustration" the black response became "still more earnest and decisive."[66]

Many black Bostonians seemed to resent any advice from even well-intentioned whites regarding their attitudes or behavior. According to the account by a white correspondent printed in Benjamin Lundy's *Genius of Universal Emancipation,* the same white clergyman had earlier in his speech almost lost his entire audience when he proceeded "to impress upon his hearers the importance of a good moral and religious character." Many in the house "immediately left the meeting with visible dissatisfaction. . . . So great, indeed, was their agitation, as to render the interference of a colored clergyman necessary." The reporter may have softened the tone of the speaker's remarks, for blacks had certainly heard countless comparable admonitions from both white and black antislavery spokespersons without similar displays of hostility. The reporter's biases are indicated by his assumption that the near walkout occurred only because the minister's language was "not adapted to the comprehension of a majority of his audience." The speaker himself claimed to be "surprised and grieved that his remarks were misunderstood." One suspects that the audience understood his meaning all too well, perhaps better than the speaker himself.[67] Taking place just a few months before the publication of David Walker's *Appeal,* this meeting in Walker's adopted city, at which he may well have been present, illustrates the growing tensions within the emerging abolitionist movement. It also marks a shift in African American public celebrations, which had already begun to cohere around a new, and potentially more promising, commemorative moment. The days of the first slave trade celebrations were passing, but their legacy reasserted itself in the celebrations of New York State emancipation that began in 1827.

The emancipation of slaves in the state of New York, effective July 4, 1827, represented to many African Americans the possible renewal of the nation's march toward liberty and rekindled their interest in public celebrations of freedom well beyond the borders of the Empire State. From New England in the North to Virginia in the South and Ohio in the rapidly developing West, black Americans took note of the abolition of slavery by one of the nation's largest and most influential states.[68] The event also renewed debate over the best means and reasons for observing special dates on the emerging African American commemorative calendar.

The most noticeably persistent component of the slave festivals that initiated blacks' formal celebratory use of public space was the procession of the black king or governor. Shane White chronicles quite convincingly the transformation of the Election Day procession into a more overtly political statement when employed by free blacks in the nineteenth century. "African American parades of the early nineteenth century," White argues, were an "important and conscious attempt by northern blacks to enter public life" and a tool for participating "in the discourse of the American republic" by representing the African American community both to itself and to whites. The connection between Election Day and Freedom Day parades was also noted by Sterling Stuckey in his reading of an 1827 parade celebrating New York State emancipation. This 1865 reminiscence by black physician and activist James McCune Smith describes the resplendent procession: "It was a proud day in the City of New York for our people, that 5th day of July, 1827. It was a proud day for Samuel Hardenburgh, Grand Marshall, splendidly mounted, as he passed through the west gate of the Park, saluted the Mayor on the City Hall steps, and then took his way down Broadway to the Battery &c. It was a proud day for his Aids, in their dress and trappings; it was a proud day for the Societies and their officers; it was a proud day, never to be forgotten, by young lads, who, like Henry Garnet, first felt themselves impelled along that grand procession of liberty; which . . . is still 'marching on.' "[69] Grand Marshal Hardenburgh, Stuckey observes, "might well have been a Pinkster king or New England governor at the Emancipation Day celebration."[70]

But Hardenburgh was not a king or governor at a slave festival. He was a free man. And that made all the difference. As free people he and his compatriots had made a conscious decision to observe New York emancipation by employing an increasingly popular form of political expression in antebellum America. Taking to the streets advertised to the general public the deeper meaning of the 1827 Emancipation Act. Public processions were generally recognized as political vehicles, having displaced eighteenth-century crowd actions as a tolerated forum for political expression by non-elites, a form of representation that would only gradually be displaced by the elective franchise.[71] Blacks' celebratory presence in public space was unacceptable to many white Americans. And black Americans knew it. The Freedom Day parade in this context was a conscious, and potentially volatile, assertion of blacks' right to engage in the political process as equal citizens of the republic.

For that very reason, some African Americans questioned the propriety of such a politically charged public display on such a hallowed occasion. Months before the act went into effect, black leaders began using the nation's first black weekly newspaper, New York City's *Freedom's Journal,* to air their opinions on the proper form, content, and date of the anticipated celebrations. In the state capital, Albany, a "numerously attended" meeting of "men of colour" assembled at the Reverend Nathaniel Paul's African Meeting House on March 27, 1827, "for the purpose of taking into consideration the expediency of celebrating the abolition of slavery in the state of New-York." The meeting unanimously resolved that it was "a duty to express our gratitude to Almighty God, and our public benefactors, by publicly celebrating" the emancipation edict. But "whereas the 4th day of July is the day that the National Independence of the country is recognized by the white citizens, we deem it proper to celebrate the 5th." A committee of twelve was appointed to oversee the arrangements. While making it clear that a public celebration was necessary, the Albany group also took into account the perceptions of their white fellow citizens. Avoiding the streets on the Fourth also avoided the inevitable confrontation with large numbers of intoxicated whites, who likely would prefer not to share Independence Day, blacks' joy in emancipation, or the right of way in the public thoroughfare. Black leaders' desire to present only positive racial representations before the broader society also is reflected in the fact that the proceedings of the meeting were to be published in two of Albany's mainstream newspapers. Undoubtedly, those accounts would, like the report in *Freedom's Journal,* include the information that "the meeting of the people of colour" was "conducted with the utmost decorum."[72]

As the first published periodical forum for African American writers and activists from across the Northeast, *Freedom's Journal* exemplifies the critical role of print media in encouraging national debates and discussions, forging national constituencies, and constructing a national black American identity. In the weeks preceding the planned emancipation celebrations, the black weekly became an important vehicle for discussions of black comportment, public commemorations, and other divisive questions facing northern free black communities. On June 22 a writer signing himself "Libertinus" expressed his hope that during the upcoming New York celebration, "no act be done to sully the sacred character of the day." At the heart of Libertinus's entreaty was his concern for the impressions formed by whites—especially those already predisposed against African Americans. "The eyes of the world are upon us," he counseled; "our enemies watch us narrowly, to catch each little failing. Let us show them, that we are men . . . by abstaining from all riotous indulgence, from unbecoming mirth and extravagance." A week later, a correspondent identified only as "R." voiced his similar fear that inappropriate public demonstrations would "injure our reputation and our interest as a people."[73] Though R.'s concerns also related to the perceptions of whites, his commentary on African Americans' public commemorations was more wide-ranging, foreshadowing a number of key issues that would again and again occupy black leaders throughout the nineteenth century.

One issue that evoked in R. "the deepest regret" was the fact "that there are to be two celebrations of the abolition of slavery in this state, one on the fourth of July, without any procession, and the other on the fifth, with a splendid procession." Such division over "an event so interesting and joyous to every one of African descent," he wrote, "is disgraceful" and "can do no possible good, public or private." R.'s position cut to the heart of the ambivalence many African American spokespersons would express regarding public commemorations throughout the nineteenth century. "So great and glorious an event," he argued, "ought to be celebrated, but it would be better not to celebrate it at all, than to be divided about it." The first source of division concerned the date to be observed. While R. felt that "[n]othing can be more evident than that the Fourth is the proper day" to celebrate, he also recognized the potential hazards involved. The reality of blacks' exclusion from July Fourth celebrations was disturbing to R. His ideal scenario would see whites and blacks *together* celebrating both national independence and New York's abolition of slavery. After all, he pointed out, "many of our [black] forefathers laboured and shed blood" in the cause of the Revolution. And "any white citizen, who has any regard to the honour, or welfare of his country," could not but be moved to celebrate any assault on human bondage. "Why then should not the whole people, coloured and white, spend it as a day of rejoicing?" This universalist vision of a nation united by the quest for expanding freedom remained central to the rhetoric surrounding most African American commemorations into the next century. Returning from his flight of idealism to the racist reality of the times, R. admitted the very real "danger of being molested by vagabonds among the whites" on the Fourth. Rather than acquiescing to delay an emancipation celebration and parade until the fifth, R. suggested that conflict could easily be avoided by foregoing a public procession that would provide a target for unruly white mobs. "Can we not," he pleaded, "manifest the joy in our hearts and our gratitude to God, and our earthly benefactors without making a parade in the streets?" R. refused to acknowledge the community-building and political empowerment functions served by public processions in the 1820s, concentrating instead on their debilitating effects. Most white abolitionists, he said, "heartily disapprove of our making a street parade . . . because they know it is hurtful to us." It would be "more pleasing" both to God and to blacks' "earthly benefactors" to refrain from any public demonstration of "pomp and pride" that would at once go against the wishes of white patrons and invite white mob violence. "A procession, therefore, on that day, would be rather a manifestation of ingratitude than of gratitude."[74]

R.'s conception of the purpose and function of the emancipation celebration seems to have been limited to thanksgiving for blacks' receipt of "this great blessing" from God and from white benefactors. His objections to a parade suggest not only his deference toward whites who had supported the emancipation act but also his disdain for elements within the black community that did not live up to acceptable standards of respectable comportment. "[O]f what use to us are processions?" he asked; "do they make us richer, wiser, or better? have they not rather a tendency to injure us, by exciting prejudice, and making the public believe we care for nothing so much as show?" R. acknowledged that "many white people are fond of such displays too. But not the more sensible part of them. Men of sense see their vanity, and only encourage them because of their effect upon the minds of the ignorant multitude, who cannot be excited by nobler motives."[75] Here R. was perhaps more perceptive than he realized regarding the political, social, and cultural potential contained within public parades and commemorative observances. For many organizers of public commemorations, appealing to "the ignorant multitude" was precisely the point.

With literacy rates generally low among free African Americans, perhaps especially among newcomers in the growing cities of the antebellum North, public commemorations provided an important opportunity to reach a segment of black communities who might otherwise remain unreachable. Many who did not attend lectures, or read pamphlets and newspapers, or go to churches, or engage in other activities where they would have come into contact with the emerging civil rights and uplift community might be—and indeed the press reports throughout the nineteenth century indicate that they were—attracted by festive public events. Once there, they could be brought into the fold of the respectable classes; introduced to new ideas about themselves, their race, their history, and their identity; and thus become foot soldiers in the campaign for abolition and racial justice. Or, as R. and others feared, they might not be receptive to the message of uplift and activism, and their presence and behavior would serve only to disrupt the celebrations and call attention to the *least* respectable elements of the black community. Concern with the presence and potentially harmful impact of unschooled and unruly former slaves in the cities was considerable. *Freedom's Journal's* editors John Russwurm and Samuel Cornish expressed their misgivings about the possible results of emancipation in a late June editorial. "It is very important, if possible, to prevent them [the recent freed-people] from flocking into our large cities, where there is but little for them to do, and where everything is calculated to draw their uncultivated minds from the line of duty."[76] At this pivotal juncture for the development of African American commemorative traditions, debating the benefits and drawbacks of public demonstrations and the participation of the black masses occupied much of the leadership community's attention.

The celebrations in 1827 show a new set of commemorative practices emerging from the precedents of slave festivals, July Fourth celebrations, and slave trade commemorations. Organizers in some cities, including New York, Albany, and Rochester, combined parades with more reverential indoor activities. In others—in New York, Cooperstown, and various out-of-state sites—parades seem not to have been a significant part of the observances at all.[77] The largest celebrations were in New York City. As with the 1809 slave trade commemorations in that city, and much to the chagrin of at least one observer, separate observances were held. On July fifth—largely in order to avoid the congestion and potential violence from white July Fourth celebrants—the parade of between two thousand and four thousand led by Hardenburgh proceeded to the site of an oration by John Mitchell, which apparently was "something of an anticlimax" after the ostentatious procession. Despite their misgivings about public demonstrations, the editors of *Freedom's Journal* did express their "satisfaction, at the great degree of order observed throughout the day . . . and notwithstanding the great concourse from the neighboring places, the day passed off without disturbance."[78]

In one account of the July 4 celebration at the African Zion Church, an anonymous newspaper correspondent applauded the "discriminating taste" shown by the organizers, and seemed especially pleased to note that "[n]o public parade added to the confusion of the day."[79] The oration by veteran black leader William Hamilton was the featured event of the day, and Hamilton took advantage of his forum to recount the history of the antislavery activism that had brought about the event being commemorated. He portrayed emancipation as an act of societal purification: the state had "been cleansed of a most foul, poisonous and damnable stain" and had been thereby "regenerated." In addition to this historical interpretation, Hamilton offered some prescriptions for blacks' behavior in the public sphere. Specifically addressing "the female part of this assembly," who "not by proud, but by modest conduct," would influence black men toward "the true line of decorum and gentle manners. First, I would have you discountenance that loud vocability of gabble, that too much characterizes us in the street: I would look upon him, or her, that hailed me with too loud, or vulgar accents, as one who had forgot what is due to female modesty." Though his critique of unseemly comportment applied to everyday street activity, the next day's planned parade could not have been far from Hamilton's mind as he voiced his dismay over the lack of "modest conduct" exhibited in African American public expressions on the city's streets.[80]

During the city's celebrations over the next several years dissension continued about the issues of whether or not to parade, and whether it was advisable to hold more than one celebration in the area. In 1828 Samuel Hardenburgh served again as "Grand Marshal of the Day" for the July fifth parade, overseeing the activities of "the principle benevolent societies" of New York and Brooklyn. With "highly emblematical" banners and "fine bands of music," the procession was reported to have been "an imposing spectacle," executed "in the most orderly manner," such that it "elicited approbation even from the most prejudiced." Religious services followed, as well as the ritual reading of the emancipation act, and an oration by John Peterson that emphasized the importance of education. The apparent success of the New York celebration was offset, in the minds of the *Freedom's Journal's* editors, by the fact that "our Brethren of Brooklyn, not satisfied with having Celebrated the *Fifth* of July with us, had another unnecessary Celebration in their village—and a pretty large one too it was, extending over half a mile, as we are informed."[81]

Though Cornish and Russwurm were apparently not present at the affair, the "narrative of the proceedings" they received was enough to inspire their unyielding derision of the Brooklyn celebration. One aspect of their complaint was simply that more than one celebration in or around the same city was both wasteful and imprudent. While generally opposed to parades, they conceded that celebrants deserved "to enjoy themselves in a rational manner: if they will after all that has been said and done, have processions— let one suffice, and let that be a grand one, and serve for the year....We had a grand procession here on the fifth, everything was conducted with order and propriety, and great credit was gained by it from all classes." But the Brooklyn celebration, and particularly the parade, was more than merely redundant; it confirmed the editors' view that almost "nothing serves more to keep us in our present degraded position, than these foolish exhibitions of ourselves." On a very practical level, parades depleted the meager earnings of impoverished community members who could ill afford to deck themselves out in the "*fine dress*" the occasion seemed to demand. The "imprudence" of putting "all our earnings on our backs" threatened to leave many blacks "*unprovided* with *food,* and *clothing,* and *fuel,* during the chilly blasts of winter." Moreover, expenditures generally went to "prepare and purchase the cast off garments of some field officer, or the sash and horse trappings of some dragoon serjeant—that we may appear as Generals or Marshals, or Admirals, on these occasions, complete and appropriate laughing stocks for thousands of our citizens, and to the more considerate of our brethren, objects of compassion and shame." This description of blacks outfitting themselves in secondhand regalia, presumably from whites, is strikingly reminiscent of slaveholder paternalism during the slave festivals. However much cultural masquerading might have been involved in blacks' appropriation of whites' garments, it was small wonder that uplift-minded men like Cornish and Russwurm saw little benefit in perpetuating the paternalistic associations of master/slave relationships when their goal was to represent blacks as respectable and independent American citizens. But the editors seemed most disturbed by the actual behavior of African Americans in the Brooklyn procession: "We have heard of officers high in authority scarcely able to bear their standards—of the insolence of certain Coloured females, and of the debasing excesses committed on that ever memorable day, all of which were we to place here, would be a disgrace to our columns. It is not and never has been our object to expose our brethren, but we do say that nothing is more disgraceful to the eyes of a reflecting man of colour than *one of these grand processions,* followed by the lower orders of society."[82]

Parades might help mobilize the masses and make powerful political statements from a people claiming their rights and their place in the national family. But parades could also threaten the image of respectable and responsible citizens that many black leaders felt was essential to project if their white fellow citizens were ever to recognize blacks as anything more than despised denizens.[83]

In Albany on July 5, 1827, the Reverend Nathaniel Paul attempted to call attention to the higher purposes many leaders saw in the commemoration of New York emancipation. He saw the occasion as an opportunity not only to express gratitude to God and to "retrace the acts of our public benefactors" but also as the commencement of "a new era in our history." Following a pattern established during commemorations of the abolition of the slave trade, the Baptist minister presented his historical interpretation explicitly as "the progress of emancipation, [which] though slow, is nevertheless certain." As William Hamilton and his colleagues had done over the past generation, Paul traced the history of slavery from "the sufferings of Africa" to the "palpable inconsistencies" the institution brought into bold relief in the United States. He also exhibited a universalist perspective regarding the duty of race elevation that came with newly granted liberty—a duty he emphatically linked with his own recognition of the consequences of public representations. "We do well to remember," Paul chastened, "that every act of ours is more or less connected with the general cause of the people of color, and with the general cause of emancipation" across the globe.[84]

Retracing the past, giving thanks, prescribing matters of conduct, and identifying with other freedom movements and with all the darker peoples of the world shared time in the minister's address with yet another purpose—Paul's very explicit effort to create in the Emancipation Day observance a legacy for the generations to come. Paul may have had the early slave trade celebrations partly in mind when he began his oration by noting that "as the nations which have already passed away have been careful to select the most important events, peculiar to themselves, and have them recorded for the good of the people that should succeed them, so will we place it upon our history; and we will tell the good story to our children and to our children's children, down to the last posterity, that on the Fourth Day of July, in the year of our Lord 1827, slavery was abolished in the state of New York."[85]

The importance of transmitting this heritage to the next generation served as the guiding principle of Paul's peroration. Only through fostering such an awareness in the coming generations could the larger project of universal race identification and subsequent emancipation be accomplished. Paul was not the first black orator to advocate the perpetual observance of Freedom Days as a means of consolidating African Americans' sense of historical memory and racial identity. But his statement came at a critical moment when the public arena was becoming a more accessible and effective vehicle for such a project.

The New York State emancipation celebrations between 1827 and 1834 represent a transitional phase during which the public practices of slave trade commemorations, whites' July Fourth celebrations, and slave festivals became intertwined. What had been primarily indoor, church-related observances "became more of a community affair" that also "sought more deliberately to attract the attention of white people." Feasts, the firing of guns, the participation of a variety of African American social organizations, and other more visible displays fused the various facets of slave festivals and slave trade observances into a new form that would serve as a template for subsequent Freedom Day celebrations.[86]

Blacks had been active in the public arena at least since the late eighteenth century. But numerous factors by the 1830s facilitated an expanded and more activist presence. Most fundamentally, black Americans had reaped the benefits of revolutions in transportation and communication that were affecting the whole nation. Blacks had their own newspapers and tracts to turn to for the exchange of opinions and ideas. *Freedom's Journal,* though it was relatively short-lived, ceasing publication in 1829, represents a remarkable black breakthrough into the public arena. Also in the 1820s, black activists Robert Alexander Young and David Walker published inflammatory pamphlets intended to foster the growth of a unified black protest movement.[87] Benjamin Lundy's *Genius of Universal Emancipation,* William Lloyd Garrison's *Liberator,* and a second wave of black papers in the 1830s augmented the existing church and fraternal networks that allowed northern blacks to keep track of antislavery attitudes and events throughout the nation and beyond.[88] These papers complemented and engaged in dialogue with oral forms— spoken poems, folk songs and tales, orations, and sermons—which previously had been virtually unrivaled as expressive vehicles for attitudes and feelings of African American communities.[89] The expanding textual formats provided outlets for African American writers to air their views on politics, history, religion, protest, and reform as antislavery agitation began to find its voice.

The voice of black protest was also inspired by the actions of the slaves themselves. The notorious slave conspiracies organized by Gabriel Prosser in 1800, Denmark Vesey in 1822, and Nat Turner in 1831 brought immediate and harsh reactions from southern slaveholders. White backlash by the 1830s included violence, the suppression of abolitionist propaganda, new restrictions on black educational and religious endeavors, and a stricter enforcement of existing "black codes." As Peter Hinks has demonstrated with his convincing linkage of David Walker with the Vesey conspiracy, the efforts by those in bondage also had a very powerful influence on black activists in the North. When enslaved blacks worked for their liberation through collective violence, they inspired northern free blacks to look for their own vehicles for united action.[90]

The free black Convention Movement, beginning in 1830, was one such vital forum for intellectual debate and political mobilization. Initially instituted in response to recent antiblack violence and legislation in Cincinnati, the conventions met fairly regularly during the 1830s and more intermittently through the antebellum period. Black leaders—mostly businessmen, journalists, and ministers—mainly from the middle Atlantic states, met to debate the potential of colonization; to address northern black issues like employment, civil rights, education, and enfranchisement; to express solidarity with their enslaved brethren in the South; and to appeal as a unified body for the support of the broader society. Though their endeavors met with little tangible success in an increasingly racist environment, they did help to maintain constructive dialogue among themselves and to keep the cause of black social justice before the American people.

Various other black institutions had become well established by the 1830s. Gary B. Nash, in his study of the black community in Philadelphia, has referred to the years from 1815 to 1840 as "an era of unprecedented institution building." Fraternal organizations, mutual aid societies, schools, and churches—all with their roots in the eighteenth century—continued to expand in the 1830s. Philadelphia alone had fifteen black churches, sixty-four mutual relief or benevolent organizations, three literary societies, and three debating societies by mid-decade.[91] These organizations played an important role in the movement for racial self-help and uplift that was very much on the minds of black leaders of the period. The formation of separate black religious denominations, the creation of schools, the organization of the Convention Movement, and the emergence of a black press were all part of a vigorous campaign for the elevation of the race. This concept of elevation was applied across the board, encompassing issues of morals, religious life, education, economics, political participation, and civil rights. In order to uplift the race to those "respectable" standards most of the leadership deemed so essential, it became necessary to reach out to blacks of all social, economic, and cultural orientations. In this project, Freedom Day celebrations also began to play an especially important role as they evolved into celebrations that had relevance for all facets of the African American community.

Even so, some communities, including ones that recognized the positive functions of a proper celebration, chose *not* to observe the first anniversary of New York emancipation in 1828. At a meeting of African Americans at the home of Austin Steward in Rochester, New York, *Freedom's Journal* reported, it was decided that "it is not *expedient to celebrate* the day." Poverty provided the sole explanation. Echoing some of the concerns expressed the same year by Cornish and Russwurm, the meeting cited the need to "pay our debts and support our families" and the fact that they owed some "$400 for the lot for the Church." With those very tangible needs dictating their priorities, the group determined that it was "impossible to celebrate the day with all the pomp and ceremony that would be proper in better times, and therefore we shall stay home and attend to our business."[92] These community leaders in Rochester seemed disappointed at having to forgo the "pomp and ceremony" that was so disturbing to others. Apparently, for some, the powerful platform provided by public celebrations outweighed the possible drawbacks.

New York Emancipation Day celebrations between 1827 and 1834 reflect a more vigorous spirit of black protest than had existed at the beginning of the century. By the 1830s the celebration of New York emancipation became more and more an occasion to lambaste American hypocrisy and injustice. The July 4 date of the emancipation act accentuated the sanctimony of an American society that refused to extend its egalitarian ethos to all its citizens. Blacks' rejection of July Fourth as an appropriate occasion for celebration intensified during the 1820s and 1830s as the hated American Colonization Society sought to fuse the meaning of American patriotism with the society's mission to deport free blacks to Africa.[93] As orator David Nickens reminded his Chillicothe, Ohio, audience in 1832, "we have met on this 5th of July, not under the mock pretense of celebrating the 4th of July, for that would betray in us a want of sound understanding. . . . This day causes millions of our sable race to groan under the galling yoke of bondage." Nickens reaffirmed the historical perspective of previous freedom orators with his inducement to "look to the history of nations . . . look through the dark vista of past ages, and read in the history of Hannibal and others, who were Africans." A knowledge of history would demonstrate that "all the now civilized world is indebted to sable Africa for the arts of civilization and learning. . . . Let the good citizens of color arise," he entreated, to continue their "goodly heritage" in the face of American dissimulation.[94] The "protest" Fourth of July tradition that emerged from New York state emancipation celebrations thus integrated the historical vision of previous black slave trade celebration orators with an intensifying—and increasingly public—spirit of remonstration. This tradition remained salient throughout the antebellum period, but after the 1830s, it came to be largely incorporated within the commemoration of a new African American freedom celebration.[95]

CHAPTER TWO

"A BORROWED DAY OF JUBILEE"

MATURATION, 1834–1862

From bright West Indies' sunny seas,
Comes, borne upon the balmy breeze,
The joyous shout, the gladsome tone,
Long in those bloody isles unknown;
Bearing across the heaving wave
The song of the unfettered slave.

—J. M. Whitfield, August 1, 1849

I like these annual celebrations because they call us to the contemplation of great interests, and afford an opportunity of presenting salutary truths before the American people. They bring our people together, and enable us to see and commune with each other to mutual profit.

—Frederick Douglass, August 1, 1857

WHEN GREAT BRITAIN'S act emancipating the approximately 670,000 slaves in its West Indian colonies went into effect on August 1, 1834, it did not immediately inspire much celebration among blacks in the United States. One reason may be that the date fell just after a July Fourth protest parade in New York City had resulted in several days of antiblack rioting. The event was, like many antebellum "race" riots, a white assault on blacks claiming their right to public political expression, and it reinforced the recent resolution by the 1834 National Convention of Free People of Colour "that we *disapprove, will discountenance and suppress,* so far as we have the power or influence, the exhibition and procession usually held on the *fifth* of July annually, in the city of New-York; and all other processions of coloured people, not necessary for the interment of the dead." The convention criticized such parades for being wasteful of limited financial resources and tending "to increase the prejudice and contempt of whites." The resolution at least implicitly denounced the persistent African-based traditions of music, dance, and "pomp in dress" that such occasions inspired. After "a very protracted debate" the resolution passed with just two dissenters, one of whom, perhaps not surprisingly, was Samuel Hardenburgh, a frequent marshal in New York's extravagant Emancipation Day parades.[1]

There was also a simpler reason for the initial lack of excitement over West Indian emancipation. The reality was that very few West Indian slaves were actually freed in 1834. Rather, the act provided for a period of apprenticeship, during which forced labor, whippings, and the other most egregious features of bondage remained intact. A handful of observances were held between 1834 and 1837, but the reawakening of commemorative Freedom Day celebrations began only after the period of apprenticeship was lifted and immediate abolition of slavery implemented in the British West Indies in 1838.[2]

In Philadelphia that year, William Douglass, the first African American to succeed Absalom Jones in the pulpit of St. Thomas's Episcopal Church, told his August 1 audience that the end of apprenticeship meant West Indian blacks were "now . . . freemen, in the strict sense of that term," and it was therefore "highly proper and becoming" for black Americans to celebrate "a glorious era in the history of freedom." But William Lloyd Garrison noted how few white Americans in 1838 "hailed the day as Freedom's noblest jubilee." Even Garrison's own Massachusetts branch of the American Anti-Slavery Society, which would soon become a regular sponsor of West Indian emancipation celebrations, apparently made no such arrangements in 1838. Many black Americans, however, did initiate public commemorations in that first year of West Indian freedom. Garrison himself was "invited, by my colored brethren in New York," to deliver an oration at their August 1 celebration. He did not expect a large crowd since "our colored friends deemed it best (as a matter of safety, probably—such is liberty in New York!) not to advertise it in any of the daily papers." Garrison was therefore surprised by the impressive turnout "of between three and four thousand persons . . . about two-thirds colored," including "friends from Philadelphia, and other places." The organizers, who apparently had concerns about white reactions to the event, were likely gratified by Garrison's report that "everything was conducted in the best possible order."[3]

Over the next two decades African Americans' August 1 Freedom Day celebrations became widespread as annual events in towns and villages across the free states and beyond. By the 1850s celebrations were being held not only in the northeastern states but also as far west as Indiana, Minnesota, and California, as well as in Canada, Liberia, and in the West Indian islands themselves. In 1848 Frederick Douglass could confidently open his oration by welcoming a familiar assembly to "this annual festival." As the tradition spread and became entrenched, it matured into a form that defined the practice of African American Freedom Day festivals into the twentieth century. Emancipation in the West Indies was a pivotal event in the construction of African American historical consciousness and in the establishment of

African American commemorative traditions. Between 1808 and 1838 American blacks had searched in vain for a suitable historical moment around which to organize their celebratory calendar. The Fourth of July was clearly a sham, not intended to include them; the abolition of the Atlantic slave trade proved an empty promise; and the various state Emancipation Days were too localized to serve as a unifying force for all African Americans. As the historian Benjamin Quarles has noted, "they did not have much to choose from."[4]

Not that West Indian emancipation was selected merely as the least odious of the available options. As Garrison's and William Douglass's 1838 comments indicate, it was seen by most black and white abolitionists as a truly epochal event that had at least partially cleansed the world of the sin of human bondage and that presaged the end of slavery in the United States. Abolitionists' attraction to the event was magnified by the fact that West Indian emancipation had been accomplished without violence. "Heretofore," one writer argued in 1838, "revolutions and changes which have shaken nations to their centre, have only been effected by violence and the hand of arbitrary power. . . . But this mighty event . . . has been peaceful as the advent of its Holy Originator. . . . No blood—no tears—no strife—no accusing recollections of violence and crime to overshadow the morning sunshine of a people's deliverance." A decade later, H. W. Johnson answered Americans who argued the "danger and impracticability of immediate emancipation" by characterizing West Indian emancipation as "a great moral triumph . . . a victory achieved, not by the sword and the bayonet, but by the force and power of truth." Johnson took pains to point out to his August 1 audience at Rochester, New York, that, given the relative isolation of the British colonies and the overwhelming numerical majority of the Africans, it would have been "not only possible, but easy, for the emancipated to have dug the grave of every white man upon those islands. . . . And yet none of those frightful evils—none of those awful scenes of blood and butchery, which we were told would be the inevitable consequences of this measure, have occurred." Prominent white abolitionist Wendell Phillips could exercise considerably less discretion than his black counterparts in commenting on the absence of black violence in the wake of West Indian emancipation. Regarding the emancipated slave, Phillips declared in 1849, "I do not care much to know what he did. There is nothing worse than slavery. If he did not cut his master's throat; if there is a white man living in Jamaica to-day, the experiment was successful." By the late 1840s many African American abolitionists were growing less committed to the Garrisonian line of moral suasion and nonviolence; however, most black speakers still refrained from seeming to condone bloody retribution quite so openly.[5]

While blacks did not frequently mention Haiti by name in this context, their references to the absence of vengeance and violence in the British colonies were clearly intended to defuse white fears of a repetition of the protracted and bloody struggle for black liberty and self-government that had taken place on that island at the end of the previous century. Of the various emancipatory events—abolition of the slave trade, New York State emancipation, and now West Indian emancipation—that black Americans had publicly commemorated, the absence of any organized public demonstrations commemorating the Haitian Revolution is conspicuous, if not altogether surprising. Given the horror with which white Americans viewed the events on San Domingue during the 1790s, black Americans must have realized that their publicly identifying with the bloody slave rebellion and revolution would only alienate and infuriate the very people they needed to convince of African American respectability. Perhaps more pointedly, public identification with the Haitian Revolution would likely have brought even more white violence to bear on black public celebrations and black communities generally. Even at other African American freedom celebrations, I have found only occasional and brief mentions of the revolution that created the modern era's first black republic on January 1, 1804. Haiti's example of black self-liberation and independent governance was unquestionably an inspiration to African Americans in quest of their own freedom, and the event and its heroes were widely admired and written about by black activists. That the event was not prominent in public festivals, even in the slave trade celebrations that shared the January 1 anniversary date, suggests the conscious avoidance of a connection with Haiti in African Americans' public demonstrations.[6]

West Indian emancipation, on the other hand, was not only more widely acceptable for its relatively peaceful initiation and aftermath, but both black and white abolitionists also took pains to demonstrate that free labor was at least as economically productive a labor system as slavery. Wendell Phillips again proved an exception, mocking the tendency to evaluate the success of West Indian emancipation on the basis of sugar production and export figures. "As if there were nothing but sugar in God's world!" he spat. "As if the American people were to test a great moral event by hogsheads of sugar and puncheons of rum! I do not care whether the slave worked or not. . . . It would not grieve me much to learn that he lay lazily under the graceful palm of his native land." Most abolitionists, black and white alike, sought rather to appease Americans' concerns regarding the possible economic impact of immediate emancipation. Black orator William J. Watkins asserted that the postemancipation West Indies enjoyed "the blessings of a glorious prosperity" and complained to his August 1, 1859, Newark, New Jersey, audience "that slave-holders and their abettors, the servile press, and paid menials, have endeavored to distort this truth so as to show an adverse condition of these islands since emancipation." Samuel Ringgold Ward, reporting from Jamaica through the *Weekly Anglo-African,* ridiculed antebellum proslavery apologists who were consistent and vocal in "crying out about the poverty and 'ruin' of Jamaica, *since* and *because of* emancipation." Ward countered those arguments with a detailed assessment of the steady profits being earned with free labor. In the face of statistics showing a decline in West Indian exports, black orator A. H. Francis argued, with some straining of both language and logic, that such figures actually reflected the growth of a prosperous "home market" made up of consumers who were formerly bondspeople. A more logical if similarly nonquantifiable argument presented in the *Pennsylvania Freeman* held that Sweden's and Denmark's 1848 emancipation of all their colonial slaves was "of itself a refutation of the stale and foolish assertions that emancipation had ruined the British Colonies. . . . They have not taken this step without counting the cost, nor without studying carefully the results of the English experiment. Such a course from old conservative monarchies is a most emphatic testimony that the cry of ruin over West India emancipation is the croaking of false witness."[7]

Black abolitionists themselves, in any case, did not need evidence of economic feasibility to convince them of the massive importance or essential righteousness of the event. In language that resonated with that of earlier Freedom Day orators, Frederick Douglass emphasized the regenerative effect of the act, depicting it as having brought about "the restoration to the broken ranks of human brotherhood eight hundred thousand lost members of the human family. It is the resurrection of a mighty multitude, from the grave of moral, mental, social, and spiritual death" that was slavery. The centrality of the black experience in this interpretation did not, however, detract from the universal import of West Indian emancipation. Using an argument that recurred persistently in Freedom Day commemorations, black orators implied that not blacks alone but all of humanity should acknowledge the event. William J. Wilson, in his August 1, 1859, address, echoed the words of early slave trade orators when he described West Indian emancipation as "one of the most memorable events in the history of our times."[8] Even more emphatic was Frederick Douglass. In a world that had "literally shot forward with the speed of steam and lightning . . . during the last fifty years," Douglass asserted in 1857, West Indian emancipation stood alone as "the most interesting and sublime event of the nineteenth century." That August 1 should be recognized as "illustrious among all the days of the year" was a fact undisputed, he claimed, among "all civilized men at least." Indeed, a year later Douglass expressed pleasure at the sight of so many whites in his audience of more than three thousand at a Poughkeepsie, New York, celebration, "for though this is our day peculiarly," he pointed out, "it is not ours exclusively. The great truths we here recognize, the great facts we here exhibit, and the great principles which truth and fact alike establish, are world-wide in their application, and belong to no color, class or clime. They are the common property of the whole human family." Similarly, at Rochester in 1848, the great orator had confidently asserted that "the occasion is not one of color, but of universal man."[9]

By midcentury words like these were reaching biracial August 1 audiences numbering in the thousands all across the free states and Canada, exposing whites and blacks alike to a historical perspective that placed freedom at its interpretive center and that touted the universal significance of acts of black emancipation. American blacks organized more than 150 August 1 celebrations, at more than 50 different locations in more than a dozen states between 1834 and 1862.[10] In addition, black orators reached diverse audiences by speaking at scores of celebrations organized by white antislavery societies. The size of the August 1 crowds and the presence of large numbers of whites suggest that Freedom Day commemorations played a broader role in antebellum popular political culture than has been previously acknowledged. Detine Bowers maintains that this "increasingly popular forum . . . was especially significant in the annals of American democracy in that it evolved into the first large gatherings where . . . diverse audiences of mixed class, race, sex, and political persuasion could congregate to hear the voice of marginal groups."[11]

As early as 1838 the white reform paper the *Emancipator* was encouraging all abolitionists around the world to commemorate August 1.[12] By the early 1840s increasing numbers of white antislavery societies were organizing their own celebrations, thereby lending further weight to black orators' claims for the universal significance of the anniversary. William Lloyd Garrison's American Anti-Slavery Society was extremely consistent in holding large and well-publicized celebrations in the Boston area throughout the 1840s and 1850s, and other Massachusetts communities followed suit. During the early 1840s the *Liberator* reported on white-organized celebrations in Fall River, Scituate, Dedham, Lynn, Weymouth, Lowell, Upton, and Hingham.[13] Gradually the practice spread among white abolitionists throughout New England, across New York, and into the midwestern states.

Whites also made up a considerable percentage of the crowds at most black-organized affairs, in large part because blacks actively solicited white attendance. They made explicit invitations to white abolitionists in addition to issuing general invitations to the entire community through newspaper advertisements. Philadelphia's Banneker Institute was typical in inviting "all lovers of Freedom and Reform" to their 1858 celebration at a commodious suburban grove.[14] Many whites attending such events were indeed ardent abolitionists, but others were merely curious spectators or even opponents of the antislavery cause. In 1857 a correspondent to Garrison's *Liberator* commended Springfield, Massachusetts, blacks for their biracial emancipation "pic-nic," at which all, regardless of their sympathies, "were made welcome." A marked contrast, it was noted, to white Fourth of July affairs. Though many communities were initially hostile to events that embodied both black initiative and antislavery agitation, whites gradually grew accustomed to August 1 celebrations as the tradition became established. The historian Benjamin Quarles, in fact, suggests that "whites were more receptive to an August 1 affair than any other kind conducted by Negroes."[15]

The evidence bears out Quarles's impression. By the late 1850s few northerners from New England to Ohio could have remained oblivious to African Americans' virtually institutionalized August 1 celebrations. The New Bedford, Massachusetts, celebration in 1843 was attended by hundreds of white citizens, including at least "two slaveholders, that heard the song of *jubilee*" on that day. The tiny central New York village of Canandaigua hosted a celebration in 1847 that consisted of some four thousand spectators, only about one-third of whom were black. In 1849 the celebration at Harrisburg, Ohio, drew an interracial crowd of two thousand, the largest ever seen in that small community. One fourth of the celebrants at Brooklyn's Morris Grove in 1855 were white. In the same year the majority of William Watkins's audience of nearly three thousand in Jefferson County, New York, was white. Crowds of five thousand at Staten Island, New York, and seven thousand at New Bedford, Massachusetts, were composed of whites and blacks from all around their respective regions. William C. Nell reported of the New Bedford celebration in 1853, that "white fellow-citizens were so numerous on the ground, and such fraternal feeling was exhibited, that a novice would have received no color of an idea that the celebration was of any other character than that in which all complexions, castes and climes had an equal interest in promoting."[16]

Though white participation continued to be a common feature in blacks' celebrations, there remained for many African Americans the conviction that Freedom Day celebrations were especially meaningful and appropriate for blacks. In 1859 Jacob C. White asserted that "we may exhaust the calender and not find another day of equal interest to our people. . . . On this day the heart of the colored man beats high."[17] In his 1843 oration at a Boston celebration held by the New England Freedom Association, a black vigilance committee, the AME Zion minister Jehiel C. Beman went further, insisting "that the colored man, as he was the injured party, could alone *feel* on this occasion. Freely acknowledging all the sympathies of our white friends, [Beman] considered they *could not,* having never been placed in the same circumstances with the colored people, *feel* as they do in celebrating this great event. Who were the slaves in the West India islands? Colored men. Who were rejoiced in the great jubilee? Colored men. Who ought now, above all others, celebrate this day? Colored men.... [Beman] hoped in the future, that every colored man in this country will celebrate this as a day of thanksgiving and praise."[18]

The timing of Beman's assertion is suggestive of the mood among black abolitionists and their evolving positions on the relationship between whites and blacks in the movement. This particular August 1 came just weeks before Henry Highland Garnet's controversial "Address to the Slaves" at the 1843 Buffalo Convention, which called for enslaved blacks to resist their oppression through "every means" at their disposal, not excluding violence. The debate this address provoked not only contributed to divisions among black abolitionists but also exacerbated divisions between blacks and whites, the latter group overwhelmingly rejecting violence as a tactic. The expanding black militancy of the 1840s also reflected some African American leaders' growing sense that the abolitionist struggle was fundamentally a black struggle. Whites, Garnet once argued, could only aspire to be blacks' "allies. *Ours is the battle.*"[19] The contention over control of the movement was not merely fought across a racial divide. Blacks and whites were also divided among themselves, and despite rising racial enmity, biracial cooperation remained an essential characteristic of antebellum abolitionism. Nonetheless, through the 1840s and 1850s, blacks exhibited increasing autonomy in directing activism, in forming community institutions, in holding meetings and conventions, and in arranging public commemorations, often with minimal white assistance.

One white observer was deeply troubled by the sentiment of black racial exclusivity he detected at an 1852 celebration organized by "two or three colored churches of Toronto," in Canada West. Writing to Garrison's *Liberator,* C. H. A. Ball expressed great disappointment that the Canadian celebration differed greatly from the more consistently biracial events he had attended in New England. Toronto's black organizers "extend[ed] no invitations to their anti-slavery friends, or to people not of their own color." The "colored people ... take the occasion, almost exclusively, into their own hands," making it essentially a " 'nigger's day.' " Whites could certainly attend the celebration and, if they purchased the required ticket, even partake in the subsequent dinner. A white minister would usually give a sermon and white newspaper editors might receive invitations, but other whites wanting to attend "must do it at the [risk?] of *seeming* intrusion." This particular celebration saw about half a dozen white men present and no white women.[20]

The following year, the Cincinnati area was the site of two separate, and apparently racially distinct, celebrations. One was held about fifteen miles from the city, along the Hamilton and Dayton railway, and "consisted principally of the colored people of Cincinnati and vicinity, but some were present from as far as Cleveland." The other "pic-nic was celebrated by the Whites, on Vine street Hill, in a wood, on a beautiful and commanding height, with a fine view of the surrounding country." In 1855 the *Liberator* noted only a single "Grand Pic-Nic Celebration" of August 1 in the city, that being organized and officiated solely by "the colored citizens of Cincinnati." At Salem, Ohio, in 1856, the white-led Anti-Slavery Society gave up their plans for an August 1 celebration upon "learning that a colored Society, named the 'Sons of Protection,' were sounding the note of preparation for the same." In this instance biracial cooperation prevailed, as the whites "cheerfully waived their own arrangements, and participated with the Protectionists."[21]

Black activists had taken the initiative in organizing their own August 1 celebrations from the outset in 1838. Through the 1840s and 1850s many black abolitionists grew frustrated with the racially defined limits to their leadership roles within white-dominated antislavery organizations, and they increasingly chose to act separately from their white counterparts. Consistent with this pattern, while biracial attendance continued to predominate at both white- and black-organized August 1 celebrations, it seems clear that blacks and whites acted separately in organizing their own observances. Blacks' initiative in making arrangements for these events was part of a larger strategy to assert their identity as leaders of their respective communities and to demonstrate their capacity to lead without white guidance. Particular black communities across the Northeast established especially strong commemorative traditions, none more notably than the seaport of New Bedford, Massachusetts. New Bedford was emerging as an energetic hotbed of abolitionism and a mecca for escaped slaves, perhaps most famously Frederick Douglass, who arrived there in 1838. Douglass's biographer William McFeely describes the New Bedford of that period as "the best city in America for an ambitious young black man."[22] The first major celebration organized by African Americans in that city seems to have been in 1843, when a procession of some three hundred black men and women passed through streets "crowded with spectators" who "looked on in amazement to see the novel sight; for such a sight was never before witnessed in the streets of New Bedford." The marchers' appearance was "very neat" and uniform, with the men wearing "white pantaloons" and the women "dressed mostly in white, in the most simple and becoming manner." The parade was "led by the Wilberforce Brass Band, a company of colored men that have been practicing for some time, and play exceedingly well." The parade's "moving spirit" on its mile and a half march to a nearby grove was not a nationally prominent leader, but a local black man "with no office" who had been "called upon" and served as marshal "by general consent." The grove accommodated a long line of tables laden with food, and the several speeches presented to the hundreds of attendees were thought to have had "a lasting effect." A correspondent for Garrison's *Liberator* emphasized "the respectability of the colored citizens" and the expressions of admiration and approval among whites in the audience. "It was," he concluded, "a grand affair, and did great credit to the colored people of that place."[23]

The following year built on that success, and attracted some four thousand participants, some from as far away as Providence and Nantucket. In an early example of what would become common practice, regional railroad and boat companies offered reduced fares from both towns. "The whole management and order of procession were conducted by the colored people," and white involvement in any aspect of the arrangements seems to have been minimal. New Bedford's numerous black benevolent societies, each "dressed uniformly alike, and each bearing its appropriate banner," were well represented in the procession, along with "two or three societies of women," a young men's society from Providence, a group of seamen, and "an excellent band of music from Bristol, R.I." A picnic was again held at the grove, at which "all persons were invited to partake without discrimination." Music and speeches were interspersed "to keep up a healthy excitement" among the crowd, which was composed of "all classes [who] wished to sympathize with us." The celebration was said to represent "the greatest move for the cause of the slave, to break down caste and remove prejudice, that has yet been made in this place."[24]

Among the numerous other communities in which blacks organized celebrations in the first years after 1838 were Pittsburgh, Pennsylvania; Buffalo, Albany, Poughkeepsie, and Troy, New York; and even Wilmington, Delaware, where slavery had yet to be abolished. Blacks in Newark, New Jersey, seem to have established a consistent commemorative tradition from an early date. The assembly at an 1839 celebration "was composed of thousands of persons, both white, and colored." After a dawn service at a Methodist church, a "large, and respectable audience" convened at "the colored Presbyterian Church" at nine in the morning. Speeches by Samuel Ringgold Ward, James W. C. Pennington, and "the Rev. Mr. Finney" were followed by a procession with a band and local schoolchildren that led the assembly to a nearby grove for more speeches and, presumably, some leisurely activities, as well. It was reported that "the day was passed pleasantly without any noise, or confusion, and we hope profitably."[25]

The 1840 Newark celebration, however, aroused expressions of disgust over public behavior, much like those Samuel Cornish had articulated regarding New York State emancipation celebrations while editing *Freedom's Journal* more than a decade earlier. Charles B. Ray, who had recently replaced Cornish as editor of the *Colored American,* voiced concerns remarkably consistent with those of his predecessor. Despite "an interesting and eloquent address" by the Reverend Theodore S. Wright, Ray reported, the celebration was "quite revolting to the feeling of the good sense of our brethren of that city." It was an impromptu parade by black folk from the hinterlands, an affair apparently not on the formal schedule of events, that drew Ray's ire. "A number came in from the country, with a drum and fife, formed a procession, which was fallen in with by a few of the more thoughtless of the place, all of whom conducted themselves in a manner deeply mortifying to the mass of our people in Newark." The editor expressed his "utter disapproval of public processions" that served only to "degrade our people." Ironically, in mid-July of the following year a writer to the paper expressed concern that the New York area, and particularly Newark, which was "generally first in this matter," had not yet made plans to celebrate on August 1. Urging that there was still time to prepare, the writer insisted that "the day should not be suffered to pass without the usual demonstrations, on our part, of joy and gratitude. . . . At all events, the committee of vigilance must not neglect their usual celebration on that day."[26] Debates about the proper public behavior of black celebrants continued, but by the early 1840s it was clear that northern free black communities had embraced West Indian emancipation as an essential commemorative moment whose annual observance must continue.

While white abolitionists continued with their own celebrations and also remained a significant presence at black affairs, I am most concerned with understanding the function and the meaning West Indian emancipation commemorations held for black communities and individuals. Jehiel Beman's insistence that only the colored man could truly "*feel* on this occasion" raises the perplexing problem of ascertaining just how the masses of black Americans *did* feel about the meaning of August 1. It is clear that not all blacks felt the same. The country folk parading in Newark in 1840, for example, had different ideas about August 1 than did their critic Charles B. Ray. Patrick Rael has argued convincingly that antebellum black activists like Ray and Samuel Cornish used August 1 freedom celebrations to assert and confirm their authority as community leaders; to demonstrate their capabilities as organizers, orators, and public figures; and to present to white America a unified racial front in the struggle for abolition and equal rights. They sought to forge a black protest movement that crossed class lines by inculcating in the black masses values and a sense of identity based on their own concern with middle-class respectability and their commitment to antislavery activism. In working toward this end—which has been usefully described as the "elevation" of the race—celebration organizers could not tolerate challenges to their control. For example, the social inversions and the mocking of white leadership that marked eighteenth-century slave festivals would have been completely at odds with free black leaders' need for public credibility and legitimacy. In this context, Cornish's disgust with black parading generally and Ray's outrage at the uninvited display at Newark make complete sense. Conversely, the paraders' apparent disregard for the desires of those who claimed authority over the celebration suggests that the masses used the celebrations for their own purposes.[27]

However difficult it is to identify the various meanings August 1 celebrations held for different constituencies, it is clear that African Americans of all classes did attend these commemorative celebrations, and they did so in large numbers. Estimates of black attendance at antebellum Freedom Day celebrations suggest that these were important social events that were looked forward to by African Americans of all social classes and cultural orientations throughout the North. More than a thousand blacks converged on Canandaigua, New York, in both 1847 and 1857. In 1858 the abolitionist and author William Wells Brown addressed a predominantly black audience of about 2,000 at Christiana, Pennsylvania, saying it "was the largest meeting of colored persons that I ever met at one time, and it was pleasant to see so many together." The village of Urbana, Ohio, whose celebration featured the popular African American orator John Mercer Langston, counted 3,000 blacks among its 5,000 participants. These numbers are especially impressive when one considers that the entire free black population outside the South totaled only around 286,000 in 1850. A high percentage of African Americans certainly made August 1 a conspicuous date on their annual calendars.[28]

These large freedom festivals—often numbering several thousand people—were usually accommodated at spacious outdoor groves similar to those used for the revivals and camp meetings that were also popular events during the nineteenth century. As early as 1836 some celebrations also included steamboat excursions as part of the festivities—a practice that was denounced by some but that remained popular during the 1840s and 1850s.[29] Whether transportation was provided by steamboat, rail, carriage, or foot, the destination was frequently a shady grove like that adjoining the Haddington Mansion outside Philadelphia. The Banneker Institute's advertisement for its 1858 celebration described the "New and Beautiful Grove" in glowing detail:

> This new, romantic and delightful place of resort is situated in the 24th Ward, at the terminus of the West Philadelphia Passenger Railway. It is in form, nearly circular, and is enclosed by thick woods, and highly cultivated farms. The surrounding country is hilly, beautiful and picturesque in the extreme. A small stream in which there are several miniature cataracts, slowly winds its way along the southern edge of the Grove. There is an excellent platform, (which is finely shaded by overhanging trees,) with swings and everything requisite for the pleasure of the Pic-Nic Party. There is also a large and fine Hotel, with a cupola commanding a most excellent view of the adjacent country and in which shelter can be taken in case of a shower. All these features, together with its comparative nearness, make "Haddington Mansion" just the place to spend a day away from the city's heat and din, and constitute it the best resort of the kind in the vicinity of Philadelphia.[30]

This type of site—usually convenient to fresh water and shade, and accessible at excursion rates by carriage, rail line, or water transport—was available in or near many northeastern communities by midcentury. In Massachusetts, New Bedford had Parker's Grove; Framingham boasted of Harmony Grove, with its spaciousness, shade, proximity to a lovely pond, and its amphitheater; Hingham's Tranquillity Grove was easily accessible by boat from Boston. Boat excursions here could be a major part of the festivities, at times packing more than a thousand celebrants in on one trip. Around New York City, Brooklyn had its Morris Grove and Staten Island Marshall's Grove; farther upstate, Geneva took advantage of the Geneva Water Cure Establishment's outdoor facilities, and Canandaigua held its celebrations "in the shade of Academy Grove." When a grove site was not available, organizers made use of fairgrounds, public parks, or public squares.[31] Indoor venues were not completely forsaken, but by midcentury the public preference for verdant and commodious outdoor facilities had helped to redefine Freedom Day commemorations.

Whether grove, park, or public square, the new outdoor sites contrasted greatly with the earlier tradition of holding Freedom Day observances in black or white churches. Not that the churches were totally dissociated from August 1 observances; for example, in 1854, the Indiana District Conference of the AME Church directed each minister to deliver an appropriate sermon or lecture during the first week of August 1855. In 1841, when August 1 fell on a Sunday, a correspondent for the *Colored American* urged that "the sacred desk" be used by "every colored minister of the gospel, and every one who professes to be an abolitionist" to "make the event which that day commemorates, one of special prayer and praise."[32] Ministers also continued to be prominent among the organizers and featured speakers at even the most secular of the outdoor celebrations. But by midcentury the excursion format at a grove site, with its far less restrictive atmosphere, had become the norm. Drawing upon the potential of these spacious outdoor venues, organizers could plan a day of activities both secular and sacred, festive and somber, in order to appeal to a broad spectrum of the black community. Fusing the patterns laid down in the eighteenth-century slave festivals and the early slave trade observances, a whole set of activities emerged that would come to define Freedom Day commemorations for generations to come.

As with all aspects of the celebrations, activities at the groves drew from both white and black cultural practices and traditions, and from what Simon P. Newman has described as a "popular political culture"—the range of commonly shared rites, symbols, and festive practices that permeated public political discourse.[33] John Collins, a white seminarian, publicized the idea of the picnic at August 1 celebrations, first through a letter to the *Liberator* in 1842 and later in his how-to guide *Anti-Slavery Picknick: A Collection of Speeches, Poems, Dialogues, and Songs*. Some of Collins's suggestions—processions with banners inscribed with particular mottoes, for example—had been applied for decades in July Fourth and other white public festivals as well as in black Freedom Day observances. But Collins's call for grove picnics to popularize the celebrations and to publicize the antislavery cause coincided with the expansion of the practice among both white and black celebration organizers. African and European Americans had used grovelike settings for religious camp meetings for some time, but not until the 1840s did the secularized Freedom Day celebrations apply that approach to link sacred observances of emancipation with the "good times" of a festive outdoor picnic.[34] In so doing, organizers were quite conscious of appealing to the desires and temperaments of various facets of black society, from the respectable classes to the (at times) unruly urban masses.

The organizers were usually identified with the more well educated, somewhat more financially secure, and generally respectable activist leaders of the community—ministers, journalists, fraternalists, business owners—but they purposely arranged events that would appeal to everyone. Celebrants enjoyed plentiful food, good company, and assorted amusements that might include boat rides, races, ball games, militia drills, and dance pavilions. There were also sermons, political and historical orations by local or national leaders, and public parades featuring floats, banners, black bands, fraternal orders, militia companies, and various voluntary associations.[35] Frederick

Douglass, for one, usually expressed his support for these public rituals because of the various functions they served for black communities. "I like these annual celebrations," he explained in 1857, "because they call us to the contemplation of great interests, and afford an opportunity of presenting salutary truths before the American people. They bring our people together, and enable us to see and commune with each other to mutual profit."[36] The great interests addressed by the celebrations took many forms, ranging from the overtly political to the social, economic, educational, and purely recreational.

One of the most meaningful aspects of West Indian Emancipation Day celebrations is that they were, in the parlance of the era, "promiscuous" gatherings, attended by all facets of the community, cutting across lines of gender, class, education, occupation, religion, color, and so on. Most black celebrants likely did not attend primarily for the contemplation of the same great interests as were emphasized by Frederick Douglass and others in their orations. It is important to remember that the masses of free blacks did not always have the same priorities as Douglass, William C. Nell, Frances Ellen Watkins, Charles B. Ray, or other community leaders and antislavery activists. For uneducated working people struggling to eke out a living in a hostile racist society that denied them opportunity at every turn, these events were fun, a pleasant break from a grueling daily routine.[37] They provided important and, for many, all-too-rare opportunities to congregate, to interact with large numbers of other blacks in a relatively safe space, away from the restrictions of their day-to-day lives. But as Simon P. Newman has argued regarding early national festivals, even those who attended primarily for a good time must also have recognized the political character of the event and of their participation in it. At times black orators made a point of reminding festive crowds of the serious object of the occasion. "We have not gathered here together for the purpose of showing our fine clothes, neither to eat or drink," admonished a speaker at Columbus, Ohio, in 1844, "but it was for the purpose of talking about the oppressed."[38]

Northern black leaders had, by the 1840s, established many institutions for political activism and agitation, including churches, mutual aid societies, fraternal orders, conventions, and newspapers. All these played essential roles in the abolitionist movement. But those institutions did not reach all free blacks, especially those who were recent arrivals from the South, illiterate and struggling to survive. And reaching all elements of the black community was very important to leaders trying to "uplift the race" and build a movement. In bringing together all elements of the community, annual West Indian Emancipation Days filled a need that other institutions did not. Frederick Douglass was not alone in recognizing the potential usefulness of

August 1 observances. Like many Emancipation Day orators, Charles Lenox Remond remarked in 1851 on the significance of August 1 and "the propriety of annually stamping its impress upon the community." A report from New Bedford in 1843 emphasized the "lasting effect" the speeches would have on the hundreds of spectators at Blackmer's grove that day. In 1849, upon reading about Douglass's plan for forming a National League of black activists, J. M. Whitfield of Buffalo, New York, suggested that annual meetings of the league should be held on August 1, arguing that "no day could be selected more appropriate for an oppressed and outraged people to assemble and devise plans for obtaining their just rights, and elevating their moral and intellectual character." Whitfield further suggested that a mass meeting be held to organize the league at Buffalo's West Indian emancipation celebration the following year.[39]

As northern black communities grew and matured, these celebrations became vital rituals of self-definition and community bonding. Orations at these events explicitly sought to educate blacks as to their identity, their history, and their prospects. Urging blacks to "place their aims higher," Jacob C. White told his Cleveland audience in 1859 that "they should remember *who* they are, and *why* they are." A Mr. Gilson, speaking to an 1851 gathering outside New York, advised that children in particular be "well informed in history, both ancient and modern, by which we would better understand our present condition, and what course we should pursue." Antebellum black orators, like their predecessors at early slave trade celebrations, took up the challenge, giving history lessons on the greatness of the African past, the accomplishments of black heroes, and the role black patriotism had played in building the nation. At Buffalo in 1849 Abner H. Francis argued that a mere "glance at the past" would refute the notion that "because the African is now enslaved . . . he always has been, and always will be." Francis was a prominent local activist and a clothes dealer whose business was in the midst of collapse; he would move from Buffalo to Portland, Oregon, within the year. In one of his last public speeches in Buffalo, Francis mocked the pretensions of whites, whose forebears were "a horde of naked savages" until "the light of science and letters . . . dawned upon their benighted visions from our Egyptian ancestors." All of Western civilization and knowledge, he argued, could be traced back to Egypt and Ethiopia, and it was to Africa "that Grecian historians and philosophers resorted to obtain wisdom and refinement no where else to be found." J. H. Perkins also maintained that "History informs us that the sciences were partial to the sable children of the sun." Moving to modern events, he chastised whites for always singling out Hottentots, Bushmen, and black thieves and prostitutes as examples of "the moral and intellectual worth of the colored citizens of the United States." Rather they should balance those negative images with the accomplishments of "such men as Toussaint L. Ouverture, the colored Washington of St. Domingo, or Alexander Dumas, the Historian of France, the scholar and gentleman." These historic figures were "not only creditable to the U. States, but would be so to any of the civilized nations of the earth." H. W. Johnson called attention to the black American patriot and to the hypocrisy of a society where, "no matter whether he be one of the last-born patriots of '76, or one of the sacred veterans of 1812" there would be "not one spot on free Columbia's soil where he can repose his weary limbs in safety."[40]

During a decade when nationalism and the invention of national traditions was on the rise throughout the Western world, many black orators emphasized the importance of African Americans' historical foundations by proclaiming that no people could *be* a people *without* a shared history and shared traditions. The very fact of having a tradition of public commemoration in itself was seen as proof of African Americans' coherence as a people. As black orators had been asserting since 1808, it was important for African Americans' sense of nationality to create a commemorative calendar since "it has been from time immemorial, a practice among all nations to celebrate certain important events" in their history.[41] The educational role of providing historical information was thus inseparable from black activists' broad political goals. Freedom Day gatherings could also promote a form of economic nationalism. One observer of a celebration between the "colored settlements" of Weeksville and Corsville, New York, explained that "the object of having it there, was not only to celebrate West Indian emancipation, nor yet to see a little pleasure, but it was mainly to congregate there from the surrounding country, on the grounds owned and occupied by our own people, and if we had anything to spend for nick-nacks, to spend it with them."[42] Black leaders were very consciously constructing a history, a heritage, and an identity for a people who were largely uneducated and who were just developing a sense of themselves *as* a people. In order to build an antislavery movement, a sense of identity, unity, and common purpose had to be spread throughout the community, not just among the educated classes.

The festivals' educational role could also be directed outside the black community to influence the thinking of whites. Patrick Rael has emphasized black abolitionists' concentration on affecting "the public mind" of white America, in order to demonstrate blacks' respectability and thereby reverse the race prejudice that prevented blacks from achieving emancipation and full equality. African American activists explicitly used Freedom Days in this pursuit, as was suggested by one description of a Harrisburg, Pennsylvania, celebration that was said to be an "occasion worthy of record" because of "the very favorable impression created and impressed upon the public mind." Likewise, Frederick Douglass called on all "friends of freedom" from two hundred miles around to gather to make the 1848 Rochester celebration "an admirable demonstration, well calculated to impress the public mind with ideas and principles which must save the nation, if it ever be saved, from the crime and curse of slavery."[43]

While these pursuits of public education and community empowerment might have been central in the minds of Freedom Day organizers, the festivals were also social events at which African Americans congregated for pleasure. Black celebrants might renew acquaintances, make business contacts, meet potential spouses, and generally have fun and let off steam.[44] Indeed, in the 1840s and 1850s, rest, relaxation, and general socializing were among the most popular attractions of Freedom Day celebrations. At a large New Bedford celebration in 1851, the afternoon hours between the dismissal of the procession and the evening's exercises were "devoted to social calls; a happy and profitable medium of keeping bright these festivals of freedom." After that evening's series of formal speeches ended, "amidst huzzas for Liberty, the friends separated again to gather as inclination led."[45]

Cannons firing, ladies fairs, banquets, and music were often among the attractions during a day that generally devoted considerable time to "feasting and hilarity." Just as Philadelphia's Banneker Institute invited participants to "spend a day away from the city's heat and din," organizers in Dayton, Ohio, emphasized their desire "to make the day one of pleasure as well as productive of good." Descriptions of celebrations mention ice cream and watermelon vendors, and tables "groaning with the delicacies of the season." While "pure cold water" was often the beverage of choice among reform-minded organizers, celebrants were known to have provided more spirited refreshment and, in any case, took enthusiastic advantage of the opportunity to make merry.[46]

Partly in concession to the tastes of the urban masses, dancing became an increasingly popular part of August 1 celebrations after the 1840s, but not without encountering continuous, if futile, opposition from more sober-minded participants. Whether under the trees at a suburban grove or at an indoor ball in the city, the light fantastic was often tripped into the wee hours of the morning. Philadelphia's Banneker Institute reserved some of the boldest and largest print in its broadside advertisement to call attention to the presence of "AN EXCELLENT ORCHESTRA" at an 1858 celebration. Dancing was often seen as the high point of the festivities, as it was for many attending the San Francisco celebration in 1855, though in this case it was not even included in the official program of the day.[47]

Concerns about the impropriety of dancing and its potential to negatively influence the "public mind" indicate that many "respectable" African Americans regretted the participation of their more boisterous brethren and remained fixated on issues of decorum and proper behavior in the public sphere. But other black leaders saw the value of attracting as large and diverse an audience as possible and were more accepting of the mix of sacred and secular activities used to celebrate the day. William C. Nell participated enthusiastically in an 1851 New Bedford Freedom Day festival and noted that many forms of public expression "whether prayer or speech, song or dance, all, all were acceptable garlands, hung on the altar of Freedom." Even the unimpeachably respectable Frederick Douglass viewed the loosening of behavioral constraints on August 1 as consistent with the central meaning behind the tradition. Douglass provided a vivid commentary on the socializing at an 1859 gathering of some three thousand celebrants at Geneva, New York:

> The ringing of bells, firing of guns, and the sound of music with the gay, fluttering throngs which arrived by every train, gave proof of the general joy. The great good nature and boisterous merriment of the colored people, as they passed to and fro, or stood in groups about the streets, shaking hands, laughing and talking, though at times not over regardful of good taste, seemed to awaken in the white people a good deal of mirth, but it was mirth without malice. The little extravagances into which a few of our people are apt to fall on such occasions, are much more painful to the judicious among ourselves than to the white people who may witness them. To many of us the first of August is like the white man's 4th of July—a day of freedom from ordinary restraints, when every man may seek his happiness in his own way, and without any marked concern for the ordinary rules of decorum. There were a few at Geneva who carried this 4th of Julyism a little too far, but they were the exceptions. The masses conducted themselves with propriety as well as freedom.[48]

William Wells Brown indicated that African Americans' public image was being well served by Freedom Day events when he noted that among the two thousand celebrants at the Christiana, Pennsylvania, celebration in 1858 "all was peaceable and quiet, not a drunken person on the grounds. All appeared to be deeply interested in the meeting, and to feel the importance of the occasion."[49] A white Providence, Rhode Island, newspaper reported that "the colored people . . . had a good time generally" at their celebration, which included a procession featuring "carriages of all kinds," from the "aristocrats" to "the humble one-horse wagon." While a gentle rebuke was offered regarding the purported "negro fondness for display and finery," the reporter granted that the crowd was on the whole "well-behaved" and exhibited "good order and good taste."[50] Despite a degree of toleration for relaxed standards of conduct, Freedom Day crowds were, according to most accounts, relatively well behaved. Frederick Douglass at times complained that the freedom festivals could be "made too much of an occasion of mirth and pleasure without doing any material good," but he remained a supporter of West Indian emancipation celebrations, so long as they served a positive purpose and blacks remained aware of their potential impact on the public mind of the broader society. "If these occasions are conducted wisely, decorously, and orderly," Douglass counseled, "they increase our respectability before the eyes of the world, and silence the slanders of prejudice. If they are otherwise conducted they cover us with shame and confusion."[51]

Douglass's concern, Charles Ray's disgust for the 1840 Newark parade, and various discussions of the issue of black public deportment suggest that black celebrations may have been rather less genteel than most reports in the abolitionist press suggested. Nonetheless, they do appear to have been more well ordered than many white Independence Day celebrations, which, one scholar has noted, "seemed bent on becoming a setting for sinful indulgence and excess" during the antebellum decades.[52] A reporter from the *Rochester National Reporter* explicitly noted the contrast in 1848, expressing "an humble wish that our fourth of July might in all future time be as orderly and appropriately celebrated by our white friends, as was the first of August by our colored citizens." The biracial nature of blacks' August 1 affairs was also noted by white abolitionists. In 1857 A. H. Raymond reported that "quite a number of white persons . . . were made welcome to the festivities" organized by "the colored people" of Springfield, Massachusetts. "I am afraid," he speculated, "that if, on the fourth of July, a company of colored persons should presume to present themselves at a white celebration, they would receive rather different treatment."[53]

African American Freedom Day events also included a broad cross-section of the black community, while white Fourth of July observances were not only racially exclusive but also seem to have been increasingly class-specific affairs. Susan G. Davis has observed that antebellum political and intellectual elites typically marked the day with a brief, decorous march to the refuge of a hotel or private club, where an elaborate dinner would be followed by patriotic speeches and toasts. Working-class whites did not enjoy the same privilege of access to suitable indoor facilities and engaged in far more boisterous activities in streets, squares, and fields, where they celebrated both the nation's birthday and a well-earned day off. Drunkenness, gambling, prostitution, and excessive violence—often directed against blacks—mixed with fireworks, dancing, and street parades in the public festivities.[54] Southern July Fourth festivities could show the most striking contrasts, as was the case at Columbus, Georgia, in 1854, when Sen. Robert Toombs chose that date for an estate sale of "between ninety and one hundred Negroes, consisting of men, women, and boys, &c." Garrison's *Liberator* noted sarcastically that the generous terms allowed payment to be delayed until Christmas.[55]

Although the firecrackers, noisemakers, and "sinful indulgences" typical of July Fourth revels seem to have been largely absent, August 1 affairs did share the white Independence Day practice of parading through the principal streets of the city. Public processions were perhaps the most visible symbols associated with the celebrations and the most obvious carryovers from the slave festivals. Building on those eighteenth-century precedents and making use of the common forms of American festive culture, Freedom Day parades emerged as important performed political statements that asserted free blacks' right to use public space and represented the African American community both to itself and to whites.

An 1847 comment in the *Liberator* by "Q." shows that at least one white observer drew a specific contrast between contemporary African American parades and Boston's slave trade processions of the preceding generation. An African American August 1 procession at Waltham, Massachusetts, according to "the sentiments of the respectable portion of the press in noticing the event the next day," was praised for having "earned universal attention and respect by its numbers and appearance." This represented "a significant mark of progress" over the preceding quarter century. "Not twenty-five years ago," Q. observed,

> when the population of Boston was not nearly as large or as miscellaneous as it is now the celebration of the colored people of the Abolition of the Slave Trade was the laughingstock of the city; they were overwhelmed with ridicule and insult, and their pretended proceedings made the vehicle of wit and satire. . . . And, at last, the celebration was abandoned by the advice of the city government which either could not protect these citizens in their rights, or did not think it worth its while to take the trouble to do so. Now, and for several years past, we understand that no molestation has been offered to a colored procession, any more than to a white one. . . . If the anti-slavery agitation has done nothing else, it has altered the condition of the colored inhabitants of Boston.[56]

While Q. appears to be sympathetic to antislavery and the protection of blacks' citizenship rights, his comments regarding the "pretended proceedings" that rendered slave trade processions a "laughingstock" during the

1820s suggest that in his view perhaps they deserved the derision of whites at that time. Moreover, any positive aspects of blacks' "altered condition" seem to be regarded as the result of the influence of the white antislavery movement. With even their supporters exhibiting such judgmental attitudes, it is little wonder that black leaders were so concerned with the face they presented to the broader society.

While the infrequency of "molestation" and the presence of cordial bi-racial crowds at many antebellum Freedom Day events were indeed notable, whites could at times still disrupt festivities with purposeful acts of violence. I have already noted the attacks on black July Fourth paraders in New York City in 1834. Similarly, in 1842 an August 1 parade in Philadelphia was at-tacked by a white mob. These and other incidents reflect the increasingly racist environment in northern cities after 1830. Proslavery propaganda was on the rise; minstrel shows were propagating distorted and damaging images of African Americans; and a wave of white immigration was beginning to aggravate job competition between lower-class whites and blacks. In this context many whites aggressively challenged blacks' citizenship and rights to full and equal use of public spaces.

Though the threat of violence loomed constantly over black Freedom Day parades, African Americans generally overcame their fears in order to main-tain the right to hold their commemorative celebrations in the public sphere. A Harrisburg, Pennsylvania, procession in 1859 featured "Grand Marshal Aquilla Amos and his aids on horseback, wearing blue sashes and decorated with wreaths"; the Philadelphia Brass Band; the Odd Fellows and the Daugh-ters of Temperance; the Carlisle and Toussaint L'Ouverture Clubs; and var-ious flags, banners, and speakers of the day. In typically inclusive fashion, these organized groups were joined in the line of march by throngs of spec-tators, some of whom, as was the custom, had traveled from as far as Phil-adelphia and Baltimore. But perhaps none of the other elements of the parade carried with it a more compelling message than the armed and uni-formed Henry Highland Garnet Guards—a black militia company.[57]

Marching black militia companies had their roots in the early republic, most notably among the *gens de couleur* in New Orleans, but these com-panies lost their legitimacy after Louisiana became part of the United States in 1803. The federal Militia Act of 1792 effectively prohibited black partici-pation in state militias, and New Orleans blacks felt the burden of American rule. This proscription was disregarded when the Hannibal Guards of New York formed a separate black militia company during the increased black militancy of the late 1840s, and the formation of numerous black com-panies in the free states became widespread during the 1850s. The Fugitive Slave Law of 1850 expanded the renewed militancy among northern blacks during that decade, leading to the formation of black vigilance committees and militias to provide protection from the anticipated onslaught of government-sanctioned slavecatchers. Reaction to the 1854 Kansas-Nebraska Act, the 1857 *Scott v. Sanford* Supreme Court decision, and several well-publicized confrontations over the abduction of blacks by slavecatchers intensified black militancy by the end of the decade. By 1861 black military companies existed in practically every state in the North and West, and boasted an enrollment of more than eighty-five hundred African American men.[58]

The militias provided a crucial outlet for African American men eager for an opportunity to demonstrate their manhood in a way that had meaning for both whites and blacks in the popular political culture of antebellum America. They also suggested blacks' readiness to strike against both slavery and white racial violence with military action. (These companies may well have contributed to John Brown's false impression that blacks would rise en masse and join him in an abolitionist guerrilla war in 1859.) The militias' vital symbolic message was nowhere more visible to a larger segment of the population than during Freedom Day celebrations. For example, the Boston celebration of 1859 was reported to have been "connected by our people with a military turn-out," as the host Liberty Guards welcomed the New Bedford Blues and the National Guards of Providence. The following year organizers of a large regional celebration at Geneva, New York, "extend[ed] an invitation to the various colored military companies from [New York City] to visit them on that occasion, promising them a cordial reception." The Henry Highland Garnet Guards at Harrisburg were joined in 1859 by military companies from Chambersburg, Pennsylvania, and New York City. The Garnet Guards made an especially imposing impression on "the crowds of people, white and colored, [who] thronged the streets through which the procession passed." The Guards were "equipped in gray coats and pants with black stripes, fatigue caps, white belts, and carrying new muskets. The company looked well, marched well, and were the 'observed of all observers.' "[59] Armed and uniformed black men marching in ranks through city streets or running through military drills on the celebration grounds must have sent chills of apprehension down the spines of many whites. But a different sort of chill—one of pride and inspiration—must have infused African American onlookers. What a stirring sight for people whose normal existence required constant monitoring of their actions lest whites take offense and retaliate. By attesting to African American self-assertion and manhood the black militias' Freedom Day performances served an important function for African American communities. They expanded the parameters of acceptable public behavior by modeling that behavior before large throngs of increasingly militant and politicized blacks on the eve of the Civil War.

The example of the militias illustrates just one of many functions that Freedom Day celebrations fulfilled for antebellum African Americans. By the 1850s West Indian emancipation celebrations were attracting thousands of blacks who congregated in large cities and smaller towns. Urban centers like Philadelphia and New York had significant black populations, and the large crowds there are not surprising. But when villages like Canandaigua, New York, or Harrisburg, Ohio, attracted Emancipation Day crowds numbering in the thousands, the implications of those figures need to be considered in order to comprehend the significance of the Freedom Day events in African American culture.

The scale of the events and the breadth of their appeal are significant. When a commemoration was held in one of these small villages, blacks representing all facets of their communities traveled many miles to attend. The huge numbers of black attendees, relative to their overall numbers in local populations, indicate that celebrations drew people from all around their respective areas, a trend that persisted into the twentieth century.[60] An 1854 celebration at Dayton, Ohio, attracted contingents of African Americans from the towns of Cincinnati, Troy, Xenia, Hamilton, and Piqua. Three years later blacks from two counties and four towns attended the August 1 observances at Galesburg, Illinois. New Bedford, Massachusetts, organizers sent out invitations to blacks and whites throughout the region. An 1860 celebration at Hudson City, New York, listed members of the official Committee of Arrangements as hailing from Poughkeepsie, Troy, Albany, Catskill, Brooklyn, and New York, as well as Newark, New Jersey, and Pittsfield, Massachusetts. Blacks in Canada West also held celebrations that drew large regional crowds. An 1854 August 1 observance in Toronto drew attendees from a dozen Canadian communities, and a subsequent gathering of 3,000 celebrants in Chatham attracted a sizable group "from Detroit, [who] chartered a steamer and came up *en masse.*" New Bedford's 1855 August 1 fete brought in an estimated 7,000 celebrants, including 250 blacks from Boston and 500 from Providence, Rhode Island. If accurate, these figures represent approximately 15 percent of Boston's and more than 30 percent of Providence's black populations.[61]

In some parts of the country, Freedom Day commemorations seemed to rotate among several interconnected cities or villages. For example, in western New York state Frederick Douglass spoke at celebrations at Canandaigua in 1847, Rochester in 1848, and Medina in 1851. The two smaller communities were each less than fifty miles from Rochester and less than one hundred from each other. In 1849 and 1850 festivals were held a bit farther west at Buffalo, with the site for each celebration generally having been agreed upon by special committees appointed at the previous year's meeting. Many of the same African Americans from the surrounding region, including contingents from Canada, seem to have attended these celebrations, thus the rigors of travel shifted from one group to another from year to year. African American leaders recognized the regional composition of the celebration crowds. Douglass, for example, advised his 1848 Rochester audience that he would not reiterate the detailed history of the slave trade and British abolitionism he had chronicled at Canandaigua the year before, "presuming that I now stand before thousands of the same great audience who warmly greeted me there."[62]

By the 1850s railroad and steamboat companies regularly offered discounted rates or ran additional lines to accommodate the travel needs of black celebrants. Organizers in Brooklyn in 1851 made special arrangements with the Long Island railroad, which provided ten cars and several omnibuses "filled with anxious passengers" from around the region. An 1859 celebration committee in Poughkeepsie, New York, chartered steamboats to accommodate the "very large delegations" that were "expected from different localities from this portion of the state." The 1859 Harrisburg celebration that featured several visiting militia companies claimed its status as "the first occasion in the history of our State on which the railway companies generally will issue excursion tickets for . . . any demonstrations among our people." Railways involved included the Cumberland Valley, Schuylkill and Susquehanna, Pennsylvania Central, Northern Central, and the Reading, with several others being contacted in order to allow the various Masons, Odd Fellows, military companies, and "citizens generally, to come by the shortest and cheapest route." A Cincinnati celebration in 1852 was attended by delegations "from several of the large towns in the State," with the Dayton railroad providing "twenty cars, containing about 3,000 persons." This was said to be "the largest passenger train which has left the city." Hotels, saloons, and other purveyors of public accommodations also profited from the increase in black travelers to freedom festivals. In fact, Frederick Douglass expressed concern that some of these white-owned facilities had "received their money [from black patrons], and appropriated it to . . . sustaining pro-slavery papers and pro-slavery men in office."[63]

While their political opponents might at times reap some benefits, the freedom festivals were orchestrated to congregate fellow blacks and their white antislavery supporters. It was typical for organizers to advertise in the abolitionist press and issue "a general invitation . . . to all Freedom's Friends throughout the State and elsewhere," as the residents of Auburn, New York, did in Douglass's *North Star* in May 1849—several months before the event. Although some celebrations were handled on considerably shorter notice, this type of advance planning was the more typical pattern and testifies to the institutionalization of the festivals by the late 1840s. The Buffalo celebration in 1849 extended its formulaic "general invitation . . . to all Freedom's Friends throughout the State and elsewhere" in the same newspaper forum a month earlier than Auburn. The arrangements behind these two 1849 events came more fully into public view than most because of some irregularities and conflicts regarding the negotiations with featured orators. The contentiousness among the principals in this discord provides a window into the complexities of Freedom Day arrangements and the occasional conflicts that they entailed.[64]

There is no inherent reason for the Auburn and Buffalo celebrations to have given rise to conflict. The two towns are approximately 150 miles apart and would not draw primarily on the same population for attendance. The fact that these two celebrations were both advertising several months in advance in Douglass's popular *North Star* is consistent with my argument that freedom festivals were important regional events that drew their crowds from up to 50 or 100 miles away. Perhaps blacks in and around the village of Canandaigua, which is roughly equidistant between the two, might be torn as to which to attend, but they would likely base their respective choices on travel considerations; their neighbors' preferences; whether they had family, friends, or business contacts in either place; or perhaps what speakers or specific activities each event offered. And each celebration would attract the majority of its attendance from communities nearer in.

The Buffalo Committee of Arrangements was able to form quite early, as the decision to hold the 1849 celebration in that city was reached during the previous year's celebration at Rochester. According to the Buffalo committee's accounts of its activities, in January 1849 committee secretary George Weir Jr. contacted prominent Syracuse minister and editor of the *Impartial Citizen* Samuel Ringgold Ward in order to engage him as one of the speakers of the day. Ward agreed, providing that the committee could pay him an honorarium of twenty-five dollars above and beyond his travel and incidental expenses, as he had received for his participation in the 1847 celebration at Canandaigua. The committee was unwilling to pay more than his expenses, but Ward nonetheless replied on March 2 that "it is probable that I will comply with the request of your fellow citizens in respect to the first of August next, on the terms that you propose." However, some time afterward Ward wrote again to say that he had reconsidered and that "owing to business matters &c." he would have to decline speaking at Buffalo. The Buffalo committee also invited Henry Highland Garnet, who initially indicated "that he would come on the same terms agreed upon with other speakers." When Garnet learned that this would cover only travel expenses, he wrote again, stating that his terms would be forty dollars plus expenses. The committee's response "expressing their regret at his receding from his engagement," prompted an apparently offended Garnet to change his mind, "stating [that] if life lasted, and Providence permitted, he should be in Buffalo on the first of August, without asking or receiving anything from the Committee." Thus assured of Garnet's participation, the committee also arranged for orations by Amos G. Beman and Abner H. Francis, and began to print and distribute publicity for the event with Garnet's name prominently featured.[65]

Nature intervened to disrupt plans for the Buffalo festival when the "dreadful scourge of Cholera" descended on the city that summer. Less than two weeks before the celebration a "Meeting of the Colored Citizens" of Rochester resolved not to attend the Buffalo event "in consequence of the prevalence of that malignant disease" and urged upon the Buffalo organizers "the propriety of defering their celebration for another year." While August 1 was "a day ever to be held in remembrance by all lovers of freedom," they found it "totally inexpedient as well as pernicious to attend the forthcoming celebration, for in doing so, we are jeopardizing not only our lives but those of our families." They expressed "sincere regret to the committee of management in not being represented by a delegation on such an important occasion" and offered assurance to "those noble and philanthropic spirits who shall assemble on that glorious day, that our hearts and souls are with them."[66]

The presence of cholera understandably had a negative impact on the Buffalo festival. Nonetheless, as planned, the procession presented "a grand and imposing spectacle," including a brass band and "carriages from which were displayed beautiful and appropriate Banners." Exercises at Judge Philander Bennett's "splendid Grove" featured songs, prayers, a reading of the Emancipation Act, an ode written by poet and local resident J. M. Whitfield, and the requisite orations. However, the disease was held responsible for "preventing the attendance of large numbers who would otherwise be present." Even the president of the day was unable to discharge his official duties "in consequence of sudden illness." A number of individuals did brave the risks to travel from afar to participate in the celebration, including Charles Lenox Remond of Massachusetts, Dr. David J. Peck of Pennsylvania, George W. Tucker and Henry Bibb of Michigan, and featured orator Amos G. Beman of Connecticut. It is not clear whether the cholera epidemic had a direct impact on Henry Highland Garnet's decision, but he chose not to be present. This unexpected absence was irritating enough to the organizers for them to publicly read his correspondence promising his attendance as "evidence of Mr. Garnet's unfaithfulness to his pledge and his wanton disregard of his moral and legal obligation." Garnet, it turns out, was at the celebration in Auburn that day, where he and Samuel Ringgold Ward gave orations, each receiving twenty-five dollars as "compensation . . . for their labors."[67]

Ward, in the August 8 editorial column of his *Impartial Citizen,* was openly critical of the Buffalo convention. They refused to pay Garnet "a single red cent over and above his travelling expenses, for his services as Orator," while at the same time they "went to great expense for printing" materials related to the celebration, including advertisements in Ward's paper. "Here," Ward complained, "lies the secret of the poverty and embarrassment of our public men. . . . When will black men learn to pay their own laborers as liberally as they pay white men?" Buffalo's George Weir responded with outrage that Ward had "taken a public opportunity of thrusting the javelin at them, and all because they would not consent to give him *twenty-five dollars* . . . for making a first of August speech." Weir expressed his indignation that Ward would dare to criticize the committee for an offer fairly made and one accepted with no complaint by orator Amos Beman, who was not "actuated by the same mercenary motives, as yourself and Mr. Garnet." He further claimed that Buffalo could indeed "have obtained white speakers as cheap as colored," but "on such occasions, we want no hireling advocates of freedom of any color, no matter how great their talents." However much esteem Ward and Garnet deserved for their activist records, Weir maintained, the fact was that "they both agreed to come to Buffalo, and both backed out" in the interest of "the almighty dollar."[68]

Black communities like Buffalo's, and even prominent ministers and speakers like Ward and Garnet, operated under enormous financial restrictions in antebellum America. With rare exceptions, even the most respected black professionals, educators, businessmen, ministers, journalists, and community leaders felt the burden of economic limitations imposed by their race and their status as activists for a generally unpopular political cause. Local figures like George Weir shouldered heavy burdens of responsibility in their quest for community empowerment and racial activism. In the instance of a single emancipation celebration, much effort and expense was employed contracting with speakers and musicians, scheduling events, arranging for food, reserving and preparing the celebration grounds, advertising, and subsequently publishing the orations and proceedings, among other responsibilities. It is perhaps because of his appreciation of the effort involved that Weir had no criticism for the Auburn planning committee, who he was sure "possessed a great deal of liberality and magnanimity" as ascribed to them by Ward. As Weir pointed out regarding his own committee, "a great deal of labor and expense was necessary in order to perfect the arrangements. This, as usual, fell on a very few individuals; and we presume it is within bounds to say, that every man actively employed on the Committee, expended as much, in time and money, as S. R. Ward or H. H. Garnet would have done, had they attended, made speeches, and paid their own expenses."[69]

Over the decade of the 1850s the complexities of organizing August 1 celebrations, including making contractual arrangements with speakers, expanded with the growth of the tradition. In June 1860 the *Weekly Anglo-African* noted that "unusual preparations are being made in various parts of the country to celebrate on an extensive scale the approaching anniversary" of West Indian emancipation. This expansion of the Freedom Day tradition reflects the growth and maturity of free black communities and activist networks, as well as the important role the festivals played in serving those communities' varied interests. But this growth, the editors suggested, also meant that "speakers for the occasion will be in great demand." As the 1849 Buffalo case indicates, making the proper arrangements was not always a smooth and cordial process. The *Anglo-African,* recognizing the development of a growth industry, made the following offer to serve essentially as a Freedom Day speakers' bureau: "Now, as we are in communication with all the talent of the country, we would suggest that committees could save themselves much time and expense by authorizing us to select speakers for them. Information in regard to the terms on which they can be employed shall be promptly furnished on application to us. No time should be lost in attending to this feature of the arrangements, for our best speakers are likely to make early engagements."[70] Walking a fine line between community service and blatant hucksterism, the *Anglo-African* editors demonstrate that August 1 freedom festivals had become deeply entrenched institutions in northern free black cultural and political life.

Northern blacks, of course, had established numerous vehicles for organization and mobilization. Churches, benevolent and literary societies, fraternal organizations, military companies, newspapers, conventions, and other institutions provided ongoing mechanisms for maintaining local and regional African American networks. Some groups met regularly throughout the year and played central roles in building coherent northern free black organizational networks. As antebellum northern free black communities grew and matured, the Freedom Day festivals themselves became vital institutions for reinforcing both regional and national networks of intraracial communication and political mobilization.

Orations served one of the most important communicative and educative functions of public commemorative celebrations: mediating between the overlapping oral and literate elements of the black community. Up to the end of the eighteenth century Americans of African descent had left scant written expressions of any kind. By most estimates, more than 90 percent of black Americans were still nonliterate at the time of U.S. emancipation in 1863. Even in the North black literacy may have barely exceeded 50 percent. Blacks—even more so than whites—lived a predominantly oral culture.[71] As the nineteenth century wore on, more African Americans, particularly in the North, had sufficient access to education to acquire at least rudimentary literacy. Those who were more highly educated and widely read began to publish written histories, and more blacks were capable of reading those documents and sharing their ideas with their nonliterate peers. But even after African American works of autobiography, history, and historical fiction became more available in the second half of the nineteenth century, the spoken and performed components of Freedom Day celebrations continued to augment their historical message and bridge the gap between the oral and literate orientations of African American communities.

The orations at Freedom Day events were thus vital tools of outreach. With a foot in each of the intermeshed and overlapping worlds of orality and literacy, Freedom Day orations were important educational and mobilizational vehicles for communicating with other blacks and with the broader society.[72] Black orators' power to inspire was suggested by one commentator who had traveled with a large contingent from Baltimore to hear Henry Highland Garnet speak at an August 1 commemoration in Harrisburg, Pennsylvania. Garnet, he attested, "has the power to fire up his auditors in such a way as to make every man feel like daring to do." After having reached large numbers of black and white auditors on their public delivery, orations often found their way to an even larger audience through publication in black and white abolitionist newspapers, which frequently were read aloud and disseminated throughout the black community. The orations thus moved back and forth between spoken and written forms of expression and promulgation. In this way the celebrations fit into the emerging impulse among community leaders to educate the masses, to instill in them a sense of history and tradition, and to mobilize the community toward political action.[73]

A June 1860 letter from "LIBERTAS" in the *Weekly Anglo-African* urged blacks from across the Northeast to "commence *now,* and make all necessary arrangements for a celebration of the day in such a manner as shall promote most effectually the colored man's advancement and elevation." He particularly called on organizers to "secure your speakers" early that they might "flash their inspirations on the hearts of the people. Let the sons of freedom and the daughters of virtue gather fresh strength and courage as the historical scenes of that day shall blaze up around them beneath the magic touch of the orator's voice. Let the tongue of eloquence and the song of freedom inspirit and energize all the friends of humanity on that glorious day." Not only should the spoken word invigorate freedom festival crowds but the written word as well. LIBERTAS also enjoined organizers to "look after your publications to distribute that day among the gathered thousands." The complex interplay between festive culture and print culture is further evidenced by an 1859 report to the *Anglo-African* regarding a New Jersey commemoration that only concluded "after the sale of a large number of your papers, which went off like hotcakes."[74]

The role of abolitionist newspapers and pamphlets in this process was crucial. As early as 1839 the organizing committee at a Newark celebration resolved that the day's proceedings and orations "be published in the Colored American and Pennsylvania Freeman." This use of the abolitionist press was ongoing. William C. Nell similarly reported that the 1859 New Bedford meeting voted to "request the publication of the proceedings in *The Liberator, Frederick Douglass's Paper,* and the *New Bedford Standard.*" This resolution reflects a lesson learned earlier by New Bedford's organizers, who in 1847 expressed their disappointment "that we had not at the meeting . . . able reporters to preserve the eloquent and spirited speeches listened to on the very interesting occasion." Like the early slave trade orations, many West Indian emancipation addresses were published in pamphlet form as well, in order to further disseminate blacks' potent ideas about history and activism.[75]

By 1844 the further expectation that festivals would be widely advertised ahead of time in the press also had been firmly established. Frederick Douglass, in explaining his failure to appear as scheduled at a Providence celebration that year, explained his absence partly on account of weather and partly due to inferences he had drawn from the press. Douglass had agreed to be one of the out-of-town speakers, along with James W. C. Pennington, but "upon looking into a New-York paper, I saw that Mr. Pennington, instead of being at Providence on the 1st, was to be at New-York. Meanwhile, there was *no notice given in any of the anti-slavery papers,* of the contemplated celebration in Providence. This threw me into doubt as to whether the celebration would go on, as all the other celebrations were thus notified." Douglass's explanation, which was written in response to published complaints by the Providence organizers regarding his absence, also corroborates that difficulties regarding the contracting of speakers were not at all uncommon. These interrelationships between print culture and public ritual reflect black activists' recognition that overlapping oral, textual, and performative vehicles of communication were all necessary tools for them to achieve their goals of education, agitation, and uplift.[76]

In their use of the public speaking platform to pursue those goals African Americans were hardly unique. The nineteenth century, it has often been said, was the golden age of oratory in the United States. During the antebellum years, at least in areas outside the slave South, a truly public culture emerged in which virtually all segments of society had some prospect of voicing their views in the public arena. By midcentury mass democracy, mass education, and related technological and cultural changes had forever disrupted patterns of social deference and neoclassical standards of speech in the public forum, opening that forum for the first time to members of what the historian Kenneth Cmiel refers to as "middling" culture, including, significantly, African Americans and women.[77]

Women played essential roles in antebellum black freedom festivals, though these most often involved behind-the-scenes activities like preparing food, decorating halls, and raising money. Elaborate feasts and banquets, both public and private affairs, were a regular part of most festivals, and these would not have come off without "the delicacies of the season and also with the dainties which only the lovely hand of woman can compound." The 1859 celebration at Harrisburg, said to be "the largest, quietest, most orderly and enthusiastic observance" ever seen in central Pennsylvania, appears to have been largely a result of "the spirit and perseverance exhibited by the ladies of the Good Samaritan Council, to whom alone the entire credit is due." The "sumptuous" banquet there was singled out as being "highly creditable to the ladies who superintended the *culinary* department." The women activists of Pittsburgh were lauded in 1848 for their efforts to raise money to support Martin Delany's recently defunct newspaper the *Mystery,* which, like most black papers, seemed always to be faced with financial collapse due to a lack of paid subscribers. Calling for more generous support of the black press generally, Frederick Douglass claimed that "had it not been for the generosity of the Pittsburghers, by the assistance of the ladies, in holding the First of August Levees, the paper would long since have stopped.[78]

Women's societies often appeared in processions, as was the case at Richmond, Indiana, when the line of march featured the Daughters of Ruth, and at Harrisburg, where the Daughters of Temperance were conveyed through the streets in omnibuses. Not surprisingly, given the gender conventions of the era, women rarely were among the featured speakers at August 1 celebrations. White female abolitionists speaking at white-run (especially Garrisonian) events appeared more frequently than women of any color at black-organized affairs. For example, Lucy Stone spoke at a white-organized First of August commemoration at Lynn, Massachusetts, in 1848, and radical feminist and socialist Ernestine L. Rose delivered her "highly effective remarks" at a Flushing, New York, celebration arranged by the New York City Anti-Slavery Society in 1853. Black women occasionally appeared on the platform, and at times spoke, usually in a minor capacity, though Miss Ann P. Ellis was said to have received "unbounded applause" for her reading of "an extract of the Act of Emancipation" at New Bedford. In the rare instance that a woman with the stature and eloquence of Frances Ellen Watkins was designated a featured orator, her topic often reflected the audience's gendered expectations. In 1859 H. Ford Douglass spoke on "The Brutality of Slavery," while Ms. Watkins discoursed on "The Home Influence."[79]

Antebellum black freedom festivals thus offered limited challenges to the era's gender orthodoxy in the public arena. But Freedom Day orators did attempt to use their public forum to extend the egalitarian promise of the "age of the common man" to include black men. Frederick Douglass exulted in 1848 that "we have this day a free platform, to which, without respect to class, color, or condition, all are invited. Let no man here feel that he is a mere spectator."[80] As Douglass implied, this free platform furnished northern blacks their first significant opportunities in the public sphere to serve as spokespersons for their own cause before large diverse audiences that cut across lines of class, color, or gender. Orators used these occasions to articulate their peculiarly black-centered perspective on the American past and to establish a sense of historical tradition within which black Americans could define themselves and their relation to the polity. August 1 orations often oriented themselves quite consciously in opposition to whites' self-adulatory July Fourth addresses (what William Watkins referred to in 1855 as "all the unmeaning twaddle of Fourth of July orators"), which were still fresh in the minds of both black and white auditors. Frederick Douglass pointed out to whites that August 1 "comes opportunely just after your National Anniversary. It laps on and supplies a deficiency, in the exercises of that day. It takes up the principles of the American Revolution, where you drop them, and bears them onward to higher and more beneficent applications."[81] Comparing the two festival days in 1860, Douglass acknowledged the recreational functions August 1 filled for African Americans, but he called particular attention to the "seriousness" of the orator's role: "The black man has no Fourth of July here, on which to display banners, burn powder, ring bells, dance and drink whisky; so he makes the first of August, in some instances, to serve this purpose. Nevertheless, the first of August speeches by such men as Henry Highland Garnet, Charles Lennox Remond, Dr. Jas. McCune Smith. H. Ford Douglass, John Mercer Langston, Wm. Wells Brown, J. W. Loguen, Prof. Reason, W. J. Watkins, Chas. Langston, and other colored men, evince a seriousness becoming the dignity of the cause of which they are advocates."[82]

Black orators used these opportunities to speak to the general public in order to revise American history—both to empower and exhort black America and to impress white America with the legitimacy of blacks' quest for equality and justice. In so doing, these antebellum Freedom Day orators built on important precedents set by early slave trade orators, thus maintaining an intellectual continuity that postemancipation leaders carried further still. The resources created by African Americans through their Freedom Day commemorations were both symbolic and tangible. Through the commemorations themselves, and most explicitly through their public orations at these events, African American leaders were constructing a set of historical traditions for black Americans and a distinctive reinterpretation of American history that was intended to inform the understanding of all Americans.

Commemorative orations in general constitute a particular rhetorical genre that differs in structure, tone, and function from other types of public address. In a public speaking text from the end of the nineteenth century, Professor Lorenzo Sears of Brown University defined the commemorative address as a "memorial" that aims at "perpetuating something which is worth saving from oblivion, and extending into the future what is too valuable to be restricted to the brief period when it was present among mankind." In the United States, especially, Sears noted "a strong inclination to celebrate anniversary days and, as a republic, to keep in constant remembrance the lessons of political wisdom left by its founders." These "occasional" addresses were well suited to the needs of a republican nation whose "continuance . . . depends upon an educated public understanding and conscience." Public commemorative addresses were to be constructed in clear and precise language—accessible to listeners from all walks of life and all educational levels—for the purpose of "mak[ing] evident to others what is seen by the speaker."[83]

African American commemorative orators, in many ways, fit neatly into Sears's delineation of a distinctly American form of public address. As he noted, the whole nation in the late nineteenth century was overcome by an unprecedented urge to commemorate the past and preserve local and national heritages.[84] African Americans, as suggested by the antebellum Freedom Day tradition, were situated squarely within this movement to recover, reconstruct, and preserve a past that would be regenerative and empowering for themselves and for the nation at large. White America's denial of the very existence of a black heritage made black Freedom Day speakers all the more concerned with "perpetuating something that is worth saving from oblivion." In the early nineteenth century African American orators began to use their Freedom Day orations to construct a black heritage so as to "keep in constant remembrance" the lessons of their own founders and their own history. America in the nineteenth century, as a new nation founded on new principles, had a self-conscious concern with constructing for itself a usable past—a set of traditions on which to build a distinctively American national identity. African Americans' concerns as a nation within that nation amplified the necessity of constructing historical traditions that lent credibility to their status—both as Americans and as a distinct people with a particular heritage that must not be lost.

Black orators in the nineteenth century surely felt peculiar desires and responsibilities as they stood before public audiences—especially those like the Freedom Day gatherings that included a goodly number of whites as well as fellow blacks. In this context African American orators needed to play at least two roles. First, in addressing the white audience, black orators had to make the case both against the institution of slavery and for African Americans' rights as equal citizens in the national family. Moreover, and perhaps more fundamentally, they felt the obligation to demonstrate, as representatives of the race, their ability to engage in public discourse during an age when the ability to speak effectively in public was far more admired and valued than we can fully appreciate today.

In addressing their black audiences, orators had to speak to a group that was extremely diverse in age, gender, education, economic position, status, religion, and regional orientation. They needed, in one respect, to present an example worthy of emulation for this disparate group, not all of whom held dear the same cultural values and sense of moral responsibility. Orations were perhaps most important as a fundamental educational tool at a time when literacy and access to other educational vehicles were denied all too many black Americans. Black speakers at commemorative events could reach hundreds or even thousands of their fellows. They took advantage of this powerful forum to provide blacks with vital information on the legacies of their past and the exigencies of their present; to reiterate the words of previous Freedom Day orators, thus reminding audiences that the day's event was part of a tradition reaching back into the past and forward toward a more hopeful future; to instill a sense of unity and cultural potency; and to incite action toward positive social and political change. They spoke to reach their entire audience with a message of freedom, knowledge, uplift, self-respect, and belonging.

Antebellum black spokespersons came increasingly to realize the crucial role that this sort of public assessment of history could play in determining the social, cultural, political, and economic fate of African American people. Free black spokespersons, in their writing and in their oratory, constructed interpretations of both world and American histories that incorporated their own lives and experiences, thereby undermining the culturally pervasive master narrative of Anglo-centric Manifest Destiny. As Detine Bowers has argued, at antebellum Freedom Day celebrations, "free blacks created a viable public address platform . . . [which] allowed blacks to restore their past through a reconstruction of histories, current events, and prophecies that challenged the white-only version of the American Dream."[85]

That white-only dream was challenged as well by African American writers in the antebellum period. Though my focus here is on the black oratorical tradition, it is important to recognize that a nascent literary tradition was also a component of a broad intellectual movement attempting to define African American history and heritage in the context of the American republic. Even as white American writers and speakers in the early nineteenth century began to define a particularly American culture and history, blacks recognized the fundamental importance of telling their own story. And the overarching guiding principle of this intellectual endeavor was that the construction and articulation of that story must be the task of African Americans themselves. As early as 1808, Peter Williams, in his oration commemorating the abolition of the slave trade, advised his "brethren, beloved Africans" that they alone "best can tell the aggravated sufferings of our unfortunate race; your memories can bring to view these scenes of bitter grief." Williams made it clear that *blacks themselves* had the responsibility of injecting an African presence into the pages of history, which up to that point had been dominated by a white, European perspective. Two decades later, pamphleteer David Walker urged American blacks to define and claim their heritage as well as their rights as Americans. Walker echoed Peter Williams's sentiment as he looked forward to the day "when the Lord shall raise up coloured historians in succeeding generations" to "do justice" to the memory of great African American heroes.[86]

The early antebellum years saw the real beginnings of African American history writing, which traced black history from the ancient civilizations of Africa to the American present. In 1836 Robert Benjamin Lewis published a four-hundred-page volume entitled *Light and Truth,* which was the first book-length work of black history. The following year Hosea Easton produced his *Treatise on the Intellectual Character, and Civil and Political Condition of the Colored People of the United States.* In 1841 another history of African Americans, *A Text Book of the Origin and History of the Colored People,* was published by James W. C. Pennington, a black minister and activist who, throughout his life, promoted the cause of black education. Black enrollment in schools and colleges continued to expand in the antebellum period, with Avery College near Pittsburgh, the Ashmun Institute near Philadelphia, and Wilberforce University in Ohio all opening their doors between 1849 and 1855. During these same years free African Americans in Boston, Rochester, New York, and other cities struggled against white opposition to enroll their children in the public schools. Historian John Hope Franklin cites these and many other examples in noting that African Americans "were part of the great awakening that swept American education in the generation preceding the Civil War."[87] During the same period a faction within the increasingly influential African Methodist Episcopal Church attempted to establish denominational publications and to require higher intellectual standards for the ministry.[88] The early history writers thus participated in a broad cultural movement intending to leave, as Pennington put it, "intellectual monuments" in the form of educational institutions and scholarly writings to inspire future generations.[89]

During the 1840s and 1850s black writers of both fiction and nonfiction began to leave the intellectual monuments sought by Pennington and others, as they established a tradition of letters that told the story of Africans in the United States.[90] But in 1857 Frederick Douglass, speaking at an August 1 celebration, could still bemoan the fact that all accounts of the fruits of West Indian emancipation "proceed from the slave-holders side, and never from the side of the emancipated slaves."[91] Douglass, like Peter Williams and David Walker before him, implied that blacks needed to act themselves to construct a meaning for the past—in this case the postemancipation experience in the British West Indies—that challenged the white interpretations that ignored or distorted the significance of blacks' experiences and accomplishments.

African American orators, and the public commemorative celebrations at which they spoke, were of central importance in this cultural and intellectual movement for the expansion of education in general and the promulgation of historical knowledge in particular.[92] Antebellum African American orators built on earlier models as they constructed a meaningful history in which blacks' experiences occupied a central place, a history whose general contours persisted through the postemancipation period. Of course, certain changes were inevitable with the shifting historical contexts, especially in the wake of the drastic social transformation wrought by American emancipation, but some of the fundamental themes addressed by antebellum August 1 orators were adapted from early slave trade orators and passed on to their intellectual progeny.

To a certain extent the connection with an African presence persisted in the orators' historical narratives, though to a lesser degree than in those presented at slave trade observances. In 1847 Frederick Douglass illustrated the tenacity of earlier rhetorical strategies as he transported his audience to the shores of Africa to experience the brutality of the slave trade. "Let us go," he bade his auditors, with imagery redolent of that employed by the first slave trade orators, "to that little village on the West Coast of Africa. The inhabitants are quiet, simple, peaceful, and happy." After further detailing the domestic tranquillity of the scene, Douglass then ushered his listeners to a more objectionable locale. "Let us leave for a moment this happy village, and go to the shore. A slave-ship is anchored off the coast." At length the audience was entreated to experience the attack and the capture of the "unsuspecting inhabitants," the march in chains back to the slaver, the horrors of the Middle Passage, and the auction at which the tender family group is forever torn asunder. Situating the by-now emotionally distraught assemblage once more in "real" time, Douglass went on to describe in more conventional tones the labors and triumphs of the British abolitionists whose work had made the day's celebration possible.[93] The narrative of Africa and the slave trade receded somewhat over the years, sharing time with the advances of British and American abolitionism and the deeds of African American heroes. But black orators continued to use the potent public forum of Freedom Day events to articulate to both black and white Americans their black-centered vision of history and their sense of historical tradition.

In their attempts to establish a viable heritage, antebellum Freedom Day orators were extremely conscious of the importance of commemorations as a characteristic defining the legitimacy of their people's collective identity. This cognizance of the role of historical consciousness and a sense of tradition was evident as early as Absalom Jones's 1808 admonition to "let the history of the sufferings of our brethren and of their deliverance descend by this means [commemoration] to our children, to the remotest generation." Nathaniel Paul reiterated that sentiment with his 1827 observation that "the nations which have already passed away have been careful to select the most important events, peculiar to themselves, and have them recorded for the good of the people that should succeed them." Amos G. Beman, a Congregationalist pastor speaking at an August 1 gathering in 1839, closely paraphrased Paul when he reminded his audience that "it has always been, and still is, customary for nations to set apart some day, or days in the year, when their orators recount the glory of their ancestors." Beman expressed his deep regret that African Americans, "as a people," had "no such day to celebrate."[94] Perhaps in 1839 Beman could not be faulted for failing to recognize that he and his people were in fact celebrating just such a day. The tradition that had begun to define itself with the 1808 slave trade celebrations had moved forward into the 1830s only in fits and starts. It had not yet matured into a fully institutionalized historical tradition.

By the 1850s Freedom Day commemorations had become widely acknowledged and enthusiastically practiced, a definitive feature of a maturing northern black culture. Not all black leaders, however, were in agreement regarding which days were truly worthy of inclusion on the African American commemorative calendar that was in the process of being defined. A correspondent to the *Anglo-African,* writing from Cleveland, commented that "seeing there is no day of our own worth commemorating, and appreciating holidays, as such, I sometimes participate in the keeping of this one, but not with the relish I should feel had the slaves liberated themselves. . . . I should prefer, therefore, commemorating the downfall of slavery in St. Domingo or the birthday of Nat. Turner."[95] James McCune Smith, by 1856, had also come to question the logic of celebrating West Indian emancipation, mainly because he saw that event as the result of white actions. Smith suggested that such celebrations would give American blacks the misleading notion that they would similarly be "given" freedom rather than having to obtain it through their own exertions. For African Americans, Smith urged, it would be more appropriate to observe the date of Denmark Vesey's death or of Nat Turner's rebellion. Robert Hamilton, editor of the *Anglo-African,* shared these other writers' contentions that, since the slaves had been merely quiescent recipients of white beneficence, West Indian emancipation was not worthy of the attention it received. The overthrow of Haitian slavery and the institution of a black republic there was for Hamilton far more deserving an object of African Americans' commemorative impulses.[96]

"Mifflin," writing from Baltimore in 1859, acknowledged that "others may question the propriety of celebrating that day [August 1], but it is not questionable with me." Connecting the race's collective memory with his own personal experiences, Mifflin commented that "I was quite young, but I shall never forget the day, nor the impression then made upon my mind" when he participated in his first August 1 celebration at New York when the edict went into effect in 1838.[97] Frederick Douglass, an ardent supporter of Freedom Day celebrations, used his August 3, 1857, address at Canandaigua, New York, to reply to these objections and to articulate a broader statement regarding the role of Freedom Day celebrations in blacks' struggle for liberation and enfranchisement. Douglass undoubtedly sympathized with Smith's and Hamilton's concerns that black heroes should be held foremost in the minds of African Americans. The exaltation of black heroes was necessary not only to rectify their erasure from dominant interpretations of history, but also "to stimulate us to the execution of [further] great deeds of heroism worthy to be held in admiration and perpetual remembrance." Though he did not call for regular commemoration of the event, Douglass claimed that "Virginia was never nearer emancipation than when General Turner kindled the fires of insurrection at Southampton." Similarly, the increasingly bellicose Douglass often called attention to the deeds of Joseph Cinque, who led the 1839 slave uprising on the ship *Amistad,* and Madison Washington, who led a similar revolt aboard the *Creole* in 1841. Douglass was so inspired by the latter incident that he perpetuated its memory in a fictional account, suggestively entitled *The Heroic Slave,* which he published in *Frederick Douglass' Paper* in 1853.[98]

Douglass consistently participated in other homages to black heroes. He was a frequent participant in the annual Syracuse, New York, celebrations of that community's liberation of the fugitive Jerry McHenry from the hands of southern slavecatchers in 1851. The October 1 commemoration of "Jerry Rescue Day" represents a more localized version of the Freedom Day tradition. The enthusiasm behind the celebration reflects the activism of both black and white abolitionists in their attempts to negate the 1850 Fugitive Slave Law, which allowed slavecatchers a virtual carte blanche to abduct and enslave blacks, whether fugitive or not, on the presentation of a vaguely worded warrant. Though they did not inspire annual celebrations comparable to "Jerry Rescue Day," similar acts of liberation in defiance of the law in Boston, in Christiana, Pennsylvania, and in Mechanicsburg, Ohio, were widely praised in Freedom Day orations and in the abolitionist press.[99]

As for the celebration of West Indian emancipation, Douglass rested his defense of the tradition on the assertion "that the slaves of the West Indies did fight for their freedom, and the fact of their discontent was known in England, and that it assisted in bringing about that state of public opinion which finally resulted in their emancipation." "Though slaves," Douglass claimed, "they were rebellious slaves. They bore themselves well." This interpretation of events turned the objections of Smith and Hamilton on their heads. Rather than being passive recipients, the slaves' active protest and rebellion had, in fact, turned the tide of public opinion and forced the expedition of the process of abolition. Though that objective had been on the agenda of British philanthropists for some time, Douglass's analysis concluded, "a share of the credit of the result falls justly to the slaves themselves."[100]

To lend credence to his assertion of the slaves' violent participation in their own liberation, Douglass pointed out that many white abolitionists quietly seethed that slave insurrections were, in fact, "prejudicial to their cause." By 1857, long removed from the paternalistic oversight of William Lloyd Garrison, Douglass was intensely aware that many white abolitionists resented any action, violent or not, undertaken by African Americans without the direction and approval of their supposed betters. He saw criticisms of black insurrection as part of a larger pattern of white desires to control black behavior, including the organization of Freedom Day commemora-

tions. "This class of Abolitionists," he scolded, "don't like colored celebrations, they don't like colored conventions, they don't like colored Anti-
Slavery fairs for the support of colored newspapers. They don't like any
demonstrations whatever in which colored men take a leading part." Black
insurrections, then, were of a piece with black-run institutions, black-
organized commemorative events, and implicitly at least, black-centered
interpretations of history, all of which threatened the power and influence
that even the most sympathetic whites were loath to relinquish. And power
was the central issue. "Power," Douglass thundered, "concedes nothing
without a demand. It never did and it never will." This oft-quoted passage
follows fast on the heels of Douglass's upbraiding of white abolitionists and
is as much a critique of their paternalism as it is a call for aggressive action
to overthrow slavery.[101]

Douglass, of course, did not fail to address the objections of the slave
power either. The specter of bloody slave revolts was a frequently used image
in proslavery attempts to instill racial fear in the hearts of white Americans.
Solidifying the connections he was making between whites' fears of black
violence and their fears of losing any degree of control or power over blacks
in the United States, Douglass noted with derision that southern slaveholders also disapproved of August 1 celebrations. Proslavery criticisms appealed
to nationalism, contending that West Indian emancipation celebrations ex-
alted British, rather than American, sentiments and accomplishments.
Douglass's caustic rejoinder ridiculed the narrowness of such objections to
the observance of what he and many others regarded as an event of universal
import. To such a small mind, the great orator jeered, "to be one of a nation
is more than to be one of the human family. He don't live in the world but
he lives in the United States. Into his little soul the thought of God as our
common Father, and of man our common Brother has never entered. To
such a soul as that, this celebration cannot but be exceedingly distasteful."[102]

In this defense of the freedom festivals Douglass evinced one of the central
threads of African American interpretations of history that pervaded Freedom Day orations. West Indian emancipation celebrations were not merely
honoring British magnanimity, nor were they only of interest to other African peoples who hoped for a similar fate to befall them. August 1 "belongs
. . . to the lovers of Liberty and of mankind the world over. . . . In the great
Drama of Emancipation, England was the theatre, but universal and every
where applying principles of Righteousness, Liberty, and Justice were the
actors." His words echoed those he had issued at the same site ten years
before: "The sentiment that leads us to celebrate noble deeds, to mark and
commemorate great events in the world's progress, is natural and universal.
. . . Neither geographical boundaries, nor national restrictions, ought, or

shall prevent me from rejoicing over the triumphs of freedom, no matter where or by whom achieved. . . . Our platform is as broad as humanity. . . . In celebrating this day, we place ourselves beneath the broad aegis of human brotherhood . . . and maintain the right and propriety of commemorating the victories of liberty over tyranny throughout the world."[103]

For Douglass, as for Freedom Day orators since the early nineteenth century, their American situation necessarily defined the particular shape of their activism. The black experience—in Africa, in American bondage, and in the ongoing struggle for liberty and justice—was the primary concern of African American activists and historical thinkers. But for all their personal stake in that very personal history, African Americans presented it as a particular variety of human experience that could, and should, inform the historical consciousness of all Americans. Their overarching vision was organized by the obvious universality of the events being commemorated, and followed logically and inescapably from the central organizing principle of African American historical interpretations—freedom.

The idea of freedom, both as an accomplished goal and as an unfulfilled ideal, provided a central image and a central message around which blacks constructed their interpretations of the past, their analyses of the present, and their prognostications for the future of not only the race, but also the nation and the world. For this reason, for example, Frederick Douglass could not but rejoice in the European revolutions of 1848, which he saw joining his own people's freedom struggle in a movement that defined a unique era in global history. "We live in times which have no parallel in the history of the world," Douglass effused in 1848. "The grand commotion is universal and all pervading. . . . The long pent up energies of human rights and sympathies, are at last let loose upon the world. The grand conflict of the angel Liberty with the monster Slavery, has at last come. The globe shakes with the contest."[104]

Douglass thus used the West Indian emancipation anniversary celebrations to promote African American interpretations of history that equated human progress with the onward march of universal liberty. He claimed that "the world owes Britain more for this example of humility and honest repentance than for all her other contributions to the world's progress." This universalizing interpretation also carried with it a great humanizing tendency. Douglass pointedly characterized blacks' freedom-centered view of history as a human-centered one, which he contrasted with interpretations emanating from white Americans' "dollar-loving hearts." Americans, he chastised in tones echoing the words of Wendell Phillips, interpreted the fruits of West Indian emancipation "as though it were a railroad, a canal, a steamboat, or a newly invented mowing machine . . . and asked with owl-like wisdom, WILL IT PAY?" Placing the experience of the former slaves (rather than technological and economic development) at the center of his interpretation, Douglass cataloged the benefits of freedom: the solidification of the family, the displacement of "pollution" by "moral purity," and the advance of education and religion. Making a comparison that would be employed frequently after U.S. emancipation, the great social critic pleaded for patience. "It has taken at least a thousand years to bring some of the leading nations of the earth from the point where the negroes of the West Indies started twenty-three years ago, to their present position. Let considerations like these be duly weighed, and black man though I am, I do not fear the world's judgment."[105]

Douglass and others recognized the importance of sustaining the Freedom Day tradition in order to present their case for equality and justice before the court of public opinion and to earn the respect and support of their white contemporaries. They also appreciated the celebrations' social functions, as they gathered together large numbers of blacks from across a given region, reinforcing networks of communication and mobilization. Moreover, Freedom Day commemorations served a vital educative function, helping to disseminate a distinctive, black-centered interpretation of history. Perhaps most important of all, the organizers of these events were deeply concerned with the judgment of posterity. From the earliest slave trade observances, black Freedom Day orators emphasized the need to establish a commemorative tradition in order to leave a legacy for future generations. Freedom Day orators consistently took note of the fact that any people with a claim to a legitimate and coherent group identity chose special days to publicly celebrate their past and honor their heroes.

By the 1850s free black Americans in the northern states had succeeded in establishing a vibrant commemorative tradition that was firmly grounded in the observance of West Indian emancipation. In 1860 Frederick Douglass noted that August 1 festivals "have been more numerous and spirited this year than ever before." Despite the increasing popularity and universal import of that event, even Douglass intimated that the commemoration of West Indian emancipation might be made obsolete for African Americans by a more immediate and personal triumph of liberty. "I hold it to be eminently fit," he pronounced in 1857, "that we keep up those celebrations from year to year, at least until we shall have an American celebration to take its place."[106] With a mature Freedom Day tradition in place, Douglass and his black brethren, slave and free, soon would have the opportunity to make that next step in the construction of their commemorative traditions as their nation approached the purifying fires of civil war.

CHAPTER THREE

"AN AMERICAN CELEBRATION"

EXPANSION AND FRAGMENTATION, 1862–1870s

> Ye sons of burning Afric's soil,
> Lift up your hands of hardened toil;
> Your shouts from every hill recoil—
> Today you are free!
>
> —Ode for Emancipation Day,
> January 1, 1863

> Not the great North and West alone should rejoice in this day. The . . .
> period will come when this day shall be celebrated as the nation's second birthday, by the people of all the states.
>
> —*New Orleans Tribune*, January 1, 1869

A S THE FORCES of the North and South aligned themselves during the early months of 1861, African Americans watched, waited, and pondered the meaning of the sectional crisis. Their attitudes covered a broad range. In Philadelphia, Elisha Weaver, editor of the *Christian Recorder*, the weekly newspaper of the African Methodist Episcopal (AME) Church, attempted to refute the notion that the nation's strife had anything to do with African Americans. In his first editorial after the firing on Fort Sumter Weaver claimed to "deeply grieve over the present condition in national affairs" and was quick "to correct what we conceive to be a very great error in the minds of many of our white friends, with regard to the relation of the colored people and the war; this is, that they are fighting about negroes. This is not true." The conflict, the editor maintained, was over territory, the control of which was sought by two sectional factions represented by "two great contending [political] parties." While he favored national unity on the grounds of loyalty and patriotism, Weaver recognized the potential for backlash if African Americans were construed to be at the root of the nation's "perplexed circumstances."[1]

In Washington, D.C., twenty-five-year-old Benjamin Tucker Tanner, who would replace Weaver in the *Recorder*'s editorial seat in 1868, was just beginning a two-year sojourn as interim pastor at the Fifteenth Street Presbyterian Church. The young clergyman felt directly the antiblack animus that inspired Weaver's disclaimer, noting in November 1860 that the election of Abraham Lincoln had kindled such "great excitement" in the capital "that I was advised not to leave church" in order to avoid becoming a target of violence. This was a circumstance Tanner "regretted . . . very much." As to his own view of the election result, Tanner cautiously confided to his diary, "As far as I can judge it is for good."[2]

As the national crisis unfolded, the future AME bishop allowed no doubt as to either its cause or the role of Divine Providence in determining its ultimate outcome. A few days after South Carolina's vote to secede he noted, "The country seems to be bordering on a civil war all on account of slavery. I pray God to rule and overrule all to his own glory and to the good of man." The young minister was clearly excited by the prospect of a war over slavery. As the new year dawned he crowed, "This a beautiful day. The cry is—War—War." On the first Sabbath of 1861 he detected a similar mood in his congregation, noting that "there was a spiritual feeling quite manifest among the people" at worship services, a feeling seemingly aroused by the war news. When Mississippi, Florida, and Alabama joined South Carolina in early January, Tanner reiterated his sense that war over slavery was imminent and again implored that "the right be made to triumph by the grace of God."[3]

Tanner's view of the conflict as a divinely orchestrated contest that would render judgment on the national sin of slavery was shared by many antislavery activists and by many African Americans, slave and free. But as the historian Vincent Harding has pointed out, a certain "ironic confusion" infused blacks' perceptions of the outbreak of Civil War. The unshakable belief that "God moved in history to deliver his people" led many African Americans to see the North, the Republican Party, and the Union cause as instruments of a beneficent Providence whose triumph would secure the liberty of those still held in southern bondage. This despite the federal government's insistence that the abolition of slavery was not a war goal, the continued legal proscriptions in effect in northern states, and the persistent racism that northern blacks encountered in their daily lives. Frederick Douglass voiced the sentiments of many abolitionists, black and white, with his conviction "that the war now being waged in this land is a war for and against slavery." Consistent with African Americans' antebellum jeremiads invoking the divine manipulation of human events, Douglass defined the war as evidence that "nations, not less than individuals, are subjects of the moral government of the Universe, and that flagrant, long continued, and persistent transgression of the laws of this Divine Government will certainly bring national sorrow, shame, suffering and death. . . . Egypt, Palestine, Greece and Rome *all* had their warnings. They disregarded them, and they perished. To-day we have our warning . . . in the terrible calamity of widespread rebellion." Over the course of the year 1861 even the initially timid Elisha Weaver came to endorse Douglass's interpretation, including the veteran abolitionist's call for the enlistment of black troops in what was "essentially an abolition war."[4]

Lincoln's 1863 Emancipation Proclamation and, more definitively, the Thirteenth Amendment in 1865, made that interpretation a reality, bringing an end to American slavery and inspiring the "American celebration" to which Douglass and others had been looking forward.[5] African Americans' many public commemorations of that momentous event in the North, South, and West through the early Reconstruction years all shared an overriding sense of joy, gratitude, and relief that the long nightmare of slavery had finally ended. Despite all that those celebrations shared, however, they also exhibited an increasing diversity of opinions about how to celebrate, when to celebrate, and precisely which of the various emancipatory events of the era were most appropriate to celebrate. By the early 1870s, the largely unified August 1 tradition had begun to expand and also to fragment, and black freedom festivals entered a new era requiring a reorientation and a reexamination of the functions and the meaning of public commemoration.

In 1861, amid black Americans' generally hopeful, but wary, reactions to the onset of the sectional conflict, West Indian emancipation celebrations continued to be "duly celebrated in many places, east and west." Frederick Douglass did note in the summer of 1861, however, that "this sublime event of the nineteenth century ... will not this first of August be extensively celebrated as in former years.—The war now swallows up everything." Even the tradition-conscious blacks in New Bedford, Massachusetts, Douglass observed, "who formerly lead in such movements, do not now display as much spirit in the observance of this festival as formerly." Despite his own conviction that the war was being waged against slavery, Douglass stressed the need to exploit the political function of August 1, in order to maintain pressure on the government to act officially against the institution. He condemned the great mistake he saw being made by "Abolitionists who have taken this war as a trump of jubilee, and a release of themselves from the toil of anti-slavery agitation. It seems to us that this of all other times is just when we should be most active and earnest. . . . Let the people speak, on the coming first of August, and ask our Government to seize the occasion which, through the operations of a natural Providence, is forced upon them, for breaking the chains of every American slave." By the following August things had changed considerably. Congress had begun to act against slavery in unequivocal ways, and Douglass was invited to speak at a West Indian emancipation celebration at Myricks, Massachusetts, near New Bedford, that was attended by about a thousand blacks from the latter city. Consistent with Douglass's call for continued agitation, resolutions passed at that event reiterated the sentiment "That this is a war of slavery against Freedom," and "That it is the imperative duty of the President of the United States to immediately . . . ORDER THE UNIVERSAL EMANCIPATION OF THE SLAVES."[6]

By early 1862 the slaves themselves had made it clear that they saw the sectional conflict as an opportunity to claim their own freedom, regardless of the stated intentions of the Lincoln administration. And it was becoming increasingly difficult for Lincoln to deny that the "contrabands" streaming into Union camps had transformed the nature of the war. Between May 1861 and May 1862 Union generals Benjamin Butler, John C. Fremont, and David Hunter separately acted to declare the escaped slaves who entered their camps "contrabands of war" and refused to return them to their owners. Fremont and Hunter went further and formally declared the fugitives free; Butler stopped short of so radical a measure. These policies reinforced the slaves' actions and lent credence to the contention that the cause of the Union and the cause of abolition were one, despite the cautious president's censure and reversal of Fremont's and Hunter's liberation of the fugitives.[7]

Support for emancipation was beginning to enjoy unprecedented (if far from unanimous) support in many northern states and, more importantly, in the legislative chambers of the nation's capital.[8] As evidence of its increasing hostility toward slavery, Congress gave official sanction to the emerging reality of the slaves' liberation by emancipating all bondspeople held in the District of Columbia, effective April 16, 1862. Black Washingtonians greeted the news enthusiastically. One resident wrote to a friend in Baltimore, describing the extent of the "rejoicing around me" and suggesting the range of African Americans' reactions to the news: "Were I a drinker I would get on a Jolly spree today but as a Christian I can but kneel in prayer and bless God for the privilege I've enjoyed this day." In New York, *Anglo-African* editor Robert Hamilton emphasized "the boon to the nation at large" in ridding its capital of slavery. This purifying of the nation's "physical heart" would insure "the return of health and vigor and freedom to the whole national body. . . . It is an act of emancipation which frees a hundred thousand white men for every individual black man."[9]

If the immediate benefits to white Americans were not so obvious to all, those enjoyed by blacks were soon made clear. This first unequivocal dent in slavery's edifice since the outbreak of the Civil War was followed by the lifting of the District's "black codes," which expanded African Americans' political rights in the nation's capital. But the rejoicing at these developments was tempered with trepidation. Black Washington's rather insular and elitist "old citizens" feared the mass influx of black field hands, whom they thought impossible to instruct in the ways of respectable comportment. The formation of the exclusive Lotus Club in 1863 was inspired at least in part by the estimated thirteen thousand contrabands who had sought refuge in and around the District, and by the desire of certain "leading Negroes" to distance themselves from those unseemly masses. This distancing manifested itself in the 1880s through a contentious debate over the commemoration of the April 16 emancipation (see chap. 6).[10]

In 1862, however, more positive sentiments predominated. Anticipating the legislation's implementation, the city's black churches set aside Sunday, April 13, "as a day of Thanksgiving and Prayer, in view of Emancipation in the District." AME bishop Daniel A. Payne, who had met several days earlier with a hesitant President Lincoln to urge him to sign the bill, delivered a predictably prescriptive sermon at Georgetown's Ebenezer AME Church. Well aware of the misgivings held by many in both races regarding the freedpeople, Payne advised those "ransomed ones" to work hard, save their earnings, educate their children, aspire to honesty and godliness, and avoid "the gambling hells, and groggeries, which gradually lead their votaries to infamy and the pit that is bottomless." "Enter the great family of Holy Freedom," he admonished, "not to lounge in sinful indolence, not to degrade yourselves by vice, nor to corrupt society by licentiousness, neither to offend the laws by crime, but to the enjoyment of a well regulated liberty, the offspring of generous laws . . . a liberty to be perpetuated by equitable law, and sanctioned by the divine." Regarding the war effort at a time when black volunteers were still being turned away, Payne recommended "supplications, prayers, intercessions, and thanksgiving" in the knowledge that "the hand of God" would direct "this nation [to] . . . do right, administering justice to each and all, protecting the weak as well as the strong, and throwing the broad wings of its power equally over men of every color."[11]

Daniel Payne, like many whites and blacks around Washington, was deeply concerned about the confusion and conflict that could result from the expected inundation of the capital by thousands of fugitive slaves from neighboring states. District emancipation was seen as a portent of things to come should the radicals in Congress extend their actions to the rest of the nation. These sentiments were reinforced over the summer of 1862, when legislation was passed abolishing slavery in the western territories, strengthening the State Department's enforcement of the Atlantic slave trade ban, and through the Second Confiscation Act, providing for the liberation and enlistment of rebel-held slaves. By July, Lincoln had broached the subject of his more sweeping Emancipation Proclamation with his cabinet, and only Secretary of State William Seward's advice that he wait for a military victory delayed action at that time.[12]

During that summer attempts were also made by African Americans at various sites in the North to incorporate District emancipation into the existing Freedom Day tradition. In Philadelphia the *Christian Recorder* advocated a joint commemoration of District and West Indian emancipations on August 1, and "mammoth" meetings to mark the event were held in both New York City and New Haven, Connecticut. Frederick Douglass spoke at a celebration in Ithaca, New York, at which "colored people for hundreds of miles around came in that day to take joyful notice of Emancipation both for this State and for the District of Columbia." It is noteworthy that this July 8 festival also recalled the July Fourth (or fifth) New York emancipation celebrations that had been largely replaced by West Indian emancipation during the 1830s. While the specific rationale for celebrating on July 8 is not clear, the fact that observances were held on a variety of dates in different locations presages the confusion that would soon arise over what date and event was most appropriate for commemorating the expansion of black freedom. Regardless of date, though, the Ithaca festival fit into the established Freedom Day pattern by providing a focal point for upstate blacks who were "scattered over the state, living in different parts of it more as individuals, and families, than as communities." "We have few occasions for meeting together for display," Douglass commented, and "the proceedings of the day made a very favorable impression upon themselves and upon the [white] people of Ithaca."[13]

Douglass was well pleased with the day's events, especially because the fine presentation by the region's blacks was more than sufficient in his eyes to neutralize an example of whites' continued resistance to black public displays. "In the morning before many colored people had come to town," Douglass reported, "two white men, in ridicule of the celebration, painted themselves black and dressed in a grotesque manner paraded the streets; but the endeavors to provoke ridicule on the occasion by their outlandish drolleries, proved an entire failure. The colored men's procession with their excellent Marshal's riding with ease and grace, on splendid horses, accompanied by both a white and a black band of Music, challenged at once the respect and admiration of all well disposed people of the place, and completely turned the tables on those who would have gladly seen them made objects of odium and derision." His ongoing concerns about black public presentations and the perceptions of white onlookers are apparent in Douglass's reaction. He was also gratified that the white attempt at mockery was so limited and ineffective, especially given the memory of his "first antislavery meeting there twenty years ago, when mob violence met us at every turn." Since that time, Douglass reflected, Ithaca "had vastly changed for the better."[14]

Recent congressional actions and the perception that white attitudes were growing more supportive of antislavery gave activists like Douglass hope by the summer of 1862. The emancipation of Washington's slaves was seen as a momentous step, both symbolic and tangible, in the long march of liberty. But within a few months its impact would be dwarfed by the prospect of the liberation of all the slaves in Confederate-held territory. The commemoration of the April 16 District emancipation act remained for some time a significant local tradition in the nation's capital. But it was the general Emancipation Proclamation put into effect by Lincoln on January 1, 1863, that was to inspire the truly "American celebration" that Frederick Douglass expected to supplant West Indian emancipation as the focal point on African Americans' commemorative calendars.[15]

On September 22, after the limited Union victory at Antietam, Lincoln issued his preliminary proclamation that all slaves held in "any state, or designated part of a state . . . in rebellion against the United States shall be then, thenceforward, and forever free."[16] During the one-hundred-day waiting period before the edict would take effect on January 1, 1863, the nation and the world debated the wisdom and the efficacy of Lincoln's thunderbolt. The reaction was decidedly mixed. Southern and Democratic northern papers decried it variously as an unconstitutional and unenforceable act of desperation or as a harbinger of bloody slave insurrection that would ultimately destroy American civilization. The abolitionist community's reaction ranged between two extremes: those who felt that the act fell too far short of the goal of universal abolition and those for whom it was the crowning achievement of the age, heralding the dawn of a new era. Frederick Douglass himself expressed a range of views. On the one hand he asserted in December 1862 that "the first of January is to be the most memorable day in American Annals." But at the same time the longtime activist doubted both Lincoln's motives and his resolve. "But will that deed be done? Oh! that is the question."[17]

Word of the impending proclamation spread rapidly among African Americans. As the New Year approached, blacks across the country—North and South, slave and free—anxiously awaited the fulfillment of the president's promise. The Sunday before that "Day of Days" Frederick Douglass expressed to his audience at Rochester's Spring Street AME Zion Church his elation at "the glorious morning of liberty about to dawn upon us." Douglass, who for years in his antebellum Freedom Day orations had emphasized the universality of the African American quest for liberty, could now rejoice at the imminent fusion of "the cause of human freedom and the cause of our common country, for these two causes are now one and inseparable and must stand or fall together."[18]

The evening of December 31 saw "watch night" meetings across the country. Since there was some doubt that Lincoln would actually follow through, celebrations in the mold of those commemorating West Indian emancipation were not generally undertaken in the North. From the contraband camps in the Federal District to towns and urban centers throughout the North, African Americans awaited the dawn that they hoped would mark the beginning of the end for their race's enslavement. Though the president did not actually sign the act until midafternoon on January 1, Washington's contrabands began celebrating with hymns and speeches hours earlier. Across town, after the proclamation had been issued, Henry McNeal Turner presided over a wildly enthusiastic celebration at Israel Bethel Church that lasted into the night. Celebrations were held all over the North during the first few days of 1863, and featured cannons firing, bells ringing, music, speeches, and spirited readings of the rather dry proclamation.

In portions of the South occupied by federal troops, slaves who had sought refuge with the liberating forces celebrated despite the fact that Lincoln's edict did not apply to them. In Norfolk more than four thousand blacks whose legal status was unaffected by the proclamation paraded through the principal streets of the city, waving flags behind a band of fifes and drums. A similar scene took place in New Orleans, likewise under Union control and beyond the scope of Lincoln's decree. In Hampton, Virginia, northern missionaries sponsored a grand celebration, but the contrabands themselves were cautious and reserved in their participation, perhaps reflecting the skepticism they felt regarding the proclamation's real meaning for their lives. Contrabands in occupied areas may not have been fully aware that they were technically excluded from the provisions of the proclamation, but regardless of their grasp of the particulars, they exhibited an expectation that slavery's long-awaited death knell had been sounded at last.[19]

While most of the celebrations held in the occupied South were organized by northern missionaries or the U.S. military, some blacks seem to have responded more enthusiastically than those at Hampton. In the Sea Islands off South Carolina, "in accordance with the orders of Gen. Saxton to the colored people of the Department of the South, . . . the negroes in this vicinity celebrated the 1st of January with all the zeal and animation which bright promises of freedom could inspire." Camp Saxton, headquarters of the all-black First South Carolina volunteer regiment, "was the scene of a demonstration of a purely African character—no less than from three to four thousand of the dusky natives having assembled, in company with their commanding general and various dignitaries of the humanitarian school, to participate in the celebration of their emancipation." In addition to the colored troops were contrabands from around the region who "commenced flocking to the ground" from an early hour. Steamers provided by the army brought well over a thousand blacks from Hilton Head, Beaufort, and the surrounding area, creating, in the caviling eyes of the *New York Herald*'s reporter on the scene,

> one of the most motley assemblages of which it is possible to conceive. There were the young and the old, of all shades, sizes and costumes; ancient domestics, feebly tottering up the grassy slope, bewildered with the glory by which they were surrounded; antiquated aunties, done up in turbans, tickled and curtseying to every one they met, gay and gaudy yellow girls, decorated with super abundant jewelry, and flashing their smiles profusely on the gay and gallant youths around them; toothless crones, furiously sucking their black pipes; young mothers, not only of the present, but of the future tense, the former violently hushing their babes, and the latter appearing painfully destitute of crinoline; while here and there gleamed the bayonet and glowed red the breeches of a South Carolina volunteer.

This group, which in fairness must have presented a remarkable spectacle to the northern reporter, formed a procession and, led by the Eighth Maine regimental band, "moved out to the spacious live oak grove, where, in olden times, the family of one of the wealthiest planters in Beaufort district had their pleasure grounds and pastimes." A platform had been erected at the center of the grove, from which General Rufus Saxton, Colonel Thomas Wentworth Higginson, and other whites controlled the orations, odes, music, and readings. Colonel Higginson "closed his speech by calling up two darkies whom he had selected as color bearers," one of whom delivered speeches "which, in the broad patois of the plantation, were less intelligible to the whites, but more enthusiastically received by the blacks, than the remarks of their predecessors." At the end of these exercises, "the crowd adjourned to the parade grounds of the regiment—the blacks to partake of a barbecue of twelve roasted oxen and illimitable quantities of hard tack, washed down with sweetened water, and the whites to witness the demolition and consumption of the edibles."[20]

The role of the military, and especially the abolitionists Saxton and Higginson, in orchestrating this celebration connects it firmly with the long-standing August 1 celebratory tradition. Many of the elements with which northern abolitionists, black and white alike, were familiar—travel arrangements, regional crowds, music, parade, speeches, odes, feasts—were incorporated into this first southern freedom celebration. The participation of the Sea Island blacks, making merry in their former owners' private grove, added a new and transformative—and for some troubling—element to the festivities. The reproachful tone of the *Herald* reporter, especially in commenting on the appearance and speech of the black participants, suggests the overly critical eye white observers cast on blacks' public presentations. The correspondent also made a point of noting that the black presence at the celebration meant "leaving plantations without field hands, wharves and depots void of laborers, and messrooms bereft of servants." The importance of black labor was also emphasized by Captain S. Willard Saxton, the acting assistant adjutant general in the Sea Islands, who expressed concern that the "ignorant, untutored, helpless creatures" recently emancipated had been "lifted too high" and were "too much petted and lionized and inflated with conceit ever to be of any great degree of usefulness to us or to themselves." White speakers at an 1866 Augusta, Georgia, celebration similarly expressed concern that the freedpeople remember their "place" in the postemancipation South. An agent of the Freedmen's Bureau advised them "to be honest, industrious and peaceable in every respect" and "to make [labor] contracts immediately," and reminded them that "it was their duty to cultivate friendly relations if possible with those who were their former masters." The white newspaper editor next on the platform told them "as a Georgian . . . that the Southern [white] men were their best friends." So while both northern and southern whites worried that newly freed blacks would cease to recognize their proper "place" in the socioeconomic order, even those sympathetic whites who participated in the celebration of black freedom imposed their authority by attempting to instruct the freedpeople in the acceptable patterns of public behavior.[21]

Northern reportage from Key West, Florida, where U.S. naval forces had maintained control throughout the war, similarly created a disparaging image of blacks' 1863 emancipation revelry. Two separate festivals were held several weeks after the proclamation's issuance, because local blacks were not informed of the act until word arrived on January 24, 1863. Due to the previous September's preliminary proclamation, the news was not completely unexpected, and it was greeted that day with a "procession, with music and banners flying." Afterward, "the party of blacks had a gay and happy time in the barracoons." As was typical at Emancipation Day feasts around the country, tables were set up which "groaned under the weight of good things, substantial and dainty." After eating their fill, the blacks and their invited guests, mainly U.S. troops and resident abolitionists, listened to the speeches by a local black leader named Sandy Cornish and a local white shipmaster. "The day's festivities concluded with music and dancing— the latter accomplishment being done up in a much better style by 'ye ladies colored' than the 'divine [white] creatures' of that little island could do." Blacks at Key West greeted emancipation with considerable jubilation. When one young man was later asked how he felt upon hearing the news, he was said to have replied, "Mighty excited, Missis, we dun sleep berry little las night."[22]

On January 29, another celebration took place. While the presence of "whitewashed niggers—i.e., abolitionists" is mentioned by the relentlessly censorious *New York Herald* reporter on the scene, the affair appears to have been largely conducted by local African Americans. The parade was a highlight of the day's events, with "about two hundred and fifty he niggers, of all sizes, ages and complexions, marching in columns of twos, with proper officers." This entourage was "commanded by 'Sandy,' a venerable nigger of huge proportions . . . [who] today evidently felt his importance. He was attired in a full suit of black, with a sash and rosette on his breast of enormous size and of the most gaudy colors; he has suspended to his side a cavalry sabre and wore an army fatigue cap. His martial bearing and the resemblance of his foot to that of a scrubbing brush, with his leg for a handle, were remarked on every side."[23] The parade's grand marshal was almost certainly Sandy Cornish, whose life experience provides some insight into his obvious pride in leading the Emancipation Day festivities. Cornish was born a slave in Maryland in the early 1790s, was hired out by his owner to Key West in 1839, and, with the help of his free wife, Lillah, was able to purchase his freedom within a few years. When a fire destroyed his free papers during the 1840s, he was kidnapped to be sold in the New Orleans market. Cornish, the story has it, managed to break free from six would-be captors and mutilate himself with a knife—cutting an ankle tendon, opening a gash in his thigh, and severing the fingers of his left hand—in order to render himself useless as a slave. While his condition as slave or freeman is not clear, "Uncle Sandie" took an active role in island life, helping to found the Cornish Chapel of the Key West AME Zion Church and becoming a leader of the African American community, which by 1860 consisted of 451 slaves and 160 free blacks. During the war Cornish was recognized by Union troops as an "aristocratic farmer" who reportedly became one of Key West's richest men by acquiring a farm and selling fruits and vegetables to the occupying Union army. Sandy Cornish died in the late 1860s, leaving most of his wealth to the church he helped establish.[24]

If we read beyond the *Herald* reporter's belittling tone, Sandy's obvious pride in leading the procession—mounted, well dressed, and bedecked with sash, rosette, and saber—suggests the bearing and appearance of early New York Emancipation Day grand marshals like Samuel Hardenburgh or even the eighteenth-century Election Day kings and governors. Like those eighteenth-century community leaders, Cornish appears to have exercised considerable authority among both blacks and whites well before the Union occupation, and possibly while he was still legally enslaved. Sandy's status and force of personality in the community were widely recognized. He was said to have been "formerly the property of Mr. Baldwin, of this place," but it was a "matter of doubt for some time before Mr. Baldwin left Key West . . . if he belonged to Sandy or if Sandy belonged to him." Even the caustic *Herald* reporter acknowledged that the parade had been "commanded" by Cornish, whose imposing physical presence is hinted at in his description as "venerable" and "of huge proportions." For Sandy Cornish the proclamation's apparent acknowledgment of his status as a free man must have expanded his already well-developed sense of self and given true cause for celebration.[25]

The activities of the day suggest that other blacks on the island were also enthusiastic about their new status. The parade was said to have been "a high time for the lads and lasses of dark hue," and presented quite a spectacle, with "all conceivable costumes . . . and all shades of [skin] color, from the light straw . . . to the blackest ebony" in evidence. The all-male procession provided its own band of music and flew numerous banners, the most "conspicuous [of which] was the stars and stripes." The line of march was flanked on both sides by crowds of women "dressed in their best attire and presenting the appearance of a walking rainbow," and large numbers of children cavorted "in advance of and following the procession." All was not joyful, however, as the paraders "were pelted with stones on several parts of the route; basins of dirty water were emptied on their devoted heads; several were knocked down, and the American flag, with which they were marching, was taken from them and the staff broken over the head of the bearer. No serious outbreak occurred; but there would have been had not the provost guard been out in force."[26]

That these attacks themselves did not constitute a "serious outbreak" indicates the sentiments of the reporter; one presumes that for the unsympathetic *Herald* correspondent providing these details only a full-scale retaliation by the blacks would have merited such a distinction. Another account from a member of the 47th Pennsylvania regiment described a lesser disruption in the form of a single man who "threw a stone at the procession as it was passing by, and came very near hitting the flag we are fighting for." One of the Pennsylvanians immediately confronted this individual, who "received a stunner from 'the shoulder' that sent him reeling to the ground . . . teaching him a lesson not to meddle with the emblem of Liberty when the 47th boys are about." It is worth noting here that the Pennsylvanians seemed more concerned with protecting the flag than with protecting the blacks who now staked their claim to flying it. It also appears that the perpetrators of the attack on the parade were explicitly antiblack, rather than generally anti-Union. That they were reacting above all to the fact of emancipation is suggested by the *Herald* reporter's comment that "not one person among those who have heretofore borne the reputation of being disloyal interfered in any manner with the celebration." The distinction between loyalty to the Union and support for black freedom was also a cause for concern around Norfolk, Virginia. At nearby Fort Monroe, Major General John A. Dix expressed alarm upon learning "that a leading citizen of Norfolk has been trying to incite the soldiers of the Ninety-ninth New York to murder negroes." In a January 1, 1863, communication to Brigadier General Egbert L. Viele in Norfolk, Dix warned that "[i]f there is such a feeling existing the procession which is to take place to-day must be watched and, if necessary, stopped . . . for the security of the negroes themselves." General Viele acknowledged that "the procession will be a source of deep mortification" to many local whites but suggested that stopping it would provide too much pleasure to "the insolent secessionists." Likely relieved that his troops had not succumbed to the alleged race-baiting, Viele reported later in the day that the parade of four thousand "passed off without any disturbance."[27]

While few of the whites at Key West and Norfolk, regardless of political or national loyalties, appear to have shared the blacks' enthusiasm for Lincoln's proclamation, abolitionists in the North were effusive. Perhaps the most notable northern celebration took place in Boston on New Year's Day. The list of attendees at the afternoon gathering at the Music Hall reads like a veritable who's who of black and white abolitionists in the antislavery stronghold. When word came that Lincoln had indeed issued the proclamation the throng erupted with shouts of joy. Later that evening a crowd of about three thousand at Tremont Temple waited for the text of the proclamation to come over the wire, some not yet believing that Lincoln had kept his word. Speaker after speaker tried to maintain morale as the evening wore on. By ten o'clock word had yet to arrive and Frederick Douglass noted "a visible shadow" falling over the throng. When verification was finally made and the proclamation read, the ecstatic audience exploded with jubilation. The celebration went on till the next morning, and, indeed, was augmented by numerous events over the next several days.[28]

Sympathetic observers saw the proclamation as a defining moment for the nation, integrating the African American quest for liberty into the American saga. William Lloyd Garrison considered the date of January 1, 1863, equal in rank with July 4, 1776, as hallowed dates "in the history of this country." Frederick Douglass went a step further, asserting that "the fourth of July was great, but the first of January, when we consider it in all its relations and bearings is incomparably greater." Wendell Phillips likened the proclamation to the voice of God, which spoke and made the prayers of the enslaved "the cornerstone of the Republic." A month after the fact Douglass was hardly less sweeping in his assessment of the act, congratulating a large and enthusiastic biracial audience at New York's Cooper Union on "the greatest event of our nation's history, if not the greatest event of the century." "It is difficult," he reflected, "to grasp the full and complete significance of President Lincoln's proclamation," but the federal government's recent authorization to form the Fifty-fourth Massachusetts Infantry indicated to Douglass that he was not amiss in using the phrase *"our* nation."[29]

After the firing on Fort Sumter African Americans had responded patriotically, and in vain, to Lincoln's call for volunteers. With the Emancipation Proclamation and its provision for the enlistment of black troops came the opportunity for African American men to fight for the liberation of the southern slaves and for the defense of the United States. But despite their consistent claims to equal rights as American citizens, not all blacks were anxious to risk their lives for a nation that had yet to guarantee those rights. Even as Frederick Douglass was recruiting for the Fifty-fourth, Philadelphian Eli T. Harmon, though he acknowledged that "slavish chains are breaking," contended in verse that

> If Afric's sons do have to fight
> They must be heirs of glory;
> And till they do receive their rights
> I don't think they need hurry.[30]

Despite such misgivings nearly two hundred thousand black men donned blue uniforms for the fused causes of liberty and national preservation. The exploits of the Fifty-fourth and of many other African American soldiers and sailors themselves were to become, for fellow blacks at least, important as subjects for historical discourse and as objects of commemoration during the generation following the war.[31]

Black troops, recruited both among northern freemen and southern freedmen, became increasingly visible on the front lines of battle during 1863. This evidence of black patriotism and sacrifice confirmed in the minds of many African Americans that the nation surely could not permit the perpetuation of slavery. William Steward, of Bridgeton, New Jersey, echoed Eli Harmon's concern regarding black military service when he questioned whether in "a country which has always denied them the right to be men[,] . . . should we be loyal to the country or to ourselves?" Steward's solution, which reflected a common point of view regarding the mass enlistment of former slaves, admitted of no contradiction between those loyalties. He denied the possibility of disarming, let alone reenslaving, the freedmen: *"The arms placed in the hands of the slaves will never be relinquished till rights are acknowledged."* This implicit threat of a black rights revolution made it clear that black soldiers, by 1863, were fighting for their nation, for abolition, and for full citizenship.[32]

As the end of that eventful year approached, African Americans began to prepare for the first anniversary celebration of emancipation. In the process, they reflected on the meaning of such celebrations and the proper manner of their observance. Many felt that commemoration of such a blessed and divinely orchestrated event should be essentially religious and involve fasting and prayer, and must primarily "offer unto God thanksgiving."[33] James H. Payne, writing from Chicago, concurred that "the first and grand anniversary of our people's liberty" must be observed "with . . . the highest gratitude to God—as a glorious day, a day when the nationality of our down-trodden race began to exist in this country." At the same time, Payne recognized that Freedom Day affairs had come to involve a variety of activities, some of which went beyond "loud shouts of thanksgiving to God." "Let me say to our people that I am not unapprized of the many ways which will be taken to celebrate the first of January. . . . But let it be remembered," he advised, "that they are not all pleasing in the sight of God. Let me say the ball room floor is not the proper place to celebrate the first jubilee year, nor is the gaming table the place, nor the drinking saloon. There is but one way with which we can properly celebrate the first of January. . . . the 1st day of January next, ought to be set apart as a day most solemnly devoted to God." Payne was aware that his admonishments could hardly eliminate secular revels held outside the purview of the churches. His plea was specifically intended to distance such foolishness from the house of God. Critical of any use of the church for anything other than worship, Payne's appeal fit in the larger context of "deliver[ing] the churches from the uncalled-for crime of holding wicked festivals and ungodly concerts to help her out of debt." If he could not eliminate churches' much-needed fund-raising socials, he at least wanted to make it clear that the divine gift of emancipation required more respectful treatment: "The noisy festival with jollifications of levity and lightness ought not to be tolerated on that day."[34]

When the day arrived, observances around the nation reflected a range of celebratory styles, indicating that not all adhered to James Payne's sense of propriety and respectability. A correspondent to the *Christian Recorder*, writing from St. Louis, Missouri, described a secular celebration on a frigid New Year's Day that was marked by speeches, the participation of both blacks and whites, and most stirring of all in that slave-holding city, "a procession . . . through some of the principal streets . . . [featuring] black men, with muskets and banners, marching to the music of 'John Brown's

Soul is Marching On.'" This scene reflects the dramatic change that had taken place in just a few years. In 1859 a St. Louis correspondent commented on an unprecedented August 1 meeting that had been arranged by antislavery sympathizers in the decidedly proslavery city. It was noted that the August 1 anniversary was "one, of late years, faithfully observed in those portions of the Northern States where Abolitionism is most rampant, and wears its most aggressive aspect." Most concern locally appeared to revolve around the fact that "at such festivals, it is customary to have an admixture of black and white orators" and a similarly mixed audience. Although the mayor had given his consent to a speech by eastern visitor Philip P. Carpenter, the proposed speaker was publicly derided as an "Abolition nigger-thieving Lecturer" and threatened with "tarring and feathering and riding you on a rail, should you dare attempt the lecture." Carpenter found the door to the hall locked when he dared to arrive for his speech.[35]

While the public, biracial, and martial display in 1864 may have elicited similar feelings among antiblack St. Louisians, they dared not threaten the proceedings as they had five years earlier. The 1864 celebration illustrates the transformation of public affairs wrought by the government's actions to attack slavery, and the procession appears to have been a proud exhibition of black manhood. The affair was marred for its chronicler, however, when the festivities moved indoors to a public hall. Singled out as particularly inappropriate were the raucous antics of "one old man" who felt the need "to get up in a corner" and "a number of old and young people fluttering around the [dance] floor like a chicken, with its head cut off." "If the Christian part of the people were to do their duty on special national days," the writer chastised, "the Hall . . . would not be turned into a ball room." Perhaps more significant than his plea for propriety was this observer's sense, accentuated by the presence of African American troops, that the affair commemorated a special day of legitimately national, rather than narrowly racial, dimension.[36]

The participation of three companies of the 8th U.S. Colored Troops similarly added to the import of a more decorous and religiously oriented celebration in Wilmington, Delaware. In this border state that, like Missouri, Kentucky, and Maryland, still permitted slavery, the black soldiers stimulated great excitement even though the celebration did not involve a formal parade and was carried on exclusively in houses of worship. The day began with prayer, choral music, and preaching at Wilmington's venerable African Union Church. In midafternoon celebrants reassembled at the East Zion Methodist Episcopal Church for singing, prayer, the reading of the proclamation, and a sermon by the respected AME minister Henry J. Rhodes. At seven in the evening yet another meeting was held, again at the Union

Church, which included more song and prayer, as well as a half dozen brief addresses whose topics included a reminiscence of slavery days (now assumed to be ending); an analysis of the nation's political state; a prediction of the race's potential in the arts, science, and business; and a "short and spicy" celebration of the expansion of liberty that was then coming to a head.

Perhaps the most broad-ranging address of the day was Henry Rhodes's afternoon sermon, which touched on a number of themes common to antebellum Freedom Day addresses. He began by linking African Americans' experiences with the prophecy in the Book of Isaiah, which describes the Ethiopian people as a nation torn and scattered, but one presently being called to Zion. Like some early slave trade celebration orators, Rhodes alluded to the greed and avarice behind the Europeans' despoiling of "the land of Africa." He quickly moved on, though, to acknowledge the long-standing greatness of the African "nation" in producing great "Bishops, Statesmen and Generals," from St. Cyprian and Hannibal to Frederick Douglass, Daniel Payne, and the leaders of Liberia and Haiti. The current circumstances represented to Rhodes the fulfillment of both Africa's biblical destiny and African Americans' rightful claim to American identity. The sermon emphasized African Americans' various duties: to themselves, to be honest and charitable as they embraced their freedom; to their country, "because it is the land of our nativity . . . [and] with all her stains, yet we should love her and be willing to defend her"; and to God, through whose beneficence their "unshaken confidence" was presently being rewarded.[37]

In Boston, despite high winds and frigid temperatures that hampered celebrations throughout the Northeast, a large gathering "of both white and colored people" celebrated the anniversary of the proclamation at several locations from the morning "until a late hour" at night. The commemorations were generally somber, consisting of prayers, speeches, sermons, readings, and musical interludes. The program assembled many of the city's well-known black abolitionists, including William Wells Brown, Lewis Hayden, Robert Morris, and the Reverend H. H. White. The latter, in his brief address, echoed Henry Rhodes's interpretation that emancipation linked the causes of race and nation: "We celebrate it *as our day*. It gives birth to our liberties. We celebrate it as *the nation's day*. This day one year ago, the brightest ray of the nation's glory burst forth from the firmament of her power." White's words also went further, recalling the universalist perspective of Frederick Douglass's antebellum Freedom Day orations, as he described the day as "beautiful and glorious for . . . the common lovers of mankind." African American speakers at this new celebration of liberty thus maintained the universalist and humanist threads of analysis established during antebellum freedom festivals, connecting the "regenerated manhood" of the race with the newly "purified and strengthened" nation and "the universal brotherhood of man [that] would be acknowledged all over the civilized world."[38]

The celebrants at New York's Cooper Institute were perhaps less confident of the universality of human brotherhood. In addition to bitter cold, high winds, and freezing rain, they also had to contend with "their fear of a mob" as they commemorated emancipation. In his description of the event, the AME minister Richard H. Cain did not specify the nature or origin of those fears of violence, but the memory of the July 1863 Draft Riots in the city was surely fresh in the minds of the celebrants. Apparently no attacks marred the day, perhaps in part due to the inclement conditions. In any case, Cain reported with obvious pride, a predominantly black crowd of one thousand "venture[d] through all the disadvantages of such a day [in order to] evidence their appreciation of the events of so much moment to the race."[39]

In a sunnier clime the freedmen in South Carolina's Sea Islands joined in "one of the grandest demonstrations ever held on Southern soil . . . in the celebration of the birth-day of liberty in the South." African Methodist missionary James Lynch worked in conjunction with the U.S. military establishment to organize a huge event in Beaufort that began with a "civic and military procession." Thousands of contrabands, "attired in their best and most brilliant garments, flocked into town from all the plantations on the neighboring islands. . . . Such a gathering was never before seen in quiet Beaufort." The procession included blacks "of both sexes, congregated together, [who] marched with numerous banners and flags." It was headed by wounded and disabled African American soldiers followed by several regiments of black troops stationed in the vicinity. Black laborers, mechanics, pilots, engineers, and sailors came next, along with black schoolchildren and their teachers, and finally, the freedmen of Beaufort, Port Royal, Hilton Head, St. Helena, Paris, and other islands, and "representatives of other states." In short, it seems that every black person in the region took part in the procession, leaving one to wonder who remained on the sidelines to serve as spectators. Ceremonies on the speakers' platform at Camp Shaw featured various readings, poems, and musical offerings, and the presentation of swords to the military governor, General Rufus Saxton, and to Colonel Thomas W. Higginson, commander of the First South Carolina Volunteers. Banners bearing mottoes were suspended above the stand that juxtaposed a range of heroes including George Washington, John Brown, Rufus Saxton, and Toussaint L'Ouverture. At the conclusion of the formal exercises the four thousand participants enjoyed "an 'Old Southern Barbecue'" that included fifteen roasted oxen and two thousand loaves of bread.

The "Great Jubilee" in South Carolina—with its grand scale and inclusiveness, its martial components, and the apparent enthusiasm of its celebration—was typical of those in other parts of the Union-occupied South.[40]

If we are to believe the report of Henry P. Jones, the *Christian Recorder*'s correspondent in Portsmouth, Virginia, the festivities at nearby Norfolk were even more grandiose, involving an estimated fifteen thousand celebrants and including four regiments of African American troops. It was important for Jones to publicize the event in order to dispel the notion held by "some of our neighbors in a more northern climate . . . that they were carrying things all their own way and alone on the 1st day of January." Consistent with the broad regional scope of the South Carolina affair, Virginia organizers made sure that "the country, for miles around, were apprized of the fact" well in advance. The turnout was obviously gratifying, and the reporter crowed that "never was there a day in the annals of Anglo-African history that was celebrated with more *éclat*." For Jones the most memorable aspect of the celebration was the procession. The black military units were clearly a source of pride and inspiration, as they demonstrated with their "splendid" marching that "they have no superiors, even in the white regiments. . . . That the colored man can and does make a good soldier, there cannot be the least doubt." In some ways more impressive than the martial display was the presence of African American civilians. Jones noted the significance of the procession being headed by "Marshall Keeling, one of Norfolk's colored citizens" and acknowledged the appearance of various African American bands, clergymen, and firemen in the line of march. Most strikingly, Jones admitted to having been "taken entirely by surprise" by the presence of "a colored Masonic society, next the Mechanics' Bible Society, and two female societies, one literary and the other secret. . . . The idea of seeing literary and secret societies, that had been organized for years in the very heart of oppression and tyranny, amongst the despised and lowly outcasts, and flourishing, too, was something beyond my comprehension. . . . Verily, and can such a race ever be slaves? As well might man, in his feebleness, attempt to calm the angry ocean when lashed into fury . . . as to again place the yoke on God's dark-hued children's backs."[41]

Jones's commentary reflects some interesting regional patterns in the celebrations. As the war raged on, and the fate of slavery remained officially unresolved, southern Freedom Day observances—dominated by the presence of large numbers of the freedmen themselves—affirmed more pointedly than any other celebrations black Americans' conviction that Lincoln's proclamation indeed represented the long-awaited fulfillment of biblical prophecy and "the death warrant of slavery."[42] The powerful presence of black troops and the organized participation of previously clandestine civil and religious societies reinforced that message through physical statements made on the public streets. These statements were not exclusive to the South, but they had their greatest impact there, when huge throngs marched, as Henry Jones put it, "in the very heart of oppression and tyranny." Fifteen thousand in Norfolk, four thousand in the Sea Islands, and eight thousand in New Bern, North Carolina, indicate the freedpeople's enthusiasm for the new celebration and their unambiguous affirmation of their freedom and their citizenship.[43]

Just as significant in their own way on that first anniversary of emancipation in 1864 were the smaller crowds in the North. Braving both the threat of white mobs and the brutal weather conditions, they gathered to commemorate an event they hoped would have meaning not just for themselves as blacks but for all Americans. Where the southern freedmen seem to have placed greater emphasis on the irrevocable reality of their own liberation, northern black commentators were more prone to look beyond the fact of emancipation toward its larger meaning for all the American people, black or white. Northern celebrations were, for largely demographic reasons, smaller in scale, and for largely climatic reasons, more likely to entail indoor oratorical and religious exercises than massive public processions. Ox roasts and parades, hardly out of place at northern August 1 freedom festivals, were impractical in January in the Northeast. And while black regiments were still being organized in the North, their numbers and their impact were far larger in the South, where they were in the field, actively liberating their enslaved brethren.

These regional variations aside, Lincoln's proclamation and the progress of the Union armies had expanded the Freedom Day tradition in two ways that would affect its continued development. First, a new date, with a much more immediate and personal meaning for African Americans, had appeared on the commemorative calendar. Second, and more importantly, for the first time large numbers of southern blacks participated in the long-standing tradition of celebrating the onward march of liberty. Taken together, these first anniversary celebrations of the January 1 Emancipation Proclamation indicate that the date almost immediately claimed a place of distinction on the African American commemorative calendar. The fact that the date of Lincoln's proclamation coincided with the date of the original commemorations of the abolition of the Atlantic slave trade went virtually unnoticed by blacks in the 1860s, all their attention being concentrated on the present cause for celebration. North, South, or West, whether focused on prayers of thanksgiving, martial parades, somber speeches, or festive barbecues, the wartime expansion of the Freedom Day tradition gave notice that the whole of the American people must acknowledge the reality of emancipation, the legitimacy of its commemoration, and the significance of both for the nation. Blacks were moving away from slavery and were more vocal than ever regarding the need for the government and the whole American people to acknowledge their rights as citizens. As William H. Meyers phrased it in a poem read at a Washington, D.C., celebration, emancipation meant that blacks would thenceforward proceed, "With our destiny linked to the nation's" in honoring a new Freedom Day anniversary:

> This day we'll hold dear—In each ongoing year,
>   From our hearts can't be blotted; no, never,
> One year to-day, this nation
>   Issued its Proclamation
> That slaves should be freemen forever.
>
> Freedom's work is near done,
>   And with gladness we come
> To honor that just Proclamation;
>   By it Abraham Lincoln,
> To the wide world has made known
>   That freedom's the aim of the nation.[44]

The immediate and widespread acceptance of the January 1 Freedom Day date, however, did not preclude the celebration of other emancipatory occasions during the 1860s and 1870s, often those having a more local significance. The nation's capital, for example, continued to commemorate April 16 along with January 1. In a similar vein, Baltimore and Philadelphia blacks celebrated the abolition of slavery in Maryland, effective with the state's new constitution on November 1, 1864. The upcoming presidential election raised the political stakes at these November celebrations; if Lincoln lost, it was not clear that a different administration would continue to support a policy of emancipation. In this context, celebrants of the Maryland act emphasized the need to "sustain" the president "by our ballots, and make emancipation a fact, fixed forever." Their appeal, of course, was directed to white voters, since African Americans in Pennsylvania and Maryland were denied the franchise until the ratification of the Fifteenth Amendment in 1870. Even after the war and the Thirteenth Amendment put an end to American slavery, the early November celebrations continued for several years at least. Outside observers, however, were at times confused as to the significance of the date. A California newspaper reported in 1869 that "[t]he colored people of Maryland and other States celebrated at Baltimore Nov 4th, the anniversary of the first emancipation proclamation" with "a procession several miles long" and the usual orations. Though this November affair in Maryland was almost surely not connected with Lincoln's preliminary proclamation, the reporter's confusion was not entirely baseless.[45]

In parts of the Midwest, especially in Illinois and Indiana, the September 22 date of Lincoln's preliminary Emancipation Proclamation did become an occasion for commemoration. But despite the date's connection with an emancipatory event, September 22 was never observed consistently or widely. Even in the Midwest it never gained the popularity of regional commemorative traditions elsewhere in the country. For example, "Juneteenth," once a more region-specific tradition in and around Texas, in the late twentieth century gained popularity across the United States, partly due to migration from its region of origin, partly due to scholarly and popular media attention, and partly due to the amenability of the summer season for public celebrations. The tradition is said to have begun on June 19, 1865, when General Gordon Granger landed his regiment at Galveston, Texas, and read General Order Number 3, informing Texans that the U.S. government intended to enforce the Emancipation Proclamation in that region.[46]

In contrast with Juneteenth's rising popularity during the late twentieth century, some local traditions remained local. In parts of southern Virginia, for example, blacks celebrated emancipation on April 9, the date of Robert E. Lee's surrender at Appomattox. One resident of Mecklenburg County explained the rationale behind the "Surrender Day" tradition on its twenty-fifth anniversary in 1890: "We do it because we held that our real deliverance was accomplished by the 'surrender.' If Lee had never been beaten and the confederacy never crushed, the proclamation would have been of no avail." Leon Litwack has observed that blacks throughout the South were hesitant to accept the permanence of their freedom until after "the surrender," and the first news of Appomattox prompted celebrations in many cities and towns in 1865. But only in Virginia did the event's date find a lasting place on the commemorative calendar. In addition to occasional observances on April 9, blacks in Richmond often commemorated April 3, the date the Confederate capital was occupied by Union troops. Despite threats from local whites that "We will wade through blood before the nigger shall celebrate the day," Richmond blacks persisted in their public observances. But throughout the nineteenth century there remained considerable debate among the city's black citizens whether to celebrate in April or on January 1.[47]

Because of the ongoing war, African Americans in some parts of the South did not have the opportunity to publicly celebrate Lincoln's proclamation until several years after the event. When Charleston, South Carolina, blacks held their first emancipation festival on January 1, 1866, the day was thought to be of sufficient import that it "must hereafter become one of the few National Holidays." The day's procession, speeches, and "old fashioned barbecue" apparently were not subsidized by the military or government, as the Committee of Arrangements explicitly asked churches to take up special collections and the public to "contribut[e] their mites to the cause of Freedom." As always, volunteer work by women's organizations on food, wreaths, banners, and the like was essential. The committee claimed "that they cannot get along without the ladies, except in the procession," making it clear that female involvement must remain behind the scenes.[48]

Blacks elsewhere in the South likewise chose to celebrate on January 1, while still acknowledging the limits of Lincoln's proclamation. In Augusta, Georgia, January 1, 1866, was observed as "the *first* Anniversary of Freedom" since it was the first New Years Day "on which our race find themselves fully secured in the liberty guaranteed by the Proclamation, and forever free from the bondage of slavery."[49] Certainly, much of the black Augustans' confidence in 1866 related directly to the Thirteenth Amendment, which, upon ratification on December 18, 1865, had erased any lingering doubts regarding the fate of slavery. The amendment generated a great deal of enthusiasm, both on its ratification and earlier when it was passed by Congress on January 31, 1865. The bill's approval in the House set off unprecedented cheering from floor and gallery, while cannons boomed in salute on the capital's streets. After ratification by the states, a celebration in Philadelphia on December 31, 1865, used the event as another opportunity to recount the narrative of black heroism during the war for freedom. Especially conscious of "demonstrating the fact [of blacks' central role in the conflict] by actual living facts in their history," the event identified "the brave colored volunteers, as THE instrument of the Almighty" in preserving the Union and ending American slavery.[50] But neither of the dates associated with the Thirteenth Amendment garnered support as fitting for sustained general observance. The amendment abolishing slavery did not enter fully into blacks' nineteenth-century commemorative traditions, though its importance was acknowledged on the fiftieth anniversary of its adoption in 1915. Perhaps blacks felt that celebrating an act of Congress would distance the new freedom too far from their own role in securing their liberty. Perhaps, like Robert Hamilton and James McCune Smith in the 1850s, they felt that celebrating the legislation of a white government was inappropriate for a people who needed to claim emancipation for themselves. In any case, constitutional abolition never carried the symbolic weight of other more widely observed dates in the Freedom Day tradition.[51]

In the South, probably due to the instigation of northern soldiers, teachers, or missionaries, some efforts were made to transplant the time-honored

August 1 tradition in the soil of the former Confederacy. An 1865 report from Charleston, South Carolina, described "the first time the First of August has been celebrated in this part of the country." The relatively modest event was sponsored by members of a local benevolent society, who marched into the hall "handsomely dressed in regalia" and supplied "ice cream, cakes, sugar plums, wines," and other delicacies. The literary program was dominated by northerners, most from Philadelphia and Rhode Island. In Memphis a more imposing display was made by "the thousands of men women and children gathered together on this interesting occasion." A nineteen-piece "colored" brass band led a procession that included several U.S. colored regiments and a three-hundred-member contingent of a "society of colored men of Memphis," known as the United Sons of Ham. Numerous white and black orators filled the day with speeches, which were "interspersed with lively music, by the band." The correspondent reporting the affair expressed his optimism, based on the pledges of white orators "to stand by the colored people," and looked forward to "a better state of things along the Mississippi valley." Before the next summer, however, those hopes would fade, as dozens of Memphis blacks would lose their lives in one of the worst riots of the Reconstruction era.[52]

Through antiblack mob violence in Memphis and New Orleans, and through countless less-publicized acts of race hatred across the South, the limits of the Union victory and of the various Reconstruction policies soon became clear. Nonetheless, January 1 continued to hold pride of place in that part of the nation most affected by the nominal end of slavery symbolized by Lincoln's proclamation. Other than a few events in 1865 the South never adopted August 1 celebrations. The date of Lincoln's January 1 proclamation had a far clearer resonance with the freedmen and remained, despite several notable localized exceptions, the most widely accepted date for southern Freedom Day commemorations.

Traditionally a day to be dreaded by the slaves, January 1 had, during slavery, marked the end of the brief Christmas holiday season and augured the initiation of new labor contracts, the resultant separation of loved ones, and the return to work. New Year's Eve "watch night" gatherings during slavery days were hardly joyous affairs, with slaves waiting up all night to greet the dawning of what some referred to as "heartbreak day."[53] The coincidence of Lincoln's choosing that day to issue his proclamation clearly changed the date's significance for the former bondspeople. On the third anniversary of the proclamation, and the first since the end of the war, Henry McNeal Turner, a black officer assigned to the Freedmen's Bureau and a prominent minister in the AME Church, addressed the crowd at a celebration in Augusta, Georgia. Turner made a point of emphasizing the transformation of the meaning of January 1 in the hearts and minds of the freedpeople:

> Associated with the first of January are peculiar interests, which in their accommodation to the world of colored men, will hereafter enshrine it in their affections with a deathless sacredness, forever and ever. This day which hitherto separated so many families, and tear-wet so many faces; heaved so many hearts, and filled the air with so many groans and sighs; this of all others the most bitter day of the year to our poor miserable race, shall henceforth and forever be filled with acclamations of the wildest joy, and expressions of ecstacy too numerous for angelic pens to note. Before this day, all other days will dwindle into insignificance with us.[54]

If January 1 predominated in the South, and other parts of the nation observed an expanding range of dates, the August 1 anniversary of West Indian emancipation maintained its strong hold in some regions, both immediately after the war and into the twentieth century. Though the event was celebrated as far afield as South Carolina, Kansas, and California, August 1 was most consistently commemorated in the northern tier of states from Massachusetts to Michigan. That the date was used primarily to commemorate U.S. emancipation is suggested by the almost unanimous presence of the reading of Lincoln's proclamation on the schedules of events. Many affairs, however, explicitly used the date to commemorate *both* U.S. and West Indian emancipations. These joint August 1 celebrations thus placed both events in the broader context of the universal progress of freedom around which African Americans constructed their historical interpretations. Many celebrations, like the one at Circleville, Ohio, in 1865, were specifically held "in commemoration of West India emancipation, *and* the glorious events that have lately transpired in our own country." This particular event was also typical of many antebellum and postbellum August 1 affairs in its use of a large grove outside of town; its combining picnic feasts, amusements, prayers, music, and orations; and its attraction of an influx of visitors from several adjoining counties. The post–Civil War Freedom Day festivals, then, were also placed in the broader context of existing African American commemorative traditions and practices.[55]

For example, in 1867 blacks in Hartford, Connecticut, met in an outdoor grove near the ancient town of Wethersfield for a series of "forcible" orations followed by outdoor dancing to "music from a fine band." Evening activities included a "grand banquet" and, later, a small private party. Farther east, black and white residents of the Massachusetts seaport of New Bedford continued their distinguished August 1 Freedom Day tradition, begun in the

1840s. Once again Emancipation Day was celebrated "in fine style," with a procession that included four separate black volunteer military companies and "a long line of citizens on foot and in carriages." Some five thousand persons from around the region assembled at Arnold's Grove for the usual addresses, prayers, and orations. The day closed with a concert "given in Liberty Hall by Miss [Elizabeth] Greenfield, the celebrated 'Black Swan,' " and a ball sponsored by one of the militia units, the Shoulter Guards.[56]

Nowhere were August 1 observances more entrenched and vibrant than in the "burned-over district" of upstate New York, named for its antebellum tradition of red-hot evangelical revival and noted as a center of humanitarian reform. As was the case with many antebellum August 1 rituals across the country, the relatively small towns around the state's Finger Lakes region drew their crowds from across the area. An 1865 celebration in the tiny village of Owego, New York, not far from the Pennsylvania border, was typical. Officers of the day included residents of the New York towns of Bath, Ithaca, Elmira, and Binghamton, and the Pennsylvania communities of Towanda, Montrose, Pittston, and Wilkes-Barre. Some of these were more than sixty miles away. Multiple gun salutes and the ringing of bells opened the celebration, but the planned parade and outdoor festivities were dampened by torrents of rain, which forced the speaker of the day, John Mercer Langston, to deliver his address inside the court house. Hundreds of disappointed participants had to be turned away for lack of space.[57]

Another representative celebration, organized in 1870 by black residents of Cortland, New York, and the nearby hamlet of Homer, featured an array of activities from morning until late at night. Festivities began with a procession that included a marching band and numerous "distinguished guests from abroad" and continued with exercises at a local grove that featured orations by Frederick Douglass and Henry Highland Garnet, both of whom had long-standing personal ties in the area. This stellar bill would have been even more impressive had Mississippi senator Hiram Revels attended, as scheduled. The presence of such luminaries in an obscure little town was not terribly unusual, even though "the two villages of Cortland and Homer do not contain over a dozen colored families" between them. As was the case at the Owego celebration, a modest local contingent was augmented by a "large turn out from Ithaca, Binghampton, Syracuse, and other surrounding towns," as well as, we can presume, a good number of white observers. The crowd totaled nearly three thousand, despite a heavy downpour that forced the speakers from the original grove venue to an indoor facility whose seating capacity of twenty-five hundred was inadequate to the task. The regional orientation of the observance is clear, given that participants on the program included residents of Ithaca, Owego, Norwich, and Elmira, towns between twenty and fifty miles distant. Considerable advance planning and regional coordination among community leaders was necessary to insure the success of the event, and the organizers were praised for "having everything done to please all concerned in the celebration." The scale and scope of the celebration indicate that a functional regional communication network was well in place and that northern African Americans continued to use Freedom Day festivals to solidify the bonds among a rather sparse and scattered regional black community.[58]

The Freedom Day tradition was just as vibrant on the other side of the country, in San Francisco, which before 1900 had the largest black urban population in the Far West. Blacks there embraced several key dates as worthy of commemoration in the immediate post–Civil War years. In contrast with the common eastern pattern, the celebration of August 1 in the Bay Area was specifically intended to celebrate the "anniversary of Emancipation in the British West Indian Islands." Within a black population of about thirteen hundred in 1870, approximately one in seven black residents was foreign born, and those overwhelmingly from the Caribbean basin. Afro-San Franciscans in the mid-nineteenth century comprised a relatively cosmopolitan group, with a high rate of literacy and considerable experience in an urban environment. The American-born black population was fairly evenly split between northern and southern origins, with migrants from Massachusetts, New York, Maryland, Pennsylvania, Washington, D.C., and New Orleans being especially well represented. Many of the northerners, like Philip A. Bell, inveterate race activist and prominent journalist, had a long-standing and intimate familiarity with existing Freedom Day traditions.[59]

The annual August 1 celebrations, organized by the West Indian Benevolent Association with the support of Bell and other black community leaders, can be traced to the mid-1850s. They included most of the components found elsewhere. The 1868 celebration at Hayes Park featured "the usual literary exercises during the day, concluding with a promenade concert at night." Addresses by the president and orator of the day, the reading of an original poem by former Buffalo, New York, celebration organizer James M. Whitfield, and several other speeches were followed by a historical "closing address" by black factory-owner and dance instructor Shadrack Howard. Howard echoed themes from antebellum August 1 orations and at least suggested the connection between British and American emancipations. His address was, essentially, "an elaborate resume of the triumphs of Antislavery principles inaugurated by Clarkson and Wilberforce in England, and in America by Benjamin Lundy, Garrison, Tappan, and their coadjutors." The attendance at the day's literary activities was sparse, "but it was considerably increased at night," when "the company enjoyed themselves until a late hour" on the dance floor. As with the city's 1855 celebration (see chap. 2), dancing was the main attraction for many San Franciscans. But the organizers still drew "great praise for their endeavors to perpetuate a remembrance of this great historical event."[60]

The 1873 August 1 affair, held at the City Gardens, perhaps reflected the organizers' growing attention to popular sensibilities, as no oratorical exercises were mentioned in newspaper coverage of the event. If any indeed took place they apparently did not warrant notice. The parade escorting the association and its guests to the picnic grounds was led by the Brannan Guards, one of several black volunteer military drill companies in the area, the United Social Club, and "a band of music," all of whom were "admired for their decorum." At the gardens the celebrants enjoyed "racing, shooting, dancing, and all the amusements the place afforded." Many "clad in picnic attire" rowed on the lake and strolled amiably around the verdant grounds. "Eating and drinking and lovers wooing were among the objects of the day." The event attracted many black Californians from outside the immediate Bay Area, especially when festivities moved to the dance pavilion that evening. There a much larger crowd, including "those from the city and interior," occupied the dance floor for a ball that extended "up to a late hour at night."[61] If West Indian Emancipation Day seems to have become a more purely social affair by the early 1870s, other freedom festivals in the region retained their focus on perpetuating historical memory and tradition.

Foremost among those days was the annual January 1 commemoration of the Emancipation Proclamation. Emancipation Day events from across the Far West were described assiduously in the pages of Philip Bell's weekly paper, the *Elevator*. From the relatively nearby California communities of Marysville, Stockton, and Sacramento to more distant centers like Portland, Oregon, and Elko, Nevada, correspondents fed reports to an editor who was quite consciously concerned with the dissemination of historical knowledge and the maintenance of historical memory and traditions. Bell, in fact, was a driving force behind the organization of San Francisco's black population. During his tenure as president of the colored citizens' executive committee from May 1869 to June 1870, the committee held twelve regular monthly meetings in addition to numerous other "public meetings for the purpose of taking the sense of the people upon the propriety of public celebrations," including July 4, January 1, August 1, and the unspecified date of the recent Fifteenth Amendment.[62]

Several years before his presidency of the committee, Bell printed a report describing the January 1, 1867, celebration in Sacramento, which reinforced the continuity between the new commemorations and themes established during antebellum Freedom Day festivals. The Sacramento affair featured many of the "usual circumstances": music, orations, processions, and a salute fired by the Grant Guards, one of the several black military companies in the area. A set of resolutions, also a common characteristic of African American meetings and conventions, artfully linked black Americans' immediate political concerns with more universal themes of liberty and equal rights for all. The assembly, by acclamation, asserted their "fidelity" to the national government in light of that government's "immortal Proclamation of freedom to our race." They emphasized their willingness to "at all times take our muskets on our shoulders . . . and go forth to fight for freedom and the laws of our country." But, these black patriots emphasized, "we therefore consider ourselves entitled to equality before the law, and we believe that the hands which held the musket should not be denied the ballot." This demand for full participatory citizenship resonated with the national political situation, as President Andrew Johnson squared off against a Republican Congress over the issues of Reconstruction policy and black rights in general, and the implications of the Fourteenth Amendment in particular. The November 1866 elections were taken as a mandate by Republican radicals, who promptly escalated a legislative agenda that was both supportive of black citizenship and punitive toward the former rebels. But the Emancipation Day resolution's context was larger still; it was linked specifically with blacks' sympathy "with the poorer classes of Great Britain, who are struggling for the extension to them of the right of suffrage." In this larger framework, African Americans in Sacramento claimed to "heartily sympathize with all nations and people who are struggling to free themselves from tyranny and oppression, and trust that the day may speedily come when all nations shall enjoy freedom in its truest sense."[63]

In San Francisco the following year, organizers again underscored the importance of black hands having wielded muskets in the nation's service as they selected Sergeant William H. Carney to be grand marshal of the procession. Carney, a veteran of the fabled Massachusetts 54th, was famous for having picked up the regiment's battle flag from the fallen standard bearer during the legendary charge on Fort Wagner and assuring his commander that the colors "never touched the ground." For his heroism in that engagement Carney was awarded the Congressional Medal of Honor. In light of Carney's symbolic significance, it is odd that Philip Bell claimed that the war hero "was not our first choice" for grand marshal. Bell gave no indication of whom he had preferred but admitted that "on mature reflection we are satisfied" that the committee made "the best appointment that could be made."[64]

New Year's Day of 1868 dawned "very stormy," and the Emancipation

Day procession did not get under way until nearly noon. At that time Grand Marshal Carney directed the line of march according to plan with military precision and aplomb. The "well-disciplined" black military company, the Brannan Guards, led the procession, followed by the Pacific Brass Band (looking splendid "in their new uniform"), the Committee of Arrangements, the Young Men's Union Beneficial Society (carrying a "beautiful banner"), the officers of the day, "two large cars decorated with American flags" and carrying African American children of the "Public and Sunday Schools," a division of horsemen, and a "long line" of carriages, buggies, and pedestrians.

The procession terminated at Turn Verein Hall about two hours later, and the literary and musical exercises began on schedule. Prayers and patriotic odes were followed by a series of orations, culminating in a remarkable discourse by the orator of the day, the Reverend Jeremiah B. Sanderson, whose comments expressed equal pride in the grandeur of ancient Africa and in the American citizenship that African Americans were anticipating as the Fourteenth Amendment moved toward ratification. Later in the evening, Bell reported two days later, a "grand promenade concert" was "numerously attended by as fashionable a company as we have ever seen." In reporting the event, Bell also expressed considerable dissatisfaction with the celebrants in the hall, whose behavior he found "not only annoying, but actually disgraceful. Crowds of men and boys in the vestibule quarreling and fighting, children running in and out, squads of the Brannan Guards marching and countermarching, committee men running back and forth, and ladies in the gallery holding conversation parties." Bell had nothing but praise for the quality of the orations, especially that of New Bedford, Massachusetts, native J. B. Sanderson, which he termed "an able production, smooth, clear, and well-written." Unfortunately, "owing to the noise and confusion in the hall on the 1st inst., the delivery was greatly marred." Indeed, the "noise at times was so great that it was impossible to hear the speakers" at all. Above all Bell laid blame for the disruptions on the committee, which, he said, "should have made better arrangements."[65]

On the bright side, Bell had some words of praise for the Brannan Guards, whose street drill was apparently more well disciplined than was the group's behavior in Turn Verein Hall. "The Guards," he reported, "received high commendation from military men for their efficiency and precision." Likewise, the editor lauded the Pacific Brass Band, who had "improved greatly" and "acquitted themselves well on Emancipation Day." Their "performances are now equal to almost any band of their number in the city." Even the Committee of Arrangements partially redeemed itself by having amassed the wherewithal to see that the band was "paid in full for their services." Finances were always a large concern at these types of events, and Bell noted that the Pacific Band was still, in fact, owed "a portion of their bill" for their performance at the last Fourth of July parade.[66]

Finances entered into another aspect of the California celebrations of 1868. Two weeks before January 1, 1868, Dr. D. C. Haynes, of San Francisco, secretary of the American Freedmen's Union Commission, appealed to readers of the *Elevator* for money. Despite their physical distance from the freedpeople in the South, blacks in the Far West understood the tenuous position in which emancipation had placed their recently liberated brethren. This plea to assist the freedpeople indicates another of the broad social functions filled by Freedom Day events across the country: reinforcing a sense of racial identity and solidarity that extended far beyond the local or regional community. In the name of the commission, Haynes "most earnestly and respectfully ask[ed] of all a donation on Emancipation Day" to help provide "the necessaries of life and schools" for the former slaves and "particularly to help the poor Freedmen through the winter and spring." After the New Year at least one community, the city of Stockton, about sixty miles inland, reported that, during its celebration, "a collection of sixty dollars was raised and sent to Dr. Haynes, San Francisco, in aid of the freedmen."[67] It is not clear what became of the funds or of the commission, but the attempt to keep blacks on the West Coast connected with their counterparts in the East—and to share responsibility for the well-being of the entire race—reflects the unifying function of the celebrations that overshadowed many of the conflicts and concerns they often engendered.

If the relatively large events held in the City by the Bay generated numerous problems of organization, finance, and control of public behavior, less grandiose affairs presented difficulties of their own. Mrs. A. L. Trask, who, writing under the suggestive pen name Semper Fidelis, provided Bell's San Francisco paper with news from a cluster of California towns about 120 miles to the northeast, complained of similar problems regarding public comportment. The January 1, 1868, emancipation celebration at tiny Nevada City, in the California mountains near Lake Tahoe, was marred for Mrs. Trask by "noise and confusion in the theatre . . . [that] was like distant thunder." Commiserating with Bell, she lamented that, as in San Francisco, "it was impossible a few feet from the stage to hear what was said" by the speakers of the day. "Why is it," she pondered, "that people are so active at such times? I think they move about to be seen, and many who have an office for the day are fearful they will not be seen in their official capacity unless they disturb several hundred."[68]

Mrs. Trask's observations are revealing. If "several hundred" people did attend the Nevada City affair, we must assume that, in addition to a number of local whites, contingents of African Americans from Marysville, Grass Valley, and other nearby towns with small black populations added to the number. Also, black families who mined, farmed, or ranched away from these settlements must have used Freedom Day festivals as welcome opportunities to commingle with their fellows. In 1860, for example, only two hundred of Marysville's nine thousand inhabitants were black, and other communities outside of San Francisco and Sacramento had much smaller black populations. Moreover, many of the region's "mountain towns and mining localities" were said to have experienced a "scarcity of single females," severely limiting the choices for black men seeking partners within the race. Steamer, rail, and coach lines connected these mountain communities with the larger lowland cities, but fares were high enough to discourage regular trips. As one San Franciscan noted regarding a fair at Marysville in 1860, the costs of travel would prohibit attendance from the larger cities, so organizers would "have to depend mostly upon our mountaineers, miners, &c."[69] It is perfectly understandable, then, that the gathering of this scattered regional black population would cause celebrants to "move about to be seen" and to see friends and acquaintances with whom they normally had limited contact. This social function of the celebrations—exchanging news, reconnecting with peers, searching for suitable mates—was perhaps even more vital in the sparsely populated Far West than in the small towns of the Northeast that exhibited similar patterns of regional participation.

Some celebrants of January 1 chose to avoid all issues of travel, noise, finance, and organization by undertaking more private observances of the day. One satirical description of a fictional event in 1869, from a gentleman signing himself "M. T. Head" (Empty Head?) of Nick's Ranch, near Marysville, demonstrates that emancipation celebrations were familiar and widely recognized components of African Americans' cultural life. The account also shows that the typical formula for reporting on, and arguing about, the freedom festivals was easily parodied. As the closest major celebration that year was held in Sacramento, and his "old woman was out of order . . . and I didn't think it safe to leave her so long," Mr. Head "commended to get up an impromptu affair on my own hook." The rancher claimed to believe, like the black leaders he was clearly mocking, "that Emancipation Day is a 'big thing on ice' . . . and demands an appropriate annual observance." The problem, he noted, was that most organizational committees were constrained by having "too much *talent*" and for being composed of "all born leaders. Somehow or other the tide of time left too much greatness on that spot, with not enough of the debris of humanity;— the understrata—to make up the rank and file. . . . Everyone has his idea; and his idea is the best, hence they fail to agree on any general plan." Mr.

Head avoided this problem easily, and declared, "I hope, without egotism, that I originated the whole thing, and I am unanimously of the opinion that it was a success."[70]

Despite invitations from committees in "Dog Flat, Rare-ripe Hollow, Pork and Beans Diggings, Sacramento, San Francisco and various other places to preside, orate and practice on the 1st," Head "resolved to go it alone," his only companion a "friend . . . dressed in black, with a light cap on—in point of fact—a cork; and although he did not speak, he assisted me vastly in the way of getting up enthusiasm." With his "friend in black" presiding, Mr. Head marched out to his speaker's platform in "a grove near the river," where he "proceeded in the most formal manner to address" an audience of livestock which he graced with comically described—and politically charged—names and personae. There was Andy Johnson, "an old pie-bald horse whom we traded for and got badly swindled"; Billy Seward, "a good horse in his day, but he has outlived his usefulness"; and Judge Chase, "once a good horse . . . he strayed into a Democratic neighbor's field, and they caught him and used him for a pack horse." Frequently addressing himself to his "chairman," Head was always acknowledged with "a very low bow— so low in fact, that his cap came off each time. It was an enthusiastic affair, and wound up with a Grand Ball, at least I think so, for the trees and everything seemed to be waltzing around when I wavered my way home."[71]

The humor in this account—as in all parody—would fall flat for those unfamiliar with the Freedom Day tradition, the frequent divisiveness and struggles for status among organizers, the formal structure and sequence of events, and the frequency with which tiny, seemingly insignificant villages hosted celebrations. M. T. Head's affair was distinctive primarily for the unanimity of its organization and the paucity (and species) of its attendants. But, like most Freedom Day festivals, it was arranged by a committee, contained overtly political commentary, was held at a nearby grove, and featured a procession, oration, distinguished guests, more than a little merrymaking, and a culminating grand ball. The correspondent, whose head was apparently not all that empty, even followed the pattern of reporting on the celebration in the regional press, being sure to note its great success. That the tradition-conscious Bell printed the account speaks well for the editor's sense of humor and indicates that he appreciated the accuracy with which the correspondent directed his barbs.

A more serious report of a celebration that actually took place came into Bell's office that same year from the editor's son, Mark A. Bell, who had recently taken up residence in Portland, Oregon. The young man's report suggests that his own sense of the importance of the Freedom Day tradition was much like his father's. The younger Bell boasted that "the colored citizens of Oregon are not behind in their appreciation of the glorious event." As was the custom throughout the United States, "the colored people came pouring in the city from all parts of the State," apparently to the dismay of many "white fellow citizens of the copperhead persuasion." The evening exercises at the court house exhibited "the utmost decorum" and even impressed some of the skeptical whites, who, in a rather derisive attempt at praise, deemed that "the exercises were highly creditable to the darkies." Bishop T. M. D. Ward of the AME Church delivered the oration to a crowd of some 1,300 persons, "most of whom were white." Black participation was dominated by local Portlanders, but the town of Salem, whose "patriotic and liberal hearted citizens" had hosted the previous year's event, "sent 30 representatives" on the forty-mile trip to support the Portland affair. Significantly, in addition to their attendance, that group was said to have "contributed materially toward making [the celebration] a success." After "the rich intellectual feast" of music and speechifying, the black guests "repaired to our own hall, where the tables were loaded with a sumptuous repast of the choicest viands." Toasts followed, and the evening ended with a ball that lasted "until a late hour." This "finest celebration of any kind ever given in Portland" was said to be a complete "success in every way, financially and intellectually." Given that the entire black population of the state probably numbered fewer than 200, with about 90 in and around Portland, the scale of the event, the attendance of a sizable percentage of all black Oregonians, and the reported financial success of the function are all the more significant and impressive.[72]

The fiscal success of the event must have been especially gratifying to the elder Bell. Despite the consistent annual observance of January 1 across the region, Bell expressed his concern in the fall of 1869 that "[t]he celebration of this glorious event should not be suffered to fall into disuse." The editor's main complaint revolved around two issues that remained persistent hindrances to African American organizational activities: lack of money and lack of unified action. As if expanding on his critique of the 1868 celebration, Bell bemoaned the fact that "[w]e have of late years failed to celebrate this day in a fitting manner, with due solemnity and appropriate ceremonies. It has been neglected until it was too late to make sufficient arrangements, and each succeeding year the celebration has fallen short of what it should be, and what the importance of this great event demands." Suggesting that financial support had been a problem in recent celebrations, Bell pleaded that "a fund should be raised sufficient to meet all expenses." He advised the early formation of a committee and subcommittees to attend to the selection of officers, orator, poet, readers, and marshals for the celebration, and urged the invitation of celebrants from across the region. "[W]e should have one grand united celebration, in which all should join. Every town and hamlet should be represented; our people should come from the most distant confines of the Pacific Coast. . . . Our sister States and Territories should unite with us and have a celebration worthy of the occasion." Within the city of San Francisco, Bell, an active member of the Prince Hall Masons, implored the local lodges "to come for once on a platform of fraternity and brotherly love. This day typifies no political event, but it celebrates the regeneration of the nation, the disenthrallment of a race. There is nothing in the ritual of our Order which forbids our taking part in such a celebration." There was nothing to prevent black Masons or other fraternal groups from joining wholeheartedly in similar celebrations across the country. In fact, in Baltimore in 1865, the Odd Fellows organized an "immense" October commemoration of emancipation that involved several months of planning and was said to have "attracted every black in the city as well as those within fifty miles of its bounds." It is unclear why the San Francisco Masonic lodges required such prodding.[73]

In any event, the January 1, 1870, affair that Bell was preparing for came off according to plan. The Committee of Arrangements, chaired by John A. Barber—perhaps not coincidentally the highest-ranking black Mason in the state—formed soon after Bell's call and met every Tuesday from mid-October through December to put affairs in order. Subcommittees on literature, music, invitations, finance, location, and the procession presented weekly updates of their activities. The finance committee issued subscription books to about a dozen highly respected black citizens in order to raise the necessary funds. The invitations committee, which included Philip Bell, issued a call for celebrants throughout the Golden State. Some regional participation was assured by the literary committee, which appointed vice presidents from Sacramento, Stockton, San Jose, Marysville, Napa, Petaluma, and Nevada City. The last two cities were also to provide brass bands for the day. Though official Masonic participation is not evident in the published line of march, the organization, probably through the efforts of Barber and Bell, did at least provide a meeting place for the committee in its hall on the corner of Broadway and Mason Streets.[74] If the January 1 event went well enough, Philip Bell encountered further obstacles to his penchant for commemorations within a few weeks.

Before Emancipation Day organizers could catch their breath and replenish their pocketbooks, a new and seemingly culminating Freedom Day event captured the attention of African Americans across the nation—ratification of the Fifteenth Amendment. The prohibition of disfranchisement "on account of race, color, or previous condition of servitude" was widely hailed by contemporary black and white reformers as the crowning achievement of Reconstruction and the ultimate victory in the struggle for African Americans' inclusion in the political nation. Many black commentators depicted the amendment as "the moral triumph of an age" or "the last grand act in the drama of a nation's justice—the enfranchisement of a race." President Ulysses S. Grant, in his ratification proclamation to Congress on March 30, 1870, concurred "that the adoption of the fifteenth amendment to the Constitution completes the greatest civil change and constitutes the most important event that has occurred since the nation came into life." And it was the right to vote, not the abolition of slavery, which justified to Wendell Phillips the dissolution of the American Anti-Slavery Society in April 1870.[75]

Access to the suffrage, whether gained through the Fifteenth Amendment or through the constitutions of the reconstructed southern states, initially had significance for virtually all African American males—rich, poor, educated, unlettered, freedpeople, freeborn, North, South, and West. Across the nation, ratification celebrations claimed their place in the Freedom Day tradition with an impressive array of parades, religious services, sermons, banquets, military displays and salutes, fireworks, poems, odes, and orations. Two black newspapers, Bell's *Elevator* and Frederick Douglass's new Washington, D.C., weekly the *New Era,* reported on several dozen commemorations during the spring and summer of 1870, in at least twenty-two states (plus the Federal District and Canada) in large cities like Baltimore, New York, New Orleans, and San Francisco, as well as smaller communities like Elmira, New York; White Pine, Nevada; and Brownsville, Tennessee. These celebrations reflected, perhaps even more than the emancipation celebrations of the late 1860s, the view that the nation, and especially its black citizens, had entered a "new era."[76]

But the new era augured by the Fifteenth Amendment did not embrace all African Americans equally. The issue of woman suffrage was, of course, hotly debated as the amendment wended its way through various drafts, congressional approval, and ratification. African Americans, male and female, expressed a wide variety of views on the subject both in public and in private. But after ratification the woman question retreated to the background and remained but a minor theme in the commemorations. Women's participation in the celebrations themselves was not unlike that in the rest of the Freedom Day tradition. Women represented the goddess "Liberty" in parades; girls personified the states of the Union; women occasionally read self-composed odes or poems (almost never orations) from the speakers' platform; they hosted balls and dinners; and they worked diligently in fund-raising activities before the fact. But the main organizers and most visible participants were males, and the prominent themes in the orations and other public expressions were dominated by a male presence and perspective.[77]

Region also seemed to make a difference in celebrations of the Fifteenth Amendment. Relatively few, and usually brief, reports came from the "reconstructed" portion of the nation (representing the states of Virginia, Tennessee, Georgia, Alabama, North Carolina, South Carolina, and Louisiana). This may in part reflect the bias of a northern-oriented press and a paucity of southern correspondents. Perhaps more significant is the fact that the Fifteenth Amendment had a greater impact in the North where few blacks had previously enjoyed the right to vote; in the former Confederacy universal manhood suffrage was a requirement for readmission under congressional Reconstruction. Furthermore, by 1870 the activities of the Ku Klux Klan and similar groups had effectively neutralized black voters and rendered ratification celebrations both meaningless and dangerous in many areas of southern and border states. And, of course, the relative newness of formal organizational structures and the severe shortage of funds probably limited the freedpeople's ability to mount celebrations.

Difficulties related to the new Freedom Day event were not restricted to the South, however. Across the nation African Americans' weak political and financial conditions could leave them, and their newly acquired voting rights, vulnerable to white attempts at manipulation. In Virginia City, Nevada, the Democrats "put forward" a black barber, William Bird, as their candidate for mayor in 1870, apparently "in the hopes of securing the colored vote." African Americans, suspecting that Bird's "political antecedents are unsound," voted overwhelmingly for the white Republican victor, and Bird's effigy was paraded unceremoniously through the streets. Sometimes white machinations could impinge more directly on Freedom Day arrangements. Blacks in Portland, Oregon, had to consider the motives of white Democrats while planning their ratification celebration in 1870. They may have had to think twice before they "indignantly rejected" the Democrats' offer "to pay the expenses of their celebration" in exchange for African American votes.[78]

White interference aside, mounting a celebration often proved difficult for reasons internal to the black community. In San Francisco, Philip Bell was dismayed that his own proposal to commemorate the Fifteenth Amendment with a grand celebration elicited "an indifference in some of our people." This is not to suggest that there was not "considerable enthusiasm manifested" among the attendants of an early organizational meeting. Indeed, Bell explained that many conscientious citizens had urged "that the Committee should make extensive arrangements for a large procession— employ musicians, procure cars, banners, chariots, and all the necessary paraphernalia to give *éclat* to the occasion, but the means are not forthcoming to enable us to meet the necessary expenses. Everybody is anxious we should have a celebration, but too many refuse to contribute, unless their way or manner of celebrating is adopted. . . . This is all wrong. We should give something—all should give according to their means, and we should give cheerfully."[79] Bell's analysis of the problem suggests that M. T. Head's parodic treatment of the workings of celebration committees was extremely accurate: not enough money and too many self-appointed leaders trying to direct affairs could often hinder the arrangements.

Bell criticized one unnamed individual who, though he had "heretofore been loud in his professions of liberality, refused to contribute one dime because the meeting adopted the plan he was opposed to." Others, Bell complained, dictated that "[i]f the Committee cannot raise sufficient money to have a procession, their subscriptions must be refunded." So despite the fact that "enthusiasm prevailed" at the initial committee meetings and the desire for a celebration was widespread, these difficulties threatened to prevent the proper observance of the day. Such seemingly petty personal obstructions to Freedom Day celebrations were hardly limited to the West. A commentator in Cincinnati in 1872 noted that "such meetings fail everywhere. The reason," he wrote, "is not hard to find. It does not arise from the indifference of the people or their lack of patriotism, but from the fact that nearly everywhere, some individual or the officers of some society seek to turn this great stream of gratitude and patriotism to their own use; to make it grind a private grist—hence the people refuse to respond when called on to assist in these celebrations. I think they do right."[80]

In their own attempt to overcome such obstructions, avoid popular cynicism, and "do right" in commemorating emancipation, the committee in San Francisco discussed two possible plans for their celebration. A modest affair involving a "national salute and literary exercises" would cost about $250. A more extravagant program, which was eventually approved, included "a procession with cars and appropriate emblems" and required approximately $800 in order to be properly arranged. By late February 1870, "two large meetings" had netted only about $80 with uncollected pledges promising another fifty. Bell hoped for $1,000 in order to accommodate "contingent expenses which cannot be calculated until they occur." As with the recent January 1 event, "outside collectors" had been appointed to gather donations and subscriptions from "our fellow citizens at large." This suggests that white money, as long as it carried no strings, was a welcome addition to the celebration's fund.[81]

On March 7, the first of many weekly, Monday evening meetings was held at the AME Church on Powell Street. The role of black churches, as well as African Americans' fusion of their history and experience with the divine orchestration of human affairs, pervaded blacks' nineteenth-century Freedom Day commemorations. The sacredness of the cause of black liberation was underscored by the Reverend J. R. V. Morgan, elder of the Powell Street congregation, who issued the remarkable statement "that he would willingly give up his usual meeting on that night, for he considered the cause a holy one, and as important as Christian worship." The meeting of nearly three hundred people (nearly 20 percent of the city's black population) spent most of the evening in "noisy demonstrations" over electing the officers of the celebration. The remainder of the meeting was devoted to collecting another $87, twenty-five of which was donated by the West Indian Benevolent Society, which garnered a vote of thanks from the committee.[82]

Two days later, after the appointment of various subcommittees and their chairs, $130 of the money was apportioned for the services of the Pacific Brass Band "for the procession and literary exercises." The meeting adjourned after a plea that subscribers quickly make good on their pledges. By March 18 Bell could report that remarkable progress had been made in soliciting funds. "We will, without doubt, have sufficient money. . . . We have now nearly six hundred dollars on hand with unpaid pledges of about one hundred more." The San Franciscans' efforts were augmented by the collection of out of town donations, as evidenced by the $16 contributed by residents of Vallejo, at the north end of the Bay. Still, Bell cautioned, continued efforts were in order since "our expenses accumulate beyond our previous estimate."[83]

All the trials of organization and fund-raising came to a happy conclusion, and the grand celebration took place on April 5, 1870. Afterward the committee proudly related that the total collections of $884.45 exceeded the total expenditures for "salutes, music, printing, decorations, etc." by $26. All that profit was later paid to Mr. L. Coleman, "who was severely injured the day of our celebration, and request[ed] the Committee to pay his doctor's bill." At their final meeting in late April, members of the Committee of Arrangements congratulated themselves on their "arduous labors," the president noting that "he had never worked with any Committee whose meetings were more harmonious. The Committee were actuated by one feeling, to carry out successfully the object for which we were appointed." Area residents were applauded for their "liberal contributions," and particular pleasure was derived from the fact that "most of the money [had] been given by colored people."[84]

Bell's faithful reporting of the committee's progress gives us an idea of the complexities of organization and fund-raising involved in a moderately large Freedom Day festival in the early years after emancipation. As with most observances of this scale, a broad participation of the city's, and the region's, black community was actively encouraged by the organizers. The committee arranged with the Board of Education for the colored "children of the public school" to be given the day off, since they were "to make a commendable feature in the procession." "Miss Bevalena Freeman was selected to personate the Goddess of Liberty" in the parade, and she was to be requested "to select 37 young ladies from the different Sabbath Schools to represent the several states." The procession would also allow various black organizations to make a public statement of their sentiments: "A Grand feature in the procession will be the Excelsior Union Republican Club, with a beautiful banner and appropriate badges. The Military will be represented by the Brannan Guard and the Independent Guard, which will turn out in full force. The civic associations will be largely represented by the Young Men's Union Beneficial League, and the West Indian Benevolent Society; and the mechanical department by the Caulkers' Association."[85]

Later in the evening a "Committee of Gentlemen" representing the cities of San Francisco, Sacramento, Petaluma, Napa, and Truckee sponsored "A Grand Ratification Entertainment" to cap off "Freedom's Jubilee," which was significantly described as both "A Holy Day and Holiday." The affair consisted of "Music, Declamation and General Rejoicing" in addition to a supper provided by a "well-known Caterer." The Independent Guards hosted a separate "Grand Jubilee and Promenade Concert" the same evening, with an admission fee of one dollar. Whether the evening activities were in direct competition is unclear, but since many prominent men served on both organizational committees it seems that the events were more likely complementary.[86]

San Francisco's Fifteenth Amendment celebration was representative in many ways of others in cities large and small throughout the nation. Perhaps the largest of these took place in Baltimore on May 19, 1870, reportedly featuring "[n]ot less than ten thousand colored people" in the line of march, with another ten thousand lining the streets representing "every class and condition." The huge biracial event was described by one historian of black Baltimore as "the definitive highlight of all gatherings held after the Civil War, at which blacks and whites could come together at their ease."[87] The procession, in five distinct divisions, included the officers and orators of the day; several bands; hundreds of black men representing numerous military companies and U.S. Army regiments; representatives of the Draymen and Cartmen's Association, Washington's Metropolitan Hook and Ladder Company, the Butchers Association, Farmers' and Brickmakers' Associations, and the Caulkers' Trade Union; several lodges of the Knights Templars, Good Samaritans, and Odd Fellows—all "in full regalia"—who constituted "a veary important feature of the procession, and made an imposing appearance"; the YMCA; a baseball club; and too many political clubs and literary and benevolent societies to list. Banners and transparencies bearing slogans and images of noted individuals were said to number nearly a thousand. The parade was led by a bell that rang continuously and, near the end of the line, a printing press mounted on a wagon reeled off small sheets bearing the text of the amendment as the procession moved along.[88]

Around the speakers' platform in Monument Square gathered from "six to ten thousand persons . . . representing every color, and shade of color, as well as every class and condition of men." An estimated two thousand women, described as being "among the most appreciative listeners," were noted amid the throng. Speakers included local black activist and labor leader Isaac Myers, John Mercer Langston, Frederick Douglass, U.S. postmaster general and native Marylander John A. J. Creswell, white Republican South Carolina senator F. A. Sawyer, and several lesser luminaries. "The best of spirits seemed to prevail" throughout the proceedings, and, among the twenty thousand black and white participants, "there was no bad feeling exhibited" and "but few disorderly or drunken persons."[89]

As in Baltimore and San Francisco, communities large and small observed the day in similar ways, emphasizing similar sentiments. The Baltimore commemoration seems to have differed from the others primarily in its scale. All the reports from dozens of celebrations indicate that the best order was maintained throughout and that whites as well as blacks celebrated the day. Exceptions to this biracial participation were common in the South, as in Richmond, Virginia, where the six thousand celebrants were comprised primarily of "the better class of colored people. . . . The whites took but little part, and apparently but little interest, in the celebration."[90]

The predominant themes in the processions and the orations validated blacks' full inclusion in the political nation, though all made a great point of emphasizing that large responsibilities and duties came with citizenship, and that political equality did not, and should not, necessarily lead to what some referred to as the great "bug-bear" of social equality. As was suggested by black Washingtonians' response to District emancipation in 1862, many blacks as well as whites had no desire to include uncouth freedpeople into their social circles. The theme of racial uplift and the responsibility of moral and intellectual leaders to stimulate black self-improvement was a central message in the celebrations. Other important themes focused on the necessity of black fealty to the Republican Party and the now even-stronger conviction that the hand of God had directed events so that blacks could fully participate in American society. These celebrations, though they often recalled the century's struggle for the end of slavery and especially the events of the preceding ten years, looked as much toward the future as the past. The optimism of the new era and the meaning of the new amendment were symbolically suggested by a transparency carried in the parade at Louisville,

Kentucky, "in which the 'Train of Progress' was depicted as a locomotive, labelled 'the Fifteenth Amendment,' with a train of twenty-nine cars attached, representing the ratifying States, and a number of jackasses harnessed to the rear car, emblematic of the States refusing to ratify, and vainly trying to pull the train backward."[91]

If the onward march of freedom embodied by the Fifteenth Amendment seemed inexorable at this high point in African Americans' aspirations toward full inclusion and equality, there remained considerable debate regarding the content and character of the Freedom Day tradition. As the eighth anniversary of Lincoln's proclamation approached, San Franciscans were far less well prepared to honor the day than in previous years. Philip Bell claimed in early December 1870 that he did not "know anything about the arrangements." A letter to Bell's paper intimated that plans were being made by some private clique, with little attempt to secure public input— quite in contrast with the early meetings for the previous Freedom Day celebration, when several hundred were on hand to vote on the initial plans. Bell reported that the present committee had considerable difficulty agreeing on the proper mode of observance, and that "[i]t was finally agreed to have the celebration 'in-doors,' with the usual literary exercises." Bell's correspondent, identified only by the pen name "Index," complained that "[t]here does not seem to be a unity of feeling in making a large display this year" and that if "something decisive" were not done soon, "the celebration this year [would] be a failure."[92]

Squabbles about how best to observe the expanding number of dates on the Freedom Day calendar were not limited to the West Coast. It seems likely that the expense of a parade was the main deterrent for the San Francisco committee. Recall that the cost of an "in-doors" affair the previous year was estimated at $250, as opposed to the more than $800 required for the actual April 5 celebration with a full procession. With annual commemorations of West Indian emancipation, Lincoln's proclamation, the Fifteenth Amendment, and now that blacks' citizenship was sanctioned, July Fourth, the expense of mounting a full-scale observance of each occasion was prohibitive for a generally poor and struggling people. Persistent concerns over the propriety of public demonstrations on any of these days began well before the Civil War. But if blacks' use of public space was more justifiable to the general public (if still sometimes dangerous to the participants) immediately after emancipation and enfranchisement, other issues came to the fore.

Most fundamentally, if expense made mounting major celebrations of each date inadvisable, if not impossible, then African Americans had to decide which of the various Freedom Days to commemorate. One Ohio minister, reporting in 1870 on some regional celebrations of August 1, addressed the problem:

> Some say that the first of January is too cold to celebrate, therefore they hold to the fourth [of August], when it is pleasant. . . . If we will celebrate, why not have one day set apart, that all may join in it; not one part celebrating the 14th of April, Cincinnati; 26th of April, Penn; 9th of April, Toledo; 8th April, Chicago, then a large number on the 4th of August. We must not forget this day, for it was our day of hope. . . . The borrowed day of Jubilee. We sung a borrowed song, but through the Providence of God we can sing the new song of freedom, and say:

> > Join in the general jubilee,
> > For God he has spoken,
> > And all our chains are broken,
> > Our nation and country are free.[93]

The dates mentioned in this passage require some explanation. The last, of course, the "borrowed day of Jubilee," refers to West Indian emancipation, which indeed was a "day of hope" and promise for African Americans before U.S. emancipation. And the sentiment that the day should not be forgotten was widely shared. The fact that the writer positions that anniversary on August 4 is only slightly unusual. The date of celebrations throughout the nineteenth century often wandered a bit from the actual anniversary, sometimes to avoid celebrating on the Sabbath; sometimes to accommodate the schedule of a featured orator; sometimes to avoid conflicts with other events, like camp meetings, which were also held in late summer; sometimes due to bad weather. In 1858, for example, a Philadelphia celebration of West Indian emancipation was originally scheduled for August 2 —a Monday. When "the inclemency of the weather" interfered, the event was postponed until August 9.[94]

Sometimes the chosen date had no apparent relation to any Freedom Day event. In 1867 a huge "demonstration in remembrance of the people's deliverance from bondage" in Hudson, New York, which drew some five thousand people from "all the river counties," was held on September 3. Philip Bell, in printing a report of the event, expressed some puzzlement at the date: "Why they chose that day we cannot imagine, but we suppose they celebrated on general principle." More likely, I think, given the region's longstanding August 1 tradition, this was a West Indian commemoration that was delayed to conform with weather, with other local events, or with the schedules of the featured orators, Henry Highland Garnet and William

Howard Day, both in demand as speakers. One clear case of a date being changed to fit the schedule of a popular speaker occurred in 1883 at Parkersburg, West Virginia, when a September 22 commemoration was held a day early, "in order that they might have the presence of two distinguished orators," one of whom was the register of the treasury Blanche K. Bruce, who was otherwise engaged on the twenty-second.[95]

But these explanations are speculative. In the 1867 example, it seems unlikely that the organization of five thousand celebrants could easily be shifted from one date to another simply because it rained. Many celebrations stuck to their original dates, rain or shine. However, accommodations to Day's and Garnet's schedules or to other local events might easily have been arranged well in advance. As to the apparent fixity of August 4 on the Freedom Day calendar in northwestern Ohio, there seems to be no obvious explanation. Even though the actual date of the celebration often shifted, most people at least *spoke* of August 1 as the date being commemorated, and even this writer, earlier in his report, did refer to "celebrating the 1st of August" in Detroit and Windsor, Canada. William Wiggins has suggested that some dates relate to state emancipation anniversaries or to the dates that blacks in particular regions first learned of their freedom. This logic clearly does not apply to Ohio, in which slavery was prohibited even before statehood by the Northwest Ordinance of 1787. It seems that the rationale for this August 4 tradition, like that for other dates Wiggins has identified but not explained, remains for the present "shrouded in mystery."[96]

Less mysterious are the other dates mentioned in our Ohioan's report. The various dates in April most likely correspond to those areas' celebrations of the Fifteenth Amendment in 1870. Though Grant's proclamation of ratification can be accurately dated on March 30, 1870, the initial celebrations could not have been planned in advance to be held on that date. They took place on different days throughout the nation, most in April or May, but many over the course of the later spring and summer. Blacks from upstate New York and Independence, Missouri, reported on celebrations as late as August, the former at least probably intended to mesh with the long-standing celebration of West Indian emancipation in that region.[97]

Of particular interest is the April 26 date identified for Pennsylvania's celebrations. A number of communities, from Philadelphia to the smaller town of Corry in the opposite corner of the state near the shores of Lake Erie, celebrated on that date in response to a proclamation by William Nesbit, president of the Pennsylvania Equal Rights League. Nesbit, a resident of the central Pennsylvania town of Altoona who had influence throughout the state, recommended setting aside the fourth Tuesday after Grant's proclamation as "a day of general rejoicing over the ratification of the fifteenth amendment." Four weeks, he said, would provide "enough time to prepare to celebrate such an event in a fitting manner." That manner should involve the opening of all the churches in the morning "for praises and thanksgiving," the closing of all businesses during the day, processions in the afternoon, and "festivities" in the evening. The appropriateness of celebrating the amendment was self-evident to Nesbit, who asserted, "Never in the past had we such cause for rejoicing, and never in the future can such an event occur. A nation is born in a day." Though Nesbit's call was directed specifically to his fellow Pennsylvanians, his language seemed to reach out to all African Americans across the nation. "It is earnestly hoped," he said, "that our people will universally accept the day above named for our jubilee celebration, and in their several localities, come together and spend one day in thanksgiving to Almighty God for His great deliverance, and with speech and music and general rejoicing, give outward expression to the joy we inwardly feel." Recalling the rhetoric of antebellum Freedom Day commentators, Nesbit was expressing the desire to create a specific commemorative moment that would give meaning to the African American experience and define his people as being on a par with other great peoples and nations. "The Jews," Nesbit pointed out, "had their set days on which to celebrate their Jubilee and Passover, and in our times the American nation have uniform days of celebration." If black Americans would "lay aside every consideration for the common good" and "let our voices rise in unison," he implied, then they too could claim status as a united people with a coherent heritage.[98]

Nesbit's call for a single date for Pennsylvania celebrations, no less than the Ohio pastor's plea that some one date for a "general jubilee" be agreed upon nationally, articulated feelings that echoed throughout the nation and related to other attempts to make the Freedom Day tradition cohere in the tumultuous decade after U.S. emancipation. In 1866 another Pennsylvanian, educator, poet, and activist, George B. Vashon of Pittsburgh, debated the merits of various possible choices for the distinction of constituting the most appropriate Freedom Day. Vashon began his letter to the *Christian Recorder* by praising his community for "arousing somewhat from last year's lethargy" and assuring that "the First of August should not pass by without some sort of demonstration." Before describing the "festive gathering" Vashon felt the need to "enter a plea" on behalf of what he called the "great criminal now arraigned before the bar of public opinion, to wit, the Calends of August." Whether the date was quite that widely or vociferously maligned is questionable. But Vashon nonetheless was responding explicitly to those who, like James McCune Smith and Robert Hamilton in the late 1850s, thought its commemoration "to be entirely wrong . . . on account of its foreign associations." For his own part, Vashon claimed that he had "no desire of disparaging the claims of any of those days I have heard suggested" to displace August first. He then proceeded to do just that. Using logic similar to that of Virginia's observers of "Surrender Day," Vashon pointed out that September 22 was the anniversary merely "of a threat of our late President," which would have come to naught had the rebels surrendered within one hundred days. The January 1 proclamation, he noted, likewise would have been meaningless had the Confederacy not been defeated. August 1, he reasoned, "which all were wont, for more than a quarter of a century" to mark with regular observance, was "a day already illustrated to the annals of humanity" for its universally acknowledged emancipatory significance. It should therefore continue to be set aside "as *the* day for commemorating the liberation of 4,000,000 American slaves." Only the Fourth of July might potentially lay greater claim to African Americans' attention as the preeminent day for commemoration. Vashon painted the Fourth in universalist tones, describing it as "a day which . . belongs not only to the United States, but to the world." But, he emphasized, only "when black and white Americans, equal before the law, can join harmoniously in the celebration of that day, then, and not till then, am I willing that the 1st of August should be forgotten."[99]

In an 1871 August 1 address before a predominantly black audience at Cincinnati, educator and activist Peter H. Clark similarly pondered the meaning of the recent proliferation of Freedom Days and the "bewildering" transition that had taken African Americans "from the auction block to the ballot box." Like George Vashon, he noted that "the 1st of August is fast taking a secondary place in the list of anniversaries kept by the colored people of this country." But he did not lament this change. Clark acknowledged that August 1 "was for a long time a date of vast significance to us. It was the only event in the long reach of centuries which bore any token of hope to us as a people. . . . It was the morning star, heralding the rise of the sun of our liberty." Yet he seemed less disturbed than Vashon regarding the decline of August 1 celebrations and did not attempt to weigh the relative merits of the newer Freedom Days. All these dates, for Peter Clark, paled in comparison with July Fourth, "which is the true anniversary of humanity. The germs of the West Indian emancipation, of the proclamations of Lincoln, of the Thirteenth, Fourteenth and Fifteenth Amendments, are all contained in the grand old Declaration, which asserts that 'all men are created equal.' " Clark claimed to "look forward to the day" when African Americans might no longer hold their separate and necessarily narrower celebrations, "which represent a partial triumph of the great principles of liberty and justice" expressed in Jefferson's prose. Even more emphatically than Vashon,

Clark anticipated the time when "we will unite with the mass of our fellows in celebrating the ever glorious Fourth of July."[100]

In the early years of Reconstruction blacks were able to take part in July Fourth celebrations somewhat more enthusiastically than before, especially in the states of the former Confederacy. But white hostility and continued obstructions of their citizenship rights dampened spirits considerably. In 1865 blacks in Louisville, Kentucky, were said to be preparing "to celebrate the approaching Fourth of July in grand style," with Frederick Douglass to give the oration. But in the recently defeated Confederacy, celebration had to be imposed by the fiat of Brevet Major General Sherman, commander of the Southern Division. The Fourth "was better observed in New Orleans than it had been for the last four years," with large crowds "throng[ing] the main thoroughfares of the city." Celebrations generally gave attention to the new reality of black freedom, most concretely by including blacks in the celebration and by reading the Emancipation Proclamation along with the Declaration of Independence. But in most southern towns celebrations were orchestrated and imposed by the U.S. troops. In Mobile, Alabama, the day was said to have been celebrated "by the colored population in fine style." Yet even with the presence of two regiments of colored troops, many in the crowd "looked daggers" at the procession, even though they "could not prevent it." In fact, one commentator reported that "most all the insults and injuries that our people received was from the hands of the men wearing the garb of the army and navy of the United States! . . . I never saw a meaner or a more negro-hating class of people than the men who are now on Provost duty here." Many in these troops, mainly from Illinois and Indiana, were overheard to bait local blacks with the comment, "I hope they'll kill every d—d nigger they come across." In 1871 it was "the colored population" of New Orleans that "monopolized 'all and singular' the patriotism inspired by the advent of Independence," featuring a procession and readings of Lincoln's proclamation and the Fifteenth Amendment. But the white citizens appeared to believe "that the reasons that once existed for observing the day were no longer applicable."[101]

By 1870 harmonious biracial celebrations of July Fourth had failed to materialize to the extent hoped for by George Vashon, Peter Clark, and others. But the ratification of the Fifteenth Amendment in that year seemed to many an event whose practical impact and symbolic significance over-shadowed that of July Fourth, August 1, or any other Freedom Day anni-versary. The tradition-conscious Benjamin Tanner, recently installed as ed-itor of the *Christian Recorder,* noted in the summer of 1869 the imminence of black male enfranchisement. "The occasion," he claimed, "is too grand to let pass." For Tanner it far surpassed any other date in its significance for

African American liberty. "Glorious are the memories of the old First of August; and we hail the newborn First of January with joy; but the day on which it is proclaimed that the XVth Amendment is ratified, that will be *the* day in the life of our people." Utilizing a time-honored biblical analogy, Tanner asserted that on that day "the redeemed Negroes of the Republic will strike the timbrels of joy, as they have never been struck since Miriam struck them on the banks of the Red Sea." But the clergyman also posed a question: "How shall we celebrate our victory?" Several weeks later a correspondent to the *Recorder*, J. T. Mahoney of Indianapolis, proposed an elaborate blueprint for a national celebration of ratification. A central committee, based in Philadelphia, would issue circulars to "the prominent men" of the race in each state and call on "all the colored people of the United States to celebrate the Amendment on the same day in each State." Mahoney even requested that "each meeting in each State be held at the same hour, so that it will be a united thing all over the United States." In a burst of pragmatism within an otherwise idealistic project, the midwesterner suggested May as a suitable month because "the farmers are busy in midsummer, and in winter they do not like much to come from home." Even as early as 1865 some African American leaders foresaw the benefits of a unified date for celebration. One movement proposed to link all the various state emancipations throughout the South into one, to be observed on April 16, since the abolition of slavery in the Washington, D.C., on that date in 1862 was the event that initiated the process.[102]

The national pretensions of these unrealized schemes were not unique, but neither were they the norm. It was more common for a community or region to define its own tradition. Some consciously fused the celebration of all the Freedom Day anniversaries into a single local celebration. In 1872 blacks in Zanesville, Ohio, chose "the glorious old first" of August for a "Grand Union Celebration" with an extremely broad agenda. They claimed "to celebrate on that day all the days or events that in any way mark any advancement on the part of our government in the protection of her colored citizens."[103] The desire for such unity of purpose—whether national or regional—echoed the rhetoric of black leaders of political, labor, and other reform activities during the same period. It also met with similar frustration.

The Fifteenth Amendment gave rise to a plethora of celebration dates in 1870, despite some notable interest in defining a single day of "general jubilee" to be infused with the meaning of African American freedom. Ratification continued to be seen by many northern blacks as a "second emancipation," even grander than the one wrought by Lincoln in 1863. A similar editorial plea for the primacy of the Fifteenth Amendment came from Philip Bell in 1873, who (inaccurately) argued that, unlike emancipation, the amendment affected all African Americans, not just the slaves.[104] But soon after the initial celebrations in 1870, the supposed capstone of Reconstruction began to show signs of weakening, as black voting was curtailed by so-called Redeemer governments throughout the southern states. By the mid-1870s relatively few communities continued to commemorate the amendment. Roger Lane's observation for Philadelphia after the end of Reconstruction in 1877 has its parallels in many areas. The celebrations of emancipation and enfranchisement, Lane notes, were not "killed . . . outright" by the effects of white sectional reconciliation, but those Freedom Day observances had, by the 1880s, "lost their old luster."[105]

The Freedom Day tradition survived the tumultuous Civil War era, but much had changed. The tradition expanded in several ways. A slew of dates appeared, each having either local, regional, or national significance in African Americans' progress toward freedom and equality. These dates competed with August 1, and with each other, for the commemorative attention of black Americans. Expansion occurred with regard to physical space as well. The entire region encompassed by the former slave states saw commemorations of freedom for the first time during the 1860s. The dates celebrated, the nature of the celebrations, and whites' responses to these assertive public statements by the former slaves combined to create a range of commemorative traditions that departed from and transformed the antebellum patterns that had been defined by free blacks in the North. As migration between North and South, and from both regions into the developing West, increased after the war, confusion over the timing and conduct of the celebrations proceeded apace. The decades after 1870 witnessed sometimes bitter debate among blacks with different ideas about the meaning and practice of Freedom Day commemorations.

In 1857 Frederick Douglass had anticipated the coming of "an American celebration" of freedom to replace antebellum blacks' "borrowed day of jubilee" commemorating West Indian emancipation. Those August 1 festivals of freedom were observed consistently and enthusiastically throughout the free states before the Civil War and formed the centerpiece of a mature and focused commemorative tradition that elicited relatively little opposition or controversy among blacks themselves. The celebrations held up principles based on a noble history and heritage in order to foster the hope and the promise of a future of freedom and equality. After the war, and especially after that promise of freedom was broken, the tradition seems to have shifted its focus and lost its coherence. Rather than a single, unified American celebration to replace August 1, U.S. emancipation and enfranchisement led to considerable confusion and conflict.

The postwar decades, then, saw not just expansion but a disruptive fragmentation. The period from 1862 to the early 1870s was at once the apogee of the Freedom Day tradition and the beginning of its dissolution. Frederick Douglass could hardly have foreseen that the coherent and unified tradition that culminated in the annual August 1 commemoration of West Indian emancipation would begin to lose that coherence after black Americans had their own freedom to celebrate. Little could he have imagined that the occasional dissents from the tradition that he encountered in the 1850s would evolve into widespread indifference to Freedom Day celebrations on the one hand and outright condemnation of them on the other. Nor could he have predicted that white Americans, who up to the 1870s had remained well-represented at freedom festivals, would steadily retreat from participating in blacks' public commemorations during the late nineteenth century.

Between the 1870s and the early twentieth century black Americans' hopes for their future in the United States plummeted as Reconstruction gave way to the age of Jim Crow. Blacks' public commemorations reflected the institutionalization of Jim Crow, becoming more racially exclusive affairs held in a more racially segregated public sphere. As they struggled to maintain some hold on their rapidly dwindling citizenship rights, African Americans also struggled to define their sense of collective history and memory. Blacks in the United States during the late nineteenth century pondered the relative merits of remembering and forgetting even as many individuals and organizations intensified their efforts to define and disseminate a positive, black-centered vision of the African American experience. Ambivalence about the legacies of slavery, the African past, and the American present intensified as African Americans considered the vexing questions of identity in the increasingly hostile nation that was the land of their birth.

FIG. 1. "The Parade of the Black Governor in Hartford." This image, produced around the turn of the twentieth century, purports to depict the processions of black kings or governors that were traditional components of eighteenth- and early nineteenth-century New England Negro Election Day slave festivals. The artist, perhaps inadvertently, suggests the multiple levels of representation and meaning, for both whites and blacks, contained within blacks' participation in election day observances. The mocking, minstrel-like appearance of the faces of the black marchers and onlookers is juxtaposed with the otherwise regal bearing of the governor and his entourage, and the respectable demeanor of the black adults on the sidewalk. A black child seen running along the sidewalk between the horses suggests some of the more boisterous elements of the celebrations. The American flag (*far left*) speaks to blacks' claims to American nationalism and belonging, though those claims actually did not become prominent in black public expression until after the demise of the slave festivals. The scene is almost devoid of whites, which was probably more typical of black celebrations in the early twentieth century than the early nineteenth. The sole identifiably white figure (*far right*) displays no interest in the proceedings, though one can imagine other white observers peering through the windows prominently featured in the middle ground. (*Connecticut Magazine* 9, no. 3 [summer 1905]: 562)

ANNIVERSARY OF
BRITISH WEST INDIA EMANCIPATION!

The Anniversary of British West India Emancipation, which was
to have been celebrated by the

BANNEKER INSTITUTE,

On the 2nd inst., is POSTPONED on account of the inclemency of
the weather to

MONDAY, AUGUST 9, 1858.

And will take place at

HADDINGTON MANSION.

☞This new, romantic and delightful place of resort is situated in the 24th
Ward, at the terminus of the West Philadelphia Passenger Railway. It is in
form, nearly circular, and is enclosed by thick woods, and finely cultivated farms.
The surrounding country is hilly, beautiful and picturesque in the extreme. A
small stream in which there are several miniature cataracts, slowly winds its
way along the southern edge of the Grove. There is an excellent platform,
(which is finely shaded by overhanging trees,) with swings and everything
requisite for the pleasure of a Pic-Nic Party. There is also a large and fine
Hotel, with a cupola commanding a most excellent view of the adjacent country
and in which shelter can be taken in case of a shower. All these features, together with its comparative nearness, make "Haddington Mansion" just the
place to spend a day away from the city's heat and din, and constitute it the
best resort of the kind in the vicinity of Philadelphia.

The members of the Banneker call upon all lovers of Freedom and Reform
to give support to this movement by honoring them with their presence at the
Grove on the day of celebration.

The Exercises will commence at 11 o'clock, and will be as follows:
Introductory Remarks, by . . . Mr. Jacob C. White, Jr.
Reading of the Act of Emancipation, by . Mr. D. Doddridge Turner.
ORATION, BY - - - MR. GEO. E. STEVENS.
Remarks by Messers S. N. Cornish, S. G. Gould, and I. C. Wears.
The Rev. Wm. Schureman and Rev. Jesse Bolden have also been invited to
make Addresses.

AN EXCELLENT ORCHESTRA WILL BE IN ATTENDANCE.
Musical Conductor, - - - - F. V. Seymour.

Excursionists will take the Cars at Eighth and Market.

TICKETS 37 CENTS.

To be had at the Lebanon Cemetery Office; at the Segar store of Mr. Geo.
Goines, Sixth above Lombard St.; at the Store of Mrs. Hawkins Lombard
above Sixth; at the S. W. cor. of Robertson and Poplar; of the following

COMMITTEE OF ARRANGEMENTS.
W. H. MINTON, J. W. SIMPSON, W. H. JOHNSON, G. B. WHITE,
A. CAMPBELL, J. SELSEY, D. D. TURNER,
And of any of the Members of the Institute.

N. B.—The Cars will leave punctually at 9, 10, and 11, A. M.; and 2,
and 3, P. M.

☞DINNER CAN BE OBTAINED ON THE GROUND.☜

Should the weather prove unfavourable, the Excursion will be postponed to the
first clear day.

FIG. 2. "Anniversary of British West India Emancipation!" This broadside advertises an 1858 celebration held outside Philadelphia that featured many of the most typical components of mid-nineteenth-century freedom festivals. Sponsored by the Banneker Institute, a literary society formed by some of the city's most prominent young black intellectuals and activists, the celebration was held at a well-appointed suburban grove accessible by excursion cars. Amusements, food, and "an excellent orchestra" were complemented by the requisite intellectual exercises and orations. Biracial attendance was sought by inviting "all lovers of Freedom and Reform." This celebration, which was planned for August 2 because August 1 fell on a Sunday, had to be rescheduled for the following Monday, August 9, on account of bad weather. (The Historical Society of Pennsylvania, American Negro Historical Society Papers / Leon Gardiner Collection)

"EMANCIPATION DAY IN SOUTH CAROLINA."—THE COLOR-SERGEANT OF THE 1ST SOUTH CAROLINA (COLORED) VOLUNTEERS ADDRESSING THE REGIMENT, AFTER HAVING BEEN PRESENTED WITH THE STARS AND STRIPES, AT SMITH'S PLANTATION, PORT ROYAL ISLAND, JANUARY 1.—FROM A SKETCH BY OUR SPECIAL ARTIST.—SEE PAGE 275.

FIG. 3. "Emancipation Day in South Carolina." This engraving from *Frank Leslie's Illustrated Newspaper* shows the platform at Port Royal, South Carolina, where the First South Carolina Volunteers celebrated the issuance of Lincoln's proclamation in January 1863. While the black soldiers most prominently positioned in the image are depicted with exaggerated and distorted facial features, several African American figures in the foreground are portrayed more realistically and manifest an intensity of emotion as emancipation is declared. An immense, if faceless, black crowd surrounds the platform, but the platform itself is populated mostly by white guests, dignitaries, and military personnel. Only the color bearers are African Americans. The large black turnout and the official white control of the formal exercises were typical of Civil War–era celebrations in the Union-occupied South. (Library of Congress)

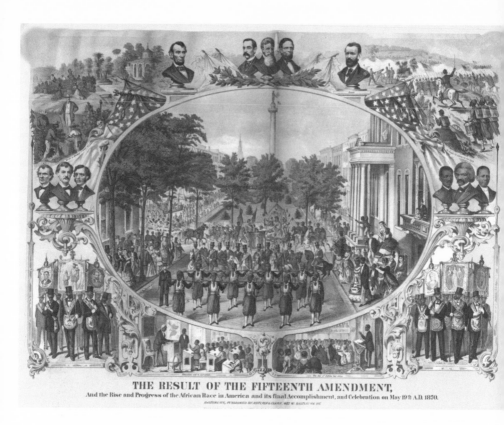

THE RESULT OF THE FIFTEENTH AMENDMENT,
And the Rise and Progress of the African Race in America and its final Accomplishment, and Celebration on May 19ᵗʰ A.D. 1870.

BALTIMORE, PUBLISHED BY METCALF & CLARK, 182 W. BALTO. ST. 5ᵗʰ ST.

FIG. 4. "The Result of the Fifteenth Amendment." Seen by many black and white abolitionists as the capstone of Reconstruction, the Fifteenth Amendment guaranteeing black men's right to vote was celebrated across the nation. Probably the largest celebration took place on May 19, 1870, in Baltimore, where tens of thousands of African Americans were reported to have participated. This commemorative lithograph's central scene depicts the procession, which was said to have taken a full hour to pass a given location. Shown are uniformed Zouaves, civil societies, the goddess of Liberty, bands, mounted militia, and what appears to be a large ship drawn by three white horses. The crowd on the sidewalk is both well dressed and biracial. Note the young black boy (*right*) waving an American flag. The lithograph also shows key individuals, organizations, and institutions in blacks' struggle for freedom and citizenship. The upper corners depict black labor under slavery (*left*) and black valor on the battlefields (*right*), the latter image carrying the caption "We fought for Liberty, we now enjoy." At the bottom are scenes showing the centrality of educational and religious institutions (*center*) and the active role played by black fraternal orders (*corners*). Individuals depicted include Abraham Lincoln, Ulysses S. Grant, Thaddeus Stevens, Charles Sumner, John Brown, Frederick Douglass, Martin Delany, and Hiram Revels, as well as several locally important white political leaders. (The Maryland Historical Society, Baltimore, Maryland)

FIG. 5. "Baltimore's African Americans Celebrate the Fifteenth Amendment (1870)." This stereoscopic print shows the 1870 Baltimore celebration commemorated by the lithograph in fig. 4. The scene contains but a portion of the massive crowd, estimated at six thousand, surrounding the speakers' platform in Monument Square. The platform, visible just right of center, collapsed shortly after it was ascended by about twenty-five dignitaries. After assuring himself that no one was seriously injured, the orator of the day, Frederick Douglass, stood atop the debris and called for "three cheers" for the Fifteenth Amendment. The crowd, reassured, maintained order, and the speakers proceeded to address them from the first-floor balcony of the nearby Gilmor House. (Reported in *Baltimore American and Commercial Advertiser*, Friday, May 20, 1870. The Maryland Historical Society, Baltimore, Maryland)

CELEBRATION OF THE ABOLITION OF SLAVERY IN THE DISTRICT OF COLUMBIA BY THE COLORED PEOPLE, IN WASHINGTON, APRIL 19, 1866.—[SKETCHED BY F. DIELMAN

FIG. 6. "Celebration of the Abolition of Slavery in the District of Columbia." This 1866 lithograph depicts an immense crowd celebrating District emancipation in Washington a year after the Civil War. Several American flags and numerous banners are held aloft. The figures in the foreground suggest the diversity of the black participants: a dignified gentleman with top hat and cane; a lady with hoop skirts and parasol; a mammy with apron and head kerchief; uniformed soldiers; roughly dressed men, women, and children engaged in conversation and revelry. The size and composition of District celebrations would, by the 1880s, contribute to heated disagreements regarding the meaning and practice of celebrating emancipation, both in the District of Columbia and across the nation. (Library of Congress)

FIG. 7. "The Procession Forming Near Citadel Square." Here the all-black state militia, along with black fire companies, prepares for Charleston's 1877 Emancipation Day parade. Blacks' military presence was described in the accompanying article as "a power exceedingly humiliating to the white citizens" and "the fearful result of the granting to ignorant, passionate negroes so much authority, and such complete means to terrorize the intelligent white masses." Despite the apparent calm and decorum of the troops, this scene was represented as "the interesting time when every one is giving orders and scarcely an officer knows where to place his men." The entire event was said to be typical of the "wonderfully absorbing love of the negro for gaudy colors, for pompous attire, and for authority over his fellows." Considering this demeaning description of an apparently respectable assembly, it is easy to appreciate black leaders' increasing concerns about African American celebrations and about blacks' public comportment generally. (*Frank Leslie's Illustrated Newspaper*, February 3, 1877; description on p. 357. William L. Clements Library, University of Michigan)

376 FRANK LESLIE'S ILLUSTRATED NEWSPAPER. [February 10, 1877.

1. Assembling on the Citadel Parade. 2. Watching the Procession. 3. The Boy Drum Corps. 4. The Thirteen States. 5. The Union League. 6. Reading the Emancipation Proclamation on the Battery.

SOUTH CAROLINA.—THE CELEBRATION OF EMANCIPATION DAY, JANUARY 8TH, IN CHARLESTON—SCENES AND INCIDENTS OF THE PARADE.—SEE PAGE 375.

FIG. 8. "South Carolina.—The Celebration of Emancipation Day. January 8th. In Charleston—Scenes and Incidents of the Parade." This 1877 lithograph indicates the extent to which African Americans in the South succeeded in claiming official public space with their large public freedom festivals during Reconstruction. The procession formed in Citadel Square (*inset 1*), which had long been the assembly site for officially sanctioned military and civic processions in Charleston. Black militias and fire companies occupied prominent places, as did the escorted wagon bearing the goddess of Liberty and her court representing the thirteen original states (*inset 4*). A marching band was present (*inset 3*), as was the Union League, led by an officer solemnly carrying a Bible with a sword laid across it (*inset 5*). The procession led a large crowd to the Battery for musical and literary exercises (*inset 6*). The lithograph depicts the celebration as having been almost exclusively black, with only two white figures apparently watching the procession (*inset 2*). This was almost certainly one of the last celebrations to successfully assert black claims to citizenship and public space in Charleston. State and national elections held the previous fall marked the end of national Reconstruction and the return to South Carolina's white supremacist "home rule." The political turmoil in South Carolina, one of several states with disputed voting results, was apparently the cause for delaying this January 1 celebration until January 8. (*Frank Leslie's Illustrated Newspaper*, February 10, 1877, p. 376; description on p. 375. William L. Clements Library, University of Michigan)

FIG. 9. Emancipation Day Parade, Elmira, New York, ca. 1880s. This stereoscopic viewing card shows a relatively modest procession in a central New York town that was one of many in the region to take turns hosting emancipation celebrations in early August throughout the late nineteenth century. The parade is led by top-hatted marshals on horseback and likely includes regional leaders, invited dignitaries, and a band. Spectators are observing from the sidewalks and from the windows of buildings. While it is small compared with earlier celebrations with thousands of participants, the several hundred people in this photograph represent a respectable turnout in a region with a relatively small and scattered black population. (Robert N. Dennis Collection of Stereoscopic Views, Miriam and Ira D. Wallach Division of Art, Print and Photographs, The New York Public Library, Astor, Lenox and Tilden Foundations)

FIG. 10. "Emancipation Day, Richmond, Virginia." Around the turn of the twentieth century, the city of Richmond, with its sizable black population, could muster a procession that appears considerably larger than the one in Elmira, New York (see fig. 9). One sashed figure on horseback and at least several instruments from a marching band are visible amid a seemingly unorganized but respectable and well-dressed crowd. Parades often included the more regimented civic and fraternal organizations near the front of the line. It is not clear what segment of the procession is shown or how large it was. This photograph may show the end of the line, which would be composed of spectators who would follow the formal procession to the site of the orations, music, and food. The streets seem to be given over entirely to African Americans, though what appear to be white faces can be seen looking on from upper-story windows. (Library of Congress)

FIGS. 11A AND B. Emancipation Day in St. Augustine, Florida, ca. 1920s. This figure probably depicts the January 1, 1923, celebration of the sixtieth anniversary of Lincoln's proclamation. While many communities had discontinued emancipation celebrations by this time, others, especially in the South, continued to commemorate various dates well into the twentieth century. The 1923 parade began at St. Benedict's Catholic Church, in a predominantly black neighborhood, and proceeded down Marine Street past the St. Augustine National Cemetery where many black Civil War soldiers were buried. (The cemetery is on the other side of the wall in fig. 11A.) The parade featured automobiles decorated with crepe and tissue, and floats carrying the St. Paul AME ushers and the goddess of Liberty and her court, among others. Fig. 11A shows a car with numerous American flags and a prominently displayed GAR pennant, which is followed by an unidentified company of smartly uniformed men who appear to be carrying swords in a salute position. In fig. 11B marching musicians are followed by a group of black World War I veterans bearing the national standard. The 1923 procession ended at the Lewis Park baseball field for speeches and a barbecue. A street festival was held in the evening, with entertainment provided by Benjamin's Orchestra. (Descriptive material from *St. Augustine Evening Record*, December 29, 1922, and from Charles Tingley of the St. Augustine Historical Society. St. Augustine Historical Society)

Souvenir Historical Chart.

FIRST PLACE OF MEETING.

FIRST BRICK CHURCH.

Pastors of Bethel Church, Phila.,
from 1816 to 1899.

RICHARD ALLEN,
RICHARD WILLIAMS,
JACOB TAPSCIO,
WILLIAM CORNISH,
MORRIS BROWN,
JOSEPH COX,
WILLIAM MOORE,
JOHN CORNISH,
WILLIS NAZERY,
HENRY J. YOUNG,
HENRY DAVIS,
RICHARD ROBINSON,
*JOHN CORNISH,
W. D. W. SCHUREMAN,
JOSHUA WOODLAND,
J. P. CAMPBELL,
*WILLIAM MOORE,
* Served two terms.

Pastors of Bethel Church, Phila.,
from 1816 to 1899.

JAMES HOLLEN,
D. DORRELL,
J. M. WILLIAMS,
*HENRY J. YOUNG,
THEODORE GOULD,
R. F. WAYMAN,
G. C. WHITFIELD,
L. J. COPPIN,
J. S. THOMPSON,
C. FELTS,
*J. S. THOMPSON,
J. W. BECKETT,
C. T. SHAFFER,
W. H. HEARD,
W. D. COOK,
*T. GOULD,
*L. J. COPPIN,
* Served two terms.

First Bishop.
Born Feb. 14, 1760. Died Mar. 26, 1831.

Successors:
2. MORRIS BROWN,
3. EDWARD WATERS,
4. WM. PAUL QUINN,
5. WILLIS NAZERY,
6. D. A. PAYNE,
7. A. W. WAYMAN,
8. J. P. CAMPBELL,
9. J. A. SHORTER,
10. T. M. D. WARD,
11. J. M. BROWN,
12. H. M. TURNER,
13. W. F. DICKERSON,
14. R. H. CAIN,
15. R. R. DISNEY,
16. W. J. GAINES,
17. B. W. ARNETT,
18. B. T. TANNER,
19. A. GRANT,
20. B. F. LEE,
21. M. B. SALTER,
22. J. A. HANDY,
23. W. B. DERRICK,
24. J. H. ARMSTRONG,
25. J. C. EMBRY.

BAND TICKET.—Bethel Church.

If ye then be risen with Christ, seek those things
which are above, where Christ sitteth on the right
hand of God.   Col. iii. 1.

Minister.

FAC SIMILE OF FIRST LOVE FEAST TICKET.

THE PRESENT CHURCH.

Observe the Landmarks.

FIG. 12. "Souvenir Historical Chart: Observe the Landmarks." This commemorative broadside, produced around 1899 by the African Methodist Episcopal Church, encouraged AME members to "observe the landmarks" of the denomination's history. The aggrandizement of the name of AME founder and first bishop Richard Allen became a major focus of the church during the late nineteenth century. Monument projects, annual Allen Day fund-raising activities, and the publication of several editions of Allen's autobiography were among the tools used by church leaders to expand Allen's recognition as both a race hero and a national hero. (The Historical Society of Pennsylvania, American Negro Historical Society Papers / Leon Gardiner Collection)

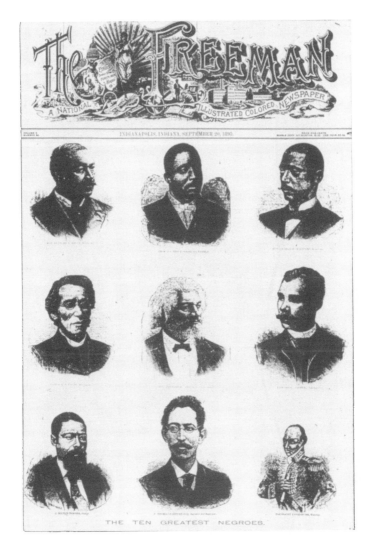

FIG. 13. "The Ten Greatest Negroes." This 1890 front-page illustration for the *Indianapolis Freeman* suggests the desire among many black intellectuals to create a pantheon of African American heroes during the late nineteenth century. With Frederick Douglass, statesman, holding the central place, the others are (*clockwise from upper left*) Blanche K. Bruce, politician; J. C. Price, scholar and educator; George W. Williams, historian; Edward E. Cooper, journalist; Toussaint L'Overture, warrior; T. Thomas Fortune, agitator and essayist; J. Milton Turner, orator; and Daniel Payne, theologian. Not surprisingly for the time, all were men. All were also contemporary figures, with the exception of Toussaint; his inclusion suggests the continued symbolic importance of the Haitian Revolution for black American activists. The somewhat idiosyncratic nature of this "top ten" list is highlighted by the *Freeman*'s editor, Edward E. Cooper, not so modestly including himself among the race's greatest men. (*Indianapolis Freeman*, September 20, 1890)

FIG. 14. "Statue of Frederick Douglass, Rochester, New York." This statue of Frederick Douglass, erected in 1897 in Douglass's longtime home city and base of operations, was one of only a few successful monument projects commemorating African American heroes during the period. (Cabinet Card Collection, Photographs and Prints Division, Schomburg Center for Research in Black Culture, The New York Public Library, Astor, Lenox and Tilden Foundations)

CHAPTER FOUR

"LET CHILDREN'S CHILDREN NEVER FORGET"

REMEMBRANCE AND AMNESIA, 1870s–1910s

[The negro] has never created for himself any civilization. . . . No monuments have been builded by him to body forth and perpetuate in the memory [of] posterity the virtues of his ancestors.

—Senator James K. Vardaman, 1914

As a race, the present is, our Heroic age. . . . The one question is: Will we embrace the present opportunity to immortalize ourselves?

—The Reverend Benjamin Tucker Tanner, 1874

BETWEEN THE 1870s and the first decades of the twentieth century African Americans' experiences as formally sanctioned citizens covered an expansive range. At first the promises embodied in emancipation and enfranchisement seemed to bode well for the future. But even as blacks celebrated ratification of the Fifteenth Amendment in 1870, they realized that those promises would not easily be fulfilled. Richard T. Greener, then a young man on the verge of becoming Harvard's first black graduate, articulated concerns that most Freedom Day orators in 1870 were reluctant to express. Addressing his audience at Troy, New York, Greener admitted to a "fear which makes my few remarks . . . more like a dirge . . . than a paean of joy. I do not believe that one-third of the American people have forgotten their feeling of caste. . . . It will take some time yet, much calm, laudable work on our part, before they do forget."[1]

This well-founded observation, however, did not prevent young Greener from using the public Freedom Day forum, as had his predecessors throughout the nineteenth century, to place the history of African Americans prominently in the larger story of the American republic. As he did so, Greener offered a profound reinterpretation of the significance of the presence of both African Americans and the institution of slavery in the United States. "It has been said," Greener recounted, "that our history in this country has been its romance; but it might have been as truly said . . . that it has also been its tragedy. The slave ship, the slave hut and pen, the overseer's whip, and the burning tears of separated husband and wife, and the equally cruel caste and prescription which has hounded the negro when free from the cradle to the grave, have mingled in far unequal proportions the romantic with the tragic. They will live in the history of the country . . . to be read as warnings against injustice, to be cited as sad examples of that perversion which noble principles may undergo, when the children drift from the teachings of the fathers." Even as the "moonlight and magnolia" view of the South and its noble "Lost Cause" was in its nascent stages, Greener challenged and refuted that view of the American past with a jeremiad that called the nation to read its history wisely and to take heed of its lessons. Unfortunately, voices like Richard Greener's were drowned out by the clamor for white sectional reconciliation that predominated well into the twentieth century.[2]

In many parts of the country, though, blacks did briefly enjoy the benefits of citizenship: educational opportunity, expanded civil rights, a voice in the courts, enfranchisement, and political officeholding. But even the jubilation surrounding the Fifteenth Amendment was not shared by many blacks in border states and in the Upper South where white Redeemer governments began curtailing African American rights well before the official end of Reconstruction in 1877. More pervasive was the anger, frustration, and despair that accompanied the solidification of racial proscription, segregation, disfranchisement, and violence by the 1890s—conditions experienced to some extent by virtually all African Americans, regardless of region. In the South, especially, blacks had by that time been ensnared in what Eric Foner has described as "a seamless web of oppression" that left them with little reason to celebrate a freedom they did not truly possess.[3]

But blacks in the South, and indeed across the nation, continued to commemorate emancipation, though more often after the 1870s in their own increasingly segregated public spaces and with rapidly declining levels of white participation and support. Through these celebrations, and through various other more or less public forums, black Americans debated many issues pertaining to the relative merits of preserving or erasing the memory of the slave past. Richard Greener longed for the day when blacks—by behaving as respectable citizens and by holding before the public their historical vision—could help whites to forget their prejudices. But at the same time many African Americans struggled with their own conflicting desires to forget and to distance themselves from the more painful and degrading aspects of the race's collective past. Perhaps the most fundamental shift in African American historical memory that distinguishes the generation after 1870 from the preceding six decades relates to the increasing tendency among many blacks to articulate a deep-seated ambivalence regarding the legacy of slavery, a sentiment that caused some to advocate discontinuing Freedom Day commemorations altogether. Paradoxically, considering the burgeoning attention to the race's history during the same period, many blacks wondered during the last decades of the century whether it served any purpose to remember the past at all.

As early as 1873 Mrs. A. L. Trask, of Marysville, California, identified the issue as she compared blacks' need for historical memory with that of the nation as a whole. She was responding specifically, and passionately, to African Americans who were not merely ambivalent or indifferent but completely "opposed to a first of January celebration, believing we ought to let all recollection of former years die out." This sentiment, Mrs. Trask argued, was "altogether wrong." National institutions and practices, she pointed out, preserved the memory of the founding fathers through the dissemination of history in the schools, "paintings for our parlors, and monuments for our public squares." The purveyors of national heritage, fearful that the people might still forget, "keep the great anniversary day—July 4. And decreed that it should be celebrated by American citizens to all coming time. Now have we not," she prodded, "more to remember than they! What was the oppression of the British yoke to slavery, taxation to stripes?" She implored fellow blacks to "cry aloud to your children, and let children's children never forget what liberty cost; never forget Emancipation Day."[4]

Concern about blacks who were "opposed to emancipation celebrations and all that pertains thereto" continued into the twentieth century. The young Baptist minister Silas X. Floyd complained in 1909 about blacks who would rather forget that "our race was once enslaved in this country." Pointing out that white Confederate and Union veterans never shrank from recalling their own experiences, Floyd bristled that "some old Negroes wish to forget all about slavery—all about the past—and stoutly maintain that we have no right to be celebrating this day that brought freedom to our race." Another celebration proponent in 1894 echoed Mrs. Trask's focus on serving the needs and interests of the youth of the race, his comments also confirming the continued importance of the freedom festivals' educative function. If emancipation celebrations were discontinued, this editor pleaded, "will these dear people tell us how they could ever satisfactorily explain to the young people of the present and coming generation the great difference in the condition and position of the two races in this country, if they are left to suppose that both started on equal footing in the great race of life upon this continent. Let us consider and use common sense."[5]

But if common sense dictated that the slave past had left blacks with more to remember—and, arguably, more *need* to remember—than other Americans, not all saw anything to be gained by perpetuating those memories. Thus a deep-seated ambivalence pervaded African Americans' individual and collective recollections of the slave past. On the one hand, blacks' perseverance and ultimate triumph over slavery—as well as their oft-mentioned progress since emancipation—was a source of race pride, representing the race's destiny as a central and redemptive component in the divinely ordained advancement of human liberty. At the same time, however, slavery was for many a personally painful and degrading experience whose recollection bred collective racial humiliation and fed the continued derision of the larger society. And the indelible imprint of the slave past could not simply be erased by the fact of emancipation. As David Blight has observed, "Looking back was not easy, but it was also unavoidable."[6] At the very least, many African Americans felt that they should be somewhat selective as to which aspects of the past were useful to recall and which were best forgotten.

For example, certain cultural practices associated with slavery were thought by many to be better left in the historical dustbin. In 1874 Benjamin Tucker Tanner, editor of the AME Church's *Christian Recorder,* expressed concern over the "danger of overdoing the business of 'jubilee' singing." While "the original Fisk Jubilee Singers," who began touring in 1871, were praised for their *"hauteur"* and "exceeding good taste," subsequent groups, including one from Samuel Chapman Armstrong's Hampton Institute, were condemned for singing the songs " 'as they were sung on the plantations.' That is, go through 'bodily exercises.' " "It is worse than nonsense," Tanner claimed, "for Gen. Armstrong to insist that they shall render their sweet songs in the dialect of the plantation. It is a crime against the very people he professes to be serving at heart." Tanner saw this "willingness to dispense with the necessary hauteur" not as a sincere desire to preserve an authentic folk cultural form, but rather as an attempt to "curry favor with the public" that resulted in "down right 'Negro Minstrelsy' of the worst kind."

He may well have been correct in his assessment. Careless and exploitative presentations of slave culture were rampant (and often lucrative) in the nineteenth century and certainly exacerbated blacks' difficulties in being taken seriously as capable and respectable citizens. Ironically, Tanner himself worked diligently to preserve selected aspects of the African American past and did recognize the positive value of spirituals as "the only original music our country has produced." Tanner had no desire to fully eradicate the memory of slavery, and he avidly supported commemorations of emancipation and other vehicles of African American historical memory. But he also felt that blacks needed to exert control over which images should be preserved in order to leave behind slavery's negative cultural associations and aspire to more socially acceptable cultural styles and manners. His own intellectual pretensions, combined with his suspicions about whites' motives and his concerns about white reception, led Tanner to the view that unrefined presentations of slave melodies placed an additional "burden of contempt . . . upon the already overburdened negro."[7]

Benjamin Tanner's ambivalence about spirituals suggests something of the nature and the centrality of blacks' debates about slavery and its place in the race's history. Though it was not Tanner's ultimate goal to eradicate slavery from the race's collective memory, that unattainable desire was hardly uncommon in the decades after emancipation. In 1876 AME minister Theophilus G. Steward went so far as to argue that blacks would never unite behind a "common history" because the race's history was centered on slavery, and "slave history is no history." In the context of a series of essays on black social life in New York City, Steward claimed that it was extremely difficult "to find a colored man even from the South who will acknowledge that *he actually* passed through the hardships of slavery. The common remark is, 'I never was so treated myself, but I have *seen others*,' and it is so hard to find these '*others*.' Our history is something to be ashamed of, rather than to be proud of, hence it has no power to unite but great power to divide. Men do not like to be referred to slavery now." This sentiment was still widespread two decades later, when a Kansas editor bemoaned "that there is a constantly increasing class among us who wish to obliterate and blot out of view all that pertains to the past history of the Negro race in this country. They would have them ignorant of the fact that they were slaves or subject to the injustice or oppression of their white brethren."[8]

If the memory of the slave past was too painful and enervating for many African Americans, their identification with Africa was no less problematic. Theophilus Steward himself, like many of the orators who spoke at the early slave trade commemorations and at freedom festivals throughout the nineteenth century, took great pride in his African heritage. But he quickly dismissed the potential of shared "African blood" for forging a united, proud, and strong African American people. Speaking particularly of black leaders, he alleged that "if you should claim them [to be] African or Negro, in high dudgeon they would probably exclaim, 'I am an American citizen' " and deny that legacy. Steward was surely overstating the case somewhat. Many blacks continued to express pride in the greatness of ancient Africa, though they were usually less enthused about contemporary cultures on the continent, which were generally regarded as heathen, benighted, and in need of "civilization." In this context, activists like Theophilus Steward were troubled by the fact that, for some blacks, the longing to claim Americanness had superseded their connection with African and racial identities.[9]

Others, however, sought to recall the more noble aspects of their shared history in order to mediate the complexities among the African, slave, and free Christian American components of African American identity. For example, the Reverend Jeremiah B. Sanderson, in his January 1, 1869, emancipation address at Stockton, California, reached to ancient Rome and beyond to establish a noble lineage for contemporary African Americans to claim as their own. The fabulist Aesop, the Roman dramatist Terence, the Christian ecclesiastics Tertullian and St. Cyprian were all identified as black Africans. "The Sphinx, the Pyramids, the Greek alphabet, the popular mythology of Greece and Rome . . . were African. The race that produced them was African. African blood and mind have contributed to the material and intellectual wealth of the nations in ages past. They will, one day re-assert the old power."[10]

As these noble lineages were being established, and as Mrs. Trask, also in California, counseled that children's children should never forget, similar sentiments concerning the need to remember were being echoed in other parts of the country. In Philadelphia, Benjamin Tanner pondered the importance of African American historical memory as it related to the definition and sustenance of both racial and national heritages. Commenting on reports of the preservation of ancient tombs in England, Tanner editorialized that here in America, too, were "Indian mounds and fortifications" worth salvaging. In addition, he wrote, "almost every one of our churches has its 'antiquities,' " in the form of class books and other records, that should be preserved for the edification of future generations. Such an undertaking was part of a larger project, in Tanner's mind. Suggesting, as would many others in subsequent years, that emancipation represented the "birthday" of the race in America, Tanner wrote in 1874 that the present was the race's youth and, as such, constituted its "heroic age." Though current events might seem "insignificant" and "exceeding tame" to many, he argued that the present was the time for black Americans to "immortalize" themselves for posterity.[11]

Tanner's defining the 1870s as the race's youth did not, however, prevent him from recalling the deeds of his predecessors, whose noble deeds must have been perpetrated in utero, as it were. A few months after Tanner's "heroic age" editorial, the Reverend John T. Jenifer, a future denominational historian, wrote from his charge in Pine Bluff, Arkansas, urging the formation of "a National Statistical Society, with the design to exhibit facts and the results of the progress of the colored citizens of America at the American Centennial July 4th, 1876." Local collection societies were to gather information on industry, education, moral and social reform, religious activities, and literary productions in order to "prove, after ten years trial, that we compare favorably in our achievements with any other nation of history in the same period of time." This desire to demonstrate "the progress of the race," especially through the use of statistical evidence, became almost an obsession for African American leaders throughout the half-century after emancipation. Benjamin Tanner himself immediately commended the plan "with more than usual feeling," asserting that "it is just what ought to be done, by us *as a people.*" In order to simplify the project Tanner suggested that Jenifer "resolve himself into a Committee of one, and go to work" assembling the data. Aware that blacks' widespread indifference to historical projects could be daunting, Tanner warned that Jenifer would encounter "petty jealousy, and almost universal inertness [that would] measurably thwart his purpose." But the editor nevertheless predicted that perseverance would assure his colleague "a [place in his people's] memory that will be immortal."[12]

Establishing an African American presence at the Centennial Exposition and generally demonstrating the race's progress in freedom were both manifestations of the intense desire to construct for the race a meaningful past that would serve as a foundation for future achievements. A future when African Americans might, as Jeremiah Sanderson put it, reassert the old power. Another attempt to define that past, and to honor the race heroes who contributed to it, was formulated in the summer of 1876, as the Centennial Exposition was attracting the attention—and stimulating the historical consciousness—of the entire nation. In June of that centennial year, a formidable group of black leaders, most of them affiliated with the AME Church, met in Newport, Rhode Island, and engaged in "a very interesting conversation in relation to the past, present and future of the colored man in America." In the course of that conversation, "the remark was made, that the character and efforts of our fathers, (but a few of whom survives) those who labored so nobly for the freeing of their race from slavery and for the moral and intellectual advancement of themselves and the rising generation, should be written by some one who is yet with us, and remembers the parties, and is personally cognizant of the efforts put forth, not only in connection with the Anti-Slavery Society, but previous to its organization." The group included, among others, senior bishop and AME historian Daniel A. Payne, Bishop John M. Brown, and George T. Downing, scion of a wealthy family of Rhode Island hoteliers and longtime activist in and around the nation's capital. These men drafted a letter to Philip A. Bell, editor of the San Francisco weekly *Elevator,* explaining that, based on his past associations, his continuing activism, his dedication to historical study, and the specific recommendation of Bishop Payne, he was their choice "to write the needed record." It was hoped that both "gratitude and the demands of those who shall succeed us" would entice Bell to "accept the responsibility." Bell's response was supportive but noncommittal. He praised existing historical work that had been published by William C. Nell and William Wells Brown, and suggested a number of other men whom he considered "thoroughly competent" to undertake the task. Since it "would be a work of years" and, at age sixty-eight, he was unsure of his ability to fulfill the responsibility, he hesitated to step forward. Bell was himself very concerned with blacks' collective place in history and worked assiduously to promote Freedom Day celebrations and generally to keep historical consciousness before the readers of his paper. He admitted in his response to the request that "we have long seen the importance of such a work, and have urged upon others the necessity of performing it."[13] Though Philip Bell lived until 1889 he did not take on the proposed project. But his and the Newport group's recognition—that a generation was quickly passing away and memory of its accomplishments needed to be preserved and passed on—defined an important orientation toward the past among blacks in the late nineteenth century. Beginning in the 1860s, and increasingly over the next fifty years, many African Americans—men and women, intellectuals and ordinary working people—actively attempted to document and disseminate the race's history.

A primary focus of blacks' historical vision in the decades after the Civil War was the role played by African American troops. Countless attempts were made to memorialize African Americans who served the race and the nation in that bloody conflict. David Blight has shown how Frederick Douglass's view of the Civil War remained unvarying over the remaining years of his life; similarly, if often less publicly, many other African Americans kept the war and its memory near the heart of their being. As early as 1866 black veterans had formed a Colored Soldiers National League in order to "perpetuate the memories and associations of the late war." Nearly twenty years later, the memories of the war experience still a defining feature in their lives, veterans of Massachusetts's three black Civil War regiments met to form the Colored Veterans Association.[14]

Generally less than welcome at events sponsored by the Grand Army of the Republic—the largest and ostensibly the most egalitarian mainstream Union veterans' group—black veterans used their own organizations and reunions to keep their particular memories of the war for freedom before the eyes of the coming generations. When African Americans did take part in GAR activities, historically conscious members of the black community urged their fellows to show support. When "heroes of the sable hue" attended the 1899 Grand Encampment in Philadelphia, one editor urged that "every Afro-American citizen of Brotherly Love, especially feel and take a personal interest in the encampment." "There are but few great events of national importance that Afro-Americans need have any interest in but this one is a marked exception." Black veterans' limited participation in Grand Army activities was regularly covered in T. Thomas Fortune's New York papers, and other writers continued to stress the importance of their presence at those affairs for relating a more "truthful history" of the Civil War era.[15]

African Americans' articulations of a more accurate version of their past were often tied to the continued need to counter prevalent white interpretations of the war. One event of almost mythic significance in blacks' collective memory was the unsuccessful assault on Fort Wagner by the Massachusetts Fifty-fourth on July 18, 1863. More than twenty years after the fact a letter to Fortune's New York *Freeman* defended the courage of the Fifty-fourth at Fort Wagner after a southern magazine had questioned the regiment's valor. In a similar defense, the presence of black troops at Appomattox was asserted with pride after a white journal questioned the fact. The writer of that rejoinder also took the opportunity to summarize blacks' military contributions to the nation from Crispus Attucks to the 1880s.[16]

By the early twentieth century little had changed. In 1913, when northern and southern whites held what one contemporary black editor called their "mock love feast" to commemorate the semicentennial of the Battle of Gettysburg, black commentators pointed out the injustice inherent in the white sectional reconciliation represented by the celebration. "The truth of history," wrote one journalist, once more "was smothered."[17] Consistent with the trend toward racially exclusive public commemorations during the age of Jim Crow, that same month aging black veterans and their supporters made their own statement regarding what was truly memorable about the war. As if to counter the message of the Gettysburg reunion, black veterans commemorated the battle of Fort Wagner in Boston with a grand "reunion of survivors of Wagner . . . and all other Colored Soldiers and Sailors." In contrast to the conciliatory commemorations that year of both Gettysburg and Vicksburg, "there was no raising of the stars and bars" at the Wagner ceremony, which was carried out "in the true spirit of the cause these soldiers represented and with respect for the principles which they espoused." It was important that the "valorous deeds" of black soldiers "shall not be forgotten."[18] Even in 1917, when a white journalist urged African Americans to fight for democracy to repay the half million white men who ostensibly had died for black freedom in the 1860s, black journalist Ralph W. Tyler, a contributing editor for the *Cleveland Advocate,* wrote to the New York *Age* to set the record straight. African Americans, Tyler asserted, would do their duty in Europe as they had done on hundreds of Civil War battlefields and as they had done "from Lexington down to Carrizal for a country that still denies us full liberty."[19] Black efforts to tell the true history intended to demonstrate that they had earned the citizenship rights that were still largely denied them. But they were continuously frustrated by white efforts to erase African Americans' patriotic deeds from public memory.

Both blacks and whites also made public statements about memory and history during these years through commemorative monuments, a form frequently used to honor military accomplishments. The impulse to raise such monuments to black Civil War veterans began early. On Decoration Day, May 30, 1870, the Colored Women's Lincoln Aid Society of Philadelphia laid the cornerstone of a two-thousand-dollar "Monument to those [black soldiers and sailors] who fell fighting to perpetuate our glorious Union." In 1877 Civil War veteran, historian, and clergyman George Washington Williams "gave his time to . . . a new Soldiers and Sailors Memorial Association." The difficulty of bringing such projects to fruition is suggested by an appeal nearly a decade later stating, "The colored soldiers who fell in the War of the Rebellion should have a monument erected to perpetuate their valor and heroism." And again, in the early 1890s, a group of blacks in Brooklyn met "to consider the advisability of erecting a monument, suitable to commemorate the heroes of our race who fell during the late war, in defence of their country." During the 1880s especially—a decade of intense black attention to, and contention about, historical memory—numerous monument projects were undertaken. Baltimore's black Lincoln Post of the GAR began a subscription list in 1881 to finance a monument to black Civil War soldiers and sailors. A marble statue depicting a soldier in a kneeling position bearing the colors was designed, at a projected cost of $2,852. Like many such attempts to honor the black past, the monument project seems to have come to naught. Nonetheless, history-conscious leaders like Charles Hendley, editor of the *Huntsville Gazette,* urged on the current generation the necessity of commemorating and paying homage "to the brave colored boys in blue, who were on the battlefields of the late war and risked life and all fighting for liberty."[20]

In Washington another black editor, W. Calvin Chase of the *Bee,* actively pushed the cause of a monument to black Civil War veterans to be erected at government expense in the nation's capital. The proposition was first discussed by the Bethel Literary and Historical Association in 1883. Noting "assurances" that Congress would appropriate money for the project, Chase reprinted an editorial from the *Petersburg Lancet,* which noted, in a frequently utilized scolding tone, that southern whites "never ceased to praise the valor of their sacred dead, and to create monuments in their honor. O! ingratitude and shame upon the colored people of the United States, who show such a little appreciation for the valor of negro soldiers who died for the preservation of the Union. . . . Let us erect a monument in honor to the black heroes, who leaped over the fortification [at Petersburg, Va.] with their muskets in our defense and suffered their bodies as it were to become breastworks while pouring out their blood most freely and willingly for our re-demption from bondage."[21]

As in the Baltimore example, black GAR posts—the Charles Sumner and Oliver Morton Posts—maintained the impetus behind the project. They held support meetings over the next several years, and Chase urged black congressman and Civil War hero Robert Smalls "to introduce in Congress a bill asking for one of the public parks for the purpose of erecting a mon-ument to the Colored soldiers." The dedication of the Washington Monu-ment in February 1885 must have only added incentive for Chase and other supporters. A bill was introduced by Senator George Frisbie Hoar, a white former abolitionist from Massachusetts who had an intense and diffuse in-terest in the perpetuation of historical memory. That the monument did not materialize even with such support indicates the uphill nature of these battles for memory that black activists were fighting.[22]

Some of that uphill terrain was congested with those who were less than enthusiastic about the erection of race-specific monuments. Regarding the proposed black soldiers' memorial, some felt that a separate monument to African American veterans was inappropriate. The editor of the *Kansas City Dispatch* felt that "if the colored people of this country desire to erect a monument to the memory of their brave who have fallen upon many a battle field, all right, if private individuals desire to donate, is well, but the government has no right to show such lines of distinction." Conversely, in responding several years later to a plan to collect $200,000 from black fra-ternal groups for a monument to Abraham Lincoln and various white ab-olitionists, E. P. Carroll of Boston urged, "It must be remembered that we are poor as a whole people and . . . cannot afford to spend such a sum lavishly in statues for whites, who have as much reason to honor the black man for aiding to save this country from division." In fact blacks did con-tribute to monuments honoring white heroes like Lincoln and Robert Gould Shaw. Carroll argued that it would be better that the race's limited finances be spent on "erecting large halls in cities" where blacks could make good use of them; even more desirable would be the building and endowing "a college for our youth."[23] Interestingly both the organizers of black monu-ment projects and their opponents often held as their top priority the build-ing of the race's future through educating the young. Whether that goal could best be achieved by nurturing race pride through historical memory and public ritual or by the construction of more mundane school buildings was often the point at issue.

Resistance to the erection of monuments, then, could come from a variety of directions, and pragmatic concern over the appropriation of limited funds was not the least of them. The financial constraints generally experienced by African Americans did much to frustrate their attempts to build monuments to honor black Civil War veterans. Equally frustrating for Charles Hendley, in Huntsville, Alabama, was his perception that fallen black soldiers were resting "in neglected graves." While that may have been the case by the 1880s for black veterans' graves in Hendley's Alabama, it is clear from newspaper accounts that many northern black GAR posts and their female supporters took seriously their annual Decoration Day obligations. Probably more widespread was the inattention to the needs of surviving veterans, to the extent that "even those suffering yet from old wounds or disease contracted in the service receive scarcely less consideration than paupers." Hendley complained in 1888 that while both northern and southern whites took pains to "honor and distinguish" surviving veterans, "the colored people pass their brave fellows unnoticed." "We may not be able to rear costly monuments," he scolded, "but let all at least while honoring the memory of the fallen, accord kind treatment and consideration to the living colored soldier."[24]

In the face of such difficulties, T. Thomas Fortune ably articulated the importance of monument building as he tried to drum up support for yet another tribute, this time to a civilian African American hero. The project Fortune advocated in 1885 was "a memorial to perpetuate the name and services of the late Dr. Henry Highland Garnet," who had died several years before. A benefit concert "by the BEST COLORED TALENT IN AMERICA" was advertised, and Fortune chastised his readers to contribute. "It cannot be denied," he bristled, "that up to this time the race has shown a phenomenal disregard for the memory of its men who have lived and labored for it. Other nations live in the memory of their great men and benefactors, and point their children with pride to statues, monuments, and charitable institutions erected to perpetuate the memory of all such. . . . It is time that we begin to build up a proper race pride by showing to our children and to mankind at large that we have produced some men to whose life and labors we can point with pardonable pride."[25]

The concert was a dismal financial failure, and Fortune despaired that there was so little "patriotism in the breast of the colored people of this country to rear a fitting memorial to perpetuate the memory of one of the best men the race has produced in the last fifty years." Two years later, due apparently to "the want of public spirit among our colored citizens," the Garnet monument plan was reported to have "died out." A correspondent to the *Age* echoed the concerns of Fortune, Tanner, Payne, Bell, and others regarding the need to "perpetuate those things among us which adorn and beautify our race development. . . . If we ever expect to become potential factors in this advancing civilization, if we would command the respect of all men and races, if we desire to leave a legacy in the form of worthy examples to future generations, we must learn to honor our own."[26]

This writer's assertion of the importance of offering tribute to the race's own heroes was stimulated specifically by Fortune's "editorial comment upon the dedication of a statue to the Italian patriot Garibaldi in Washington Square, New York City, by his fellow countrymen dwelling here." Michael Kammen has described the years between 1870 and 1910 as "the most notable period in all of American history for erecting monuments in honor of mighty warriors, groups of unsung heroes, and great deeds." Indeed, Eric Hobsbawm argues that the same period was one during which traditions were invented "with particular assiduity" in many European nations as well. Hobsbawm identifies "the mass production of public monuments" as one of several vehicles for this project, along with the creation of public holidays and ceremonies, and the inculcation of nationalist traditions in the schools. Kirk Savage points out that a "monument industry" emerged in the United States during the postwar generation in response to the demand for the generic Civil War soldier monuments erected in small towns and cities in both North and South. During this period blacks could hardly avoid noticing the wave of statues and monuments, both to Civil War soldiers and to a wide variety of notable historical figures.[27]

A particularly galling spectacle was provided by the 1890 dedication of the Robert E. Lee statue in Richmond, which Kirk Savage has aptly described as southern whites' "brilliant effort to re-present white mastery in the postwar world." "Afro-Americans," the *Age* reported, "took no part in the ceremonies." "Perhaps no celebration ever took place in the history of mankind in which a whole race stood by, silent and unsympathetic, while another race was simply deliriously vociferous and enthusiastic." The *Age* quoted from a southern paper the words of two "respectable darkies" who claimed that "We is Mars Jubal [Early]'s niggers, we is, and we come over two hundred miles to pay our specs to him." Early, one of the graying Confederates at the ceremony, was one of the white southern "irreconcilables" who refused to countenance any black participation in public life except as servants. The *Age* contended with ire that, if Early's former slaves actually had appeared, it "illustrates forcibly a woeful condition." The analyst in Fortune's paper suggested that some of the older members of the race were better dead and forgotten if, alive, they perpetuated the more degrading aspects of slavery's legacy: "Until such relics of the dead past . . . representing the arrogance and insolence of the master and the cringing cowardice of the slave, have passed away . . . it will be impossible for the white man and the black man to adjust themselves to the condition of free and equal citizens." The lack of freedom and equality in the South in 1890 is hinted at by the more circumspect commentary on the "imposing ceremonies" at the Lee monument offered by Charles Hendley. More vulnerable to possible white hostility than his northern counterparts, the Alabama editor noted merely that Lee was "by long odds the greatest and most thoughtful man on the Confederate side in the late unpleasantness."[28]

If monuments to Confederate heroes could be troubling to African Americans, southern white attempts to honor the "faithful slave" and the "mammy" could be even more so. Their own memories of the slave past fraught with pain and emotion, blacks generally found former slaveholders' proposed memorials misguided, at best. One exception may be the plan put forward by a Reverend Dr. Landrum, just two years after the Lee unveiling, to "erect a monument in Richmond to the memory of the colored slaves who so faithfully served their masters during the war." If the focus on black subservience was familiarly unsettling, at least the form of the monument met with some blacks' approval. For the monument was not to be "one of marble or bronze, but of brick," in the form of "an old folk's home" to care for those no longer able to fend for themselves. More typical were the resolutions passed at successive reunions of the United Confederate Veterans in 1914 and 1915. Here more conventional monuments were to be erected "to commemorate the fidelity to their masters by the slaves during the war." Robert Abbott of the *Chicago Defender* responded that "the very loyalty of the slaves seems pathetic," in that "they did not know enough to strike for themselves the blow" for their freedom. "Monuments are all right in their way," Abbott conceded, "but the colored people of the South need justice far more than they do monuments." Abbott, perhaps more hopeful than accurate, took the Confederate veterans' resolutions as an indication that "even at this late date they realize the right was not on their side." Still, he would rather see "these worthy gentlemen" build and finance a school or work to "better conditions" for southern blacks than to waste their money and energy on meaningless "heart ease." "The soldier in gray will soon be a memory; why not leave something behind worthwhile?"[29]

Blacks did not find all monument unveilings nearly so troubling as these efforts, but they surely had to question the relative merits of the slew of statues that appeared around the turn of the century. A casual reader of the Washington, D.C., black weekly the *Bee* between 1904 and 1906 would have encountered articles on several dozen commemorative statues covering a bizarre range of subjects: statues of Baron Von Steuben, George McClellan, Oliver P. Morton, Ethan Allen, Virginia Dare, Sacajewea, Lord Calvert, Giuseppi Verdi, Robert Fulton, Benjamin Franklin, Pocahontas, Robert

Burns, and Civil War nurse Mother Bicker-Dyke only begin the list. In addition to other monuments honoring assorted battles, grave sites, and famous prayer meetings, one monument was erected in tribute to a mule that stumbled onto an Idaho gold mine. As if to emphasize the extent of the monument craze, and apropos of Hobsbawm's discussion of the "mass production of tradition," one article reported the invention of a statue-making machine in Europe. African American monument drives, then, were part of a national, or even international, trend between the Civil War and World War I. Blacks were caught up in what one journalist described as "monument fever" as they erected, or at least proposed, monuments to William C. Nell, Crispus Attucks, Nat Turner, Frederick Douglass, Harriet Tubman, John Mercer Langston, and others in the fifty years after emancipation.[30]

One noteworthy monument plan that achieved its goal involved a bust of AME Church founder and first bishop Richard Allen, which was unveiled in Philadelphia's Fairmount Park during the National Centennial Exposition in November 1876.[31] Benjamin Tanner's 1874 "heroic age" editorial comment on the preservation of the past related very particularly to his spearheading the drive to erect the Allen Monument. Tanner, editor of the *Christian Recorder* from 1868 to 1884, was one of many black journalists with an intense desire to perpetuate the memory of black history and heroes, and to have those heroes recognized as *American* heroes. From 1874 to 1876 he used the *Recorder* to drum up support for the Allen Monument in order to challenge "the popular thought that we colored Americans have not contributed anything to the moral grandeur of the common country—anything in the shape of heroes."[32] Tanner believed that a statue of Allen would create a tangible site of historical memory to help blacks balance the racial and national components of their identity. The Allen Monument would nourish African Americans' race pride, and perhaps more importantly, it would assert black citizens' collective right to be represented in a national ritual that Tanner shrewdly perceived to be a "mighty Presentation of the nation to itself and to the world." "The negro," Tanner argued, needed to "put in [an] appearance" to "show the American people and the world what he is, and what he can do."[33] Making an appearance at the centennial—a national ritual of self-definition—was designed to break down white resistance to the idea of blacks' fundamental Americanness and to foster in blacks a sense of both racial identity and national belonging.

This message was made explicit at the June 1876 dedication of the monument site. In his oration, the Reverend John T. Jenifer called attention to blacks' African past, and the centrality of the African American presence in America's national destiny. Jenifer noted how becoming it is for us, the children of ancestors who were the founders of the earliest civilization, the establishers of great cities and vast empires, the patrons of arts and sciences, to emerge from the darkness of centuries, to show our appreciation of industry and art, by joining this feast of nations in this our own beloved country at this her first Centennial feast. With a history written in blood and baptised in tears, we are here to-day; here to-day upon the soil where we have suffered; here to-day with those by whom we have been degraded; here to-day with the wisest in scientific learning, the greatest in power, the most famous in art, and with the best in Christian philanthropy; here to-day to show that the spirit of our fathers has not expired; but with a purpose grander than that which built the Pyramids or founded Carthage, we come to make our contributions to the New World's Fair, which shall stand forever as the first national scientific effort of a race heroically struggling to shake off the degradation of centuries.[34]

In this moving address, Jenifer next offered a poignant counterpoint to the lily-white reading of history and the message of white sectional reconciliation that dominated the centennial (and would dominate the rest of the century). Blacks had earned the rights of American citizens, Jenifer asserted, through their "patriotism and bravery" displayed on the many battlefields of various American wars. The black folk had enriched American culture with the soulful gifts of song, poetry, and Christian devotion that had sustained the race through the ordeal of slavery. Jenifer interpreted the history of two and a half centuries of bondage as the history of "negro industry" which, he asserted, had "placed [the Negro] prominently upon the pages of [American] history as foremost among those whose productive labors have developed the staple resources of" the South. After thus situating black labor as the defining presence in the American South, Jenifer proceeded to situate "the Southern question" as a central issue for the destiny of the entire nation. Jenifer criticized the nation first for its continuing tolerance of "Kuklux Klans and White Leagues" and then for its "impatien[ce]" with the progress of the freedpeople. Rather, he argued, much as he had two years before in suggesting a statistical survey of the race, their "progress [in] . . . the past fifteen years has been marvelous, all things considered. The mistake these people make who despair is that they do not read history wisely."[35]

Jenifer took this very public opportunity to address a racially mixed audience that was reported to be "quite large," in the context of a huge national ritual of self-definition, in order to offer a striking reinterpretation of American history that placed African Americans in a central and defining role in that history. He incorporated the African past into a positive African American identity and then proceeded to construct the story of American bondage as one not primarily of humiliation and indignity but of industry and nation-building. Similarly, the story of blacks' brief and troubled freedom became a story of remarkable progress. Jenifer's oration was intended to be a tool for shaping public views of black history and identity.[36]

But the fact of the monument itself was also intended to deliver a historical message. While defending the monument plan against its opponents in 1874, AME minister Andrew Chambers emphasized the usefulness of monuments and other public, nontextual expressions of historical consciousness for imparting a sense of history and tradition to a largely nonliterate people. Such expressions were essential, he claimed, for "pointing our illiterate race toward . . . loftier institutions." An unlearned people, he asserted, need visual displays like statues and monuments in order to "arouse the masses" to support more high-minded enterprises like publishing houses and universities. Chambers emphasized the educative value for the present generation and particularly the importance of leaving a legacy for subsequent generations: "This generation intends to leave traces of its existence for posterity to look upon. . . . [The Allen Monument] shall work an epoch in the history of our race. It shall be a stepping stone to the colored men of America to rise higher in self esteem and the esteem of all nations. We intend to leave Philadelphia in 1876 as did the heroes in 1776, with a fixed resolve to achieve noble results; and in 1976 we expect our progeny to gather around the Monument in question, shed tears of gratitude for the example we have left them, and call us blessed."[37] After numerous delays, the marble bust of Richard Allen was unveiled "with appropriate ceremonies in the presence of several hundred colored people" in Philadelphia's Fairmount Park. African American educator, politician, and journalist, John Mercer Langston, speaking several weeks later at Allen's Mother Bethel Church, informed his audience that the Allen Monument was the first ever erected by black Americans to honor one of their own.[38]

Other efforts to hold up positive components of the past involved commemorating other key figures and signal events in the race's history, besides emancipation days. In 1883 a resident of Norfolk, Virginia, suggested that "no day ought to be more hallowed, no event more appropriate for commemoration by the Negroes of the United States, than the 5th day of March." On that date in 1770, during the so-called Boston Massacre, Crispus Attucks "shed the first blood in defence of liberty in our country." Significantly, the day was said to be far more meaningful for blacks than Washington's birthday, which was "clearly a white man's day." Attucks Day, by contrast, was "the day that a real slave struck at the power that held him a slave; therefore the Negro ought to celebrate that day."[39] Boston blacks had observed the occasion for decades and in 1888 succeeded in raising the Attucks monument on the Boston Common, one of the most significant black projects, and one of only a few successful ones during the postemancipation generation. Though it was thought by some to bestow "only tardy justice" to Attucks's memory, it was nonetheless a "fitting recognition of that Negro hero" and represented "an important step in the right direction" toward blacks' inclusion in the national story. Blacks in Boston had been working against considerable opposition since the 1850s to secure funding and support to bring the project to fruition in order to call attention to blacks' patriotic contributions to the nation's founding and to lay claim to the democratic promise of the Revolutionary victory. As much as paying tribute to Attucks as a black founding father, the monument would also serve contemporary African Americans by earning for them "the honor of preserving in marble the heroic name and deeds of the first patriot whose blood was shed for American Independence." The idea expressed here reflects an attitude blacks had been articulating as early as the first 1808 slave trade celebrations: that the act of commemoration itself was an important legacy that would bring credit to those taking such initiative.[40]

Other black founding fathers were recognized during the 1870s and 1880s, as African Americans began to construct their pantheon of race heroes. In 1884 black Masons commemorated the one hundredth anniversary of Prince Hall Freemasonry in the United States, and Hall himself was praised for his labors to "educate and elevate the race" and designated as a black hero whose "name should ever be remembered."[41] In conjunction with the movement to erect the Richard Allen monument at the Centennial Exposition, the prelate's name and legacy were kept before the readers of the *Christian Recorder* with a series of front-page extracts from Allen's slim autobiography, "The Life, Experience and Gospel Labors of Rev. Richard Allen," which ran through the summer and fall of 1875. Beginning in the 1880s, around the founder's February 14 birthday, readers of the *Recorder* were urged to familiarize themselves with, and to emulate, the great leader's life. In addition, Allen Day exercises first began to be systematically celebrated in AME congregations across the nation to commemorate the founder's natal day. In 1887 Allen received additional attention as the AME Church celebrated the Centennial of Philadelphia's Free African Society, an organization cofounded by Allen in which the independent black church had planted its roots. This event prompted a lengthy essay that paid homage to the founder, comparing him variously with Moses, Martin Luther, Jan Hus, George Whitefield, George Washington, and Thomas Jefferson. Further literary homage to Allen appeared with the publication of two separate editions of his autobiography and J. F. Dyson's pamphlet *Richard Allen's Place in History: A Commentary on the Life and Deeds of the Chief Founder and First*

Bishop of the African Methodist Episcopal Church. These 1887 centennial publications suggest an increasingly literary approach to honoring Allen, along with the continued use of nonliterary forms for disseminating historical and biographical knowledge about this African American hero. AME leaders thus worked on various fronts—through public commemoration, published books, and the press—in their efforts to instill historical consciousness in the minds of their literate and nonliterate constituencies.[42]

Perpetuating the memory of past heroes during the late nineteenth and early twentieth centuries was integral to constructing meaningful versions of both the recent and the more distant history of the race. In this project AME activists represented a growing trend conjoining the use of public ritual, monuments, and commemorations with written historical accounts in fiction, nonfiction, and autobiography.[43] On rare occasions African Americans could point to the inclusion of blacks in mainstream historical works, as when the *Age* reported with satisfaction in 1891 that the compilers of *The Official Records of the War of the Rebellion* were seeking information on black troop records. But even then the article noted that George Washington Williams's works on black troops were being used extensively by the research team.[44] African Americans thus had to rely primarily on their own literary and historical efforts in publicizing their contributions. And African American writers faced immense problems of access to an audience. Blacks in the late nineteenth century were making steady progress in raising literacy rates, but limited reading skills and lack of disposable income made the production of literary material of any kind for a primarily black audience an unprofitable undertaking.

Between the 1880s and the turn of the century, journalist and author T. Thomas Fortune devoted considerable space in his several New York papers to promoting works by and about African Americans, usually appealing to his readers' sense of race pride. An 1886 article in the *Age* chided that "no race can hope to occupy a conspicuous place in the opinion of the world which has not demonstrated high literary capacity." The writer went on to list a host of black authors from Phillis Wheatley through David Walker, Frederick Douglass, and William Nell to John Mercer Langston, George Washington Williams, and Fortune himself. The piece criticized fellow blacks for their "failure to indemnify the authors" of the race through the purchase of their books.[45] Supporting black writers was seen by some as one way to speed the progress of the race. One editor noted: "As a people advance in civilization, culture and refinement, they develop a taste for literary acumen. . . . So it has ever been; in all countries and in all climes, the sorrows and joys, the successes and failures of a people have been sung by their native bards."[46] In supporting those bards, black newspapers printed numerous reviews and advertisements for works like William Still's *Underground Railroad,* Williams's *History of the Negro Race,* Joseph Wilson's *Black Phalanx,* Fortune's own *Black and White,* the Reverend George C. Rowe's volume of poetry *Our Heroes,* E. A. Johnson's *School History of the Negro Race,* and many other "race books." In addition editors occasionally offered free copies with paid subscriptions to their papers.[47]

T. Thomas Fortune especially touted the efforts of other race journalists who tried to raise readers' historical consciousness. Though Fortune may have surpassed others in this concern, most black journals printed historical sketches, letters, and editorials that encouraged African Americans to attend to their history. Fortune's New York *Globe,* in 1884, offered for sale a wall chart displaying heroes like Frederick Douglass, Hiram Revels, and Blanche K. Bruce. And Fortune often printed letters like the one in 1886 that pointed with pride to the likes of Richard Allen, Douglass, Toussaint, and Daniel Payne in order to illustrate that the African American "belongs to a race that has a history and a literature of proud mention dating back many centuries ago." John Mitchell Jr., editor of the *Richmond Planet,* offered for sale (or free with a paid year's subscription) a series of historical chromolithographs featuring black Civil War engagements at Fort Wagner, Olustee, and even the tragic massacre at Fort Pillow, along with "The Capture and Death of Sitting Bull" and the "Battle between the Monitor and Merrimac." In 1912 the *Chicago Defender* planned "to issue a series of souvenir pennies bearing the picture of Frederick Douglass" during that year's meeting of Booker T. Washington's National Negro Business League. The Wizard of Tuskegee indicated that the pennies "will help out a whole lot" in making the meeting a success.[48]

One could find, in a variety of black papers, discussions of blacks' role in the American Revolution and the abolitionist movement, and biographical treatments of Philip Bell, Sojourner Truth, Richard Allen, and the African ecclesiastic St. Cyprian, to name a few.[49] In 1885 W. Calvin Chase's Washington, D.C., *Bee* urged young African Americans in particular to study and emulate the lives of the race's "representative men." And in 1890 Edward E. Cooper's Indianapolis paper, the *Freeman,* printed several full-page pictorials featuring, for example, "The Great Leaders of the West Indies," including Dessalines, Toussaint, and others, and "The Ten Greatest Negroes," including Douglass, Fortune, and Cooper himself. A similar "Souvenir Historical Chart," printed by the AME Church in 1899, featured a large portrait of Richard Allen surrounded by engravings of the several historic sites of Allen's Bethel Church in Philadelphia, along with lists of the mother congregation's pastors and of all the denomination's bishops, living and dead. The caption encouraged blacks to "observe the landmarks" of their history.[50]

As with so many aspects of black activism and leadership during this era, the black press was at the forefront of African Americans' *intellectual* activism in addressing these concerns about history and memory. Before the professional study of black history was well established, black journalists' access to a written forum gave them a powerful tool for spreading their views and having those views recorded for posterity. Editors used their papers to critique the dominant white-centered interpretations of history; to structure and moderate debates regarding the contested memories of slavery and the African past; to promote books on black history, monuments to black heroes, commemorations of historic events, and historical societies to preserve and disseminate black history. They also, of course, spoke on current political and social issues facing their communities. J. A. Arneaux, editor of the *New York Enterprise*, commented on the responsibilities and rewards he accepted with his job: "Editing a newspaper is my heart's delight, not for the sake of being an editor, for the position of an editor in the estimation of the masses of Afro-Americans is no more than any other position, but because it is within my province to combat those who dare trample upon the rights of the race. I wish to give what advice I am capable of giving to my people and warn them of impending danger."[51]

Moreover, many journalists were orators, speaking their truths and issuing their warnings at emancipation celebrations and other public events. Black newspapers were also read aloud within black communities. Thus black journalists' voices reached large numbers through both written and oral forms of expression—an important breadth of coverage among a people rooted in an oral culture yet very concerned with the expansion of literacy. The black press and black journalists—by speaking to both literate and nonliterate components of the black community—were central to this pursuit to establish and maintain a tradition of historical study and a concern for heritage and collective memory.

Among the efforts of his fellow black journalists, Fortune especially applauded "the standard of excellence" set by the initial number of the *AME Church Review* in 1884, which contained both literary and specifically historical essays. Fortune predicted that "every intelligent member of the race will find both pleasure and profit in its pages."[52] But profit of the monetary variety was hardly to be expected by the publishers of the *Review* or other race periodicals. Benjamin Tanner, after completing his sixteen-year tenure at the *Christian Recorder*, experienced considerable difficulty in attracting paying customers for his rather erudite new quarterly. After two years in print, with only 1,200 subscribers ("out of a colored population of 7,000,000 people") paying $1.50 per year for the journal, the *Review's* receipts did not nearly match the estimated $3,000 annual publication costs. Other newspapers fared no better in their efforts to attract paying subscribers. J. A. Arneaux was forced to cease publication of the *New York Enterprise* after four years due to lack of funds. "The Afro-American press is [a] necessity, and would be sadly missed if wiped out tomorrow," he complained in 1887. "It is a burning shame that our people do not see the necessity of their newspapers and give them that support they merit." One commentator placed part of the blame on some of the actual recipients of blacks' money, a group that, tangentially at least, included freedom festivals: "Think of the hundreds of thousands of dollars we squander every year on balls, picnics, excursions, receptions and gew-gaws, and then think of the miserable pittance we contribute to the sustentation of race enterprises. It is more than enough to make an honest man sick of the work that must be done. Let the race brace up!"[53]

Another struggle to present the history of the race to the American reading public in the 1890s was undertaken by an increasing number of black writers of fiction. Perhaps no better advocate of a positive historical interpretation was at work during this period than Frances Ellen Watkins Harper. Faced with the same problems as writers of nonfiction, and additional obstacles because of her sex, Harper wrote numerous poems, speeches, essays, and novels (both serialized and formally published) that attempted to present a positive and usable interpretation of the race's recent history. The most famous product in Harper's decades-long writing career was one of her last major works, the novel *Iola Leroy, or Shadows Uplifted,* published in 1892. Here Harper provides a prime example of her literary efforts to uplift the race's self-image. *Iola Leroy,* set during the Civil War and Reconstruction, was possibly the most widely read African American novel of the nineteenth century, going through five printings in its first year.[54] The title character is the virtually white daughter of a planter and his fair-skinned slave. The planter eventually frees and marries his slave and installs her as mistress of the plantation. After the planter's death both his wife and daughter are reduced to slavery. The rather didactic plot centers on the decision by Iola and other key characters to reject the option of passing for white, assert their identity as blacks, and work for the elevation of the race.

Within that larger project of uplift, Harper also uses her characters to comment on the importance of historical memory. Harper, like many blacks, perceived the hand of Providence in history and saw the Civil War as an act of national suffering to purge the national sin of slavery. The destiny of the nation, in this view, was to embody justice through welcoming the Negro into the national family. Recognizing the importance of African Americans' service in the war, Harper at one point has a character express the hope that "some faithful historian" would one day make that service widely known. A regular participant in Freedom Day celebrations, and well aware of debates over the relative value of perpetuating or eradicating the slave past, Harper especially pointed out the need for young blacks in the late nineteenth century to remember "the hardships [of slavery, Civil War, etc.] through which we older ones passed." "Instead of forgetting the past," she intoned through one protagonist, "I would have them hold in everlasting remembrance our great deliverance."[55]

But even as widely read as Harper's novel was, its reach was still limited. As if to compensate for their lack of attention to written material, African Americans after the 1870s began to escalate their organization of other vehicles for historical memory in the form of historical and literary societies. In 1877 Benjamin Tanner claimed to "know of no more hopeful 'sign of the times' than the Literary stir manifested in almost every section." Especially since so many African Americans had minimal literacy skills and were too overburdened with family and work obligations to attend school, Tanner felt that "with a history such as ours, no better means could possibly be adopted to the general enlightenment of the people." The Negro Authors Literary Society, established in Kansas City, Kansas, in 1894, embodied Tanner's vision of the potential of these organizations for race development. The club was determined "to devote its efforts in rearing monuments of sentiment to Negro genius and in rescuing from obscurity those bards who have tuned their harps 'neath the blight of caste and prejudice. . . . May the club that has taken the initiative along this line," intoned one of its advocates, "ever live to inspire the hearts of our youth with a pride of race, and to instill in the minds of our people the fact, 'that all our strength is in our union.' " The importance of literary clubs was still recognized in the early twentieth century, when the *Pittsburgh Courier* noted that "there should be two or three such organizations in every large city where our people form any considerable number of the population. Nothing is more helpful to the young men and women as the opportunity to develop their intellectual knowledge through the agency of the literary society."[56]

Though many literary societies were strictly local organizations, some, like Washington, D.C.'s Bethel Literary and Historical Association, attracted the attention of blacks across the nation. From its founding by Daniel Payne and others in 1881, "the Literary" provided a forum in which many of the leading African American intellects of the day—both men and women— read papers on the racial identity and accomplishments of ancient Egyptians and Ethiopians; reflected on the successes and failures of Reconstruction;

or debated the benefits of separate schools, industrial education, woman suffrage, and a host of historical, philosophical, political, and literary topics.[57]

Historian George Washington Williams, however, saw the subject matter of the Bethel Literary as too broad to serve as a true institution of historical inquiry and advocated, in 1883, the formation of "the first historical society of Negroes in the world." The proposed "American Negro Historical Society" would meet yearly, present scholarly papers, and work to preserve files and records germane to the race's history. The society never materialized, and four years later the prominent Philadelphia journalist and educator Mrs. Gertrude Bustill Mossell was herself writing to Fortune's *Freeman* regarding the creation of an African American historical society. She praised the ephemeral collection of fellow Philadelphian William Dorsey and asserted that black Americans "should feel it a privilege to gather [the] scraps of history of our people." Mossell was suspicious of the motives of whites who were actively working to collect abolitionist "pamphlets and books" and other "relics of slavery." Well aware of the ambivalence many felt toward the slave past, Mossell nonetheless urged that blacks needed to lay claim to their history, for only they could make it serve the interests of the race. "[H]owever *painful* the memories [those materials] have stirred to life," she implored, blacks should "not be ashamed of what is rightfully ours. Let us make use of it. Let us get to work and gather up the fragments. . . . Let us begin to form an historical society."[58]

One week later the prominent minister Harvey Johnson of Baltimore proposed that the society be located in Philadelphia and that Mrs. Mossell, as "the prime mover in the matter," be designated "president *pro tempore*." He offered twenty-five dollars toward the purchase of materials for the collection and urged one hundred other concerned members of the race to do likewise. Mrs. Mossell's essay on the subject of race history had rekindled an awareness in Johnson's own historical consciousness of "a long felt need that I have thought on with painful anxiety." A month later Johnson noted the financial contributions of a few colleagues among Baltimore's black clergy and the endorsement of the then little-known Memphis journalist Ida B. Wells. Furthermore, Johnson added to his original proposal with the suggestion that the organization not be "a Historical Society pure and simple, but let it be in its nature a book depository and circulating library, where not only race relics and rare works are to be kept, for reference and review, but where they may be purchased by those who wish to have them." That such sales of items would defeat the archival purpose seems not to have entered the minister's mind. Johnson and the other proponents, of course, remained ever aware that the race faced enormous difficulties in guarding blacks' basic human rights during the 1880s. Stemming the rising tide of discrimination, disfranchisement, and racial violence clearly took precedence over comparatively less urgent concerns about history and memory. But the field of history and memory, too, was recognized as a key battleground in that larger struggle. Johnson put the importance of the proposed historical society in perspective when he stated that it was probably secondary to the formation of "a National League" to insure "race protection and race freedom and liberty." But, nonetheless, a formal mechanism for the collection and dissemination of race history was, for this man and for others, "one of our needs and one of our great needs too."[59]

This proposed society, like its predecessors, was stillborn, though William Dorsey continued to attend to his own idiosyncratic pursuit of race-related materials.[60] In 1890 T. Thomas Fortune, whose papers seem to have been the main vehicle for such discussions, noted that "several suggestions and attempts have been put forward in past years to organize an Historical Society, for the purpose of gathering the scattered literature and historical records of the race and properly preserving the same, but nothing tangible has grown of it all." Fortune's comment accompanied yet another proposal, this one from Thomas L. Cottin, professor of Greek Language and Literature at the AME Church's Payne Institute in Augusta, Georgia. Cottin proposed that "[i]nasmuch as all nations have bodies of learned men who pry into the past and present to the living the records of the dead, would it not be well for our race to have some such body? Our history, meager as it is, has never been placed before the race. To the great mass of our people, there have never been any Negro heroes; no actions worthy of emulation. For the rising generation ought there not be effort made to train them in the paths of honor and glory?" Fortune, of course, supported such an endeavor, but he pointed out that "there are no Negro records, simply because there is no Negro race, in history or out of it." This objection does not reflect the editor's feelings about race history but rather his growing aversion to the term "Negro." Fortune assumed wryly that "what he really wishes to suggest is an African Historical Society; if so, we heartily endorse the suggestion as a pertinent and happy one."[61]

A year later a group of Sunday school workers in Connecticut reported the acquisition of "well preserved copies of the conference minutes of the 'African Methodist Episcopal Church in America,' from 1830 to 1845." In advertising this find, Fortune declared, "It is to be hoped that before many years a society will be organized for the special purpose of collecting and preserving in proper form . . . documents relating to the early history of our churches and race that is now scattered throughout the country. A well organized historical society would be a decided benefit and some day *The Age* may start the project and carry it through successfully."[62]

If the paper never fulfilled that role, other individuals were just as eager to see such a project succeed, in part to prevent racist white societies from monopolizing the interpretation of black history. In 1890, as the study of American folklife began to attract considerable attention at both local and national levels, Fortune noted the organization, by southern-born Harvard geologist Nathaniel Shaler, "of a society for the collection of data and the study of the history and the character of the African in the United States, past and present." After indicating Shaler's decidedly racist positions on issues like race mixing, social equality, and black intellectual capacity, Fortune concluded "that Prof. Shaler knows entirely too little about the history and character of the African in the United States to write so learnedly about them."[63] Far better for blacks themselves to take on that urgent task.

In that very year the Society for the Collection of Negro Folk Lore was organized in Boston by a number of black socialites and literati including Josephine St. Pierre Ruffin and a young Harvard student W. E. B. Du Bois. The society adopted the mission "to collect and perpetuate the anecdotes, stories, legends and experiences of the colored people" in America. A few years later the Hampton Institute formed a separate folk and ethnology section to serve the same purpose. By the late 1890s Alexander Crummell's American Negro Academy and Philadelphia's American Negro Historical Society (ANHS), though less interested specifically in folk culture, were also beginning to fill the pressing need to encourage the scholarly study of the African American past. This was especially true of the ANHS, which, in addition to sponsoring commemorative events and readings of historical papers, also worked to collect and preserve documents germane to the race's history.[64]

The members of the ANHS were extremely conscious of the need to continue their efforts and to enlighten the public as to the importance of their particular endeavor. A 1904 address to the members stressed that although the society "may appear to many as having done not much . . . it is not so." The organization had a growing archive and was possessed of "so many very interesting facts and reminiscences of events of people . . . of the past who [have] given us an example of everything to make us proud of our ancestry." The ANHS's project was especially vital for two reasons. First, despite many staunch supporters "among our Anglo-Saxon friends, . . . among the writers of history the Negro is only sparsely noted." Second, and perhaps more important in light of blacks' widespread ambivalence regarding slavery and African identity, the ANHS felt the need to counter "the disposition of many [who would prefer] to forget the African side." More-over, responsibility for passing on historical knowledge dwelt not just with historical societies but at every level of African American social organization: "We want the newspapers, the Churches and the parents to tell their children what our past condition was, and about those dear people who are dead and gone of the sacrifices they made in our behalf, and the grand oppor-tunities [that] are now offered."[65]

By the 1910s decades of intermittent efforts to create institutions of African American historical memory culminated in two organizations that would have far-reaching and long-standing effects on the preservation and study of black heritage. In 1911 former slave and journalist John Edward Bruce and Puerto Rico–born bibliophile Arthur A. Schomburg formed the Negro So-ciety for Historical Research in New York in order to explore the history of the black diaspora, encourage the incorporation of black history in school curricula, and stimulate race pride. The grandeur of ancient Africa was, for both men, a key point of interest in understanding the history of blacks in the Americas and in defining a noble heritage of superior accomplishment. Several years later, in Washington, D.C., Dr. Carter G. Woodson formed the Association for the Study of Negro Life and History in order to likewise collect documents and sponsor research pertinent to the history of African peoples on both sides of the Atlantic. Woodson, a Harvard Ph.D., also pub-lished the *Journal of Negro History,* which was widely praised, not least for preserving "memories of noble forebears" and a "tradition of honor and courage."[66] The *Journal* provided an important vehicle through which blacks' interpretations of their past began, slowly, to have some influence on the larger historical profession, if not the whole of the American public.[67]

On the literary front, W. E. B. Du Bois spearheaded a similar, if less institutional, drive to place black history in the public eye. Du Bois proposed a multivolume *Encyclopedia Africana* to appear in conjunction with the 1913 "Jubilee of Emancipation" in order to cover "the chief points in the history and condition of the Negro race." Around the same time, Daniel Murray, for many years an assistant librarian at the Library of Congress, attempted a similar project, garnering the support of numerous black scholars and activists. Neither project could accumulate the funds to get under way at that time, but Du Bois accomplished part of the purpose with his "Star of Ethiopia" historical pageant, first presented in 1913 at the New York Expo-sition celebrating the fiftieth anniversary of emancipation, and with the 1915 publication of his remarkable historical and sociological study *The Negro.*[68]

Whether through the preservation of records, the observance of momen-tous anniversaries, the building of monuments, the writing of fiction and nonfiction, or the founding of institutions of memory, African Americans between the 1870s and the early 1900s engaged in a conscious effort to interpret the history of the race and to make that history serve the larger project of race uplift. These efforts were hardly unanimous or without detractors. Some felt that the elevation of the race could only proceed with the erasure of large portions of its past. Those blacks who were most concerned with building and disseminating knowledge about the past repeatedly had to scold, cajole, and beseech their fellows to support such endeavors. They were not always successful.

Black proponents of memory used various literary, commemorative, and performative vehicles to address contemporary concerns and to shape the legacy they passed on to future generations. Their constructions of historical memory, their contributions to a commemorative tradition, and their role in establishing a foundation for black historical writing were part of an important cultural struggle that was shouldered by numerous black intellectual and political leaders in the late nineteenth century. Their example suggests that African American tradition-builders during this period increasingly chose to emphasize the educative function of commemorations for a people straddling the worlds of orality and literacy. Much of that education was directed outside the black community as well and was intended to provide white Americans with black perspectives on social and political issues of the day. Black Americans were often advised at commemorative events regarding the political and social needs of the present. At the same time, many older black leaders, in particular, consciously used commemorations to instruct younger generations of African Americans in the lessons of history, as the race grew progressively further removed from contact with the African past, the experience of slavery, and the antebellum tradition of abolition and rights activism. Efforts to maintain a continuity with those aspects of the past represent a vital component in African Americans' challenge to establish a sense of history, a set of traditions, and a pantheon of heroes that would legitimate, to the nation and to themselves, their inherent worth as a people and as American citizens.

CHAPTER FIVE

"LESSONS OF EMANCIPATION FOR A NEW GENERATION"

REORIENTATION, 1860s–1900s

Emancipation Day has many advantages for the race. It gives a grand opportunity for our scholars to make known the ancient glory, the heroic labors and celebrated actions of Negroes, and point out the path of future success. It is a period of instruction.

—Anonymous correspondent, 1894

The Negro has a part in the history of this country of which he need not be ashamed. Let it be told for his own vindication. Let it be told as an answer to those who would slander the race. Let it be told for the encouragement of the rising generation. Let it be told for the sake of truth and eternal justice.

—Abraham Lincoln DeMond, January 1, 1900

BETWEEN THE 1860s and the turn of the century African Americans across the nation struggled to maintain their rights and their collective sense of self-worth in the face of a white sectional reconciliation that placed scant value on blacks' concerns or condition, let alone their history and heritage. The various monument projects, publications, literary and historical societies, and public commemorations undertaken during this trying period demonstrate that these deteriorating circumstances hindered, but could not fully expunge, the efforts of many black leaders to define and disseminate African American history and traditions. The worsening conditions may actually have stimulated some to action. African American leaders during these decades used an array of strategies to advance their complementary pursuits of racial uplift, rights activism, and full inclusion in the republic, infusing those pursuits with positive and functional interpretations of African American history. Freedom Day festivals continued to play a significant role in this enterprise as black Americans entered what has been termed the nadir of African American history. As Jim Crow solidified, white support declined and black celebrations gradually retreated into a more racially segregated public sphere in both the North and the South. Debates over the propriety of celebration and ambivalence about the memory of the race's past continued to divide black communities. In their reorientation to this new context, committed organizers increasingly employed the rhetoric of education as they used emancipation celebrations to teach a variety of "lessons" to both blacks and whites in the public sphere of the late nineteenth century.

In Philadelphia, even if historian Roger Lane is largely correct in his assessment that freedom festivals had "lost their old luster" during those years, the January 1 Emancipation Proclamation was still periodically commemorated at least through the 1890s.[1] If mass demonstrations in a racially inclusive public sphere seem not to have been a prominent feature of most late-century affairs, the list of distinguished guests, organizers, and orators, at least, had retained its brilliance. At a celebration held indoors at Association Hall on January 2, 1889, William Still, representing the Pennsylvania Society for Promoting the Abolition of Slavery, invited an impressive slate of speakers, including Frederick Douglass, Booker T. Washington, Samuel Chapman Armstrong, Frances E. W. Harper, George Washington Cable, Robert Purvis, and several other black and white luminaries. Cable, a southern white novelist sympathetic to African Americans' plight, declined the invitation, despite his confidence that "the interests of the nation at large will be benefitted" by "the utterances of the important gathering." The not-yet-famous Wizard of Tuskegee also found it "painful and disappointing" that he could not attend due to his wife's ill health. But Washington's enthusiasm for such affairs was clear. "I agree with you," he wrote to Still, "that the occasion is one that should not pass unnoticed and it furnishes food for thought. You deserve gratitude for providing such a celebration." The remaining guests apparently did attend, Armstrong noting his gratitude for having been "counted worthy to appear in it . . . in the presence of an orator like Frederick Douglass." The race's old man eloquent himself (who like Armstrong had received a remittance for his travel expenses, but apparently no other compensation) found the event "a most useful demonstration." Significantly, Douglass considered the celebration useful to a wider audience than merely those in attendance. As Cable had suggested it might, the gathering drew notice from blacks and whites in distant and more racially oppressive sections of the country. Douglass observed with satisfaction that "that which was said on that occasion has attracted a large degree of attention even in the South. I wish it were possible," he mused, "to have such meetings in our large cities oftener."[2]

As Douglass intimated, many large cities, even those with long and distinguished histories of black activism and commemoration, held emancipation celebrations only irregularly. In 1889 New York editor T. Thomas Fortune noted that it had "not been customary to celebrate Emancipation

Day in this city. There has never been a sympathetic public opinion to inspire and sustain it." Fortune attributed this lack of commemorative zeal not to the accelerating deterioration of black rights, but rather to the desire of many African Americans to distance themselves from the slave past. Consistent with Theophilus G. Steward's 1876 observations regarding blacks' ambivalence toward the memory of slavery, Fortune contended that "[a] great many of our people are decidedly opposed to celebrating any event in their history which refers to their former condition of servitude, or anything which recalls that period of woe and debasement. These people would like to forget that the race was ever held in bondage."

The tension between selective memory and selective amnesia regarding the slave past was persistent. Fortune saw many others interpreting slavery as "a Divine method of chastisement," the deliverance from which "should be kept alive not only as a grateful remembrance, but as a lesson which should serve as a reminder when temptations to transgressions are strong upon us." This was only one of the lessons blacks derived from slavery and emancipation during the late nineteenth century. Many African Americans emphasized different messages for different audiences. Whatever the lessons held by the past, and however high a value Fortune himself placed on the definition and transmission of black history and heritage, the editor had to admit that by the late 1880s "our people are not at all agreed upon the wisdom and propriety of celebrating their emancipation from the slave condition. It is only here and there in widely separated sections, that the sentiment is strong enough to make such celebrations a success."[3] All across the nation other communities, large and small, did host freedom festivals, though not always on January 1 and not always in commemoration of emancipation. Black New Yorkers held occasional celebrations of the Fifteenth Amendment during the 1880s, perhaps because enfranchisement was an event slightly removed from the negative associations of bondage.[4] But, as Fortune observed, most communities did not maintain vibrant and consistent commemorative traditions during this period.

Where celebrations were held, black organizers consistently intended their messages for a biracial audience, even though most public commemorations of emancipation, like other black endeavors, generally took place with less white cooperation and participation in the years after the 1870s. The decline in interest among white government officials is particularly striking. Southern emancipation celebrations during and immediately following the Civil War were often orchestrated by white military and political leaders who attempted to impose their own notions of acceptable public commemoration on freedpeople who had not been steeped in antebellum popular festive political culture. The southern black masses had their own ways of celebrating freedom that often conflicted with those both of white officials and of middle-class, northern blacks who came south. Members of both groups were often disdainful of the folk culture of slavery and felt a paternalist need to control the public expressions of the freedpeople. Especially in areas with a prominent governmental presence—New Orleans, Richmond, the Sea Islands, and Washington, D.C., for example—local blacks' control over the celebrations was limited during the early Reconstruction years. The platform and program at an 1867 celebration at Arlington Heights, Virginia, was dominated by about a dozen white Republican congressmen, Freedmen's Bureau officials, and clergymen. The condescending correspondent for the *Washington Independent* reflected many whites' attitudes toward the former slaves. Mrs. Mary C. Ames reported that the chapel was filled with hundreds of freedpeople, from tiny infants to "the old 'uncle' and 'aunty' of the plantation," whose "dusky faces" were "full of child-like enthusiasm, and unquestioning faith." The only black involvement mentioned as being on the program was the recitation of scripture by "several little colored boys and girls, with neat dresses and bright faces." Even the feast, at which some of the tables were attended to by "young colored women from Washington," appears to have been arranged under the supervision of the white Washington, D.C., postmaster. Mrs. Ames suggested that she attended primarily for the entertainment of "hear[ing] the freed-people sing and talk, and see[ing] them eat their goodies." One must wonder about the deeper feelings of an "old uncle" who may have been telling his interviewer merely what she wanted to hear regarding his view of the festival: "A purty day, Mis', a purty day! We's havin' a very good time."[5]

Whites' political abandonment of African Americans over the decades that followed is reflected in an 1891 celebration at nearby Alexandria, Virginia, regarding which there is no evidence that any white officials or reporters were present at all, despite dozens of invitations having been sent. The "colored citizens" of Alexandria were said to have "turned out en masse" for the event, and Lannon's Opera House was overflowing, with "both floors groaning under the weight of the assemblage." But no whites were reported to have been in the house. The committee received nearly thirty letters of regret from white Republican politicians. One was in fact a long and apparently sincere letter from former Lincoln cabinet member Hugh McCulloch, which was read at the celebration. The rest were polite, yet perfunctory, notes indicating that "other engagements" would occupy the writers on January 1. In an attempt to put the most positive spin on this inattention, the orator of the day, James M. Townsend, the black recorder at the U.S. Land Office, suggested that the mere fact that the invitations had been answered represented a great stride for the race. "There was a time when your communications would have been regarded as insults, or found their way to the wastebasket unanswered." The celebration organizers, he declared, should be proud that the "great men of this great Republic" deigned to "stop the wheels of government to write you . . . to give expressions of their good will, and regrets that they cannot be present." Townsend may well have been aware of the bitter irony in his assertion that "these letters of regret, which I hold in my hand speak volumes."[6]

Indeed they did. As black rights receded from the national parties' political agendas and racial proscriptions stiffened, those letters illustrated the extent to which African Americans' use of public space had become increasingly circumscribed. Some festivals still were attended by local white officials and residents, but black celebrations by century's end were increasingly confined to a racially segmented public sphere. While their messages to the broader society were not completely eliminated, celebration organizers began to focus their attention more pointedly on conditions within the black community. And those conditions were steadily deteriorating during the late nineteenth century, most disconcertingly in the South. One black clergyman, in his 1892 Emancipation Day address at Raleigh, North Carolina, asserted that the "lessons of the hour" required both blacks and whites to "adjust ourselves . . . to changing times and conditions." Joshua A. Brockett promised that blacks would continue to provide "the brawn of black hands and the loyalty of true hearts" and would protect "the virtue of [white] wives and daughters." But he also demanded that whites "keep your hands off of ours [black wives and daughters]" and to "utterly destroy the . . . incubus of lynch law."[7] The increasing prevalence of lynching represented the most horrific aspects of the antiblack animus of the period. Prominent southern black newspapers like the *Huntsville Gazette* and the *Richmond Planet* regularly railed against the practices of "Judge Lynch" after the early 1880s, and the latter paper periodically printed "Lynch Lists" documenting names, dates, and the alleged offenses of recent victims of the "reign of lawlessness." Lynching also exemplifies the reasons that southern blacks took particular care in monitoring their public behavior. Violence always lurked just beneath the surface of the white supremacist culture of the New South.[8]

Given this context, public Freedom Day commemorations persisted in the South to a greater extent than one might expect. Despite rapidly declining opportunity and escalating racial violence, many black southerners did continue to commemorate occasions that held aloft those unfulfilled promises made in the heady days immediately following the war. They were, however, usually extremely careful not to alienate or offend white southerners. Preparing for a celebration in April 1866, Richmond blacks felt it necessary to "respectfully inform the public that THEY DO NOT INTEND to celebrate the failure of the Confederacy" but merely to give thanks to God for their own liberation. The Reverend Emanuel K. Love, speaking at a large Savannah, Georgia, celebration in 1888, expressed his pride in his race and called for black unity, self-help, and race uplift. Love was no weak-kneed accommodationist. In other addresses he had pointed to the greatness of ancient Africa and predicted that blacks would again rise to a position superior to whites. He remained a staunch Republican and was critical of white Americans' indifference "to the murdering, lynching, injustices, outrages and countless atrocious crimes" committed daily against blacks. But Love also emphasized that blacks should remain in the South and have the "good sense to cultivate the confidence and friendship of those who live nearest us . . . [and] can do us the most good if they would and most harm if they try." He was also critical of Frederick Douglass for marrying a white woman. The "dreadful sin of Amalgamation," he argued, "is damaging alike to both races. While we should be friendly as common citizens of a common country, socially, we ought to be as distinct as a race as the turkey and the chicken."[9]

Love's position had more to do with race pride than with Washingtonian accommodation to white dominance, but many parts of his address encouraged the kind of thinking southern whites appreciated in southern blacks. Others went much further toward appeasing whites. Prominent educator Daniel Barclay Williams, dean of the Collegiate Department at the Virginia Normal school in Petersburg, was the orator of the day at a celebration near Roanoke, Virginia, in 1893. His address "was permeated with the sentiment that the white men of the south are the colored people's friends." He urged his two thousand black auditors to "keep out of mischief" and appreciate that "the white men of Virginia had done much for the colored people." Counseling patience, he predicted that whites' "good sense and general good feeling" would lead them "to give us greater opportunities and larger privileges as the mass of the race evinces a greater capacity for citizenship." Similarly urging patience in 1903 was Robert H. Terrell, who the year before had been placed by black power broker Booker T. Washington as the first black judge in the District of Columbia. In looking at the race's history, Terrell chose not to honor Africa's heritage, asserting instead that "the ancestors of American Negroes were savages, inhabiting a vast continent dark with the shadow of an unrecorded past." Utilizing the Washingtonian model of slavery as a school for uplift, Terrell asserted that through "contact with a great civilization" blacks had "learned to work" and "acquired the language and adopted the religion of a great people." Continued study in "the training so eloquently advocated by Booker T. Washington" would prepare them as cooks, chambermaids, waiters, and other positions suitable to those with "the veriest rudiments of education." To his credit, Terrell spoke strongly against lynching and mentioned blacks' contributions to the country, but he was silent on the issues of citizenship, political rights, and social equality.[10]

Perhaps the most telling example of southern blacks' cautious public insistence that racial harmony prevailed in the New South came in North Carolina in January 1898. Later that year the city of Wilmington would see one of the worst race riots of the era, which would result in a dozen or more black deaths and force at least another thousand to flee the city. But at a Raleigh celebration on January 1 the emphasis was on racial cooperation. To be sure, North Carolina's "fusion" government during the 1890s engendered a remarkable degree of black political participation and officeholding. In fact, the Wilmington slaughter was perpetrated at least in part to curtail blacks' political influence and reestablish white-only rule in the state.[11]

On January 1, at what was said to be the largest and most dignified Emancipation Day Raleigh had ever seen, the "fine assemblage" at Metropolitan Hall included numerous white political leaders, along with "quite a number of white ladies and gentlemen" in the audience. North Carolina's unique biracial Fusion Party composed of black and white Republicans and Populists allowed a degree of official public interaction that would have been unlikely elsewhere. The governor, secretary of state, superintendent of the penitentiary, register of deeds, and several other white officials joined the various black celebration organizers and officers of the day on the stage. Surely well aware of the growing white hostility toward black involvement in the biracial government, the Committee on Resolutions attempted to reassure antifusionist Democrats with some of their more obsequious declarations. "Our rejoicing today," one asserted, "carries with it no spirit of hate. We have none other than the kindest feelings for the race that once held us as slaves." "We love North Carolina," proclaimed another. "We desire to cultivate the friendship of our white fellow citizens and live in peace" and would "seek no encroachments upon the sacred precincts of their social lives." Addressing the political issue, they admitted to blacks' "limitations and weaknesses" and acknowledged "the superior governing power of our white fellow citizens as a race." "We seek not to dominate the government of the State."[12]

The rest of the proceedings, including the oration by black recorder of deeds Henry P. Cheatham, followed a similar conciliatory tack. Cheatham encouraged "industry, economy, integrity and knowledge" among the blacks so they could aspire to "the same high intellectual and moral qualifications which these white fellow citizens have displayed in building and steering the ship of our good old State." A celebration at the nearby town of Louisburg carried similar messages about the two races "working together harmoniously" and emphasizing whites' clear superiority. The speaker of the day commented on "the past and present of the negro" and the race's progress since emancipation, but also "pointed out the immoral tendencies of the race" and cautioned that industry was necessary if they were to keep "their liberties." Other speakers offered similarly "wholesome advice," and the program continued with a band that "discoursed popular music." "Dixie," we are told, "was played with a will." Such conciliation would not forestall that autumn's tragedy at Wilmington and the return of white rule in North Carolina.[13]

The disruption of the superficial racial calm in North Carolina was in keeping with white Americans' refusal to recognize blacks as legitimate members of the national family. Not surprisingly, then, the relationship between African Americans and July Fourth remained problematic, especially below the Mason-Dixon line. As late as 1883, one southern black paper deemed it a "novel" development for whites in Jackson, Mississippi, to celebrate Independence Day. The editor ruefully added that "[t]he [white] South seems determined to take care of the 4th this year." Gradually, southern whites did reclaim July Fourth as their own holiday and at times used force to exclude blacks. During the 1870s whites murdered African Americans attempting to celebrate the Fourth in Mississippi and South Carolina. In some southern communities it appears that neither whites nor blacks were quite sure whose celebration it was during this transitional period, and the day went unobserved. This was the case in Huntsville, Alabama, in 1885. "Time was," a local black editor recalled, "when grand barbecues, processions and orations would be filling the air at this time, set to martial music." That year there was "no further observance in Huntsville" beyond the closing of the post office, banks, and government offices. Many black leaders clung firmly to the idea that if African Americans were to continue to assert their fundamental Americanness and their citizenship rights, they needed to maintain their right to participate in national rituals. Many emphasized the role of Crispus Attucks, asserting that "Negro blood was the first shed for American Independence. Why then should he not celebrate the Fourth?" Nonetheless, sometimes because of their fears of white violence, sometimes out of utter disgust, some blacks abandoned a day that seemed to be primarily of interest to whites. Noting that whites and blacks held separate observances in one Alabama community, a black commentator said he could not see "why the black man should rejoice over the 4th. . . . It certainly brought no light to him."[14]

By the end of the century, then, Emancipation Day was considered by many, white and black, to be "the Negro's Fourth of July," indicating that blacks had no more success in claiming the national ritual than they did before black citizenship and enfranchisement were ostensibly guaranteed by the Fourteenth and Fifteenth Amendments. In the South, emancipation was celebrated on September 22 in Tennessee and some parts of Virginia. Texas blacks observed Juneteenth. African Americans in the District of Columbia maintained their April 16 tradition. April 9 Surrender Day observances survived at least into the 1890s among "the colored people especially of Mecklenburg and neighboring counties of Virginia." Black Richmonders continued to commemorate September 22, April 3, and the first of January.[15] Despite the persistence of these regional traditions celebrating emancipation on a variety of dates, it was the January 1 anniversary of Lincoln's proclamation that continued to capture the commemorative attention of blacks throughout most of the South. Blacks in numerous Virginia communities maintained January 1 Freedom Day traditions that thrived at least through the 1880s. Norfolk festivals received considerable attention in the national black press, but consistent with many African Americans' widespread indifference toward history and tradition, it was observed that not all the city's black residents "know what such a day means and why it is celebrated. . . . Hundreds and hundreds of our race," one correspondent reported from Norfolk in 1886, "who should with keen remembrance cherish the importance of such anniversaries, walked on the sidewalk and looked on [during the Emancipation Day parade] in the most absent manner."[16]

That indifference may have been preferable in the eyes of some black leaders compared to celebrations at Hampton, which brought out the whole community and often involved far more drinking, firing of guns, injuries, and general rowdiness than Hampton's black elite deemed acceptable. One reason for elite concerns about the celebrants' behavior is suggested by the patronizing reportage of an 1886 celebration. The procession included several school bands, the Oystermen's Association, resplendent in their "glorious effulgence of red shirts" and carrying a silken banner, and a group of older black men wearing blue scarves and representing the Sons of Abraham. A "ragged crowd" of "pickaninnies" harassed the line of march, and a "motley company" of black social groups "marching in all the pride and circumstance they can muster" were said to have been "too happy with the misguided happiness that comes from imbibing ardent spirits." The (apparently white) reporter purported to understand that this "amusing" scene was rooted in "the childlike enjoyment that [blacks] take in little things." He assumed that "thoughtful persons" would realize that the "inextricable confusion" suffusing the "common folks" and their "poor little parade" must be all that could be expected from the freedpeople for many years. This was not the public image black leaders wanted to convey.[17]

Around the turn of the century, at the northern end of the Chesapeake Bay, Baltimore blacks hosted numerous public January 1 commemorations, and the remote community of Cumberland, Maryland, in 1902, held what was apparently its first ever freedom festival on that date. Like their counterparts elsewhere, Cumberland blacks celebrated in order "to observe the anniversary of our liberation and to impress its lessons upon the rising generation."[18] Other outlying towns around the state, including Frederick, Hagerstown, and Easton, chose to impart the lessons of emancipation at freedom festivals held in August. It is not clear why and when Marylanders abandoned the commemoration of the state's November 4, 1864, abolition of slavery. Nor is it obvious why August celebrations became the norm in some communities. National newspaper accounts of August 1 celebrations around the country, or perhaps the presence of individuals who had grown up with the August 1 tradition, might explain the late summer gatherings. But since events were held even at the end of the month it seems that the general convenience of the season may have been as important as any other factor. In any case, these celebrations across Maryland were often quite impressive, as in Frederick in 1901, where some five thousand celebrants converged in what was said to have been the largest commemoration in many years.[19] The regional crowds drawn to such celebrations were aided, as they had been throughout much of the nation during the second half of the nineteenth century, by special excursion rates offered by rail lines.[20]

For example, in 1897 an estimated six hundred Washingtonians took advantage of the reduced fare as they accompanied the orator of the day, *Bee* editor W. Calvin Chase, to Frederick for an event. The Washington contingent added to an August 12 Freedom Day throng that equaled the 1901 affair's five thousand. As at many celebrations, the orations and the behavior of the masses at the event were often at the forefront of commentators' considerations. This was evident in the comments of Revel H. Fooks, chairman of Baltimore's Colored Citizens Executive Committee. At a time when African American activists in the Monument City were tireless in combating the onslaught of antiblack legislation and practices, Fooks encouraged Chase to use his address to advertise the "deplorable" conditions among Maryland blacks and to "advise the masses" as to the best means to improve their lot.

Since Frederick's Freedom Day event was expected to "attract considerable attention from the press," Fooks must have been pleased by the "respectable and well behaved" crowd of five thousand. He may have been a bit puzzled and perturbed, however, by Chase's admonitory address, which

blasted blacks for public behavior that presented to whites "a shifting, vac-
illating character in the body politic," thereby contributing to their own
lowly conditions. The *Bee*'s acrimonious editor alternately criticized "cow-
ardly leadership" and "stupidity" among the masses, asserting that "the negro since his emancipation has been doing little but organizing secret societies to enable him to put on a red, white and blue uniform. . . . He appears
happier behind a tooting of horns and the beating of drums than he is in
the school house, or at home teaching his sons to become citizens in the
broadest and most acceptable sense." On a more positive note, Chase emphasized the need for national organization and unity of action to ensure
the race's "power in advancing the cause of humanity and the dignity of
American civilization."[21]

Chase's typically feisty oration also addressed questions about the purpose
and propriety of freedom festivals themselves. His comments about the attraction of gaudy uniforms and parading bands cut to the heart of a bitter
enmity over public celebration in which blacks around the nation's capital
and across the nation had been embroiled since the first freedom festivals
nearly a century before. Much of the current debate, as Chase made clear,
revolved around the relative tangible benefits produced by raucous public
displays as opposed to more sober and practical enterprises that encouraged
education, self-improvement, hard work, and mutual assistance. But just as
important to Chase and others was the public face that blacks presented to
whites—"[t]he picture . . . that the white man carries in his brain." "Do not
our celebrations appear ridiculous," he chided, "to the eyes of those in whose
hands the Republic is entrusted?" Not that the curmudgeonly editor was
entirely hostile toward the commemoration of African American freedom.
"Don't understand me to be opposed to Emancipation Day Celebrations,"
he hedged. But Chase clearly had his own ideas regarding the proper form
and function of such observances (see chap. 6). In his August 12 oration
Chase also took a stand on the proper date for Freedom Day commemorations. Harkening to his theme of race unity, he claimed to "oppose the
different dates observed by different sections of the country" in the observance of emancipation. After joining the chorus rejecting July Fourth as
exclusively "the day for the white man," Chase asserted that "there is but
one day for the negro and that is the first day of January, for it was on that
day that President Lincoln declared freedom to all slaves."[22]

This unequivocal statement seems odd coming from a man who participated in Freedom Day commemorations on numerous dates other than
January 1. Keep in mind that the speech itself was delivered in mid-August.
And the plethora of emancipatory dates was not based simply on regional
idiosyncrasies. Even in and around Chase's own home turf several dates

attracted residents' commemorative zeal. Various January and August dates in Maryland, the April 9 Surrender Day in southern Virginia, the April 16 observances of District emancipation, and occasional September 22 celebrations in Richmond, Hamilton, and Alexandria, Virginia, all drew sizable crowds, as did January 1 affairs in the latter city. Similarly, during a September festival at Richmond in 1890, in another odd twist that spoke to the ongoing debate over the proper date to commemorate, the convention officially designated January 1 as "the most fitting for the celebration to be observed in the future."[23]

The plethora of dates created some confusion and generated some debate in the black press regarding which date was most appropriate. Black Texans who relocated sometimes tried to introduce their Juneteenth tradition in new locales. While this enthusiasm for expansion began to see some results during the last decades of the twentieth century, it had little impact during the nineteenth. One transplanted Texan found himself the target of gentle gibes as he attempted to implant the Juneteenth tradition in northern Alabama and Tennessee. "Uncle Billy Williams" was said, in 1881, to have been quite upset "over the indifference with which his resolution setting aside the 19th of June as an Anniversary of Emancipation, is observed." After the date passed it was reported that "the 19th of June is tided over and the world still moves." Despite this lack of general support, other Texans in the area did continue on their own to "duly celebrate the . . . 19th day of June as Emancipation Day" at least into the mid-1880s. Blacks in Texas, of course, celebrated enthusiastically, not only with toasts and orations but also with parades, baseball games, military drills, music, dancing, feasting, croquet, tennis, boat rides, and the whole gamut of amusements typical of most warm-weather freedom festivals. In Galveston, in 1883, prisoners were released from the city jail to celebrate the day. The tradition did spread outside the Lone Star state to some degree. In an anomaly that raises interesting questions about the diffusion of traditions, blacks in the small town of Covert, Michigan, departed from the August 1 tradition that generally prevailed in the area and began to hold regular Juneteenth celebrations during the 1870s. More typically, Juneteenth's expansion remained within the Southwest, so that Tucson, Arizona, and the Oklahoma of Ralph Ellison's youth were holding Juneteenth celebrations by the early twentieth century.[24]

At times the attempt to institute a Freedom Day tradition in a particular locality failed miserably. Tradition-conscious blacks in northeastern Pennsylvania made an effort during the 1880s to conduct the annual commemoration of the Fifteenth Amendment each June 18. Whether this date has some connection with the Texans' June 19 or if it has any relevant provenance at all is unclear. In any case, the 1884 affair was said to be "a grand success," highlights including an elaborate procession, music, and an address by the noted African American orator and activist William Howard Day. A reception and a grand ball attended by "about one hundred couples" carried the celebration to the next morning. Though most of the listed participants hailed from the immediate vicinity, both Day and the Steelton Cornet Band traveled from the Harrisburg area, a hundred miles to the southwest. The event was a joint effort by blacks in Scranton, Wilkes-Barre, Pittston, and other adjacent communities, and though Wilkes-Barre served as host, the celebration's expenses could not have been paid without help from the neighboring towns. In fact, the reporting correspondent, probably B. F. Towns of nearby Plains, obviously felt that the hosts' enthusiasm was sorely lacking. "The indifference manifested by many of the colored people of this city," he scolded, "is reprehensible."[25]

The following year seems to have seen the last attempt to instill this tradition among apparently reluctant celebrants. The schedule of events mirrored the 1884 arrangement, this time featuring an oration by the former Mississippi congressman John R. Lynch. The presence of this national figure and gifted speaker (whose address was deemed excellent, despite being marred by "the smack of political partisanship") should have drawn quite a crowd. And indeed white Scrantonians "warmly greeted" the parade "with elaborate decorations . . . and the waving of handkerchiefs by ladies, gentlemen and children." But the turnout among blacks, it seems, was disappointing. In particular, "[t]he procession was not as large as it should have been. There might have been double the number in line, were it not for the lack of patriotism on the part of the colored people of Wilkes-Barre." Though the Scranton hosts were praised for their efforts and the whole affair was again described as "a grand success," the correspondent's report a month later told a truer tale. Despite cajoling that echoed numerous other efforts to call attention to history and heritage projects during this period, the movement to "organize a club for the purpose of celebrating the passage of the Fifteenth Amendment" in the area was doomed to failure. The initial idea may have been a response to the Supreme Court's 1883 overturning of the 1875 Civil Rights Act, a decision that symbolized the Republican Party's, and the nation's, abandonment of black rights. Perhaps that blatant rejection by the highest judicial body was also part of the reason for Wilkes-Barre blacks' lack of enthusiasm. Why waste time and resources on the commemoration of a meaningless suffrage and a citizenship that existed in name only? Still, the frustrated activist who reported on these events was scathing as he blamed blacks themselves for their failure to appreciate the underlying meaning of their own freedom: "The colored man who lacks the patriotism to commemorate the event that clothed him with the inestimable boon of American citizenship is totally unfit for liberty, and the indifference manifested by the people of this community both this year and last, is a disgrace."[26]

The cessation of Fifteenth Amendment celebrations around the nation was virtually complete by the 1890s. But other dates continued to compete for African Americans' commemorative attention into the twentieth century. In parts of the Upper South and especially the Midwest, the September 22 date of Lincoln's preliminary Emancipation Proclamation remained an occasional inducement for commemoration. In Memphis in 1889 both black and white residents were said to have "caught the spirit of the occasion" during a celebration organized by a local black newspaper, the *Negro World*. "It was a glorious and proud day for the Negro," and the celebration was apparently "worth a great deal to the colored people of this section." Stressing the inclusive nature of the proceedings and imparting a broad meaning to such commemorations, the reporter (probably the orator of the day, T. Thomas Fortune) noted that the event "has been worth quite as much to the white people. There have been mutual lessons learned which we hope shall help us solve the great problem." Fortune left the nature of the lessons undefined. That the "great problem" did not have to be named only emphasized how urgent was the perceived need to revive dwindling white support during this disheartening time for black Americans.[27]

In addition to numerous September 22 affairs in Illinois and Indiana, the date also was celebrated, if more sporadically, in Virginia, West Virginia, Missouri, Pennsylvania, and Ohio. West Virginia provided the setting for two such celebrations in 1883 and 1891, events that each featured an oration by Blanche K. Bruce and that drew participants from the adjoining states of Pennsylvania and Ohio. The earlier affair attracted well over a thousand and the latter was expected to draw thirty thousand. Actual attendance figures are not available, but it seems highly unlikely that anywhere near that number took part.[28] Cleveland celebrated the autumn date in 1904 with a parade featuring various black fraternal organizations, a band, a GAR post, numerous carriages, and a platoon of the city's police force. Later the celebrants moved indoors to enjoy "an extended program of songs and instrumental music and patriotic speeches" at the Forest Street Armory Hall. Washington, D.C., Recorder of Deeds John C. Dancy's oration "was largely confined to a review of the history of slavery in the United States," though he also used the opportunity to recount the progress of the race since emancipation. It was becoming a common practice in Freedom Day addresses and in other public statements by black writers and orators to catalog race accomplishments, as did the *Baltimore Race Standard* newspaper in its January 2 "Emancipation Edition" of 1897. Among other items, half an editorial page column was devoted to brief notations of black accomplishments: 100 pharmacists, 150 dentists, 700 physicians, 600 lawyers, an aggregate wealth of more than \$300 million, more than 200 patents, numerous newspapers and publications, and so on. Dancy, in his 1904 address, similarly listed the number of professional people and college graduates the race had produced and made the particular point "that the negro race to-day is producing more of the national wealth than any other class."[29]

The tendency, hinted at by John Dancy, not only to call attention to race accomplishments but also to compare them favorably with other "classes" of Americans escalated around the turn of the century and was particularly intended as a lesson to white Americans. Blacks used a variety of media to contrast African Americans' accomplishments and loyalties with those of the millions of immigrants then pouring into the nation. Though Dancy's presentation understated that comparison, focusing more positively on blacks' accomplishments, others were far more explicit and judgmental vis-à-vis the newcomers. Blacks' anti-immigrant tirades had begun to appear decades earlier. In 1874, as part of his agitation to erect the Richard Allen monument at the Centennial Exposition, *Christian Recorder* editor Benjamin Tanner compared blacks' Americanness and patriotism with that of immigrant Catholics, who were planning to erect a commemorative fountain. "As a people," he spat, "we are surely to be credited with as much patriotism . . . as the alien Romanists, who are not and cannot be truly American."[30] Black nativism grew stronger as southern and eastern European immigration expanded, and job competition stiffened, during the difficult economic conditions of the 1890s. These sentiments were never more ardently expressed than in the months following the 1901 assassination of President William McKinley by Leon Czolgosz, an avowed anarchist and the son of Hungarian immigrants. That tragic incident at the Pan American Exposition in Buffalo, New York, was all the more telling because the man who, according to some accounts, accosted and disarmed the attacker, preventing him from firing a third shot at the president, was James "Big Jim" Parker, a black man. This juxtapositioning was exploited by various black newspapers and in a stinging September 21 Emancipation Day address delivered in Hamilton, Virginia, by *Bee* editor W. Calvin Chase. Conjuring up images both of antebellum slaves' loyalty to their masters and free blacks' contributions as citizens and workers, Chase pointed out that the nation had reached a sad state when "the anarchist has more rights than the black man."[31]

The long-standing tradition of using the Freedom Day platform to demand justice, and otherwise to provide whites with blacks' perspectives on social and political issues of the day, was less perilous in the North and West than in the South, and agitation continued to be an important function of the festivals in those regions. But the dates were more frequently used to impart a variety of messages to African Americans. The September 22 date in particular, though it had a clear connection with an emancipatory event, also fell shortly before November elections and thus lent itself easily to appropriation for political purposes. In gearing up for the national canvass of 1888, for example, some prominent black Republicans made a tour of midwestern states during September, addressing several celebrations in Indiana on or around the anniversary of the preliminary proclamation. The Indianapolis *Freeman,* a black-run weekly that espoused an "Independent" political posture and urged African Americans to be "a slave to no political party," complained that one event "was not a success" because of "the widespread impression that it was merely a campaign meeting, under the auspices of local Republican managers." Reminiscent of John Lynch's 1885 speech at Scranton, the New York clergyman and hopeful Republican office-seeker William B. Derrick delivered an address that day that was criticized as "simply a partisan effort." A few weeks later Frederick Douglass, described as being "in his dotage," was denounced as an "idolator" who was "fanatic in his political wanderings." His recent Emancipation Day address was condemned as "one of the most partisan Republican speeches that has been delivered here this year." These critiques by *Freeman* editor E. E. Cooper reflected a broadening black dissatisfaction with the Republican Party that intensified as that party consciously distanced itself from African Americans during the 1880s. Beyond his condemnation of some blacks' seemingly blind and illogical fealty to a party that had abandoned them, Cooper expressed outrage that so sacred a day could be coopted by partisan political climbers. Cooper claimed to speak for many African Americans who felt "that celebrations, of a social nature, as grand and National as the emancipation of the slaves, should be kept clear of politics. . . . The emancipation of our race was a red-letter day in its history, and when it is celebrated and held above party lines, it will be what it should be—the Negro's fourth of July."[32] The last phrase in the editor's political critique implicitly reinforced the notion that, though blacks indeed deserved all the rights of citizens, they remained for the most part outside of national commemorations and retained the need to observe their own separate celebrations.

In the 1880s the enthusiasm for maintaining a distinctive commemorative tradition was still strong, despite occasional confusion over which date to celebrate, widespread indifference to commemoration, and the disturbing ambivalence about the past displayed by many blacks. Cooper's ostensible desire to keep blacks' commemorative celebrations separate from their political maneuverings was likewise not shared by all. The criticisms from

Cooper and from the Wilkes-Barre correspondent regarding orators' partisan harangues indicate that the public platform provided at freedom festivals could be used to deliver a wide variety of messages, political and otherwise. Political statements at these events in the 1880s were, in fact, quite common, a tendency that ran counter to what some have identified as blacks' turn away from national political issues toward more locally defined problems after the end of Reconstruction. Furthermore, Republicans were not the sole practitioners of partisan proselytizing. One orator at a Kansas celebration, a supporter of the Prohibition Party, was chastised for his "ranting political speech, which proved only that he has a grievance against the republican party." The growing number of Democratic and Independent black political commentators also made frequent use of Freedom Day platforms to air their views. Perhaps no person of this ilk was more outspoken and well known than T. Thomas Fortune. A prominent exponent of both commemorative activities and the promulgation of historical knowledge in general, Fortune was nationally recognized as one of the most vocal proponents of blacks' abandoning their blind loyalty to the Republican Party. A popular speaker during his heyday in the 1880s and 1890s, Fortune often used Freedom Day events to publicize his advocacy of black political independence.[33]

In central New York, near enough to Fortune's New York City base for him to be an occasional visitor, the antebellum August 1 tradition maintained its role as the region's Freedom Day of choice. One of Fortune's most pointed political statements came at a regional celebration at Owego, on August 5, 1886. Two days earlier, the steadfast black Republican John R. Lynch had delivered one of his predictably partisan speeches to a crowd of eight thousand at an emancipation celebration in nearby Binghamton. Just a year after Grover Cleveland took office with the first Democratic presidential administration since the war, the former Mississippi congressman harshly condemned the recent movement of some black politicos away from the Republican fold. "The Democratic party has been the bitter enemy of the colored race," Lynch reminded his audience. "Colored men would have a reasonable excuse to support that party if it were friendly to the race now. But we all know that it is not. A colored man, therefore, who calls himself a Democrat is devoid of principle, manhood and self-respect."[34]

Though Fortune regarded himself as a political independent and not a Democrat, he may well have perceived himself to be a target of Lynch's epithets. Never one to take an attack on black manhood lightly, Fortune spoke true to his contention that "on an anniversary of this nature it is well to talk plainly to each other." "Occasions like unto this," he argued from his Freedom Day platform in Owego, "should teach us lessons which shall serve to advance us on the scale of honest manhood and good citizenship." The explicit political lesson the editor chose to impart that day was that blacks had for too long "sacrificed our civil rights upon the spurious altar of unreasoning and misguided gratitude for favors received [from the Republican Party]. But we have come into a new manhood, and have learned what our rights are and are learning how to demand them as brave men and as sovereign citizens." Part of that sovereignty, it seemed obvious to Fortune, involved making far better use of their votes, which currently were being blindly cast for Republican "white politicians who profit by your loyalty and treat you with contempt after the election is won." Critical both of black voters and of black Republican leaders, the fiery editor pointed out that "[y]ou are simply a political cipher in the South and a voting machine in the North; and your Douglasses, Lynches, Bruces, Langstons and the rest have no more influence on the politics of the country nor the policies of parties than so many Aunt Dinahs. The million and a half voters they represent have no more potentiality than they have!"[35]

Fortune claimed to be no more sanguine toward the opposing party, though he expressed mild approbation of the appointment of two blacks to "high and important offices" in the Cleveland administration.[36] The young editor noted that he had been as often accused of being a "fire-eating Republican" as a "hireling of Democrats." Just as he had never, in his journalistic career, "spared the Republican party when it has been recreant to its promises to the race . . . it can not be shown that I have ever minced my English in denouncing Democratic opposition to our rights. . . . I have not coined my cheek to gain the cheap favor of the politicians of either party. When the rights of the race have been trampled under foot, I have not paused to see who the offender was; I have simply resented the injury by telling the truth." Fortune claimed to speak for "the younger and more progressive men of the race" as he attempted to define for African Americans a new political identity that placed race unity and loyalty above party considerations: "If you should ask me if I were a Republican, I should answer you, 'No!' If you should ask me if I were a Democrat, I should answer you, 'No!' If you should ask me, 'what are you, anyhow?' I should tell you that I am a Negrowump! A Negrowump! And I say to you, as I have said in my paper for five years, 'If this be treason, make the most of it.' "[37]

Fortune's stormy address illustrates the variety of roles played by Freedom Day celebrations. In addition to providing a platform for political sparring and civil rights agitation, the celebrations continued to be recognized as indispensable vehicles for the definition and dissemination of a distinctive African American sense of history and tradition. As was typical for celebrations in central New York State, the small town of Owego was filled that day with "well-dressed colored people, representing nearly every town in Southern, Central and Western New York and Northern Pennsylvania."[38] In addressing this primarily black assembly, Fortune interspersed his activist, political commentary with an equally clear message regarding the importance of maintaining a vibrant commemorative tradition. Early on he made clear the broader purpose of the event:

> We meet here today to attest to our fellow-citizens of all races and nationalities that, while we revel in the glories of the promised land, whereunto we were led by the anti-slavery hosts, we are not yet unmindful that for thrice forty years we wandered in a howling wilderness of unutterable darkness and desolation. We meet here today to keep fresh in our minds and the minds of our children the wrongs which have been righted, and to insist upon the full concession of all rights still denied us as coequal members of the State or Federal Government. In returning in this manner thanks to the God of nations for the measure of right and justice conceded to us . . . we do but exercise that magnificent prerogative which our forefathers wrested from the avarice and cunning of British tyrants more than a hundred years ago. Fellow-citizens, we do wisely to assemble ourselves in this manner once a year. We do wisely to thus come together that we may review the past and the present and to philosophize upon the future. We do wisely to thus meet in vast concourse that we may rejoice in the conscious might of numerical strength and to renew those tender sympathies of race which pulsate in the hearts of all who feel a pride in the ethnological divisions into which God has divided the children of Adam. Therefore, fellow citizens, if the periodical commemoration of the emancipation of the race shall serve the purposes here indicated, we do well to perpetuate it.[39]

In this introductory passage the young editor touched on many of the central functions that organizers intended for nineteenth-century freedom festivals. In reviewing past struggles and victories, celebrants reminded themselves—and, more importantly in the 1880s, their children who had not experienced those struggles—just how far they had come and what efforts were required for further advancement. Neither the howling wilderness of slavery nor the sacrifices of white and black abolitionists were ever to be forgotten. They reminded themselves of the role of Providence in delivering a chosen people from bondage as part of a divine plan whose ultimate end was universal liberty and justice. By meeting together in a large public gathering, they maintained regional communication networks and fortified their symbolic connections with blacks in more distant places, reminding themselves in the process of their numerical strength. Finally, they nurtured a pride of race that distinguished them from their fellow citizens without denying that ineradicable Americanness that their forefathers had claimed over the course of American history through their contributions to the creation and perpetuation of the nation.[40]

Three years later Fortune reiterated many of these sentiments in an editorial in his New York *Age*. But first he chose to emphasize the importance of emancipation for the nation as a whole. "No event in American history," he claimed, "is more significant than the emancipation of the slaves of the Republic. It is an event which the whole people should unite to commemorate." Well aware of the steady withdrawal of white participation in Freedom Day commemorations, Fortune attempted to rekindle biracial cooperation by calling attention to emancipation's meaning for all working people. As elements within the Knights of Labor and the Farmers' Alliances, as well as other individuals during this period, tried to activate the potential power of a biracial working-class movement, Fortune argued that whites as well as blacks could and should find meaning in the commemoration of emancipation. In freeing the slaves, he argued, the nation had also "liberated and enobled American labor, which slavery had shackled and degraded. If for no other reason it is an event in American history worthy of commemoration by all the people." Though the various attempts at working-class cooperation across race lines were to collapse during the 1890s, Fortune's 1889 statement indicates his desire to impart his historical interpretation to both blacks and whites, and to expand the meaning of freedom festivals to embrace broader issues and serve additional functions beyond the black community.[41]

But the editor remained well aware that the event's significance for African Americans was unique. Even though blacks' citizenship rights were being whittled away, Fortune claimed, perhaps more hopefully than accurately, "that the observance of August 1 is becoming more and more popular among the colored citizens." But, he argued, "[t]here should be a uniformity in the celebration that has not heretofore been true." Weighing into a discourse that engaged historically conscious blacks across the nation, Fortune proceeded to identify some of the central functions he saw in the proper commemoration of emancipation: "It should be a time of great rejoicing among us. It should be a time when the wisest and best of our men should tell the people the whole truth concerning their condition, moral, religious and political; and when the shortcomings of the government, the persecutions and the designs of the enemy and the duplicity and treachery of friends should be unsparingly exposed and denounced. The light should be turned on." This task was especially crucial as blacks entered the nadir of the 1890s. Much as he did in Owego in 1886, Fortune stressed the importance of "race pride and mutual dependence," the need to "return thanks to the God of nations for delivering them from bondage," and the justice in "pay[ing] homage and reverence to the memory of the great, good and wise men He used to accomplish the work." But this last point—expressing gratitude for benefits received—declined in importance for Fortune and many others of his generation as blacks had less and less in the way of political and civil rights for which to be thankful. Above all Fortune urged blacks to continue with their annual celebrations primarily for the sake of the race. "Let the colored citizens of the Republic celebrate August 1 with a will," he implored. "It will do them good."[42]

Fortune's sentiments regarding the need for commemorative traditions were echoed in emancipation celebrations nationwide during the 1880s and 1890s, but few black communities implemented those ideals more consistently than those around the Finger Lakes in central New York State. In the postwar decades blacks in a number of communities, all roughly within a forty-mile radius, consciously took it upon themselves to share the responsibility of perpetuating a Freedom Day tradition that dated back to the antebellum years. Between 1883 and 1891 alone, at least fourteen celebrations were held in twelve different communities in this sphere of interaction, all no more than eighty miles distant from one another, and all fairly accessible to one another by road, rail, or water transportation. An 1889 report from a Corning, New York, celebration pointed out both the tenacity of this vibrant tradition and the regional coordination involved in its perpetuation: "For years the people [of central New York] have been accustomed to celebrate the Emancipation of slaves by Abraham Lincoln. They hold the demonstrations at different places each year and the surrounding towns and villages pour a flood of human being into the locality where the celebration is held. There is always a street parade and public speaking. Douglass, [Blanche K.] Bruce, Lynch, Fortune and [the prominent educator and activist, Joseph C.] Price have been orators in previous years. . . . Trains with reduced rates came [to Corning] from Elmira, Ithaca, Binghampton, Owego, Syracuse, Williamsport [and] Wilkes Barre, Pa., and other towns and villages."[43]

The correspondent, who most likely knew otherwise, gave the false impression that the tradition began after 1863. In fact, West Indian emancipation celebrations in the area date back at least to the 1840s. That longstanding tradition and the continued participation of nationally prominent orators suggest that blacks in the area recognized the importance of freedom festivals as vehicles for political activism and the preservation of historical memory. The well-established practice of social activities—picnics, parades, music, barbecues, dancing, foot races, baseball matches, and so on—also continued to attract hundreds or even thousands to gather at the outdoor groves and parks where the events had been held since antebellum days.[44] The cooperation of rail lines, which regularly offered reduced rates for the events, facilitated even more involvement for a people whose disposable income was limited.

As the Corning report indicates, communities from outside the immediate Finger Lakes sphere also participated in these regional gatherings. The cities of Rochester, New York, and Scranton, Wilkes-Barre, and Williamsport, Pennsylvania, for example—each about fifty miles outside the primary Finger Lakes sphere—hosted their own celebrations and also sent delegations to the Finger Lakes communities. These more-distant towns were part of this vital regional communication network and helped keep the Finger Lakes towns connected with an even broader area through their contacts with centers like New York City, Buffalo, and Philadelphia. These networks were sustained throughout the year primarily by communication and interaction among the various church, fraternal, and other voluntary organizations that thrived in most postbellum black communities. But the celebrations provided important annual gatherings that reinforced those groups' ongoing pursuits of social activism, community uplift, and regional coordination.[45]

Although a few of the Freedom Day events around the Finger Lakes during the 1880s were April commemorations of the Fifteenth Amendment, most were early August observances of emancipation. The importance of that date was emphasized by Cortland, New York, resident Abraham Lincoln DeMond in a letter to Fortune's *Age* in 1888. DeMond was attending the State Normal School at Cortland, which he would soon leave as the institution's first black graduate. He later studied theology at Howard University and went on to enjoy a career as a respected minister in the South. The young DeMond began with the customary injunction that "it is well for any nation or any people" to celebrate "those events which make landmarks in its history." He then outlined a familiar litany of reasons why such days needed to be commemorated: "The proper observance of their annual return will tend to bring together and unite the people, giving them the strength that there is in union. It is upon such days and occasions that the voices of their leaders are heard, eloquently relating the achievements of the past, earnestly discussing the questions of the present and sounding the battle cry of the future." After thus establishing the broad agenda of commemorative events, DeMond turned to the particularities of African Americans and proposed the adoption of a single date for the celebration of the signal event in their history. In the process he shed further light on the intensity of the commemorative spirit and the degree of interaction, across the central New York region in which he lived. "In the history of the Negro race in America," he wrote,

> there have been many names and events worthy of such commemoration. But the greatest of these is the name of Abraham Lincoln and the event of issuing the Emancipation Proclamation. In years past the colored people have not been negligent in yearly celebrating this event, but they have had no fixed day for its general observance. For various reasons, in the Northern States it is not convenient to hold these celebrations upon the first of January, the day upon which the proclamation was issued. In most of these states it has been held on or about the first of August. Would it not be better and unite us more as a people, if there could be a fixed date which from year to year should be known as Emancipation Day—a day which every colored man, throughout the length and breadth of this land might call his day, when our people might leave (for one day) the workshop and the farm, the haunts of business and the marts of trade, and unite in properly celebrating the prominent events in their history in America? A committee, which met in Ithaca, during the recent celebration there, decided upon the first Tuesday in August of each year for holding such celebration throughout central New York. Should not this date be generally adopted?[46]

DeMond's plea for continuing the annual emancipation celebrations and establishing a single date for their observance elicited no response in the *Age* and met with the same fate as other postbellum attempts to create a nationally unified commemorative tradition. Yet his views were shared by many African Americans across the nation, including regions where the celebratory tradition had attenuated by the 1880s. In 1881 Charles Hendley Jr. of Huntsville, Alabama, noted that during the first years after emancipation "the race seemed given over to rejoicing." "Public expression of this joy was given in numberless picnics, grand barbecues and great meetings at which . . . public thanks" were offered to both God and Lincoln. He bemoaned the recent decline in celebrations in his own community, which he attributed largely to blacks being brought "face to face with the stern wants and realities of life." Hendley recognized that the race had made progress in establishing churches and schools, and by accumulating property, but he feared that the "barriers of prejudice" and other "discouragements" were "dampening [blacks'] love and appreciation of liberty." He advocated the embrace of "anything that would stimulate the masses to renewed hope and spirits . . . inspiring their minds with higher ideas . . . firing their hearts with the love of liberty." Nothing, he believed, would be "more appropriate than an annual celebration of the Emancipation of slavery, the day for commemoration being the same throughout the Union." Hendley's missive had little effect, for in 1888 he was still bemoaning the fact that "Emancipation Day, Jan. 1st, was very generally observed in other towns and cities by the colored people. Why is it that Huntsville lags so far behind, taking no notice of the anniversary in any way?"[47]

Similar problems of generating enthusiasm for freedom festivals appeared all over the country by the turn of the century. In Portland, Oregon, in 1907, one community leader complained that there would be "no celebration of the 1st of January; in fact, it seems of late that our organizations have ceased to take advantage of opportunities to appear before the public." The Knights of Pythias was the only organization to take to the streets on a cold and snowy 1899 New Year's Day in Richmond. "None of the others seemed patriotic enough to observe the Emancipation day or no one took steps in that direction." Among the exodusters in Kansas, those blacks who left the South after Reconstruction in search of a new start in the West, commentators noticed in 1891 that "for a long time, the Negro has celebrated [emancipation] in a half hearted manner." The United Sons of Progress, a local voluntary association, "determined to arouse the proper enthusiasm and pride" for that year's August 1 celebration. But there, as elsewhere, the debate over the appropriate date for commemoration contributed to a lack of unity in generating support. Leavenworth resident W. B. Townsend questioned the August 1 date and tried to provoke discussion regarding "the right day." He welcomed debate only from those "who may see fit to do so in an amiable manner, without resorting to abuse or personalities."[48]

So while some blacks lacked enthusiasm for commemorations of emancipation, others might argue vigorously about the appropriate date and other minutiae of the events. Alabama's Charles Hendley did not lobby for one particular date for his proposed national celebration, but he was well aware that the regional fragmentation of Freedom Day traditions had rendered "the date to select . . . a question of propriety." A few localized traditions, like Texas's Juneteenth, Richmond's April 3, and Washington's April 16, resonated deeply for blacks in those areas. But most vocal proponents of a single date for national celebration promoted either August 1 or January 1. August 1 had been entrenched in the customs of the North and West for half a century. Younger residents of those regions simply had never celebrated on any other date, and many older blacks were loath to sever the bonds of memory that infused August 1 with so much personal meaning. AME bishop Benjamin W. Arnett in 1888 still vividly recalled his first August 1 procession, four decades before, from which "the drum and tune of freedom is still beating in my memory."[49]

But August 1 had no relevance for southern blacks, and many in all sections thought it obvious that January 1 was the only logical choice. It was, after all, "the day made memorable by the emancipation proclamation." Some also argued that celebrating freedom on January 1 represented an especially meaningful inversion of the date's former connection with the separation of enslaved families as new work contracts went into effect on New Year's Day. Therefore, it was obvious to many that "January 1 is the date that should be generally observed and intelligent persons admit it." Even so, intelligent people also had to admit that festive outdoor celebrations were simply not possible in the dead of winter in much of the country. On the frosty Great Plains, the Kansas City Emancipation Association, "comprised of all our business and professional men," was charged with arranging "suitable programmes or exercises, for the commemoration of the freedom of the slaves." While they agreed that January 1 was the "proper time, it was decided that owing to the condition of the weather at that season of the year— September 22nd of each year was chosen." The editor of the *Southwest Christian Advocate,* however, contended that "the temperature and state of the weather have nothing to do with the occurrence of national events, and should have no influence in fixing the date of their observance." *Cleveland Gazette* editor Harry C. Smith responded that had the gentleman experienced a few Great Lakes winters "he would not have such set opinions." Smith did concede the logic of the argument and promised to "*think* about January first being the day." But he seemed most concerned with arriving at some resolution to the issue. "Let us settle upon a date." A group of Richmond's black civic leaders called a national convention in 1890 to do just that, but their efforts bore little fruit. After considerable, and often petty, disagreement, January 1 was decided on, but the convention's verdict was unenforceable. Just as many Kansas blacks celebrated August 1 despite the Kansas City Emancipation Association's decree specifying September 22, most Richmonders seemed to prefer their April 3 observances to January 1.[50]

The debate over dates presupposed that there existed a consensus to support *some* commemoration of emancipation. The lack of unanimity on this point is demonstrated by the complete absence of celebrations in some areas and the steady appearance in the press of complaints about blacks' lack of enthusiasm for celebrations where they did take place. A case in point is the large September 22, 1888, celebration in Kansas City, where exercises, amusements, and a "monster parade" were "arranged to suit all classes." Thousands of blacks from around the region turned out, but "many negro businessmen" were censured in the press "for not taking part in such a worthy and magnificent display of negro advancement." The root of the problem was traced by one critic to the seemingly endemic discord and lack of unity within the race. Whenever blacks collectively undertook some great project, lamented the editor of the Kansas City *American Citizen,* "how many want to be head and first one thing then another. If he is not in or consulted about matters he is ready to throw cold water on everything. In the recent Emancipation celebration we learn that because some Negro firms and representative men were not extended invitations on a silver platter they took no part. Now this is wrong."[51] Such bickering and disunity was certainly not a new development among black leaders, nor was it a problem confined only to emancipation celebrations. But these squabbles could destroy any potential for good the celebrations might provide.

Some African Americans argued that the celebrations actually did the race more harm than good. One commentator thought it unconscionable for blacks to get so "worked up over the annual celebration of the Emancipation of the slaves. . . . Money is recklessly spent. Excursions, picnics and balls are the order of the day." While claiming that no one appreciated the meaning of Emancipation Day as much as he, the writer still felt "that this wholesale spending of our summer earnings, when the imperative needs of the race demands strict economy, should be discouraged." It would be far more beneficial to "help the needy of our own race, and it would reflect more to our interest than the hollow mockery of our usual summer pleasure." Indeed, these events could be expensive. One calculation of the expense of a large Washington, D.C., street pageant in 1890 estimated that each of the four thousand men in line paid at least fifty cents to prepare. The "dozens of fine carriages filled with twenty-four-hour rich colored men and women" cost from three to seven dollars each for the day. Expenditures on untold quantities of beer, whiskey, cigars, and other indulgences "pushed the cost of the day's frolic way up into the thousands and flattened the purse of an element of our population who can not afford the yearly and senseless luxury."[52]

But many African Americans weighed the positive aspects of the celebrations favorably against those costs and continued to derive great value and meaning from perpetuating festive public commemorations of emancipation. Many believed, with T. Thomas Fortune and A. L. DeMond, that freedom festivals continued to serve enough important functions for black communities across the nation to warrant their continuance. That sentiment certainly resonated in and around the Finger Lakes, where the meaning of August 1 maintained its hold. The region's attachment with the date of West Indian emancipation was thoroughly reviewed by George A. Johnson of Ithaca, at a celebration in that town on August 6, 1883. Johnson began by recounting the celebrations of New York State emancipation after 1827, which many blacks chose to hold on July 5 in order to avoid white violence on the Fourth and to protest their exclusion from Independence Day celebrations. Johnson explained that "[i]n these little demonstrations they endeavored to show to the world their love of freedom" until, on August 1, 1838, England fully abolished slavery in the British West Indies and invested the former bondsmen with full citizenship rights. At that time African Americans began to commemorate August 1

> for it was [that] national legislative act that lifted from many of our race in bondage, the galling yoke of slavery and at the same time invested them with the full dignities of enfranchised manhood. In 1838 no act of similar import could be found on the statute books of any State in the Union.... Thus for many years we were forced to laud the act of a foreign nation, while America,— the so-called *free* America, still clung to a slavery more damnable in its foul abominations, than any other that ever polluted the face of God's foot-stool! ... These are the reasons why we have a peculiar regard for the 1st of August, and regard it as the birthday of African emancipation on this continent, for, on that day, in 1838—Great Britain—unlike the State of New York, made her slaves enfranchised freemen![53]

In this critical interpretation, Johnson thus placed equal weight on abolition and enfranchisement in his praise for the British act. He also explicitly contrasted Britain's enlightened policy with the horrors of American slavery, reviewing the various acts of government that upheld the institution during the antebellum period and compelled blacks to continue observing West Indian emancipation at celebrations which became, during the 1850s, the foundation for a mature commemorative tradition.[54]

Johnson also made a concerted effort to use the celebration to transmit specific historical memories to his audience. Relying on the authority of his own personal recollections and experiences, Johnson testified, during the remainder of his address, to "the younger portion of this generation," for whom "many of these statements seem [too] monstrous and impossible to have existed, ... but they are only too true." Grounding his point in the physical world surrounding his auditors, Johnson emphasized events "even here in Ithaca during my memory" that would disgust his audience. "In the pulpit of one of the churches still situated in this beautiful park, I heard during my boyhood days sermons delivered sustaining human slavery as a divine institution, and the Bible quoted to justify the sum of all villainies." There were more noble recollections as well. In contrast with the more presentist orientation of many younger orators, Johnson found it equally appropriate to praise by name "many of the good men and women who, despite their pastor's teaching to the contrary, aided the slave by both prayer and purse to escape from their bondage." Though many individuals had "escaped my memory, but I still remember and revere" the acts of all those, living and dead, who occupy "the roll of honor" for their work to advance the cause of African American liberty.[55]

Johnson's very personal reminiscence was a strategy employed by other orators who used the Freedom Day platform to impart the lessons of the past to the younger generation. AME bishop Benjamin W. Arnett spoke in Columbus, Ohio, at a September 22, 1888, celebration commemorating both U.S. emancipation and the centennial of the Northwest Ordinance, which had prohibited slavery in the old Northwest Territory. Though speaking in September, Arnett echoed Johnson in asserting that black Americans should "never forget the first day of August; it was a great day with us." He also emphasized the power of the Freedom Day tradition through his own rec- ollections, connecting those early influences and memories with his ongoing quest for universal liberty: "I remember the first time I marched in a pro- cession. It was in 1849, in Brownsville, Pa. I remember the tunes that were played by the fifer; the drum and tune of freedom is still beating in my memory, and will continue to beat and encourage my heart until the last fetter is loosed from the limbs of my fellow-men. . . . Then with all hearts and minds emancipated, we shall join the universal shouts of freedom, which shall be heard to the utmost part of the habitation of men." Arnett brought in more of his personal history in order to strengthen the connec- tion between the young northerners in his audience in 1888 and the race's slave past, pointing out that he had, in his youth, "touched the hand of the slaves of New York with my own hand. I have seen the children first born to freedom in the Empire State, and we have rejoiced together at the jubilee of freedom." Even in Pennsylvania in 1840 he knew one of the few slaves who remained in bondage, unaffected by the state's 1780 gradual emanci- pation act. Two of his grandparents had been slaves. "So you see," he drove his point home, "how near I am to slavery. Only link between me and slavery."[56] Arnett and George Johnson used the public forum of the freedom festival to insure that their personal memories of the community's, the race's, and the nation's engagement with the experience of slavery and the aboli- tionist struggle would be preserved.

Several years earlier Frederick Douglass had mounted another central New York platform to impart a similar (if more politically driven) message, one he deemed important enough to include, in edited form, in his auto- biography. In his August 3, 1880, address at Elmira, unambiguously entitled "The Lessons of Emancipation to the New Generation," Douglass delivered his message to "hundreds of colored people [who] flocked to Elmira from 100 miles around." The venerable activist began by noting that he was indeed "standing mainly before a new generation." Though some younger men like

Fortune and DeMond also expressed the desire to preserve the memories of the old days, that task was more central in the minds of those leaders whose day was passing. Along with Benjamin Arnett, Daniel Payne, Philip Bell, and many others in his own rapidly disappearing cohort, Douglass voiced his concern that "[t]here are but a few left to tell the story of the early days of anti-slavery." Like Ithaca's George Johnson, Douglass placed great value on the continued retelling of that story, and he proceeded to enlighten the uninitiated in his audience as to the meaning of the date being observed. "In the history of our struggle with American slavery," he explained, "West India emancipation played an important part. It was the first bright star in a very dark, stormy and threatening sky; a smile from the inner folds of a frowning Providence. It brought to us the first ray of hope of the possibility of freedom to our race, in this and in all other countries. Whoever else may forget or slight its claims, it will always be held memorable and glorious by the colored people of the United States, as well as by the colored people of the West Indies. Though familiar to most who hear me, the story of it may be briefly told for the edification of our young people, who may know but little about it, and who ought to know all about it." A local newspaper reported that Douglass went on "at great length" to detail the circumstances of the British act, especially taking pains to discuss "the moral aspects and results of freedom upon the colored race" and to justify yet again "the American celebration of English emancipation."[57]

But the lessons Douglass imparted that afternoon were not limited to the history of transatlantic abolitionism. He divided his audience's instruction between past deeds that must not be forgotten and present political questions that must be acted upon. After briefly commenting on "the state of affairs in the South"—taking yet another opportunity to condemn the ongoing "exodus" of black migrants to Kansas—the Hayes-appointed marshal of the Federal District devoted the remainder of his two-hour oration to stumping for Republican presidential candidate James A. Garfield. "While this is not a political gathering," Douglass maintained, "it is not improper on this free occasion, to call attention to the fact, that we are now fairly within the currents of a political canvass of . . . pressing interest to us as a party of an oppressed and proscribed people."[58]

Blacks in the 1880s increasingly questioned whether the Republicans were indeed the party of their people. But Douglass remained steadfast, arguing that "[a] thoughtless and foolish exercise of our political power, was [will?] become a fountain of trouble to our fellow men and ourselves." Intelligent voting, for Douglass, resulted in large part from an exercise in historical memory that would keep clearly in blacks' minds the recent history of the two contending parties and would forever prevent them from casting votes for the Democrats. "I admit that the American people have a tolerably good memory, but they are more likely to forget too soon than remember too long the actions of parties during the late war." Democrats at that time "worked in a common cause of treason" though the party now "shrinks from its blood-stained path." "Oh, Fellow Citizens! Those were terrible times and we do well to remember them, and to remember what followed."[59] Douglass thus attempted to make the lessons of the past serve the political needs of the present.

As the historian David Blight has demonstrated, much of Douglass's rhetoric during his later years was devoted to making his deeply held memory of the Civil War a matter of public record and emphasizing the political implications of such a position. He tried to fuse the need to address the exigencies of the present with the need to remember the past.[60] Though few approached the great orator's dedication to that cause, Douglass's views were shared by many and were often promulgated at Freedom Day events. During the 1880s, as a segment of black political thinkers turned away from the Republicans, these large, public gatherings became important as forums for debate among the various positions on blacks' partisan identity. Celebrations in central New York generally attest to this tendency toward an explicitly partisan political content in Freedom Day addresses. They suggest the continued significance of Freedom Day events in solidifying regional communication networks and in perpetuating black history and commemorative traditions, not least by stressing continuities with the antebellum abolitionist struggle for the benefit of the younger generation. And like similar events across the country, they exemplify the continued importance of Freedom Day commemorations in African Americans' dialogues on a variety of social and political issues, both among themselves and with the broader public.

In the South those public dialogues needed to be approached far more cautiously than at the northern venues where Douglass and Fortune, for example, usually held forth. But even there, and despite the numerous dates observed and the polemical nature of some of the oratory, the lessons imparted at celebrations across the country usually fit into similar categories. Orators used Freedom Day platforms to extol the virtues of particular political parties, to comment on local and national concerns, and to agitate more generally for blacks' civil rights. Perhaps the most widespread use of Freedom Day commemorations related to their educative function for a generation of black Americans who had not experienced either slavery or the battle to abolish it. Even in the Deep South emancipation celebrations attempted to fix in the minds of black celebrants the lessons—and the necessity—of remembering the past. In Greenville, South Carolina, in 1894, one reporter expressed a view shared by proponents of commemoration across the country when he stressed the educative value of Freedom Day observances. "Emancipation Day," he asserted, "has many advantages for the race. It gives a grand opportunity for our scholars to make known the ancient glory, the heroic labors and celebrated actions of Negroes, and point out the path of future success. It is a period of instruction."[61]

Like the other strategies for advancing African American historical memory, the celebrations became sites of contestation over the content and meaning of that memory. Especially during the 1880s—a decade that saw both a dramatic expansion in public attention to historical memory and a steady erosion of black rights—celebrations of emancipatory events increasingly had to share the attention and imagination of historical thinkers with numerous other projects, including monument schemes, written works, historical societies, and veterans' organizations. Just as important, the erosion of blacks' citizenship rights began to gnaw away at the very freedom being commemorated, enshrouding emancipation celebrations in a more disquieting atmosphere than that which had predominated immediately after the Civil War. Largely because of this social and political context, the rhetoric surrounding them explicitly emphasized education and agitation as much as celebration. Blacks throughout much of the South had to exercise great restraint in their public statements and often chose to mollify whites with the rhetoric of patience and accommodation, biding their time in hopes of future gains. If the Freedom Day tradition remained intact, and even thrived in some areas, it also underwent a significant reorientation as new issues presented themselves during the turbulent decades that followed Reconstruction.

In the North, celebrations in central New York State in particular demonstrate the remarkable persistence of the Freedom Day tradition in some areas and suggest its continued importance in solidifying regional networks. Annual freedom festivals helped maintain connections among African Americans both across space through physical contact and over time through the construction and transmission of historical memory. Commemorative observances of emancipation were widespread in the South as well, even during the worst years of this era that the historian Rayford Logan has described as "the nadir" of African American history. Local commemorative traditions could be as vibrant below the Mason-Dixon line as in other parts of the nation, even if blacks there often treaded very lightly so as not to become targets for white repression. One area where commemorative traditions maintained a strong hold on the black community for an extended period was in the nation's capital. A close examination of the particularly intense tradition of April 16 District emancipation celebrations reaffirms many of the functions Freedom Day commemorations displayed elsewhere, including the potential for contestation over the meaning of com-memorations. Moreover, tracing the trajectory of Emancipation Day in Washington, D.C., into the twentieth century illustrates the transformation of the tradition as black Americans approached a transitional era in their history.

CHAPTER SIX

"A GREAT OCCASION FOR DISPLAY"

CONTESTATION IN WASHINGTON, D.C.,

1860s–1900s

We are not to be governed by the rabble and mob that has been a disgrace to this community. What the people desire is a respectable gathering.

—*Bee* (Washington, D.C.), 1884

These annual celebrations of ours should be so arranged as to make a favorable impression for us upon ourselves and upon our fellow-citizens. . . . If they fail to produce, in some measure, such results, they had better be discontinued.

—Frederick Douglass, 1886

WHILE EMANCIPATION celebrations were held in many cities and towns across the United States during the late nineteenth century, no single African American community maintained the commemoration of a Freedom Day anniversary more continuously than in the nation's capital. Blacks in Washington, D.C., held occasional January 1 celebrations, but they were far more consistent in their commemoration of the April 16, 1862, abolition of slavery in the Federal District, which was observed annually at least up to the turn of the century.[1] This commemorative tradition remained an important touchstone for District blacks, but over time the observance of April 16 became less a celebration than a forum for airing personal animosities and a point of convergence for various debates over black politics, intraracial class relations, public deportment, and the memory of slavery. In many respects, Washington's black population was unique. Its proximity to the national government made the city a mecca for talented and ambitious black professionals and office-seekers. The presence of Howard University (founded 1867), the Bethel Literary and Historical Society (1882), and the American Negro Academy (1897) defined Washington as a center of black intellectual activity. The presence of a deeply entrenched, light-skinned free black elite accentuated intraracial color and class divisions beyond those experienced in most black communities. Washington between the Civil War and the Harlem Renaissance was arguably the preeminent intellectual, cul-

tural, and political capital of black America. Still, the practice and the meaning of emancipation celebrations in the District during this period suggest
patterns of reorientation and transformation that were experienced to some
degree in black communities across the nation.

Class divisions within black Washington were well established even before
the war. The 1862 liberation of the District's slaves, and the subsequent influx
of fugitives from the surrounding area, elicited an ambivalent response from
black Washingtonians. In 1863 the exclusive Lotus Club was formed by a group
of mulatto servants, waiters, and coachmen, most of whom were themselves
outside of the black elite's inner circle, explicitly to maintain their own
distinction above the burgeoning black masses. Though fearful of the expanding numbers of poor and uneducated freedmen, the city's black middle
and upper classes nonetheless offered considerable aid and support even as
they maintained their distance from a people they saw as their social infe-
riors. This ambivalence did not prevent the regular commemoration of District emancipation, but even in the early postwar years these freedom festivals presented conflicting images and messages to the broader public.[2]

In 1867 visiting contingents of African Americans from Baltimore and
Annapolis "manifested no little displeasure" when rain caused the Washington organizers "to postpone the celebration until the first clear day."
Indecisive leaders aborted and resumed the festivities twice before a trun-
cated procession of understandably frustrated marchers finally formed in
the late afternoon and wended its way through the muddy streets, passing
thousands of spectators on the crowded sidewalks. As the parade returned
from Georgetown toward the Fifteenth Street Presbyterian Church, an altercation arose between participants and the drivers of several streetcars
whose progress was "impeded" by the procession. Violence "was prevented
by the timely interference of the police," but the fracas further marred an
already chaotic celebration. Despite "all the disadvantages surrounding" the
celebration, the sympathetic observer from the Washington, D.C., *Daily National Intelligencer* still declared that "it was by no means a failure."[3]

That paper's reporter the following year did not share his colleague's respect for the black celebrants. The 1868 affair included a much larger procession and "speechifying" by various black and white figures on the
grounds of the executive mansion, but the columnist was less interested in
describing the event than in mocking it. He implied that the "[t]wo fine
looking darkies" in the rear of one "open barouche" had displaced a white
city councilman from his rightful place. After suggesting that the contingent
had acquired a "strong" odor after "tramping through the mud for several
hours," the acid critic contemptuously noted that "the crowning and most

ludicrous feature of the parade was the chariot containing several colored damsels." By contrast, Philip Bell's *Elevator* described the procession of "upwards of three thousand persons" in some detail, noting with considerable pride the presence of black military and fraternal organizations, as well as the "light-complexioned colored girl" representing the goddess of Liberty in the evergreen- and banner-bedecked chariot. Wagons carrying, respectively, a working printing press (reeling off copies of the Emancipation Act), a blacksmith at his forge, and a carpenter at his workbench also were said to have made a fine impression. Even the *Intelligencer*'s snide chronicler had to admit that the affair was well ordered and that all the participants were "satisfied with the style in which they had passed their holiday."[4] If such was the treatment African American celebrants could expect from the mainstream popular press after an apparently dignified and smoothly run commemoration, it is not surprising that members of the city's black elite and civic leaders like *Bee* editor W. Calvin Chase were concerned with the public face they presented to whites.

The celebration in 1869 must have further reinforced those apprehensions, though this time it was black disorder, rather than white derision, that was to blame. It was a very popular event, the scale seeming to have dwarfed previous affairs. One commentator noted that "[i]t appeared as though the entire colored population of the District had been reinforced by their neighbors from Virginia and Maryland." Addresses at City Hall by distinguished black activists George B. Vashon, John Mercer Langston, and the Reverend J. Sella Martin lent further dignity to the proceedings. Unfortunately, however, the procession, which proceeded from K Street, through Georgetown and down Pennsylvania Avenue to the speakers' platform, was tainted by a skirmish between marchers and spectators, described in detail by the local press:

> While the procession was passing along the avenue, at the corner of Thirteenth Street, several stones were thrown from the south side of the street by colored men, in consequence of one of the crowd having, it is said, been struck with a sword by a man in the procession, a short time previously, and immediately a rush was made for the men who threw the stones; but the police (mounted men and officers of the Fifth Precinct) took three of them in custody, and by great exertions succeeded in taking them down Thirteenth Street into D, where a number of the friends of the captured parties made efforts to rescue them, while others intended to administer mob law to them. At the corner of Twelfth street, one of them broke away, but was recaptured, and finally the officers succeeded in locking them up in the Central Guardhouse.

"With the exception of the above and a trifling disturbance among themselves," the reporter asserted without a hint of sarcasm, "the procession was
orderly."[5]

Little wonder then that some African Americans looked forward to District emancipation celebrations with as much trepidation as pride. But the
commemorations continued to be conducted through the 1870s. Detailed
coverage of the 1872 observance indicates something of the event's continued
attraction for the local community. The huge procession included seventy-
nine marshals, aides, and officers representing twenty-two of the city's legislative districts. Six bands and a drum corps, interspersed through the line,
provided accompaniment for seven military or militia units (many bearing
muskets), ten district workingmen's clubs, several fraternal lodges, three
"pioneer's clubs" (some "armed with axes"), one Republican Club, and the
Lincoln Hook and Ladder Company. Numerous carriages and floats, the
chariot bearing the "Goddess of Liberty" and her entourage, and a "large
detachment of mounted men" filled out the line. Local participants were
joined by groups from Philadelphia, Baltimore, and New Jersey.[6]

Members of Washington's most prestigious black families were conspicuously absent from the list of officers and aides in the parade. Frederick
Douglass's youngest son, Charles Remond Douglass, and the fourteen-year-
old future federal judge Robert Terrell were the only representatives of the
black upper crust listed, and it may be significant that their families were
relative newcomers among the District's elite, both having taken up residence only after the Civil War. The speakers' platform in Judiciary Square,
however, was graced with the presence of "many noted individuals," including John F. Cook, scion of perhaps the most patrician of the colored
aristocracy's "old citizen" clans. From the stand the "vast multitude" in
attendance was addressed by two of the most respected black figures in the
nation, Philadelphian Isaiah Wears and South Carolina congressman Robert
B. Elliott. As was typical at large Freedom Day gatherings, both these gentlemen used their forum to instill the lessons of the past in their audience.
After reviewing the past "sufferings of his race" and the "noble deeds" involved in their liberation, Elliott asserted, as did many others in the wake
of black male enfranchisement in 1870, that the anniversary of emancipation
should serve to remind African Americans that certain responsibilities came
with their newly acknowledged rights. The most important of these in his
estimation was to fulfill the obligation owed "to those of our race who died
without the right" by passing on to the next generation "a heritage enriched
by our accumulations and adorned by our triumphs." Wears, for his part,
was less concerned with heritage than with broadening the meaning of
emancipation during an era that saw the steady withdrawal of white partic-

ipation from Freedom Day events. Wears suggested that whites should show more interest in such celebrations "so as to learn the lesson of liberty, which they have not the slightest idea of compared to the colored man." Wears's primary message for blacks was overtly political: emancipation celebrations should "occur frequently" and should be used explicitly "in the interest of the great Republican party."[7]

These same concerns—party loyalty, passing on the lessons of liberty (to members of both races), preserving the memory of slavery and the abolitionist struggle—continued to appear at District emancipation celebrations, as they often did elsewhere, through the 1880s. But during that decade the rift that separated most of Washington's black elite from the parading masses grew ever wider. This division may have been exacerbated by shifting race relations after legislation in 1879 ended home rule in the city and denied District citizens the right of suffrage, effectively severing the political ties between whites and the black elite. In the wake of this development, the historian Jacqueline Moore argues, "Washington became two distinct communities, one white, one black, the black one struggling for identity and control of the few matters that were left in its hands." Given the additional factor that many whites thought District blacks "incompetent to manage their own affairs," these developments set up a crisis of community self-definition for black leaders.[8] If there had been hints of a lack of unanimity in the celebrations during the 1860s and 1870s, by the early 1880s signs of discord were overt and incontrovertible. The observance of 1883 stands at the crossroads.

On the one hand the affair appears to have been truly magnificent. The *Bee* reported that "never before in the history of the colored race, was there ever such a demonstration in the District of Columbia." The mile-and-a-half-long line of march, under the oversight of Chief Marshal Colonel Perry Carson, who had also commanded the 1872 parade, far surpassed any previous processions. It included a dozen military companies; an equal number of fraternal and benevolent associations; ten social clubs; numerous workingmen's groups, bands, drum corps, and minstrel troupes; and more than two hundred hacks, wagons, and chariots representing various trades and miscellaneous organizations. Addresses that evening at the First Congregational Church were delivered to an appreciative, racially mixed audience by the Reverend Dr. Robert S. Laws; the Civil War hero, prominent banker, and local officeholder Milton M. Holland; and, in the first of several District Emancipation Day speeches, Frederick Douglass.[9]

The addresses were stirring and touched on many of the themes common to Freedom Day commemorations throughout the nineteenth century. In his opening oration, Holland emphasized the universal appropriateness of such celebrations of freedom for preserving the heritage of the past and passing it on as a legacy for subsequent generations: "Let all the anniversaries of all the nations and of every race and clime, which brings back the memories, the traditions, and the triumphs of human liberty, be held sacred and dear by all the people. . . . It is well that with full and grateful hearts you celebrate [this anniversary's] annual return. Teach your children its importance, and hold it in high and sacred remembrance. Prize it as your dearest legacy from man, and cherish it as the richest gift of God." Holland next introduced Douglass, the orator of the day, as "a man whose name is inseparable with the cause we celebrate." The graying abolitionist lion, midway between two crushing personal blows—the August 1882 death of his wife, Anna Murray Douglass, and the October 1883 Supreme Court decisions that effectively repealed the 1875 Civil Rights Act—delivered a well-received and widely reprinted address that suggested his willingness to pass the mantle of leadership to the coming generation "of aspiring and promising young colored men." Assessing his own purpose on this commemorative occasion, Douglass felt that it was "well to have something of the past mingled with the present" in order to instruct "the legitimate children of the great act we are met to celebrate."[10]

Douglass, as was his wont, interpreted the past for his listeners, reminding them that District emancipation "was one of the most important events connected with the prosecution of the war for the preservation of the Union, and, as such, is worthy of the marked commemoration we have given it today." In assessing the significance of the act, Douglass harkened back to a theme from his antebellum Freedom Day addresses, offering a distinctively humanist reading of the doctrine of progress that placed universal liberty and moral justice as higher criteria than economic gain or territorial expansion. The liberation of the District's slaves, that "great step in national progress," he maintained, "imparted a moral and human significance to what at first seemed to the outside world, only a sanguinary war for empire." Though he warned that "the present hour is full of admonition and warning," Douglass saw blacks' "steady, vast, and wonderful" progress since the war as further reason for the race to feel pride in its accomplishments. Douglass thus maintained his own race pride even as he advocated the abandonment of racial distinctions. The aging warhorse advised young black leaders to seize control of the race's destiny and "to make ourselves . . . a part of the American people in every sense of the word. Assimilation and not isolation is our true policy and our national destiny."[11] That position would increasingly attract censure from his growing number of critics—especially after his controversial 1884 marriage to a white woman—but at the time it drew little negative comment, perhaps in part because the local black elite was obsessed with its own assimilation and acceptance by the white community.[12]

The final speech of the evening, by Robert S. Laws, ranged widely over past, present, and future, touching on numerous issues including discrimination, party identity, office-seeking, and race amalgamation. But his most telling words had to do with the ubiquitous Freedom Day themes of freedom, equal justice, and the need to remember and honor the past. Though the institution of slavery had a painful "history which makes the living shudder to recall the sufferings of the dead," it was necessary, Laws insisted, "to leave on record by transmission to all coming generations" those "living recollections which must be commemorated throughout life existence by every man, woman and child of the race." Like Douglass, Laws also emphasized blacks' essential Americanness and the strength that came with the nation's diversity: "we have one nation, but a part of all races: different complexions, but one people . . . [all of whom should] unite in the celebration of one grand principle, freedom."[13]

Laws's address was a fitting conclusion to an affair that was recognized as far away as Boston to be "the most successful celebration that has been held in the District for many years."[14] In addition to the generally acknowledged success of the proceedings, it seems to have been a more inclusive gathering than were many previous affairs. Among the organizers and officers of the day were representatives of several of the most renowned and long-standing of black Washington's aristocratic families, including the Grays and the Cooks. Other participants who had been admitted to exclusive social circles by marriage or by accomplishment included Medal of Honor recipients Christian A. Fleetwood and Milton M. Holland, Richard T. Greener, and Frederick and Lewis Douglass. Even the procession was graced by an elite presence, with Fleetwood and W. P. Gray leading black military units, Gilbert Gray marching as an aide to the chief of staff, and Miss Margaret Gray personifying the ever-present goddess of Liberty in her chariot.[15]

But the event was hardly dominated by the upper crust. Unlike the exclusive Emancipation Day dinner hosted by Blanche K. Bruce and his wife, Josephine Willson Bruce, that evening, the day's public celebration was a decidedly mixed-class event. One Ohio visitor observed that "[t]ogether were assembled the most intelligent and cultivated of the colored race and the worn-out relic of the inhuman traffic."[16] While we can assume that the largely respectable classes that fell between these poles were also well represented at this and other observances, it was the tendency of Washington's black community to dichotomize these two elements. The juxtaposing of these two extremes of black Washington lay at the heart of subsequent controversy. The presence on the streets of vast numbers of the city's many alley-dwellers in particular sparked a conflagration over the purpose, meaning, and practice of District emancipation celebrations that was to expose a malicious factionalism that would ultimately bring about the demise of large public commemorations of District emancipation.

The seeds of enmity were sown at least as early as the 1862 Emancipation Act itself. On the eve of the Civil War, more than 75 percent of District blacks were free, and many of those individuals' families had been free for generations. Almost overnight most of Washington's rapidly growing black population consisted of former slaves or the descendants of slaves. This new reality forever changed the demographic and social arrangement of the community and stimulated the elite's concern with differentiating themselves from the black masses.[17] Little mention of any overt factionalism or conflict marred the April 16 observances, however, until the 1880s. Coverage of the 1883 celebration adhered to this pattern, except for a few scattered bits of information, including the Ohio correspondent's poignant observation. The detailed account in Chase's *Bee*, while lauding the event, noted in passing that Chief Marshal Perry Carson and "others interested in the success of the celebration" had to overcome considerable "opposition" from undisclosed quarters.[18] The nature of the discord remained undefined, though its persistence was made clear a few weeks later when Carson was "summarily" removed from his position as "an employee of the marshal's office," a post to which he had been elected "by acclamation" before the celebration. On May 11 a meeting was called by the "emancipation celebration association," apparently a permanent body by this time, whose stated "primary object" was, oddly, not to mount celebrations but rather "to reclaim the orphan sons and daughters of the colored poor from lives of vice and crime and lift them up by finding trades and occupations for them." The association resolved to investigate Carson's dismissal "and to make arrangements for a public mass meeting to discuss and give the views of the colored citizens of this district" on the matter.[19]

By the spring of 1884 tensions had expanded somewhat. At a March meeting in south Washington many "expressed considerable dissatisfaction" on the election of Perry Carson once again as chief marshal, claiming "that Mr. Carson carried his point at the meeting by allowing women to vote, a thing which, the dissatisfied ones say, never occurred before." Calvin Chase revealed no opinion on the matter in the *Bee*, confining his remarks largely to boosterism. "Let every citizen come out and make the emancipation celebration a success," one editorial blurb exhorted. This seemingly inclusive invitation, though, was tempered by another column on the same page that demonstrated the editor's differentiation between worthy and unworthy participants. "We are not to be governed by the rabble and mob that has been a disgrace to this community," he chastised. "What the people desire is a respectable gathering." Such a result, Chase suggested, could be achieved in part through the participation of "the military" under the direction of the likes of Christian Fleetwood and others who should "come out and make our emancipation one of honor and distinction."[20]

Chase neither identified the "rabble" nor specified the nature of the growing division among Washington's blacks regarding their annual commemorations. That division was also affirmed by a pseudonymous letter to the *Bee* accusing the recently established Bethel Literary Association of attempting to undermine the celebration by scheduling its own "public entertainment at Lincoln Hall on emancipation evening. It has always been the custom of the managers of the annual Emancipation Celebration," wrote the correspondent, "to close the parade of that day with appropriate exercises." Was the leadership of the literary association "so badly informed," he wondered, "that they did not know that Emancipation Celebration would be carried out as heretofore on the day and evening of April 16, or do they mean to run an opposition to the day we celebrate?" Even in Baltimore inklings of dissension were reported for that city's own observance of District emancipation. A parade by the Hod Carriers Association, an entertainment by the Monumental City Guards, and speeches at the Douglass Institute by local and national notables of both races promised a successful event. But attorney William Ashbie Hawkins, who must have been exposed to District emancipation fever while a law student at Howard University, nonetheless despaired of "the efforts of some who have been working strenuously against" the celebration.[21]

The 1884 festival in Washington was celebrated "with unusual gusto" by a "prodigious throng of negroes of both sexes and of every age and shade." Apparently the affair came off without any major public conflicts, despite many blacks having taken the day off work, "intent on making the most of their holiday." The procession was more than a mile in length and included some five or six thousand "persons of all colors, classes and descriptions." There was much "pomp and circumstance" surrounding the parade, which was reviewed as it passed the White House by President Chester A. Arthur. It included "a dozen brass and martial bands, several well disciplined military companies, innumerable civic organizations, flags and banners in profusion, wagons with canopies beneath which sat dusky queens with their maids of honor dressed in white, [and] scores of vehicles of every description filled with enthusiastic celebrators. . . . There was much uproarious cheering and the entire colored population seemed to be in a high state of enjoyment."[22]

Evening exercises featured speeches by Frederick Douglass and a number of representative men of the younger generation, including the minister and historian George Washington Williams and Howard University dean James M. Gregory, both thirty-five; forty-year-old Howard Law School dean Richard T. Greener; and the thirty-year-old W. Calvin Chase. This group of young lions was joined by Edward A. Forrest, the youthful correspondent from the *Cleveland Gazette*, who had not yet turned twenty-one. The age of these men is suggestive, especially in light of Douglass's comments the year before regarding the responsibilities of the coming generation to shoulder the burdens of race leadership. The generational transition of the 1880s is important for understanding black leaders' shifting approaches to the problems and possibilities faced by African Americans two decades after emancipation. Young Forrest, who had not yet been born when District emancipation was declared, delivered a powerful address that indicates the younger generation's willingness to confront the challenge of race leadership.[23]

Forrest admitted to feeling some "diffidence" on account of his "inexperienced youthfulness," but nevertheless he boldly claimed his place as "the junior representative of a new order of things, an era hitherto unknown, one of true progress and large freedom." After paying tribute to those who fought to secure black enfranchisement, he launched into a tirade—just months after the Supreme Court's abrogation of the 1875 Civil Rights Act—against African Americans' current civil and political disempowerment at the hands of "the Red Shirt Democracy." "The Negro stands to-day," he declaimed, "a nonentity" in political affairs. Showing no concern for mollifying southern whites, this representative of the rising generation praised the patriotism of Nat Turner and cast shame on the southern whites who acquiesced to "political misrule and tyranny" in the South. Taking to heart the lessons men like Douglass were trying to instill among his generation, Forrest compared his cohort with the "young men [who had] helped to wipe out human slavery" during the war. He claimed his generation's responsibility to work "to blot out political slavery forever from the land."[24]

The young orator's idealism, however, was belied by his own bitterness over recent political maneuverings that exacerbated rifts among the city's black Republican partisans. Shortly before the 1884 celebration, Colonel Perry Carson, a well-known south Washington saloon keeper and "one of the 'old leaders' " of the city, had been selected as a delegate for John A. Logan at the 1884 Republican National Convention in Chicago. According to Forrest's account in the *Cleveland Gazette,* the meeting of the District Republican Association that elected Carson was so "disorderly, unruly and boisterous" that it took a full twelve hours merely to put an organization in place. The convention was said to have been dominated by "an element" more disgraceful than anything found *"even [in] the South."* The agitation seems to have had much to do with the 1879 removal of suffrage from the District's citizens. While all present sought to have those rights reinstated, that cause, Forrest contended, was severely injured by the "roughs" who "manipulated the entire business of the District Convention." The capable and articulate James M. Gregory and Richard T. Greener (both of whom would share the celebration platform with young Forrest) were passed over, and Carson imposed, by the alleged deal-making of "unprincipled politicians." According to later reports in Chase's *Bee,* Carson went on to engage in some "treachery" at the convention that apparently damaged both Logan's bid for the nomination and black Washington's influence within the party. Once a supporter of Carson in Emancipation Day politics, Calvin Chase had become his bitter enemy.[25]

The rift became more clearly defined in 1885 in the aftermath of Grover Cleveland's election as the first Democratic president since the Civil War. As the factions took shape it became clear that Calvin Chase spoke for one group while Perry Carson was the dominant figure in the other. The full details of the schism are unclear, but it appears to have hinged initially on two issues: Carson's alleged personal ambition, pursued at the expense of race and party loyalty, and Chase's growing obsession with controlling the public deportment of Washington's black residents. There was surely a far more complex set of circumstances involved in defining the factions; indeed, more than two polar positions were articulated at any given time and their compositions shifted periodically, often due to the capricious loyalties of Calvin Chase. But the fundamental existence of a "Chase faction" and a "Carson faction" seems to have been consistent into the 1890s.[26]

Chase, once a supporter of Carson, was firing broadsides at his new nemesis in mid-February 1885. After praising his own "large and enthusiastic meeting" for the planning of the emancipation celebration, Chase dismissed a competing organizational meeting as "bogus, and in the interest of a ring for the Carson faction—a man who sacrificed the rights of the people for self-aggrandizement." It seemed for a time that there might be two competing celebrations, with each faction expressing its "determination to celebrate if it only has five persons in line."[27] That situation was avoided, and it was with great satisfaction that Chase reported Carson's defeat in his run for chief marshal of the 1885 emancipation parade. The election of Charles H. Marshall, by a vote of 77 to 30, was interpreted as a "just rebuke" to Carson from "the colored people whom he deceived" in Chicago. Especially important to Chase was the fact that the meeting was the largest and "most representative" ever held, including 150 delegates from "every organization and twenty legislative districts in the District." It was also a meeting at which he could claim that "the best elements in the city" persevered.[28]

Chase made a point of emphasizing the near "unanimity" of African American sentiment for celebrating emancipation. "During previous years," he reported, "the northern and western sections of the city, took a very little interest in the Emancipation, but to day we are pleased to note that the people [from those areas] honor this day." Northwest Washington was the home of the District's black elite and the location of many of the prestigious churches and organizations patronized by that group. That these race aristocrats were now joining the celebration, along with Perry Carson's consistently enthusiastic working-class south Washington contingent, suggests the elite's growing recognition of the need for unified race activism, but it also set the stage for a showdown over the nature of black Washington's public displays. Even with the expanded elite participation and support, Chase did have to acknowledge that a significant number of District blacks "are ashamed of the day and will not aid in its success." The editor was unequivocal in his judgment of this third faction, which preferred to do away with the event entirely: "Let no black citizen be ashamed to celebrate the 16th day of April," he reproached. "It is a day that should be honored by the colored people in the District of Columbia." Those who turned away from that responsibility, he resolved, "have no respect for themselves or the freedom and liberty which are being enjoyed." They "should never have been liberated." That "class of people who are ashamed . . . to honor the day of our freedom" were never clearly identified by Chase or the other commentators who denounced them in the *Bee*. But it was Chase's position that both patriotism and "good sense and judgment" on the part of "the sensible portion of the colored population" would induce them to fulfill their "duty . . . to turn out and celebrate on the 16th day of April."[29]

Another focus of black opposition to the event, in addition to the desire to sever connections with the slave past, was the view held by many that fiscal mismanagement had marred previous affairs. "The people," Chase claimed, "asked for a reform in the management of this anniversary, and with the assistance of honest men, we have endeavored to give it to them." Those honest men, including presiding officer Blanche K. Bruce and the orator of the day Frederick Douglass, were presented as the antitheses of the purportedly disreputable Perry Carson and his supporters. Operating under financial constraints that were experienced by celebration organizers across the nation, Chase still periodically reminded his readers of the managers' need for money to mount "a celebration worthy of the name we bear." The committee of arrangements finally resolved that District churches "set apart the fifth Sunday in March to take up a collection for the exclusive benefit of the Emancipation Celebration."[30]

The celebration, at least according to the slanted account in Chase's *Bee,* presented "the grandest procession in the day and the finest exercises at night ever had on such an occasion." The parade was reviewed by President Cleveland and his cabinet, taking a full hour to pass the stand. One report estimated only about a thousand people in the parade, a figure well below previous years' numbers, yet the size of the procession itself gave Chase satisfaction, since it was more exclusive than previous ones, and was tightly controlled by the marshal's aides. Where the 1883 parade, for example, contained hundreds of carts and hacks, many of questionable condition and appearance, the 1885 line of march listed no such entries. That the carts were excluded from the parade and not merely from Chase's coverage is corroborated by the report in the *Cleveland Gazette.* Marching bands, military companies, GAR posts, workers' organizations, private clubs, and fraternal orders were the only designated marchers aside from the various officers, aides, and featured guests of the day. Chase made a special point of noting "the great opposition of strikers and bummers, who thought themselves highly necessary to a successful parade." "The ruffians were not out," the editor crowed, "but the procession went on just the same." Chief Marshal Charles Marshall, District Register of Deeds Blanche K. Bruce, and Chase himself came in for glowing praise, and Frederick Douglass was said to have outdone himself in his oration. "Taking the celebration in all, it was a most brilliant success, and the *Bee* congratulates the respectable citizens of the District upon their emancipation from ruffian and ignorant Negro rule." Another black paper reported that the "grand style" of Washington's celebration "reflects credit on the race."[31]

A report in T. Thomas Fortune's New York *Freeman* was considerably less effusive in its praise of the celebration. The reporter did call Douglass's address, which focused mainly on his concerns about the new Democratic administration, "a bold, noble effort, worthy of the man and the occasion." He also deemed the procession "quite creditable." More critically, however, he noted that "the ranks of several [military] companies were far from full . . . and there is a widespread feeling among the better class of citizens—the substantial, tax-paying class—to do away with the ostentation of a parade, which fills the sidewalks with the idle, thriftless class of the worst elements and entails an expense of not a few thousand dollars. . . . It is very likely that this will be the last of the street demonstrations, which are not sufficiently hearty to be imposing, and thus [to] counteract the impression made by the great unwashed."[32]

The *Freeman* report echoed Chase's crude designation of the factions as representing the "ruffian" and "respectable" elements of black Washington. Note that the respectable class is not defined by membership in the tiny black elite but rather by the fact of employment and "tax-paying." The ruffian/respectable dichotomy seems to be linked primarily to work ethic and adherence to a particular code of moral behavior, not merely wealth, education, or pretensions to high culture. The account in the New York paper also defines a third position that would do away with public displays entirely, and observe emancipation, if at all, with subdued and inexpensive literary exercises. The poles of debate, then, are not altogether unlike those in San Francisco in the 1860s and 1870s or in various locales through the late nineteenth century, where fiscal concerns attenuated the scale of some celebrations. Similar questions regarding the logic of squandering scarce financial resources on commemorations were debated in the AME Church's discussion of the raising of the Richard Allen statue at the 1876 Centennial. But in Washington the pronounced enmity among various cultural divisions within the black community added a significant variable that made the situation even more volatile than these other instances. In 1886 these various and vehemently held positions divided black Washington in an embarrassingly public display.

In early February the *Bee* reported that Charles Marshall would again command the procession, after Carson was denied delegate status at the Emancipation Convention. Carson "demand[ed] to be recognized" and was finally given the floor where he protested his exclusion from the proceedings, but Marshall's election stood and the meeting adjourned. Carson's response to being railroaded out of the celebration was to call his own convention and organize a separate observance on the sixteenth of April. The *Bee* criticized the Carson faction as "a certain element . . . that is determined to degrade the day rather than to celebrate it." These proponents of "rum-ism" and "rag[-]ism" were said to be opposed by the vast majority of "the quiet law abiding citizens of this District" who would "turn out and make this day one to be long remembered."[33]

Chase's *Bee* also lashed out at those who preferred *not* to remember—the "few in this city who oppose the annual Emancipation celebration." Those who wanted to do away with the tradition found "the custom . . . degrading," primarily because of its "tendency to recall the former condition of the race which should be forgotten." While Chase admitted that "there are certain things in the history of all races that should be forgotten," others, he insisted, needed "to be forever remembered." The editor offered no specific criteria for determining which events required selective memory and which selective amnesia. But Chase and his columnists argued that simple respect for "the honest mothers and fathers who have felt the pangs of slavery" demanded that a day be set apart for them to express gratitude for their deliverance. As for that "certain class that are ashamed of their parents, such people should be relegated to oblivion. Let every honest man and woman turn out and celebrate this day."[34]

As the date of the dual celebrations approached Chase shifted his criticisms from those who would forget back to the competing, and apparently quite popular, Carson faction. The editor predictably called for "all respectable people" to "look out and join the right party." Constructing the situation as a choice "between respectability and rowdyism," Chase continued to denigrate that "notorious class of Negroes" who "were endeavoring to gain power and rob the people." The two camps, up to the day of the celebrations, openly competed for the participation of a variety of bands and military companies, and perhaps most notably on a symbolic level, the sanction of President Grover Cleveland.[35]

Cleveland wisely removed himself from the fray by declining to review either procession, though Carson led his contingent past the locked gates of the executive mansion anyway. Carson's group appears to have been the larger, despite Chase's estimate that his own line of march contained some four thousand of "the best element of the colored people." Both ended their respective parades with speeches, Carson's at Lincoln Park and Chase's at the Israel Bethel Colored Methodist Episcopal Church. The editor praised his followers for their patriotism and manliness in the face of opposition from the "maudlin bummers and worthless men" who comprised "the whisky element." Carson in particular was condemned as an "ignoran[t] . . . man, who puts himself up as a leader of the people." Amid this bitter divisiveness, Chase could still manage to extract some lessons from the commemoration of emancipation. Though a "harmony which would not brook factions" might be preferred, "even dual celebrations of the same event are instructive in their way. They suggest what meanness, self-interest and ignorance can accomplish toward defeating the best wishes of the grateful and law-abiding people."[36] A larger lesson, one less burdened with personal animus, involved the merit in holding public processions on Emancipation Day at all. The *Bee* noted that "processions have now become unpopular by the antagonisms, bickerings, and faction strife. . . . Now that it seems that we cannot have a united parade, it is hoped that parades in such occasions will be dispensed with and instead, have meetings in churches and halls where men of ability, character and worth may speak and give thanks for the wisdom and goodness of that Providence which demanded that the oppressed of the District should be free and that soon thereafter every American should be freed from the shackles of physical, moral and intellectual thraldom."[37]

This particular sentiment was articulated most eloquently by Frederick Douglass, who devoted considerable attention to the subject in his April 16 oration. Douglass ranged over a wide array of topics, including plans for the 1889 national centennial celebration of the Constitution, which, he claimed, "like our own" commemorations, would have varied and "large uses." He also expressed the desire that "[a]s part of the people of this great country, we may feel ourselves included" in that national ritual. Most of the address was a severe castigation of the Democratic Party and of racial injustice in the nation at large. Douglass tried to link the day's significance with the painful reality of that injustice. He spoke of emancipation as an act of national progress and purification that was as beneficial to the master as to the slave. The venerable abolitionist implicitly acknowledged the growing white disinterest in black public commemorations of emancipation by lamenting that "it is left to us alone to keep it in memory." The veteran of scores of Freedom Day platforms emphasized the importance of continuing to commemorate emancipation, explicitly advocating the "use of this annual celebration" not just to construct historical memory but also "to keep the subject of our grievances before the people and government and to urge both to do their respective parts in the happy solution of the race problem."[38]

Given the context of the dual celebrations, Douglass could hardly avoid commenting on the race's internal problems as well. He insisted at the outset "that no apology is needed for these annual celebrations" whose "demonstrations of popular feeling . . . are consistent with and creditable to human nature." He did, however, express remorse over "an incident connected with [the celebration], and by which it is greatly marred." His concerns were, like Calvin Chase's, partly about the face black Washingtonians had presented to the larger society. The dual celebrations "have said to the world that we are not sufficiently united as a people to celebrate our freedom together." He personally found the division "unfortunate, disgraceful, and mortifying," and he appealed to the tolerance and patience of the "disgusted public" with the excuse "that colored men are but men" who would surely behave better and act more wisely "[w]hen we have enjoyed the blessings of liberty longer." Douglass also warned blacks that "a repetition of this spectacle will bring our celebrations into disgrace and make them despicable." Warming to this tone of rebuke, Douglass continued to upbraid an audience comprised "mainly [of] colored men" for having lost sight of their larger common goal of race progress. In so doing he made clear the importance of carrying on commemorations so as not to call undue attention to the most unflattering elements in the black community:

The thought is already gaining ground, that we have not heretofore received the best influence, which this anniversary is capable of exerting; that tinsel show, gaudy display, and straggling processions, which empty the alleys and dark places of our city into the broad daylight of our thronged streets and avenues, thus thrusting upon the public view a vastly undue proportion of the most unfortunate, unimproved, and unprogressive class of the colored people, and thereby inviting public disgust and contempt, and repelling the most thrifty and self-respecting among us, is a positive hurt to the whole colored population of this city. These annual celebrations of ours should be so arranged as to make a favorable impression for us upon ourselves and upon our fellow-citizens. They should bring into notice the very best elements of our colored population, and in what is said and done on these occasions, we should find a deeper and broader comprehension of our relations and duties. They should kindle in us higher hopes, nobler aspirations, and stimulate us to more earnest endeavors; they should help us to shorten the distance between ourselves and the more highly advanced and highly favored people among whom we are. If they fail to produce, in some measure, such results, they had better be discontinued.[39]

Despite the warnings of Douglass, Chase, and others, the 1887 Emancipation Day committee once again anticipated "a big procession" as part of the commemoration of the day. The embarrassing events of the previous year surely made their mark, however, and a single celebration was planned, one that included both Chase and Carson as members of the various organizational subcommittees. The procession seems to have been pleasing to all, despite (or perhaps because of) a heavy downpour that kept participants' numbers well below the twelve thousand that organizers claimed to have expected. Still, even the mustering of the line before the march began presented quite a spectacle, as the following account suggests:

After ceaseless galloping of messengers and aid[e]s, ordering and countermanding orders, the chief marshal of the day, a large, well-fed minister, mounted on a prancing charger which he vainly tries to gracefully manage, rides to the head of the line. He is followed by a dozen or more deputies, captains and supers on horses of all sizes, ages and conditions of repair. Behind these come a few hacks with the "big guns" of the day, and following them the main body of the procession, consisting of captains and their companies, wagons, carts, carriages, drays, buses and coupes, men women, boys and girls, in almost endless number and variety. When these have all been arranged, a deputy dashes madly down the line to see if all is ready to start. Returning to the same pace he salutes the commander-in-chief, who gives the signal to the drummers and the procession moves off to the inspiring strains of a dozen bands of music.

After wending its way through "the principal streets" lined with thousands of "eager and this year, wet and shivering" spectators, the procession filed into the White House grounds where President Grover Cleveland reviewed the line of march.[40]

Despite the intense controversy surrounding recent celebrations, the masses of Washington's black citizens looked forward with great pleasure to this annual day of revelry and were not about to let the festive tradition die. "For a month before it is the common topic of conversation, the constant food for newspaper gossip." Not only was April 16 a great opportunity for "real as well as would-be orators," it was also viewed by the military companies as "the best dress parade of the year." "The white people," District blacks felt, "turn out on General Washington's birthday, the Irish have their St. Patrick's day, the Dutchman has his day, and we are going to have ours, too. This 16th of April is our day, and we are going to celebrate it." The social and recreational functions of the day were clearly foremost in the minds of the working classes. It was an opportunity not only to visit with fellow Washingtonians but also to meet with visitors from out of town. "The people living here are up by times on the 16th . . . and all the married sisters, cousins and aunts from the bordering States swarm out upon the streets, sometimes twenty thousand strong, to see the sights and to be seen by sightseers." In the evening, celebrants could choose between listening to the orations "or else betake themselves to the numerous balls and hops given in honor of the occasion."[41]

If the procession produced considerable excitement in the streets, it was the orator of the day, George Washington Williams, who stimulated the most controversy in 1887, with a long-winded address that "occupied the time intended for him and also the space allotted to . . . everybody else who were billed to follow him." The speech was roundly criticized for its harsh arraignment of President Cleveland and for its condemnation of black Cleveland appointees as racial Judases for failing to criticize the president's inaction on southern racial violence. Most vociferous of the critics was T. Thomas Fortune, who was at one time one of Williams's closest allies. After reproaching Williams for his "absurd and injudicious and demagogical outburst of petulance," which branded him as "a traitor to the race," Fortune expressed sadness that one he once considered "our friend" had "fallen so low." Williams defended himself ably in Fortune's paper, claiming that some remarks were taken out of context. He pointedly stood by his condemnation of black "Judases" in federal posts, explaining that Cleveland's failure to address the escalating racial violence and proscription in the South should have been protested by those blacks who served under him.[42]

The controversy generated by this Freedom Day oration provided Fortune, in his critique, another opportunity to comment on the political importance of Freedom Day commemorations in African Americans' quest for both their inclusion in the American historical narrative and their equal and just treatment in the nation's present and future. It was, of course, "right and proper" for blacks to celebrate their emancipation. "But," Fortune continued, "the colored people of the District owe it to themselves and to the race at large to select as orator for such occasion a man not only competent to deal with the historical features of the occasion, but who is competent also to draw correct lessons from history and comment on contemporary conditions with wisdom and judicial fairness." In Fortune's view, Williams had failed to live up to these criteria. In the political context of the mid-1880s, "correct lessons" for Fortune meant, in part, recognizing Republicans' abandonment of black civil rights even as continuing Democratic sins were exposed. Just a year after his "Negrowump" speech at Owego, New York, in which he proclaimed black political independence from either major party, the fiery journalist condemned Williams as a "partisan demagogue" who had publicly besmirched the reputation of black men in order to curry favor with the Republicans. "The colored employees" in Washington, Fortune postulated, "most of them Republicans to the core, must have felt their flesh creep when they read in the daily papers that a black orator, upon the commemoration of District emancipation, had likened them to" the "degraded" betrayer of Jesus.[43]

The political issues that shaped Fortune's reaction were still relevant a year later. The 1888 celebration also fostered a new schism in black Washington, which this time was defined in part by the growing animosity between two of the race's leading lights—John Mercer Langston and Frederick Douglass. "There is a fight again this year," reported the *Cleveland Gazette*. "Are the colored people of Washington, D.C.—as a mass—retrograding?" The complex rift between Douglass and Langston was both personal and political. The two had been opposed for years over issues like the Kansas exodus, but in 1888 Douglass drew the ire of Langston and his allies by opposing Langston's run for Congress in Virginia. Douglass's support of white Republican William Mahone over Langston exemplified his stance in later years against using race alone as the criterion for political action. His opposition to Langston's candidacy revived criticism of Douglass's lack of race pride that began when he married a white woman, Helen Pitts, several years before. That the second Mrs. Douglass was herself attracting negative attention for having recently questioned black women's capabilities in women's rights activities only fanned the flames. Among the many blacks who turned away from Douglass was one of the most vocal and contentious black men in the nation's capital—Calvin Chase.[44]

Though Chase's enmity toward Douglass lasted until the latter's death in 1895, the editor placed another issue before Washington's African Americans in 1888 that would prove even more persistent. The question of whether or not to parade on Emancipation Day gave rise to competing celebrations in 1888 and hovered over District celebrations into the twentieth century. The featured orators at the two celebrations—Douglass and Langston—attracted considerable attention, but the debate over the propriety of public processions and the related issue of the financial needs of the black community are more important for understanding the transformation of African American Freedom Day commemorations in the new century.

Cost and public image were early defined in the *Bee* as crucial concerns for black Washingtonians. Citing Douglass's 1886 diatribe against processions, Chase made a sound case for transforming District emancipation commemorations in a way that would please everyone and benefit the black community in several ways. "It costs over $5,000 to run the Emancipation street parade," he argued, with most of the money solicited from sympathetic whites. Chase's estimate was based on statistics that considered the rental or purchase of horses, carriages, hats, sashes, bands, chariots, printing, and hall rent, and that figured in expenditures of $800 "drank up in whiskey." Furthermore, the editor claimed, "bogus collectors" with subscription books had bilked thousands of dollars from black and white contributors over the years, pocketing money ostensibly collected to finance the celebrations.[45]

Weekly reminders on the *Bee*'s editorial page warned readers to "beware of bogus books" as the editor presented the alternative drawn up by his emancipation committee. "Street parades on April 16," he claimed, "are universally condemned and disapproved by the more intelligent colored citizens . . . as being detrimental and disgraceful" and "the money that is collected is misappropriated." Chase's faction, which appears to have bolted from the original committee, announced that an attenuated public procession on Emancipation Day should be conducted solely by the District's black militia companies, which "can parade without expense, and which will reflect credit on the colored people of this city." Anyone wishing to make a contribution to the black community, the *Bee* suggested, should send funds "directly to the managers of the Colored Orphans' Home and matrons of the Industrial School for Colored Children." The only donations that would be taken during the celebration would be at the literary exercises, and those would go to the National Association for the Relief of Destitute Colored Women and Children and the Women's Christian Association for Indigent Colored Girls. Chase garnered considerable support for this ambitious plan to transform a rowdy and wasteful exercise in excess into a mechanism for lifting up the race's worthy poor and serving the long-term interests of the black community.[46]

But many District blacks resented being denied their day of freedom and revelry on the public streets. After some vacillation on the part of Frederick Douglass, and some last-minute scrambling by "the old man's son Lewis" to organize the line, a procession of militia companies, floats, bands, and clubs wended its way past President Cleveland's reviewing stand late in the afternoon. Chase denounced the parade as completely "void of dignity, uniformity and respectibility." "Never before in the history of the colored people in this city has a greater disgrace befallen them, than that apology for a parade on last Monday." After more than five hours' delay the procession that formed was said to have consisted largely of "disgraceful carts, wagons, and other things that would have been disgusting to the courtesans of murders bay," a notorious black vice district in the city. "The parade," he complained, showed only "that class of colored people who live in poverty and spend all their money for one day's festivity." Chase claimed that the president "had to send guards" to prevent the rabble from entering the executive mansion.[47]

Such unrelenting opprobrium was to be expected from the hyperbolic editor of the *Bee*. Yet his assessment was corroborated by the Washington correspondent to the *Age*, Lemuel Livingston. Livingston was a twenty-seven-year-old native Floridian who had graduated from Howard University Medical School several years earlier and was employed at the U.S. Treasury Department. He would later serve as a delegate to the 1896 Republican National Convention and, in 1898, be appointed U.S. consul to Haiti. After praising the evening orations by both Douglass and Langston, a point on which Chase was typically one-sided, Livingston addressed the question of whether emancipation celebrations served any useful purpose for black Americans. His appraisal hinged on the relative merits of remembering or forgetting the slave past. "The only plausible objection advanced by the anti-celebrationists," he stated, "is the desirability and advantage of forgetting entirely the system which the act of emancipation put an end to." Livingston himself found "nothing objectionable" in commemorating emancipation; indeed, he argued that the "specious reasoning" of those who would discontinue the tradition would, by extension, "do away with the celebration of all great revolutions and reforms." July Fourth, he pointed out, did not serve as a painful reminder of British tyranny, but as an empowering assertion of American independence. By the same token, "[t]he effect of the emancipation celebration is not to remind us of slavery—we can never forget that—but to commemorate the day of deliverance. . . . It is a reminder not of the night of bondage but of the dawn of freedom." The nearness and the intensity of the pain wrought by the slave past, Livingston astutely implied, explained both the desire to erase its memory and the impossibility of so powerful an amnesia coming to pass. Despite the ineradicable nature of such memories, annual reminders, he argued, could and should be used to serve the interests of the black community. "If properly celebrated, then, the occasion may be productive of positive good, resulting from the competent discussion of the great questions of the material progress and political status of the race." Like other black commentators in the 1880s, some of them his seniors by nearly half a century, Livingston stressed the educative function of Freedom Day events, especially as they pertained to the race's young people. "The masses," he asserted, "can . . . be enlightened as to their past achievements and future possibilities. Aspiring youth can thus be stimulated to noble exertion by enlarging the sphere of their mental vision and teaching them the proper solution of vexations and discouraging problems."[48]

Turning to the question of the proper manner of commemoration, Livingston claimed that this potential for good work could only be realized "by confining the exercises to discussion within doors. If improperly observed the occasion may easily be made a disgrace rather than a credit. It may be made to do positive harm instead of good." He was particularly critical of the parade on April 16, using language as strong as that of Calvin Chase. "There is no sort of doubt in the mind of any intelligent person that the shabby parade which is annually made the 'big show' of a celebration in Washington is a real set-back to race progress." He went on to describe in some detail the procession that so "disgusted" him, taking particular note of the gaudy sashes of the officers, a "tenth-rate military company," "a squad of young dudes in the garb of minstrels," crude and disorderly workmen shouting the praises of their trades, and a number of other unflattering features. Most offensive of all was the "grand *finale* of rickety country turn-outs filled with unprogressive humanity, crowds of riffraff on the sidewalks and in the streets murdering English, indulging in vulgar exclamations, showing off flashy cheap dresses and shabby-genteel outfits and in a thousand ways provoking smiles of derision and contempt from passing whites who are only too glad of such an opportunity which gives them a semblance of reason for their prejudices." The event was "a bad exhibition of a very bad custom. . . . This annual parade undoes the good work of the whole year in creating favorable opinion."[49]

By 1890 the District's black elite had largely abandoned the practice of rowdy street parades, though another took place that year. The closest Chase, Livingston, and other like-minded Washingtonians came to realizing their goal of using Emancipation Day to do "good work" came in 1891, when the event provided a forum for displaying "the progress of the colored people of the District." That year there was no parade. An oration by Langston highlighted the afternoon exercises. "The evening meeting was devoted to the work of the school children, this being deemed the best way to celebrate emancipation day." Exhibitions of products from woodworking and metalworking classes at the manual training school for boys were set up. Even a working pair of telephones assembled by the students was on display. Awards were given to the creators of these manufactured items as well as to essayists who wrote on half a dozen different biographical and social topics. Proceeds from the event went to the Home for Destitute Girls. The 1891 event was in some ways similar to the AME Church's effort during the same period to make the name of Richard Allen especially meaningful to the youth of the race. Church officials instituted the annual commemoration of Allen Day each February 14 in order to honor a black hero, and also to raise money, which was primarily directed toward saving the church's publishing house. Both the Allen Day project and Chase's plan for Emancipation Day indicate that concern for the younger generation—both their sense of the past and their preparation for the future—was of vital importance to many organizers of commemorative activities. The transformation of Emancipation Day in the District, however, met with less success than the commemoration of Richard Allen.[50]

Over the remaining years of the decade the 1891 format was not duplicated. Black Washingtonians continued to debate the propriety of the Emancipation Day parade and to allow personal and political disagreements to mar what many hoped could be a day of dignity, unity, and instruction. Chase continued to complain about "bogus" collectors embarrassing the race by pocketing money. In some years dual celebrations split the community, eliciting familiar diatribes in the *Bee* regarding public displays and fiscal extravagance. At times a tenuous truce was attained that permitted a single commemoration. Compromises often sanctioned a parade so long as the despised carts, wagons, and disorderly persons were prohibited. Often the proceeds from the literary exercises were remitted to a worthy cause, like the Home for Destitute Colored Girls. And always the speeches—by Douglass, Langston, Chase, William Derrick, and others—attempted to instruct and inform the black community about its past, present, and future in America. While some celebrations during the last decade of the century, like the one in 1899, did include both "patriotic addresses" and a parade,

Washington's freedom festivals in the 1890s never approached the scale, or attracted the public attention, of similar events in the previous decade.[51]

After the turn of the century public processions on Emancipation Day were only a memory. By 1906 Chase and most of the other community leaders in the city did not even consider publicly debating the issue of holding a parade. But as that forty-fourth anniversary of District emancipation approached, the veteran journalist still bemoaned the existence of a "bogus emancipation committee." "Even to-day there is a class of shysters collecting money from the merchants in this city under the pretense of having an emancipation celebration." The only commemorations held on the sixteenth consisted of indoor exercises, the most elegant of which was an evening gathering at the Metropolitan AME Church sponsored by the Dunbar Literary Association.[52]

The impressive list of speakers at that affair was headed by the Reverend Francis J. Grimke of the Fifteenth Street Presbyterian Church, Professors Kelly Miller and William Tunnell of Howard University, and Chase himself. Despite the subdued, almost private nature of the commemoration, Mrs. Helen A. Davis, who chaired the meeting, noted that "[t]here is no occasion that inspired the colored people of this city more than this day." Kelly Miller presented statistics demonstrating the progress of the race, an increasingly common occurrence at black meetings in the early years of the century. Other speakers emphasized the need for black men to respect black women, to adhere to religious faith, and generally to assert their manhood. When Calvin Chase stepped up to the rostrum he first called for African Americans to wake up from their slumber of nearly three hundred years and take action to secure their place in American society. Then he pondered the past and "cited amidst applause and laughter the time when he and Col. Carson had two Emancipation Day street parades." He also noted Grover Cleveland's refusal to review either parade "because there was a division among the negroes. However," Chase recalled, "we paraded just the same. To-day we have adopted other methods in celebrating this day. . . . 'We want to be united,' said Mr. Chase, 'and show to the American white people that we are good citizens.' "[53]

Chase and his companions felt sufficiently removed from the heated conflicts of the 1880s to smile and wax nostalgic as early as 1906. A quarter century later another journalist pondered "the emotional abandonment with which the masses of people used to 'turn out' to celebrate the anniversaries of the emancipation of slaves in the District of Columbia. There is no gainsaying the importance of the event in the lives of the masses of the people." The editorialist seemed to be well informed regarding the old celebrations despite the broad gulf of time that separated him from the events. He was also cognizant of the class distinctions that still caused dissension within the race. "That the old methods of 'celebrating' should displease native sons and daughters who were slowly arriving at 'middle class status' is to be expected, but that they did not turn the event into a more dignified occasion is cause for comment." This hinting at unrealized possibilities recalls Chase's own unsuccessful attempts to make the tradition do good for the race during the 1890s. The 1931 editorialist's description of the "old methods of celebrating" was unflattering to elite and masses alike, but indicated that a great opportunity had been lost when the tradition was discontinued:

> In the former "celebrations," one might witness hordes of the unwashed, partly clothed, slow-dragging to bands with . . . drums and trombones in crescendo while beribboned marshals pranced astride spavined cart horses back and forth along the belated line of march. Prominent citizens, many long since passed into the great beyond, were seen to loll importantly in open carriages bedecked with strings of scanty bunting. Uniformed organizations with every man an officer, and others with greenish frock coats and stove-pipe hats of veteran service composed the line which was reviewed by city officials and even Presidents. It was a great occasion for display, emotion, and expression. Though it but crudely expressed freedom, it was impressive and had in it the elements of an annual custom for which music could have been written, poems composed and dramas enacted, but were not.

At least those celebrants of days gone by had tried to make a statement that mattered about who they were, what their history was, and what their expectations were of participation in American public life. "As crude as that celebration was," he judged, "it was far superior to the smug, middle class, suppressed life of today." Harshly critical of assimilationist middle-class blacks who aped whites while exploiting the black masses, the editorialist chastised them to remember that racial unity is the essential ingredient in the recipe for racial progress. And even in 1931, he believed that freedom festivals could play a role in that project. "Emancipation is a continuing process; it should be celebrated."[54]

In 1906 Calvin Chase stood midway in time between the escalation of community conflict over public freedom festivals during the 1880s and the lamentation for their abandoned potential for community empowerment in the 1930s. If the "lessons of Emancipation" defined a major theme in late nineteenth-century black commemorative culture, he had learned much. During his two and one half decades of District emancipation celebrations,

Chase absorbed lessons that his journalistic descendent in 1931 probably could not fully appreciate. The largest of those lessons had taught him that an era of large, public African American commemorative festivals was coming to an end, and that new methods and new strategies were required to address the challenges that faced the New Negro in a new century.

CHAPTER SEVEN

"THE FAITH THAT THE DARK PAST HAS TAUGHT US"

DISSOLUTION, 1900–1920

Sing a song full of the faith that the dark past has taught us,
    Sing a song full of the hope that the present has brought us,
Facing the rising sun of our new day begun,
    Let us march on till our victory is won.

              —"Lift Ev'ry Voice and Sing,"
                James Weldon Johnson, 1900

Just fifty years—a winter's day—
    As runs the history of a race;
Yet, as we look back o'er the way,
    How distant seems our starting place!
. . . .
Then let us here erect a stone,
    To mark the place, to mark the time;
A witness to God's mercies shown,
    A pledge to hold this day sublime.

              —"Fifty Years,"
                James Weldon Johnson, 1913

EMANCIPATION DAY celebrations in the nation's capital were in many ways distinctive: for their commemoration of a locality-specific date and event; for taking place in a city of such national prominence; for their long years of uninterrupted observance; for their magnitude; for the size and complexity of the city's black community; and for the intensity with which that community often engaged the issues surrounding the commemoration of African American freedom. These factors do not render Washington's Freedom Day tradition anomalous; rather, they combine to draw in bold relief a number of patterns that affected Freedom Day commemorations across the country in the late nineteenth and early twentieth centuries.

One of the most important patterns—one that illustrates African Americans' most fundamental predicament—involves the increasingly segregated public sphere in which Freedom Day celebrations took place. Coincident with the accelerating Redemption of the South after the early 1870s, white America began to turn its attention away from black America's concerns and toward the process of white sectional reconciliation. In particular, the institutionalization of Jim Crow and the abandonment of black rights issues by the race's erstwhile allies in the Republican Party augured profound changes in the nature of African American commemorations. By the 1890s the large, biracial affairs of midcentury had given way to more exclusively black celebrations in more exclusively black public spaces. Within this increasingly segregated social context, black Freedom Day organizers after the Civil War all strove to define the meaning of emancipation and to extract appropriate lessons from its commemoration.

Despite vocal minorities who sought to put an end to the tradition, it persisted into the twentieth century in cities and towns where local activists valued the need to remember the past enough to overcome numerous obstacles to commemoration. At times a single inspired individual might take the responsibility for establishing and maintaining a local commemorative tradition. In the western Michigan community of Dowagiac, Thomas Jefferson Martin was a leading black activist and is identified by one historian of the region as "the founder of the First of August celebration protest festivities" during the mid-nineteenth century. In the early twentieth century, the western Pennsylvania town of Butler held what was said to be its first commemoration due to the efforts of John W. Dixon, who "was given a vote of honor as father and founder of the first celebration."[1] In Elbert County, Georgia, Dr. James Thompson. a black graduate of Brown University and Shaw Medical School, is credited with starting emancipation celebrations there in the early twentieth century. One resident recalled years later that "I don't think they [some whites] liked it 'cause Thompson started that [the Emancipation Day celebration]." While many local blacks enjoyed the festivities and speeches, the festivals were especially resented by the "people who owned the fields. They thought your place was out there in the fields." In 1915, at the age of forty-two, Thompson was shot and killed by a white physician. There were no witnesses, and the shooting was ruled an accident by an all-white jury.[2]

The potential for violence inhibited emancipation celebrations in the South more than elsewhere. In all parts of the nation, though, one of the most troubling obstacles faced by Freedom Day supporters who urged the race to remember its past was the fact that many African Americans expressed an equally strong desire to forget. Not that those who had lived through the days of slavery ever could forget. But the transmission of those memories to generations that had not experienced them firsthand became ever more crucial after the 1880s as many of the old abolitionist warhorses died and a cohort born since emancipation came of age. This generational transition had a profound impact on the lives of individual black activists and on the communal world they inhabited. Should the rising generation not be instructed in their distinctive history and heritage, should the definition of their sense of the past be left to the historical interpretations dominant in the larger society, then much of what was unique and valuable and empowering in the black experience would be lost. In 1912 former congressman George W. Murray argued that "a way must be found to teach Afro-American youth to be self-respecting and proud of their racial connections," and whites could not be trusted to accomplish that end. Given the relative paucity of "text-book instruction" in black history, Murray asserted that "to counteract the pernicious teachings of three centuries of slavery, unwritten instructions for this purpose must be given orally to the young by members of their own race." While Murray's suggestion focused on the role of ministers, teachers, and journalists, it is clear that public orations and family discussions would have a function as well. Women played a particularly important role in this process, if not usually in public at emancipation celebrations, then certainly in the home. "A race cannot be greater than its women," Bishop Benjamin Arnett told his audience of five thousand in a September 22 Emancipation Day oration at Chicago's 1893 Columbian Exposition, "The women are the teachers and molders of the thought and sentiment of the rising generations." Time and again during the late nineteenth and early twentieth centuries blacks articulated and acted upon their recognition of that need to interpret their own history and to transmit the knowledge of both their singular experience and their essential, ineradicable Americanness to the younger generation.[3]

Certain messages had to be transmitted to whites as well. Calvin Chase ended his 1906 Emancipation Day speech by stating his desire to "show white people that we are good citizens." To demonstrate their citizenship—both to whites and to themselves—and to assert their right to partake fully in all the opportunities of American society was a central goal for the organizers of African American Freedom Day celebrations and other commemorative activities throughout the nineteenth century. As they struggled to overcome white America's resistance to their full inclusion in the republic, black leaders, especially after U.S. emancipation, also grappled among themselves regarding the meaning of the important dates on their commemorative calendar. Some internal dissension was, in part at least, a product of their marginal position in American society. As Frederick Douglass's biographer William McFeely has suggested, when African Americans of high ability and ambition found themselves shut out from the positions of leadership they were capable of holding, they often vented their frustrations in acrimonious debate within their own racially circumscribed domain.[4]

Largely within a separate black institutional framework African Americans developed their leadership skills and their sense of place in the world. Notwithstanding considerable internal contestation, and fully cognizant of the limitations placed on them by American racism, they worked to define common goals of race progress. Freedom Day celebrations were by no means the only mechanisms through which those goals were defined and pursued. More important in many respects were the continuous organizations that structured life in every black community. Churches, benevolent societies, fraternal orders, veterans associations, military companies, literary societies, businesses, and in some larger cities, institutions like newspapers and publishing houses provided a network of associations and touchstones within a dominant culture that was fundamentally hostile and unwelcoming.

To the extent that blacks' commemorative activities were integrated into this structure and served a positive function for African American communities, they constituted a tradition worth maintaining. In the antebellum North and in all sections of the country during the Civil War and early Reconstruction, there existed a broad consensus among African American leaders that Freedom Day events—especially commemorations of West Indian and U.S. emancipations and of the Fifteenth Amendment—were indeed useful tools for pursuing the goals of race progress. Their functions were numerous. Perhaps most fundamentally, antebellum Freedom Day commemorations in the northern and western states were central to blacks' construction of a coherent heritage and a historical tradition—the cultural inheritance that black leaders insisted any people must possess to demonstrate their legitimacy and gain the respect of their fellows. In order to establish that heritage and also to counter white distortions of the African American past, commemorations offered black-centered interpretations of history that blacks themselves could best articulate. In the process they placed in the public eye capable and articulate race leaders whose oratorical and analytical powers—indeed, whose very presence—negated popular perceptions of black inferiority. Bridging the worlds of orality and literacy, antebellum and Civil War–era freedom festivals also served as forums for political mobilization and civil rights activism, and provided important vehicles for strengthening local, regional, and national networks of communication. And they accommodated leisure-time interactions among large numbers of African Americans who did not often have the opportunity to commingle freely in a recreational setting. These functions were carried out at large-scale, biracial gatherings in a shared public sphere. Freedom Day events through the Civil War era commanded the attention of the larger society, and thus allowed African Americans to combat slavery, stake their claim to citizenship rights, and articulate their historical vision before a significant portion of the American people. The celebrations' very public character complemented other, often less visible, mechanisms for enabling the construction of a positive African American identity within an unappreciative American society.

But imposing, public Freedom Day celebrations, in part because of their very visibility, gradually fell out of favor as the nineteenth century drew to a close. The decline in white participation and support was accompanied by increasing ambivalence on the part of many blacks, as the positive images the celebrations presented in the public sphere were accompanied more frequently by other images that were less inspiring. As was strikingly apparent in Washington, D.C., some African Americans abhorred the idea of displaying unflattering representations of the race—whether the behavior of black alley-dwellers or the internal dissension among black leaders—before the white public. By the turn of the century, in an era that came to be defined by the adjective "progressive," it did not seem worthwhile to many black leaders to organize events that might emphasize something other than the race's progress.

The vehement rejection of street parades by many of black Washington's self-defined "respectable" classes reflects a longstanding concern among many African Americans regarding the opinion of the race held by whites and the effect that blacks' public appearances had on that opinion. Early in the nineteenth century, commentators on slave trade, New York State, and West Indian Freedom Day celebrations had voiced their distaste for the public behavior of certain elements in the black community. For example, recall that the 1834 National Negro Convention explicitly condemned the "pomp in dress" at New York's July Fifth parades and called for their cessation on the grounds that they wasted scarce resources and tended "to increase the prejudice and contempt of whites."[5]

By the 1880s this desire to control the public behavior of the black masses had intensified. Postbellum African Americans struggled to come to terms with the memory and legacy of slavery and the image of race progress that many defined in terms of respectable and sober comportment as much as educational and economic attainment. During the late nineteenth century it became increasingly common for ministers, newspaper editors, and other cultural arbiters to condemn in general terms the "crying evil" of black excursions, not only for the negative public images they conveyed but also for the damage they did the race on other fronts. AME minister James Handy focused on economic effects when he railed before an 1879 Decoration Day audience that it was inexcusable to spend thirty thousand dollars annually on excursions. Handy also condemned blacks' behavior at such events and implied that they must distance themselves from the vestiges of slave culture, noting, "We must forget the dark past, live in the present, and remember that we are American citizens." In 1886 one pseudonymous commentator in northern Alabama waged "war and no quarters" against the many excursions that the black masses found so appealing. At a time when local workers earned barely a dollar a day, "Solonite" estimated that blacks along the railroad lines connecting Huntsville, Alabama, with Chattanooga and Memphis, Tennessee, spent twenty-five thousand dollars a year on excursions, most of which were run by "men whose only aim is to make money by beguiling the silly and robbing the poor." Excursions were not merely a "financial evil," they were "a business which would yield the greatest harvest of evil" facing the race and "soon make prodigals of all our young people." Their "moral evil" was especially dangerous to "our women and girls," who were "turned loose like so many tramps" when they ventured sometimes "a hundred miles away" from their home communities to "wonder over town and rove the streets unprotected and without shelter." Beyond these inherently damaging effects, excursions also hurt blacks' public image. If blacks could "ever expect to gain the recognition and confidence" of the broader society, they "must quit exposing our girls and boys and our women to every evil influence in the land.... The way to be respected is to be respectible."[6]

Such proscriptions and prescriptions were not limited to criticisms of excursions, urban street manners, and Freedom Day parades. The historian Lawrence Levine has noted a trajectory for the John Kuners, or Jonkonnu, festival in North Carolina that is remarkably consistent with debates over public behavior surrounding District emancipation celebrations—and the Freedom Day tradition in general—in the late nineteenth century. According to Levine, the festival, which had its roots in slavery, "reached its peak of popularity in the 1880s when it became an eagerly anticipated annual event among blacks in the region. By 1900 it seems to have disappeared because of the growing opposition of the Negro clergy who felt it was an undignified exhibition, and a growing number of Negro residents, especially among the middle class, who were convinced that the event lowered their status in the eyes of whites."[7]

Even the lack of "decency" in funeral processions was an issue, one Louisville, Kentucky, paper contending that too much money was wasted and "too much display [was] incident to these occasions."[8] Others took note of the popularity and scale of some funerals. One in New York was distinctive for its use of a "$6,800 automobile hearse." Especially after 1910, as increasing numbers of southern migrants appeared in the urban North, a general consensus among prominent spokespersons in that section contended that it was "more obligatory upon Negroes than upon other sorts of people to so conduct themselves in places of public amusement, accommodation and transportation as gentlemen—modest, quiet, unobtrusive, [and] without . . . any display of vulgarity, uppishness, [or] bumptiousness."[9] Excursions and other public festivities were roundly condemned as venues for the kinds of "objectionable" public behavior that "contribute[d] toward creating a strong sentiment . . . against the great body of colored people, who are not only industrious, sober and law abiding, but profoundly grateful for the respect and good opinion of their white neighbors." These "disorderly mobs" were guilty of "injuring our good name and rendering our advance, so much the more difficult."[10]

The desire to present a united and progressive face to white America was only part of the reason behind this aversion to certain cultural practices and patterns of public comportment. At least as important was the sense of moral responsibility and personal conduct that guided many blacks' individual lives regardless of the perceptions of the outside world. Criticism from within the black community on unseemly public behavior was not simply a matter of genteel urbanites lording it over less sophisticated bumpkins, though these perceptions surely existed in both northern and southern cities. Nor was criticism merely a function of bias based on socioeconomic status or educational attainment. In part such attitudes reflected a particular moral code that was deeply rooted in antebellum black abolitionist circles and in many African Americans' sense of Christian identity and racial destiny. The black clergy—men like Daniel Payne, Benjamin Tanner, and many others with more limited, often only local, influence—were at the forefront of this moral community, but they were hardly alone. Joining them were black Masons, Odd Fellows, Pythians, and True Reformers; members of veterans' organizations and temperance societies; clubwomen; laymen and laywomen active in their local communities; and vast numbers of unremarkable working folk who shared a belief in a just and Divine Providence that guided human affairs and a common commitment, based on that belief, to moral rectitude, right living, and the quest for justice and equality in the land of their birth and citizenship.[11]

Concerns about the public face presented to whites and the basic aversion of many blacks to what they viewed as immoral behavior on the streets help to explain the decline of large, public African American freedom festivals—especially those with elaborate, and often raucous, parades—after the turn of the century. But other factors were at work as well, some of which were peculiar to the black community. Celebrating emancipation in any manner excited opposition from some blacks who would rather not call attention to a shameful past dominated by slavery. Celebrations, monuments, and other commemorations designed to honor blacks as a separate people at times were objected to by African Americans who preferred to assert an undifferentiated American identity to the virtual exclusion of participation in what they saw as narrowly race-specific enterprises. At times the urgent need to address issues pertaining to the erosion of blacks' civil and political rights superseded the need to commemorate the past. And commemorative activities, like most projects undertaken by black community leaders, were constantly hindered by the scarcity of financial resources among a poor and struggling people. But many of these factors existed earlier in the nineteenth century as well, when the Freedom Day tradition was thriving, and thus are insufficient to explain the decline of the celebrations in the early twentieth century. That process can be better understood by appreciating that African American Freedom Day commemorations were firmly rooted in the broader context of American culture and society.

Over the course of the nineteenth century, African Americans' efforts to engage the past were both similar to and vastly different from those of white Americans. To a considerable degree, blacks' and whites' attention to the past followed similar trajectories. Michael Kammen, David Waldstreicher, Simon P. Newman, Len Travers, and others have shown that between the 1790s and 1830s a number of white American intellectuals and political leaders were paying close attention to the construction of a set of traditions around the Revolutionary experience. July Fourth commemorations were central components of this tradition-building among elites, while the working classes were making use of public festivals in their own ways.[12] Black Americans were generally excluded (often forcibly) from participating in these national rituals. But blacks' construction of their own distinct commemorative traditions was not merely a response to this exclusion. Their observances of the 1808 abolition of the Atlantic slave trade illustrate African Americans' early desires to establish a pattern of commemoration that highlighted their own experiences and served their own purposes.

Moreover, as Kammen has observed, before the Civil War "a great many Americans wished to carry little or nothing of the past with them." Though interest in the nation's history was gradually expanding among antebellum whites, Kammen argues that "public policy was infrequently discussed within any sort of historical context. Americans were much more likely to allude to the *burden* of the past than to the possible *uses* of the past." Nor were most white Americans in the early nineteenth century "very consistent about the observance of historic anniversaries."[13] In contrast, by the 1850s African Americans' antebellum Freedom Day celebrations had formed an extremely consistent and well-defined tradition of commemoration around the well-attended public observances of West Indian emancipation. The orations at these, and earlier, commemorative events indicate that blacks, counter to the national trend, very consciously manipulated a version of the history of the slave trade, slavery, emancipation, and blacks' role in the American republic in order to provide a historical context and a rationale for the radical public policy decision to eradicate American slavery and recognize blacks' equal citizenship rights.

Another point of divergence involves the purported "indifference to [historical] ruins that persisted for most of the nineteenth century in the United States," an indifference that was in marked contrast to Europeans' use of the icons of fallen civilizations to impart solemn moral lessons. Those icons, Kammen observes, offered a "homily . . . [from] the past to the present: Take heed." The jeremiads of antebellum Freedom Day orators had more in common with the European pattern than with the white American one. Though they had no physical ruins at hand, black orators explicitly held up examples of ancient slaveholding civilizations that had crumbled before the judgment of Providence. They warned modern nations, especially the United States, to mind the lessons of the past, and, in the words of one postbellum orator, to "read history wisely."[14]

In some respects, then, the nature of black and white public commemorative rituals remained distinct. Most fundamentally, they differed in their uses of the past. In the United States as a whole after 1870, "more often than not, memory . . . served as a bulwark for social and political stability—a means of valorizing resistance to change."[15] For African Americans the preservation of the status quo was far from desirable. Change was the underlying objective of practically every social and political action or movement undertaken by black Americans, commemorations included. During the last several decades of the century the need for drastic change in their collective political, economic, and social status was as pressing as ever. Blacks' uses of the past and applications of historical knowledge during this period were largely dictated by their ultimate goals: freedom, equality, and justice, most immediately for themselves, but also universally, for all humanity.

As the words and actions of individuals like Benjamin Tanner, T. Thomas Fortune, Calvin Chase, and others suggest, African American spokespersons in the generation after the Civil War continued to use the remembrance of the past to an even greater degree than had their intellectual and activist forebears. By the time of Reconstruction the rest of American society's attention to history had proceeded apace. Indeed, as Kammen has pointed out, "Anyone who probes historical sources for this period [between 1870 and 1915] will be figuratively assaulted by the nation's arsenal of memory devices and by the astonishing diversity of its stockpile." Both black and white Americans utilized similar weapons from that stockpile—monuments, historical societies, written histories, and, of course, public commemorations. The historian Ellen Litwicki has called attention to the "frenzy of holiday creativity" during this period, and her overview of Labor Days, Memorial Days, Emancipation Days, and various white ethnic holidays shows considerable similarities in their practice and function. Litwicki notes that these holidays all interacted in complex ways with the press, through both advertising and coverage; all were organized and intended to be expressions of middle-class planning and sensibility; all were sites of contestation on various levels, both within the group and between that group and the broader society; all used these public venues at least in part for the edification of the masses; and, perhaps most significantly, all were used by their respective constituencies to forge, promote, and legitimate particular varieties of American identity.[16]

As Litwicki's study demonstrates, after the 1870s both black and white Americans emphasized the educational function of their commemorative rituals. Even a singular national ritual like the 1876 Centennial, for example, was touted as an educational experience, though profit was as much a motivation as was devotion to country. For centennial organizers this ostensible use of memory to educate was largely "lip service" and did not accurately reflect the reality behind the rhetoric.[17] African Americans were, for the most part, more earnest in their attempts to appropriate the past for a range of educative purposes, even if, at times, they too attempted simultaneously to address financial needs, political agendas, or personal ambitions. Even in the antebellum period the use of Freedom Day commemorations to teach the lessons of history to both white and black Americans was among the most important of their functions. After the 1870s the use of those events to impart lessons to both races in history, memory, citizenship, race pride, and politics became even more explicit. This increasing cognizance of the importance of educating the public meshes with another broad trend in American culture not directly connected with public commemoration or historical memory.

The historian Michael McGerr, in his study of popular politics in the postbellum North, has identified the 1880s as a "turning point in . . . [American] political style." The style that political historians have traditionally ascribed to the middle decades of the nineteenth century was defined by white male voters' intense personal identification with political parties and avid participation in popular democracy. Campaigns were spectacular partisan displays featuring massive political rallies that were climaxed by huge parades and torchlight processions. Not unlike the multifunctional Freedom Day celebrations that matured during the same period, these rallies were festivals of popular amusement and entertainment as well as tools of political mobilization. By the mid-1880s this popular approach to campaigning was giving way before what McGerr calls the ascendancy of "educational politics." Jean H. Baker attests to the educative function of partisan celebrations, referring to them as "one of the best civics lessons the nineteenth century offered." By the 1880s white political campaign managers had begun to see torchlight processions as "a silly sort of show" that was "exceedingly costly" and of minimal value in attracting voters. In an interesting parallel with both the persistent financial strains and the expanding educative functions of Freedom Day commemorations, managers advocated redirecting campaign money toward "enlighten[ing] the voters" through education. Political organizers increasingly "played schoolmaster to the electorate" and instituted a tradition of rather dull campaigns that "alienated many people" and contributed to a marked decline in popular political participation by the turn of the century. "Spectacular parades," McGerr observes, "almost vanished in the first decades of the twentieth century. . . . Elaborate all-day rallies, with speeches and parades, declined after 1900" and were "quite rare" by 1908. Baker charts the same general chronology for such affairs, which were "commonplace" by the 1850s but "had largely disappeared" by the 1910s.[18]

The parallels here should not be overdrawn. There were fundamental differences—in scale, in objective, in audience—between national political campaigns and African Americans' relatively modest commemorations. What is significant is the general trajectory they shared. From the 1850s to the 1870s both types of events featured large, spectacular public displays that served their respective purposes well, attracting broad popular appeal and participation. By century's end, both had gravitated toward a more subdued presentation that focused on practical goals with less concern for catering to the tastes of the masses. The educational campaign style was mirrored by a more explicit attempt on the part of many Freedom Day organizers to instruct the public in a variety of areas. Many African American commemorations by the start of the new century were more likely to promote comparatively pallid essay contests and displays of black industrial talents, and were otherwise conceived as vehicles to raise money for worthy causes in the service of the race, as was the case with Allen Day and with Calvin Chase's efforts to transform District emancipation celebrations in the 1890s.

Many festivals did continue to include an expanding array of popular amusements like beauty pageants, popularity contests, tugs-of-war, fat men's races, and ball games, but often these types of affairs had been divorced from any commemorative, educational, or political meanings. An August 4, 1897, "Grand Union" celebration in Kansas City heavily advertised all of the above amusements without any mention of the event being an emancipation anniversary. All in attendance "went away feeling the importance of [an] annual good time." In 1912 Chicago also witnessed a huge "Grand August Carnival and Negro Exposition" during the last two weeks in August that was not connected in any way to the commemoration of emancipation. The "two big weeks of mirth, merriment and review" took over the segregated space of South State Street between 31st and 39th Streets with nightly parades, electric light shows, beauty pageants, and assorted amusements. At a Cleveland emancipation celebration on the first Monday in August 1917, one newspaper account claimed to have no knowledge of, or concern for, that date's historical relevance. "What's in a date when 20,000 people wish to get together once a year and 'talk it over'?" The celebration was valued primarily for providing a good time and "weld[ing] a good feeling" among people expected to come in from all across the state.[19]

Organizers both of national political campaigns and of commemorative festivals could hardly have been unaware of the momentous transformation in American popular culture that directly impinged on their own abilities to connect with the masses of their respective constituencies. Around the turn of the century a whole slew of mass entertainments appeared and vied for the attention of a working- and middle-class public that was less constrained by Victorian standards of civic conduct and social order. According to the historian John Kasson, dance halls, vaudeville, amusement parks, nickelodeons, movie houses, and other attractions "became meccas for a public eagerly seeking recreation." While African Americans did not play a central role in developing all these new recreational forms, black voices undeniably played a large part in defining the popular arts and entertainment culture of the ragtime era. Bob Cole, James Weldon Johnson, and J. Rosamond Johnson helped redefine American musical theater between the 1890s and 1910s. Musicians like Scott Joplin, Thomas Dorsey, Buddy Bolden, and W. C. Handy helped create new categories and standards in American popular music. Bandleader and composer James Reese Europe provided the accompaniment for the 1910s dance craze, during which the team of Vernon and Irene Castle adapted and popularized black dance styles, making them more accessible to the wider American public. Performers like Bert Williams contributed distinctively black interpretations of the minstrel tradition to the emerging form of vaudeville.[20]

Black Americans had limited opportunities to enjoy the new amusements offered by urban culture, but they embraced them wholeheartedly when they had the chance. Separate amusement parks were opened for blacks in a few southern cities, but none lasted long. Most parks across the country only admitted blacks on certain days, sometimes as seldom as once a year.

Most cities had at least one segregated black theater, and most vaudeville theaters and movie houses allowed blacks in a segregated balcony. The *Pittsburgh Courier* condemned the fact that blacks were "being discriminated against by the proprietors of the nickolodeons," even as the paper expressed concern that so many were attracted by an entertainment it deemed void of "moral uplift." While spokespersons for the "respectable" classes viewed the growth of urban amusements with some anxiety, the masses of black city dwellers took to them as enthusiastically as local discriminatory laws and customs would permit.[21]

Concerns of black cultural arbiters notwithstanding, a new cultural acceptance of the pursuit of leisure for its own sake made both newer and older forms of spectator or participatory activities—bicycling, ball games, races, boxing matches—more legitimate pursuits, especially for the working classes. McGerr has noted that the "traditional forms of [political] campaigning" simply "could not compete with these new diversions." Campaigns in large cities had for many years had to contend with the attractions of urban recreation, but in the twentieth century "the contest was uneven." By the 1910s even residents of small, isolated northern communities showed a "lack of inclination . . . to turn out." "The people," one journalist reported, "don't attend meetings as they used to." McGerr points out that New York City experienced a decline in the popularity of political parades earlier than other places largely because New Yorkers' pretensions to sophistication rendered such activities too quaint to take seriously. Perhaps the absence of a vibrant African American Freedom Day tradition in that city, as noted by T. Thomas Fortune in the 1880s, can be explained in part by a similar logic. In any case, by the early 1900s, African Americans increasingly had at least limited access to many of the diversions of a transformed public sphere in urban America. Some of the black press's criticisms of public behavior explicitly identified the worst culprits as unemployed "gentlemen of leisure."[22]

Journalists and ministers especially took note of some of the new leisure-time attractions, usually characterizing them as sinful and socially damaging. Charles Stewart, who wrote a column for Baltimore's *Afro-American Ledger* under the pseudonym "Col. J. O. Midnight," complained in 1901 about activities at a Quincy, Illinois, emancipation celebration. After listening to some rather tedious speeches before a sparse audience, Stewart was disturbed to find a much larger gathering at an adjacent dance hall, where men and women "turned and turned and hugging [rather than dancing] seemed to be in order. I said that I wanted to know if that was a hugging celebration instead of an emancipation." Even more offensive was the liquor concession where "even a little baby girl was given part of a glass of beer by her parents." That the ten-cent admission fee was supposed to go to the church seems not to have justified the situation. A visit to Quincy the following year convinced Stewart that the people there "were going to the devil with their eyes wide open."[23]

After 1910 critics increasingly condemned the "scandalous conduct" associated with the new wave of "public entertainments" that included "dance halls and gardens" as well as automobiles, amusement parks, and movie houses. The attraction of these and other forms of leisure-time activities, carried out largely in less structured and more anonymous public spaces, posed a direct threat to the oversight of the ethnic community. Even in the realm of popular politics, Michael McGerr has suggested that the dissolution of "the communal experience" contributed to the breakdown of vibrant local political traditions. More directly germane to African Americans' disrupted communal world and commemorative tradition is the analysis of the historian Roy Rosenzweig, whose study of leisure among white ethnic workers in Worcester, Massachusetts, indicates a similar pattern. Rosenzweig argues that the "commercialization of leisure" in the early twentieth century eroded workers' "commitment to an ethnic community" and resulted in "the loss . . . of communal control over popular recreation," even in that relatively small industrial city. It is particularly striking that Rosenzweig singles out commemorations of July Fourth as a key site of this cultural transformation. "The ethnic July Fourth picnics had been held under the watchful eyes of community leaders, particularly . . . ministers." Mass cultural amusements appealed to individuals primarily as individuals and therefore challenged "the traditional bases of authority in Worcester's ethnic communities." Just as important, the masses' gradual abandonment of community leaders' organized activities also "threatened their economic base." The historian William H. Cohn similarly argues that the "loss of community spirit" engendered by early twentieth-century urban life was a large part of the transformation of July Fourth as a public ritual.[24]

Perhaps the presence of the equally watchful eyes of African American community leaders helps explain the widely reported (if perhaps exaggerated) absence of drunkenness and rowdy behavior at mid-nineteenth-century Freedom Day commemorations. Certainly by the turn of the twentieth century the reportage had swung to the opposite extreme. To the extent that large, public Freedom Day festivals still took place, the behavior of their once well-ordered crowds appears to have deteriorated considerably. This despite the apparent fact that the scale of those events, with rare exceptions, did not approach that of affairs a half century earlier. Part of community leaders' response to this transformation of the Freedom Day tradition mirrored another cultural pattern in Progressive America. John Kasson has suggested that, as part of their "struggle to regain their cultural authority" and "rekindle a sense of common purpose," community leaders turned to pageantry.[25]

A number of African American pageants were produced surrounding the fiftieth anniversary of U.S. emancipation. The "Pan-American Kermiss" was a "spectacular drama" with a cast of five hundred actors and singers and a fifty-piece black orchestra that was produced during a week-long celebration in St. Louis in 1914. It used several camels and elephants in its African segment, and used "realistic scenes and characteristic music" to depict "Slavery Days," "The Negro as a Soldier," "Reconstruction Days," and "Negro Religious and Educational Life." A widely publicized semicentennial exposition in Richmond in 1915 included a somewhat less elaborate "pantomimic pageant" entitled "The Answer to the Birth of a Nation," which featured "300 of the colored school children of the city."[26] African Americans' most well-known use of that form came with W. E. B. Du Bois's "Star of Ethiopia" historical pageant, which was first presented to an opening-night audience of five thousand African Americans in conjunction with the 1913 New York Emancipation Proclamation Exposition celebrating the semicentennial of Lincoln's edict. The exposition as a whole was conceived by Du Bois and his fellow commissioners to be "distinctly and impressively educational."[27] The pageant in particular was said to be "eliciting the liveliest attention and promises to be a great educational influence." It was hoped that it would rectify "a very great lack of information [among both blacks and whites] regarding the part the Negro has played in the civilization of which he is a part." The "Star of Ethiopia"—a three-hour extravaganza utilizing hundreds of black actors—was by most accounts a magnificent panorama of African American history and progress from prehistoric times to the present. Some critics, however, found little in the pageant's depictions of ancient African civilizations that was relevant to "the progress of the Negroes of New York or of the country." Fred J. Moore, a mouthpiece of Booker T. Washington who took the reins of the *Age* after T. Thomas Fortune had been removed for a variety of financial and personal reasons, was chief among the critics of Du Bois and the exposition in general. He especially condemned the attention given to the focus on the African past, deeming it an insult to modern black New Yorkers. Du Bois presented the pageant again in Washington in 1915 and in Philadelphia in 1916 at the commemoration of the AME church's centennial. In keeping with the educational function of the Freedom Day tradition, Du Bois hoped that the "Star" would "teach on the one hand the colored people themselves the meaning of their history . . . and on the other . . . reveal the Negro to the white world."[28]

In 1915 a sympathetic reviewer of the Washington production affirmed Du Bois's intention, perceiving that "the one idea that dominates the whole [of the pageant] is that the Negro has a past of which he should be proud." Regarding the clarity with which Du Bois communicated that message, he noted that "the historical truth in the episodes is evident, the symbolism simple and in no sense obscure." But one reviewer of the 1913 New York pageant contended that the educational message in that first production may have been less accessible to the masses. In a generally positive review in the *Age,* drama critic L. H. White praised the "historical value of the play." But that message, he felt, was "so involved in splendor of imageric language that it is lost to the conception of the average mind."[29]

The *Bee* pointed out that the 1915 pageant also tested the reach of "the average mind." But Calvin Chase's journal found the "Star of Ethiopia" especially pleasing in part *because* it did not pander to the tastes of the masses. The commentator singled out the pageant's musical selections, which featured refined renditions of slave spirituals and original works based on African themes written by several black composers. Selections from Verdi's *Aida* and a rousing version of "Le Marseilles" rounded out the score. These pieces, the reviewer noted admiringly, "must be played accurately and absolutely on time," in marked contrast with the "syncopated jingling dance music" so popular among black musicians and audiences during the ragtime era. David Glassberg has interpreted the *Bee's* stance as being similar to that of other self-appointed guardians of public morality in the broader society. This class of observers, he argues, "looked to historical pageantry not only to foster a greater appreciation of history but also to elevate that community's taste in amusements."[30]

This desire to separate popular amusements from commemorative events was not new. But in the 1910s the transformation and proliferation of those amusements made their threat to the vitality of the Freedom Day tradition and the black community in general loom larger than ever. Several observers of the 1913 New York Exposition "were surprised and disgusted to find that even this exhibition was turned into a great big ball. Another appeal to the weakness of our race simply to get money out of their pockets." The Reverend Adam Clayton Powell Sr., prominent pastor of Harlem's Abyssinian Baptist Church, complained that "[t]he Negro Race is dancing itself to death. We could not even celebrate our fifty years of progress without advertising 'dancing every afternoon.' "[31]

These were not the only voices expressing dissatisfaction with the way the exposition was conducted. Other complaints, however, had less to do with the frivolity of the affair than with the composition and management of the Exposition Commission. Fred Moore of the *Age,* an ardent Republican, was bitterly critical that the commission was dominated by black New York Democrats with close ties to Tammany Hall. His paper regularly reported factional strife among the commissioners, including a $5,000 libel suit brought against Du Bois by Director General Sumner H. Lark. Though internal dissension was undeniably a problem, the commissioners responded that Moore's "malicious and pernicious lies" were largely a result of the fact that the editor had "failed in his bid to become a member." Other conflicts related to DuBois's plans to spend money on "an exhibition consisting of charts, sociological congresses and African curios," when the state's $25,000 appropriation specified "an exposition illustrating the work and progress of the negroes of the state of New York." Du Bois was also reported to have been "involved in a heated argument" with fellow commissioner James D. Carr, during which the two demonstrated "the progress of the race at hurling uncomplimentary epithets. . . . Luckily, no blows were struck." Several witnesses were reported to have declared that the altercation was "the feature of the exposition."[32]

Despite substantial press coverage in several northeastern cities, the New York Exposition, like similar affairs held in Philadelphia, Chicago, Richmond, Louisville, and Atlantic City between 1913 and 1916, was less than a resounding success. The intent of the expositions was to use historical and industrial displays of black accomplishment to demonstrate the rapid progress of the race during the fifty years since emancipation. Some African American commentators wryly noted that continued disfranchisement, segregation, exclusion, and lynching raised some doubts about the extent of that ostensible progress. The *Chicago Defender* did eventually promote that city's "Lincoln Jubilee" in 1915, but as plans were developing several years earlier the paper complained that in the absence of "full citizenship" for black Americans, the "former chattle" were about to celebrate the semicentennial of their "semi-freedom."[33]

Black critics of these events also pointed out the common difficulties all the organizers had in responsibly handling the considerable sums of money involved. A number of black New Yorkers were disgruntled enough over the commission's alleged misuse of funds to threaten a mass boycott of the celebration. Rumors of huge deficits despite large gate receipts led to "much dissatisfaction" over the handling of money at the New York Exposition. "Wherever one or more dollars are gathered together in one place and Negroes have the management, there war will be found," one reporter wryly noted. The Senate passed an appropriation bill setting aside $250,000 for a national emancipation celebration, but the House voted it down on the grounds that fifty years was too short a time to warrant such an event. The states of Illinois, New Jersey, Pennsylvania, and New York, however, each allocated between $20,000 and $100,000 to their respective celebrations of emancipation. And Congress ended up earmarking $55,000 for the Richmond affair. In each case black organizers were accused of mismanagement, if not outright embezzlement. In Philadelphia, the home of exposition organizer Harry W. Bass was "beseiged" by "a crowd of colored women" clamoring to be paid for services rendered during the celebration. The reporter "hoped that the country and the race will be spared the disgrace of a controversy over accounts of the Exposition." Bass was also taken to court by a sculptor who was not paid, and in New York, there were "many complaints being made by former employees of the exposition that they have not been paid what is due them."[34]

Even without the specter of fiscal impropriety, the events generally were seen as less than helpful to the race. Regarding the "dismal failure" of the 1913 Philadelphia Exposition, the *Age*'s correspondent expressed the hope that "this exhibition of our failure, right in the heart of the North, will go far to teach our race that in the future when we undertake anything that is to come before the public we should be very careful to see that everything is so planned as to bring about success and not failure." When "more than a score" of black delegates from other states arrived in Philadelphia for the opening ceremonies, they found that the buildings had barely been started and could not find any of the organizers to assist them. The exposition opened more than two weeks late. The affair was less spectacular than New York's, consisting primarily of meetings and speeches that rendered the exposition "a dismal, gloomy and disappointing failure." "What does a big speech amount to," pondered the reporter, "when the speaker has behind him and in front of him and on each side of him evidences of racial failure? A speech on such an occasion means little or nothing." To be fair, some reports positively glowed with praise for the "indescribable inspiration" elicited by the fair. The opening parade was said to have included five thousand in line and been witnessed by more than fifty thousand spectators. One observer hoped whites would be so impressed with the exhibitions of black progress "that these celebrations may be the opening wedge to the door of opportunity," which had been closed to blacks for so long.[35]

By and large, the boosterism of such reports was countered by more critical and less optimistic accounts regarding whites' impressions. The 1915 Negro Historical and Industrial Exposition at Richmond presents an interesting case in that virtually all the praise for the event appeared in the white press. The sole African American organizer, Giles B. Jackson, was a former slave, a Richmond lawyer and entrepreneur, and an avid supporter of Booker T. Washington, who was generally mistrusted among Richmond's other black leaders for his subservience to the city's white elite. Jackson was also deeply involved in black commemorations in Virginia, having organized the Negro exhibit at the 1907 Jamestown Tercentennial and already beginning to plan the three hundredth anniversary of the first landing of Africans at Jamestown in 1619. Jackson received the enthusiastic support of white spokespersons and the consistent condemnation of other black Virginians. The Richmond Exposition had the support of national, state, and local government; received $55,000 from Congress and smaller allocations from Richmond and New York State; and was billed for some reason as "the first negro exposition ever held." Unlike the other semicentennial fairs, its "creditable midway" featured "amusements galore," including a Wild West show, vaudeville performances, and "scantily attired" white female springboard divers (these "shapely aquarian artists" having somehow managed to gain the approval of the Board of Censors). The midway attractions were described as "the equal of any state fair ever given in this city." Of course, like other expositions, there were also historical and industrial, educational, and handicraft exhibits intended to demonstrate the progress of the race since emancipation. The crowds were reported in the white press to have been consistently large, but other than an opening day estimate of "several thousand negroes" in attendance, the fair seems to have attracted mostly whites. "The white people," according to several accounts, "have manifested a great deal of interest in the exposition and have patronized it in a very liberal manner." Black attendance was clearly lagging. Shortly after opening day the fifty-cent admission charge was lifted and free admission to the grounds allowed. But two weeks later the *Richmond Leader* still commented on the large white attendance and scolded that "the colored folk should realize that it is their exposition and they should patronize it to the fullest extent."[36]

Many black Virginians apparently did not see it as their exposition at all. One problem in the segregated city of Richmond involved there being "but one colored hotel of any size," and that, combined with the few boarding houses, "could not accommodate 150 negroes." The presence of so many white patrons in itself may have discouraged blacks from attending. Giles Jackson's sycophantic reputation among local black leaders may also have worked against the exposition's popularity within the race. White observers had nothing but the highest praise for Jackson and the exposition, including a glowing account in the *American Review of Reviews*. The *Richmond Dispatch* saw him as a Negro "of the old school" whose "own effort raised him to leadership among his race in Virginia and the South." He was the "guiding spirit" of the fair to whom all "credit is due." To the editor of the *Richmond Planet*, however, the exposition was "a miserable farce" and Jackson the "chief offender." Once more it was allegations of fiscal misconduct that brought matters into the public eye. Jackson and other "promoters of this scheme," asserted the *Planet*, "had their heads and both feet in the trough" and were "so indiscreet as to row among themselves over the contents." In doing so they aroused the "disgust and contempt" of blacks and also "re-vealed themselves in their true light to the white folks." Contrary to white characterizations, Jackson's "insatiable greed" marked him as a "miserable and obnoxious" excuse for a leader. Personal and political differences had alienated Jackson from other black figures long before the exposition, es-pecially his pride in what he considered "his influence with the white race." That influence made for a well-financed exposition, plenty of good press, a large attendance at the fair, and profits in Jackson's pockets, but did little toward fulfilling the "larger aims and purposes" semicentennial celebrations hoped to achieve for race progress. According to the *Colored Virginian,* "Mr. Jackson and his self-appointed associates were the wrong men on the right job." Jackson countered that his critics suffered from "a great deal of jealousy."[37]

None of the other semicentennial celebrations fared well in impressing whites with the progress of the race. New Jersey's Atlantic City celebration, despite the promise that it would be "one of the largest gatherings of colored people ever held in the state," was reported to have taken place "on a small scale" and with "a paucity of results." In New York, despite Du Bois's massive pageant, it was "estimated that less than two hundred white citizens attended the exposition to note the advancement made by the Negro" since emanci-pation. Despite the participation of state governors and other local white political officials at each celebration, the relative inattentiveness of whites, except at Richmond, reflects the racial segregation of the public sphere by the early twentieth century. White Americans at the time were far more in-terested in the semicentennial commemorations of the Civil War, with their emphasis on reconciliation and national unity.[38] But some African American analysts had entertained the possibility that the celebrations would augment the expansion of historical consciousness that accompanied the growth of black literacy, education, and scholarship during the 1910s. The *Chicago Defender* editor Robert Abbott had hoped that "the different expositions and celebrations will be as much of an eye opener to our own race as it doubtless will to the white race. How many of those who consider them-selves fairly intelligent know what the race has done or what they are doing today? And yet we should be as familiar with such things as we are with an American historical fact, for the Negro plays an important part in American history, in fact there is no American history without the Negro."[39]

The semicentennial fervor did not serve the interests of either race pro-gress or black (and white) historical consciousness hoped for by optimistic commentators like Abbott. But the hoopla surrounding the semicentennial probably helped inspire blacks across the nation to hold emancipation cel-ebrations between 1910 and 1920. Booker T. Washington, by the 1910s in the waning years of both his political power and his life, added to the fiftieth anniversary fervor by advocating that black communities across the nation hold local celebrations during the third week of October 1913, which would be designated "Fiftieth Anniversary Week." Washington's general view of the celebration's importance and function is consistent with that of other black leaders. "There are two things that can be accomplished by a celebration," he maintained in a letter to the prominent Washington, D.C., educator and lawyer Jesse Lawson. "One is the encouragement of our own people, and secondly, letting the world see what we have accomplished. Now if we keep these two central thoughts in mind, the mere technicality covering the date means but little."[40]

The proposed date, the scale, and the question of leadership of the celebration all caused some division among various parties. Since 1909 Lawson had been president of Washington, D.C.'s National Emancipation Commemorative Society and had been planning a massive national celebration of the semicentennial to be held September 22, 1912. In addition to being adamant about the date, Lawson also insisted that a single, grand national celebration be held in the nation's capital, rather than the coordinated local ones proposed by Washington. Since "Congress refused to make any appropriation" to adequately finance a single grand event, Washington felt that only a series of smaller localized events, coordinated through branches of his National Negro Business League, could properly represent the progress of the race. Lawson needed to "face facts. It is impossible to get together in Washington or anywhere else any large sum of money to be used in financing an enterprise of national character. . . . [However,] when the responsibility is placed on each local community, they do raise considerable sums of money and will do it in this case." Should Lawson attempt to centralize the commemoration, Washington wrote in August 1912, "I fear that the whole thing is going to prove a fiasco." The Wizard of Tuskegee's assessment demonstrates the depth of his experience, and his knowledge of the limits of the possible when organizing in African American communities.[41]

While the week-long celebrations hoped for by Washington did not attract significant support, many black communities did experience a revival of commemorative spirit during the 1910s. There were attempts to maintain August 1 commemorations in old strongholds like New Bedford, Massachusetts, and Binghamton, New York, as well as celebrations on various dates at sites as far-flung as Keokuk, Iowa; Peoria, Illinois; Montgomery, Alabama; Savannah, Georgia; Milwaukee, Wisconsin; St. Paul, Minnesota; and Spokane, Washington. Charleston, South Carolina; Alton, Illinois; Los Angeles, California; and Knoxville, Tennessee, each observed the fiftieth anniversary of Lincoln's proclamation in January 1913.[42] The Knoxville celebration may have been arranged by migrants from Virginia, since it was held on the "Surrender Day" anniversary of April 9. This event maintained much of the established Freedom Day tradition, with special trains bringing in "hundreds of negroes from all parts of East Tennessee," a "pretentious" mile-long parade, an evening banquet, and an oration that "forcefully reviewed the history of the colored race in America." Many "white friends" were also said to have come out to see the procession. The parade exhibited black Americans' sense of Du Boisian double-consciousness, as the schoolchildren marching in the procession carried " 'emancipation' flags and American flags, alike celebrating that particular day and at the same time demonstrating their allegiance to the old flag—the Stars and Stripes." At September 22 celebrations in Lima, Ohio, and Terre Haute, Indiana, political partisans engaged in another familiar Emancipation Day activity as they urged large crowds to cast their votes for particular candidates.[43]

In Texas the Juneteenth tradition remained vibrant, though in one instance there was a campaign to abandon the state's distinctive anniversary in order "to concentrate on the observance of the real emancipation day, according to history, the anniversary of which is January 1." The issue here was according to *whose* history would the date be determined? This 1918 report from El Paso indicates that the relatively new National Association for the Advancement of Colored People (NAACP) was behind the movement to alter the deeply entrenched local Juneteenth tradition. This top-down attempt to impose an official version of history on a vibrant folk culture must have infuriated El Paso's black population. The history and experiences of black Texans were quite clear on the matter of their emancipation, and they no doubt made short work of this utterly futile effort to impose a replacement celebration date.[44]

Barbecues, baseball games, picnics, dancing, red lemonade, Budweiser, parades, beauty contests, and general merriment dominated the festivities in Dallas, Houston, Galveston, Hillsboro, El Paso, and other communities across the state. Dallas whites fully expected that their black employees would take the day off from work. One 1914 commentator from that city was pleased that "not a single arrest was made" during the celebration, a welcome departure from previous celebrations. He expressed concern, however, that in the midst of the merrymaking, "we are not taking our freedom seriously enough. We have not fully realized that freedom means opportunity instead of a 'big time.' . . . While the recreation and amusements enjoyed by the thousands of colored people present were perhaps good in their places, it would have meant so much more had this followed an appropriate program including the reading of the Emancipation Proclamation and an inspiring address." That these features were not even on the program represents a dramatic shift from the celebrations of the nineteenth century. There was nothing in the day "reminding them of the deep significance of the occasion." It was especially disturbing for this writer "that many of the young people in particular passed the day away in pleasure without giving the object of their celebration one minute of serious thought. These celebrations should not be merely 19th of June festivals to be had annually, but they should be real emancipation celebrations, during which we should briefly but carefully review our slavery days and the years that have passed since our freedom."[45]

The problem was that everybody liked to have a day off and a good time, but not everybody really wanted to think about slavery on their holiday. The Reverend Silas X. Floyd had expressed his own concerns about blacks' relationship with Emancipation Day in 1909. At a January 1 celebration in Augusta, Georgia, Floyd touted Emancipation Day as "the grandest day in American history." "But," he continued, "and I regret to say it—there are some colored people who know so little what important factors tradition and sentiment are in the lives and characters of races and individuals that they are not willing to enter heartily into the observance of Emancipation Day." Many would eschew even the festive aspects of the celebrations, holding that "we have no right to celebrate this day, while others declare that we ought to try to forget that our race was once enslaved in this country."[46]

In 1914, even in the midst of the semicentennial excitement, the editor of the *Afro-American Ledger* wondered in print "just why we take so little interest in the celebration of Emancipation day." It was, he puzzled, "somewhat of a mystery. Having the example of the American people in its constant and regular celebration of the Fourth of July . . . it does seem just a little bit strange that our people take such little interest in a matter of which we were, if possible, more interested in than that of the American colonies." As the year 1915 drew to a close, the same editor took note of the semicentennial of the ratification of the Thirteenth Amendment, pointing out that "it is not generally known that Saturday of last week [December 18] was the fiftieth anniversary of the birth of freedom to the colored people of these United States. Some day, possibly, we will get it into our heads that such occasions should be properly celebrated."[47]

Emancipation celebrations had long been used to instill historical consciousness among blacks generally and in the younger generations in particular. But if some African Americans saw value in maintaining that practice, others who were just as committed to race history thought the time had come for a more structured approach to developing and utilizing historical knowledge. In late 1911 the young black Rhodes Scholar Alain LeRoy

Locke had presented his paper "The Negro and a Race Tradition" at a meeting of the Negro Society for Historical Research at the Yonkers, New York, home of the society's president, John Edward Bruce. Locke spoke of African Americans' collective "duty toward a racial past." Any people, he asserted, had a responsibility for "their acquisition of historical mindedness in the establishment of a tradition." Though American blacks stood "between two heritages," Locke's unavoidable conclusion, given the realities of American society, was that "the desire to preserve our past commits us to a racial consciousness. . . . One cannot raise the question of history without raising the question of race or nationality." But Locke also felt that blacks needed to "change [their] attitude toward the past." It was no longer appropriate to cling to the "sentimental ties" that bound blacks to the "abolitionist period of our history." Young people of the race like himself could not really "care for race history in the same way" as those who had lived through emancipation and had a particular set of memories to preserve. Locke's argument suggests that yet another generational transition was in process that required a different approach to the study and teaching of black history. It was Locke's expectation that the "younger generation" would reject the sentimentality of their elders and through a "scholarly attitude toward history" solve the "great American problem"—"whether a race can exist within a nation without disrupting the nation or contradicting itself." Locke insisted on a new orientation toward history that did not attempt to forget slavery, but that, at the same time, moved beyond what he saw as the race's sentimental connections with abolition and emancipation. The "sentimental" approach had freed blacks physically, he asserted, but bound them to only one brief period in the race's history. Mentally they were "blinded" to the larger history, "the remote racial past," in which lay the key to understanding the race's present and future.[48]

A January 1913 editorial in the *AME Church Review* also prescribed a new direction for blacks' relationship with emancipation and with their history. Dissatisfied with the refrains of "the progress of the race," the editor argued that it was not appropriate, "either in jubilation or self-praise, to be counting the milestones of our progress or enumerating our material wealth or intellectual gains." It was time, he insisted, for a "new emancipation." T. Thomas Fortune had given voice to the older attitude in the 1880s when he called for blacks to never forget the wilderness of slavery through which the race had wandered for so long. Black Americans in 1913, said the *Review* editor, "had been wandering for these past forty years in the wilderness of political serfdom and drinking the bitter water of the Merah of Jim Crowism. Within the next fifty years there must come to the Negro a new emancipation . . . from social degredation, industrial and commercial exclusion, political inequality and all discrimination based on race and color." Ever conscious of the importance of posterity, he recognized that "fifty years hence the Negroes of this generation will be reviewed by our children's children." Contemporary leaders, he contended, must "fully emancipate ourselves" to earn the respect of their posterity.[49]

If the editorialist did not call for the complete abandonment of freedom festivals, the celebrations of emancipation had in fact dwindled. "By the 1920s," one historian of blacks in western Michigan has noted, "the idea and festive protest parade [on August 1] ceased to occur." In 1924 the *Chicago Whip* reprinted an editorial from the *Norfolk Journal and Guide* that called attention to "a steady decline in attendance upon Emancipation Day observances." Street parades still attracted "a creditable crowd," but "speeches and recitations appropriate to the occasion" no longer held people's interest. His language echoed that of the *AME Church Review* editorial from a decade before: "A close study of the situation reveals that the Negro of the latter day as a whole is indifferent about and not interested in celebrating emancipation from chattel slavery. In the first place any reference to American slavery fosters into his imagination a picture of the abhorrence of the times. In the next place he realizes that there is yet so much to be done to break the bonds of economic slavery, proscription of opportunity, injustice before the law and denial of citizenship rights, that his attention is focused more upon gaining a newer emancipation."[50]

A 1929 call from Gary, Indiana, to "end Emancipation Day celebrations" made a similar point. Noting the numerous different dates celebrated every year, the writer suggested that "this lack of uniformity and agreement on a day to celebrate is merely one of the inanities of such a celebration." "Emancipation day celebrations have a habit of leaving us too well satisfied. We get drunk on words" glorifying the progress of the race when that progress was often difficult to see. He also implied that a new emancipation was needed to make the old one seem real. It was still sadly the case that "many Negroes who live in Mississippi and other places will never know that they are 'free' unless they accidentally drop around where one of the celebrations is in progress. . . . The sooner the Negro forgets that he was once a slave, the better. The sooner he quits celebrating the day when one white man took him away from another, the better." Not all who opposed celebrations, or called for more complex understandings of race history, were quite so ready to completely dissociate from the slave past, but most expressed some version of the idea that "we are emancipated but in many ways we are as yet not free." By 1930 even the space of the celebrations themselves was no longer as free as it had been. In Warrenton, Georgia, blacks had planned to invite Benjamin J. Davis, radical editor of the *Atlanta Independent,* to be the orator of the day. Unhappy with that choice, local whites put pressure on the sheriff, who "felt it his duty to tell the 'niggers to call it off.' " The celebration did not take place.[51]

There were many reasons for African Americans' declining interest in organizing or attending freedom festivals, and the long absence of any real freedom for most blacks surely ranked among them. The numerous and expanding diversions of mass culture also contributed to the erosion of the Freedom Day tradition by providing recreational activities that were far more interesting to most twentieth-century African Americans. Many black community leaders had their own reasons for discontinuing the celebrations, but those who had for generations put such stock in the annual commemorations for their political and educational functions were prepared to carry on their responsibilities through other means. Even during the nineteenth century black leaders had utilized formal institutions for the preservation and dissemination of African American historical memory, the organization of civil rights activism, and the mutual uplift of the race. Benevolent, fraternal, and church-based organizations maintained their importance in these endeavors during the age of the New Negro. Around the turn of the century many other formal institutions emerged that helped compensate for the decline of the Freedom Day tradition. The Afro-American League and Council, the Niagara Movement, and with considerable white cooperation, the National Association for the Advancement of Colored People provided a structure from which to work for the reinstatement of blacks' civil and political rights. Similarly the National Association of Colored Women, the National Federation of Afro-American Women, the Urban League, the YMCAs and YWCAs, and a number of more locally oriented groups worked for civil rights, education, and mutual aid, especially the Urban League, which was designed to ameliorate black Americans' adaptation to the urban, northern environment.

In terms of the transmission of historical knowledge, the 1890s saw the beginnings of Washington, D.C.'s American Negro Academy, Boston's Society for the Collection of Negro Folk Lore, and Philadelphia's American Negro Historical Society. By the 1910s Arthur Schomburg and John E. Bruce had founded the Negro Society for Historical Research, and Carter Woodson had begun to publish the *Journal of Negro History* through his Association for the Study of Negro Life and History. These institutions fit the bill Alain Locke had called for in 1911, when he argued before Schomburg and Bruce's organization for serious academic research and scholarship to replace what he called the "sentimental" approach to historical understanding. In addition to increasing numbers of research societies and published works of black history, more vocal movements were afoot to incorporate black history in the public schools in order to teach the youth "the valorous deeds of their ancestry" and to satisfy "a thirsting and a craving for this kind of literature by the young Negro."[52]

During this era, which historian August Meier has defined by its "institutionalization of self-help and racial solidarity," blacks built on nineteenth-century precedents in institution building. The proliferation of institutions of memory and activism by the 1910s came at a crucial time, when other traditional modes of disseminating knowledge and organizing activities among African Americans were beginning to crumble before the cultural changes of the early twentieth century, especially in the urban North. Shifts in the African American Freedom Day tradition were in some ways distinct, but they remained deeply rooted in the developments of the broader society. This particular transformation of American culture unarguably took shape with the assistance of blacks themselves, partly through their influence on music, dance, and theater, but perhaps even more strikingly through the beginnings of a massive migration, which was itself extremely disruptive of the traditional roles and structures within African American communities. The Freedom Day tradition was one component of the vibrant, community-oriented culture that was fading.

As the folklorist William Wiggins has demonstrated, emancipation celebrations have persisted throughout the twentieth century. His own "Freedom Trail" of participatory research, however, suggests a significant demographic slant to this persistence. Wiggins's fieldwork was conducted primarily in the South. While he did attend a few celebrations in Pennsylvania, Ohio, and Indiana, the vast majority of the celebrations he discusses took place in the southern states of Kentucky, Tennessee, Alabama, Georgia, Arkansas, and Texas. Ironically, it seems to have been in small towns in the southern part of the country—not in the Northeast where the tradition was born and where increasing numbers of blacks had migrated after 1910—that Freedom Day commemorations retained their greatest significance for African American communities. The affairs Wiggins describes seem rather quaint compared with the enticements of the urban mass culture that, after the 1930s especially, extended its reach throughout the nation. When one critic of the 1913 Philadelphia Exposition compared it unfavorably to a small country fair, he made a telling statement concerning the future of the Freedom Day tradition. A marked resistance to change and a certain stability in these smaller communities made them a much more fertile ground for the celebrations to continue to flourish than the impersonal and anonymous life that many found on the streets of urban centers in the North or South. As Toni Morrison observes in *Jazz*, black migrants to early twentieth-century cities soon left their country ways and mentalities behind, exchanging them for more urban sensibilities. "[T]hey were country people, but how soon country people forget. When they fall in love with a city, it is forever, and it is like forever. As though there never was a time when they didn't love it. The minute they arrive at the train station or get off the ferry and glimpse the wide streets and wasteful lamps lighting them, they know they are born for it. There, in a city, they are not so much new as themselves: their stronger, riskier selves."[53] The "riskier selves" of twentieth-century black urbanites may not have discarded their former selves as quickly or completely as Morrison suggests, but gradually they did find less and less of value in the festivals of freedom that had served so many functions over the preceding century.

The dissolution of the Freedom Day commemorative tradition in most of the United States after the 1910s need not be regarded nostalgically as a tale of declension. It is more usefully considered as a process of adaptation. Social, political, and cultural contexts are in constant flux, and a people's cultural practices need to adjust to those shifting contexts if they are to survive. Black leaders' priorities were to preserve and transmit the race's heritage, to fight for civil and political rights, and to work for the improvement of the educational and economic state of the race. These interconnected goals were part of a more sweeping project requiring the generational continuity of an African American collective identity that maintained blacks' legitimate claim to the rights of American citizens and their own singular identity as a people with a distinct history and heritage. If freedom festivals were no longer useful in the pursuit of those goals, then their time was past and their fate was just. The modest resurgence of the tradition under the rubric of Juneteenth celebrations in the late twentieth century may augur a meaningful revivification of this once potent cultural expression. But for the present Juneteenth remains a pale reminder of what the festivals of freedom once meant to African American communities more than a century ago. That vibrant nineteenth-century Freedom Day tradition has itself become a small part of a large history that must, in the service of larger goals, still be preserved and passed on.

NOTES

Introduction

1. James McPherson, "A House Divided: Historians Confront Disney's America," *OAH Newsletter* 22, no. 3 (August 1994): 1.

2. For a thoughtful discussion of historical memory and lynching in one southern county, see Bruce E. Baker, "Under the Rope: Lynching and Memory in Laurens County, South Carolina," in *Where These Memories Grow: History, Memory, and Southern Identity*, ed. W. Fitzhugh Brundage (Chapel Hill, 2000), 319–45.

3. For a discussion of modern Americans' ideas about their historical knowledge, see Roy Rosenzweig and David Thelen, *The Presence of the Past: Popular Uses of History in American Life* (New York, 1998).

4. I use the generic terms "freedom festival" or "Freedom Day" to refer to public commemorations of emancipation in individual states, the British West Indies, and the United States, as well as related emancipatory events commemorating the abolition of the slave trade, ratification of the Thirteenth, Fourteenth, and Fifteenth Amendments, and other similar landmarks of African American freedom. The phrase "festivals of freedom," which I chose for the title of this book, was coined by the black activist and historian William C. Nell during the 1850s. I refer to 1915, rather than 1913, as the fiftieth anniversary year since it was the Thirteenth Amendment in 1865, not Lincoln's 1863 Emancipation Proclamation, that fully abolished U.S. slavery. Blacks generally focused their attention on Lincoln's proclamation but

organized semicentennial celebrations at a variety of locations between 1913 and 1915.

5. Turner and Payne quoted in Reginald F. Hildebrand, *The Times Were Strange and Stirring: Methodist Preachers and the Crisis of Emancipation* (Durham, 1995), 58.

6. Clear articulations of this orientation of black social activism around ideals of personal responsibility and Christian morality can be found in David E. Swift, *Black Prophets of Justice: Activist Clergy before the Civil War* (Baton Rouge, 1989), and Nick Salvatore, *We All Got History: The Memory Books of Amos Webber* (New York, 1996). Swift, as his title implies, deals primarily with prominent antebellum minister-activists, while Salvatore's work illustrates the extent to which a similar moral orientation permeated the black working and middle classes throughout the nineteenth century.

7. David Blight has explored these developments in his *Race and Reunion: The Civil War in American Memory* (Cambridge, Mass., 2001).

8. Many studies attest to this fact, the most thorough being Leon F. Litwack, *Been in the Storm So Long: The Aftermath of Slavery* (New York, 1979).

9. Emancipation celebrations have been grouped with school homecomings, town and family reunions, Memorial Day observances, and other events as "celebrations of community identity" by the organizers of a museum exhibition on African American celebrations in the southeast. The exhibit's catalog asserts that "by identifying with the community and showing it off to the larger society, every member of the community is affirmed." Regarding emancipation celebrations in particular, the text claims that they became "forums for political solidarity" and "important symbols in the struggle for equality" after the hopes of the immediate post–Civil War years were quashed. I contend that these statements applied to antebellum celebrations as well and will emphasize those continuities. In addition I suggest that, while solidarity remained a goal, the events also display some of the significant factional and cultural divisions within African American communities. See William H. Wiggins and Douglas DeNatale, eds., *Jubilation! African American Celebrations in the Southeast* (Columbia, S.C., 1993), 72–78. *Jubilation!* is a catalog of an exhibition held September 12, 1993, to May 1, 1994, at the McKissick Museum, University of South Carolina, and afterward at other museums.

10. Iwona Irwin-Zarecka, *Frames of Remembrance: The Dynamics of Collective Memory* (New Brunswick, 1994), 133.

1. "A day of publick thanksgiving"

1. On race and class in colonial America, see Gary B. Nash, *The Urban Crucible: Social Change, Political Consciousness, and the Origins of the American Revolution* (Cambridge, Mass., 1979); Gordon S. Wood, *The Radicalism of the American Revolution* (New York, 1992); James Oliver Horton and Lois E. Horton, *In Hope of*

Liberty: Culture, Community, and Protest among Northern Free Blacks (New York, 1997), chap. 2; Graham Russell Hodges, *Root and Branch: African Americans in New York and East Jersey, 1613–1863* (Chapel Hill, 1999); Thomas J. Davis, *A Rumor of Revolt: The "Great Negro Plot" in Colonial New York* (New York, 1985; Amherst, 1990).

2. The late historian and folklorist William D. Piersen made a strong argument for the African influence on not only African American cultural forms but also the culture of the broader American society. My concern here is not to support or refute such claims but to use Piersen's, and others', research to describe the forms and functions of eighteenth-century black public festivals as a baseline for my analysis of nineteenth-century public commemorations. See William D. Piersen, *Black Yankees: The Development of an Afro-American Subculture in Eighteenth-Century New England* (Amherst, 1988), 117–40; and Piersen, *Black Legacy: America's Hidden Heritage* (Amherst, 1993).

3. Piersen, *Black Yankees,* 117–40; Shane White, "'It Was a Proud Day': African Americans, Festivals, and Parades in the North, 1741–1834," *Journal of American History* 81, no. 1 (June 1994): 16–31; S. White, "Pinkster: Afro-Dutch Syncretization in New York City and the Hudson Valley," *Journal of American Folklore* 102, no. 403 (January–March 1989): 68–75; A. J. Williams-Myers, "Pinkster Carnival: Africanisms in the Hudson River Valley," *Afro-Americans in New York Life and History* 9, no. 1 (January 1985): 7–17.

4. S. White, "'It Was a Proud Day,'" 30, 31.

5. Benjamin Quarles, *The Negro in the American Revolution* (Chapel Hill, 1961); Arthur Zilversmit, *The First Emancipation: The Abolition of Slavery in the North* (Chicago, 1967); John Hope Franklin, *From Slavery to Freedom: A History of Negro Americans,* 3rd ed. (New York, 1967), 138–41; Horton and Horton, *In Hope of Liberty,* chap. 3.

6. Gary B. Nash, *Forging Freedom: The Formation of Philadelphia's Black Community, 1720–1840* (Cambridge, Mass., 1988); Horton and Horton, *In Hope of Liberty,* chaps. 3–6; Sylvia Frey, *Water from the Rock: Black Resistance in a Revolutionary Age* (Princeton, 1991). As David Waldstreicher has noted, the first recorded black freedom festival occurred in New York City on July 5, 1800, in commemoration of the passage of the state's Gradual Emancipation Act. This appears to have been a singular event that did not lead to an ongoing tradition of commemoration, as did the slave trade celebrations. See David Waldstreicher, *In the Midst of Perpetual Fetes: The Making of American Nationalism, 1776–1820* (Chapel Hill, 1997), 328–29.

7. S. White, "'It Was a Proud Day,'" 29.

8. Russell Parrott, *An Oration on the Abolition of the Slave Trade* (1812) in *Two Orations on the Abolition of the Slave Trade Delivered in Philadelphia in 1812 and 1816* (Philadelphia, 1969), 10.

9. Numerous works treat this Christianization process in great detail. On the pre-Revolutionary Christianization of southern slaves, see, for example, Mechal

Sobel, *Trabelin' On: The Slave Journey to an Afro-Baptist Faith* (Westport, 1979), and Margaret Washington Creel, *"A Peculiar People": Slave Religion and Community Culture among the Gullahs* (New York, 1988).

10. Carol George, *Segregated Sabbaths: Richard Allen and the Emergence of Independent Black Churches, 1760–1840* (New York, 1973); Swift, *Black Prophets*, quotations on 7, 10. Swift's study deals particularly with six prominent Presbyterian and Congregationalist ministers. Peter P. Hinks, in his study of the world of the pamphleteer and activist David Walker, notes the central impact of evangelical Christianity among southern slaves, as well as on the views and actions of both Walker and South Carolina rebellion organizer Denmark Vesey. See Hinks, *To Awaken My Afflicted Brethren: David Walker and the Problem of Antebellum Slave Resistance* (University Park, 1997), esp. 31–39.

11. On the importance of pamphleteering and print generally among blacks in the early republic and antebellum years, see the introduction to Richard Newman, Patrick Rael, and Phillip Lapsansky, eds., *Pamphlets of Protest: An Anthology of Early African-American Protest Literature, 1790–1860* (New York, 2000). For an extremely insightful approach to assessing the interplay between press reporting and public ritual in the broader society, see Waldstreicher, *In the Midst of Perpetual Fetes*.

12. Nash, *Forging Freedom*, 210–11. The relationship between signing ability and functional literacy is not absolute. That said, I think these figures suggest that most blacks had, at best, a limited degree of comfort with print media.

13. On the interpenetrations of cultural practices among African and European colonists and on African influence on American culture generally, see Mechal Sobel, *The World They Made Together: Black and White Values in Eighteenth-Century Virginia* (Princeton, 1987); Joseph E. Holloway, ed., *Africanisms in American Culture* (Bloomington, 1990); and Piersen, *Black Legacy*. David Waldstreicher (*In the Midst of Perpetual Fetes*, 323–28) has also commented on the cross-fertilizations across a "culturally porous racial divide" (325) that necessarily shaped both "black" and "white" versions of American culture. See also Eric Lott, *Love and Theft: Blackface Minstrelsy and the American Working Class* (New York, 1993). On the origins of colonial American public rituals, see Waldstreicher, *In the Midst of Perpetual Fetes*, 17–30; and Len Travers, *Celebrating the Fourth: Independence Day and the Rites of Nationalism in the Early Republic* (Amherst, 1997), 16–20.

14. Quoted in Waldstreicher, *In the Midst of Perpetual Fetes*, 17.

15. Travers, *Celebrating the Fourth*, 43–46.

16. On the analysis of parades in late eighteenth- and nineteenth-century America, see, for example, Susan G. Davis, *Parades and Power: Street Theatre in Nineteenth-Century Philadelphia* (Berkeley, 1988); Mary P. Ryan, "The American Parade: Representations of Nineteenth-Century Social Order," in *The New Cultural History*, ed. Lynn Hunt (Berkeley, 1989), 131–53; Sean Wilentz, "Artisan Republican Festivals and the Rise of Class Conflict in New York City, 1788–1837," in *Working*

Class America: Essays on Labor, Community, and American Society, ed. Michael H. Frisch and Daniel J. Walkowitz (Urbana, 1983), 37–77. On the form and function of parades in early national July Fourth celebrations, see Travers, *Celebrating the Fourth,* and Waldstreicher, *In the Midst of Perpetual Fetes.* On black marching bands, see Horton and Horton, *In Hope of Liberty,* 157.

17. Anonymous commentator quoted in Waldstreicher, *In the Midst of Perpetual Fetes,* 75.

18. Quoted in Travers, *Celebrating the Fourth,* 56.

19. My condensed summary of early national July Fourth proceedings is based primarily on Travers, *Celebrating the Fourth,* and Waldstreicher, *In the Midst of Perpetual Fetes.*

20. The decline of blacks' acceptance in public by whites by the early nineteenth century is discussed in Paul Gilje, *The Road to Mobocracy: Popular Disorder in New York City, 1763–1834* (Chapel Hill, 1987). On the impact of Haiti, Gabriel's Rebellion, Denmark Vesey's plot, and other actual or planned uprisings, see also Horton and Horton, *In Hope of Liberty,* 109–10; Douglas R. Egerton, *Gabriel's Rebellion: The Virginia Slave Conspiracies of 1800 and 1802* (Chapel Hill, 1993); and Hinks, *To Awaken My Afflicted Brethren,* xiv, 30–62, 149–50.

21. Nash, *Forging Freedom,* 176–77; Travers, *Celebrating the Fourth,* 142–44; Waldstreicher, *In the Midst of Perpetual Fetes,* 327–29.

22. David Waldstreicher offers an extremely valuable discussion of African American slave trade observances and their role in shaping early black nationalist ideologies and practices; *In the Midst of Perpetual Fetes,* chap. 6.

23. Travers, *Celebrating the Fourth,* 20.

24. On the Boston celebrations, see William B. Gravely, "The Dialectic of Double-Consciousness in Black American Freedom Celebrations, 1808–1863," *Journal of Negro History* 67 (winter 1982): 303. On the influence of the Haitian revolution and French radicalism on American blacks, see, for example, Alfred N. Hunt, *Haiti's Influence on Antebellum America: Slumbering Volcano in the Caribbean* (Baton Rouge, 1988), and James Sidbury, "Saint Domingue in Virginia: Ideology, Local Meanings, and Resistance to Slavery, 1790–1800," *Journal of Southern History* 63, no. 3 (1997): 531–52.

25. S. White, "'It Was a Proud Day,'" 34–8; Gravely, "Dialectic of Double-Consciousness," 303; Hinks, *To Awaken My Afflicted Brethren,* 83–84.

26. Report from the *Boston Daily Advertiser,* July 17, 1817, quoted in S. White, "'It Was a Proud Day,'" 35–38. For further discussion of the significance of the "bobalition" literature, and of black public rituals, see Waldstreicher, *In the Midst of Perpetual Fetes,* 335–42.

27. For different views on black nationalism, activism, and identity during this period, see Mia Bay, *The White Image in the Black Mind: African-American Ideas about White People, 1830–1925* (New York, 2000); Hinks, *To Awaken My Afflicted*

Brethren; and Patrick Rael, *Black Identity and Black Protest in the Antebellum North* (Chapel Hill, 2001).

28. Genevieve Fabre has noted that these celebrations constitute "the first site [of memory] chosen for a national black celebration." Fabre, "African-American Commemorative Celebrations in the Nineteenth Century," in *History and Memory in African-American Culture,* ed. Fabre and Robert O'Meally (New York, 1994), 77. Fabre uses the term "site" in keeping with Pierre Nora's conception of *les lieux de memoire*—events that are imbued with meaning for the collective memory and history of a people. See his "Between History and Memory: *Les Lieux de Memoir,*" *Representations* 26 (spring 1989): 7–25.

29. Fabre, "African-American Commemorative Celebrations," 77. The order of events at representative indoor exercises is reproduced in Russell Parrott, *An Oration on the Abolition of the Slave Trade* (1812) in *Two Orations,* 1, and in Dorothy Porter, ed., *Early Negro Writing, 1760–1837* (Boston, 1971), 33–34, 344–45, and 363–64.

30. Jeremiah Gloucester, *An Oration Delivered . . . in Bethel Church on the Abolition of the Slave Trade, January 1, 1823* (Philadelphia: John Young, 1823), Black Abolitionist Archives, University of Detroit Mercy; Thaddeus Mason Harris, *A Discourse Delivered before the African Society in Boston, 15th of July, 1822, on the Anniversary Celebration of the Abolition of the Slave Trade* (Boston: Phelps and Farnham, 1822), 12, in Daniel A. P. Murray Pamphlet Collection, digital ID: (h) lcrbmrp t2202, accessed at the Library of Congress *American Memory* Web site at http://memory.loc.gov. Biographical information on Gloucester in Nash, *Forging Freedom,* 200, 236, 245, 262.

31. Harris, *A Discourse Delivered,* 13, Murray Pamphlet Collection.

32. Ibid., 11, 15, 16. Harris's oration is consistent with the argument presented in Joanne Pope Melish, *Disowning Slavery: Gradual Emancipation and Race in New England, 1780–1860* (Ithaca, 1998). Melish argues that white New Englanders engaged in a sort of collective amnesia about the region's long participation in slavery and constructed an ideology of black racial inferiority connected with their fears that disorderly blacks needed to be controlled by whites, lest they threaten the stability of the republic.

33. Gloucester, *An Oration Delivered,* Black Abolitionist Archives.

34. On the politicized use of public festivals in the early republic, see Simon P. Newman, *Parades and the Politics of the Street: Festive Culture in the Early American Republic* (Philadelphia, 1997), and Waldstreicher, *In the Midst of Perpetual Fetes.*

35. Many of these themes, singly and in various combinations and emphases, have been noted by numerous scholars. The historian Dickson D. Bruce Jr. identifies the slave trade orations as "arguably the first African American–initiated literary genre in the early republic" and asserts that they contributed more than any other form of expression to establishing the framework for nineteenth-century African

American literary conventions. See Dickson D. Bruce Jr., *The Origins of African American Literature, 1680–1865* (Charlottesville, 2001), chap. 3, quote at 106. On blacks' views of Africa, see Bruce Dain, "Haiti and Egypt in Early Black Racial Discourse in the United States," *Slavery and Abolition* 14, no. 3 (1993): 139–61, and Bay, *The White Image in the Black Mind.* On Christianity, the Revolution, and natural rights, see Hinks, *To Awaken My Afflicted Brethren,* 30–46, and Frey, *Water from the Rock.* Regarding blacks' positions on more general political issues, Joseph Sidney, for example, in 1809, devoted more than half his oration to a critique of the policies of the "Virginia junto," and especially the Embargo Act of 1807. Sidney identified "the mad democracy of the southern states" as a threat to American commerce as well as a threat to African American liberty. Citing Washington's manumission of his slaves and "the blood of the martyred Hamilton," Sidney urged all his auditors—black and white—to cast their lot with the Federalists rather than the "Slavery-hole of democracy" (in Porter, *Early Negro Writing,* 366–73). It should be noted that the Embargo Act did have a disproportionate effect on African Americans, many of whom were employed in the shipping industry, which was severely damaged by the decline in trade that resulted from the embargo. See W. Jeffrey Bolster, *Black Jacks: African American Seamen in the Age of Sail* (Cambridge, Mass., 1997). On black associations with the major political parties, see Waldstreicher, *In the Midst of Perpetual Fetes.*

36. My interpretation of the content of slave trade orations is based on my perusal of twelve addresses delivered by African Americans in New York and Philadelphia between 1808 and 1822. These include the eight in Porter, *Early Negro Writing;* William Miller's *A Sermon on the Abolition of the Slave Trade: Delivered in the African Church, New York, on the First of January, 1810* (Philadelphia, 1969 [1810]); two by Russell Parrott in *Two Orations;* and one by Jeremiah Gloucester in Philadelphia in 1823. I have also made use of one address by a white minister, Thaddeus Mason Harris, at Boston in 1822.

37. Genevieve Fabre observes that slave trade commemorations stimulated among American blacks "a heightened consciousness of Africa as a *lieu de memoire*" and a more profound sense of "the importance of the African component of their identity"; Fabre, "African-American Commemorative Celebrations," 77–78.

38. For thoughtful analyses of African American intellectuals' views of Africa, and especially Egypt, see Dain, "Haiti and Egypt" and, for a later period, Dickson D. Bruce Jr., "Ancient Africa and the Early Black Historians, 1883–1915," *American Quarterly* 36, no. 5 (1984): 684–99.

39. W. Miller, *A Sermon . . . 1810,* 4; Porter, *Early Negro Writing,* 392–95; Absalom Jones (1808) in Porter, *Early Negro Writing,* 337.

40. Russell Parrott (1814) in Porter, *Early Negro Writing,* 384.

41. Peter Williams (1808) and William Hamilton (1815) in Porter, *Early Negro Writing,* 346, 35.

42. In Porter, *Early Negro Writing*, 384–85.

43. In her provocative study of antebellum Emancipation Day orations, Detine Bowers refers to this rhetorical technique as "visual enactment." She identifies it as "the single-most employed temporal strategy" in Emancipation Day orations that exemplifies the African-derived worldview based on a "recurring cycle of interactive events"—a worldview that remained embedded in the black American psyche long after explicit ties to Africa had been severed. She sees this pattern as distinctly African in its dissolution of rational, linear conceptions of time in favor of a cyclical and regenerative conception. This traditional African orientation invokes audience participation, shifting the audience from a profane to a sacred temporal sphere in which past, present, and future are one, and all events are immanent. See Bowers, "A *Strange* Speech of an Estranged People: Theory and Practice of Antebellum African-American Freedom Day Orations," Ph.D. diss., Purdue University, 1992, esp. 1–14, 116–60.

44. In Porter, *Early Negro Writing*, 348, 396–98.

45. Joseph Sidney (1809) in Porter, *Early Negro Writing*, 363.

46. Williams and Lawrence in Porter, *Early Negro Writing*, 350, 379, respectively; Parrott (1816) in *Two Orations*, 8.

47. Henry Sipkins (1809) in Porter, *Early Negro Writing*, 367–68.

48. In Porter, *Early Negro Writing*, 378.

49. Parrott (1812) in *Two Orations*, 7; Hamilton in Porter, *Early Negro Writing*, 394.

50. In Porter, *Early Negro Writing*, 389.

51. Russell Parrott (1812) in *Two Orations*, 3–4; Gloucester, *An Oration Delivered*, Black Abolitionist Archives.

52. In Porter, *Early Negro Writing*, 356–57.

53. George Lawrence (1813) in Porter, *Early Negro Writing*, 382.

54. Sidney (1809) in Porter, *Early Negro Writing*, 363; Sipkins (1809) in Porter, *Early Negro Writing*, 372; W. Miller, *A Sermon . . . 1810*, 16; Jones (1808) in Porter, *Early Negro Writing*, 340–41.

55. Jones (1808) in Porter, *Early Negro Writing*, 340–41.

56. In Porter, *Early Negro Writing*, 33, 355, 363–66, italics added. See n. 35 above for a sample of Sidney's antiembargo comments.

57. *An Oration Delivered*, Black Abolitionist Archives.

58. Russell Parrott (1812), in *Two Orations*, 9.

59. A more thorough discussion of the issues of "uplift" and the broader goals of northern black activists in the early nineteenth century can be found in Frederick Cooper, "Elevating the Race: The Social Thought of Black Leaders, 1827–1850," *American Quarterly* 24 (1972): 604–25; Gravely, "Dialectic of Double-Consciousness"; Leonard I. Sweet, *Black Images of America, 1784–1870* (New York, 1976); Benjamin Quarles, *Black Abolitionists* (New York, 1969); Jane H. Pease and

William H. Pease, *They Who Would Be Free: Blacks' Search for Freedom, 1830–1861* (New York, 1974); Horton and Horton, *In Hope of Liberty;* and Rael, *Black Identity and Black Protest.*

60. Numerous works speak to the multifaceted cultural practices and styles of early nineteenth-century American cities. See, for example, Christine Stansell, *City of Women: Sex and Class in New York, 1789–1860* (Urbana and Chicago, 1986); Richard B. Stott, *Workers in the Metropolis: Class, Ethnicity, and Youth in Antebellum New York City* (Ithaca and London, 1990); Stuart M. Blumin, ed., *New York by Gas-Light and Other Urban Sketches by George C. Foster* (Berkeley, 1990).

61. Nash, *Forging Freedom,* 213–23. Peter P. Hinks, based on his research into black Boston in the 1820s, has also been critical of Nash's analysis. Hinks argues, as I do, for a more complicated and nuanced approach to understanding the various strata in black communities and the range of cultural choices available to individuals within those communities. See Hinks, *To Awaken My Afflicted Brethren,* chap. 3, esp. 73n. 23, 84–90. Thoughtful discussions of antebellum black culture can also be found in Horton and Horton, *In Hope of Liberty,* esp. chaps. 7, 8, and 9; and Shane White, "The Death of James Johnson," *American Quarterly* 51, no. 4 (December 1999): 753–95.

62. Bay, *The White Image in the Black Mind,* 33–37, and chaps. 1 and 2; Walker quoted on 35.

63. Peter Hinks makes a similar argument in *To Awaken My Afflicted Brethren,* 109–11. See also Rael, *Black Identity and Black Protest.*

64. Porter's *Early Negro Writing* includes eight such texts. William Gravely, "Dialectic of Double-Consciousness," 313n. 9, notes that fifteen orations have survived in published form. Waldstreicher, *In the Midst of Perpetual Fetes,* 338–44; Hamilton quoted on 343.

65. Floyd J. Miller, *The Search for Black Nationality: Black Emigration and Colonization, 1787–1863* (Urbana, 1975); Horton and Horton, *In Hope of Liberty.*

66. "African Celebration in Boston," *Genius of Universal Emancipation,* September 2, 1829, 7.

67. Ibid.

68. Gravely, "Dialectic of Double-Consciousness," 303.

69. S. White, "'It Was a Proud Day,'" 49; *A Memorial Discourse by Reverend Henry Highland Garnet with an Introduction by James McCune Smith, M.D.* (Philadelphia, 1865), cited in S. White, "'It Was a Proud Day,'" 49–50.

70. Sterling Stuckey, *Slave Culture: Nationalist Theory and the Foundations of Black America* (New York, 1987), 144. Genevieve Fabre makes this observation in "African-American Commemorative Celebrations," 79, and Detine Bowers suggests an Afrocentric trajectory from the slave festivals through celebrations of August first and beyond in, "*Strange* Speech," 50, 76–77.

71. By the 1830s virtually all adult white males had the vote, as property quali-

fications were removed for that class of citizen. But parading continued as a popular form of political expression until the end of the century. On the analysis of parades in nineteenth-century America, see, for example, S. Davis, *Parades and Power;* M. Ryan, "The American Parade,"131–53; Wilentz, "Artisan Republican Festivals," 37–77. Michael E. McGerr discusses the decline of parading in *The Decline of Popular Politics: The American North, 1865–1928* (New York, 1986).

72. "Abolition of Slavery," *Freedom's Journal,* April 20, 1827, in Black Abolitionist Archives Clipping File, item no. 31774, University of Detroit Mercy, hereafter referred to as BAACF.

73. Letter from "Libertinus," *Freedom's Journal,* June 22, 1827, in BAACF, item no. 31799; letter from "R.," *Freedom's Journal,* June 29, 1827, in BAACF, item no. 31804.

74. Letter from "R.," *Freedom's Journal,* June 29, 1827, in BAACF, item no. 31804.

75. Ibid.

76. Editorial, *Freedom's Journal,* June 22, 1827, in BAACF, item no. 31800.

77. Quarles, *Black Abolitionists,* 120–21.

78. Quarles, *Black Abolitionists,* 120, gives the larger figure, based on the report in the *New York Daily Advertiser;* a *Freedom's Journal* editorial, July 13, 1827, estimates the attendance as "near two thousand." Quotations from Quarles, *Black Abolitionists,* 120, and editorial, *Freedom's Journal,* July 13, 1827.

79. *Freedom's Journal,* July 6, 1827.

80. Hamilton (1827) in Porter, *Early Negro Writing,* 97, 101, 103–4.

81. "Celebration," *Freedom's Journal,* July 11, 1828, in BAACF, item no. 31960; "The Brooklyn Celebration," *Freedom's Journal,* July 18, 1828, in BAACF, item no. 31965.

82. "The Brooklyn Celebration," *Freedom's Journal,* July 18, 1828, in BAACF, item no. 31965.

83. For a different perspective on blacks' uses of clothing as a form of positive expression and an example of black agency, see Shane White and Graham J. White, *Stylin': African American Expressive Culture, from Its Beginnings to the Zoot Suit* (Ithaca, 1998).

84. Paul (1827) in *Negro Orators and Their Orations,* ed. Carter Godwin Woodson (New York, 1969 [1925]), 64–77.

85. Ibid., 64.

86. Gravely, "Dialectic of Double-Consciousness," and Fabre, "African-American Commemorative Celebrations," 81, also recognize the transitional nature of New York emancipation commemorations. New York emancipation celebrations, and the class divisions they illustrate, are also given attention in Alessandra Lorini, "Public Rituals, Race Ideology, and the Transformation of Urban Culture: The Making of the New York African-American Community, 1825–1918," Ph.D. diss., Columbia University, 1991.

87. Walker's *Appeal* and Young's *Ethiopian Manifesto* are reprinted in Sterling Stuckey, ed., *The Ideological Origins of Black Nationalism* (Boston, 1972). See also David Walker, *David Walker's Appeal to the Coloured Citizens of the World*, ed. Peter P. Hinks (University Park, 2000); Hinks, *To Awaken My Afflicted Brethren;* and Newman, Rael, and Lapsansky, eds., *Pamphlets of Protest.*

88. Bernell Tripp, in her *Origins of the Black Press: New York, 1827–1847* (Northport, 1992), 30, notes the publication of the following: *African Sentinel and Journal of Liberty* (Albany, N.Y., 1831); *National Reformer* (Philadelphia, 1833); *Spirit of the Times* (New York, 1836–42); *Weekly Advocate,* succeeded by *Colored American* (New York, 1837–41).

89. Roland E. Wolseley, *The Black Press, U.S.A.,* 2nd ed. (Ames, 1990), 28.

90. Hinks, *To Awaken My Afflicted Brethren,* chap. 2.

91. Nash, *Forging Freedom,* 259. See also Horton and Horton, *In Hope of Liberty,* chap. 6; American Moral Reform Society, *Minutes and Proceedings of the American Moral Reform Society* (Philadelphia, 1837), 17.

92. *Freedom's Journal,* July 25, 1828, in BAACF item no. 31967.

93. Leonard I. Sweet, "The Fourth of July and Black Americans in the Nineteenth Century: Northern Leadership Opinion within the Context of the Black Experience," *Journal of Negro History* 61 (July 1976): 260.

94. Reprinted in John H. Bracey Jr., August Meier, and Elliott Rudwick, eds., *Black Nationalism in America* (Indianapolis, 1970), 34–37.

95. Bowers, *"Strange* Speech," 66–69.

2. "A borrowed day of Jubilee"

1. *Minutes of the Fourth Annual Convention . . . of the Free People of Colour* (New York, 1834), 14–16, reprinted in Howard Holman Bell, ed., *Minutes of the Proceedings of the National Negro Conventions, 1830–1864* (New York, 1969). On blacks' use of dress and bodily adornment as a form of cultural expression, see White and White, *Stylin'.*

2. See Gravely, "Dialectic of Double-Consciousness," 304, 305, 311–12; and Quarles, *Black Abolitionists,* 123. On West Indian abolition and the apprenticeship system, see Robert S. Shelton, "A Modified Crime: The Apprenticeship System in St. Kitts," *Slavery and Abolition* 16, no. 3 (1995): 331–45, and Henrice Altink, "Slavery by Another Name: Apprenticed Women in Jamaica, 1834–1838," *Social History* 26, no. 1 (2001): 40–59.

3. Douglass's address reprinted in the *Colored American* (New York), August 11, 1838; *Liberator,* August 24, 1838. Biographical information on William Douglass from George F. Bragg, *Men of Maryland* (Baltimore, 1914), 47–50.

4. Speech at Rochester, New York, August 1, 1848, in Douglass, *Frederick Douglass Papers,* ed. John W. Blassingame et al., ser. 1, *Speeches, Debates, and Interviews* (New

Haven, 1979–92), 2:133–34, hereafter referred to as *FDP*. Quarles, *Black Abolitionists*, 118.

5. Anonymous letter, "The 'First of August,'" *Pennsylvania Freeman*, August 2, 1838; Johnson's oration reprinted in *North Star*, August 21, 1848; Phillips's oration at a West Indian emancipation celebration in Worcester, Mass., reprinted in *North Star*, August 31, 1849.

6. Numerous scholars have made references to African Americans' commemorations of the Haitian Revolution, but I have yet to see a specific source documenting an actual observance publicly commemorating Haitian independence. The closest approximation of a commemoration involves an 1825 address by William J. Watkins commemorating not the revolution itself, but France's recent acknowledgment of Haiti's independent status. See *Genius of Universal Emancipation*, August 1825. This address was cited by Ira Berlin as evidence of frequent African American celebrations of the Haitian Revolution, and other scholars have continued to repeat this inaccuracy without any additional documentation. See Berlin, *Slaves without Masters: The Free Negro in the Antebellum South* (New York, 1974), 314–15; Christopher Phillips, *Freedom's Port: The African American Community of Baltimore, 1790–1860* (Urbana, 1997), 174; S. Newman, *Parades and the Politics of the Street*; and Ellen M. Litwicki, *America's Public Holidays, 1865–1920* (Washington, D.C., 2000).

7. Phillips's Worcester oration, *North Star*, August 31, 1849; Watkins's and Ward's statements reported in the *Weekly Anglo-African*, August 20, 1859; Francis's oration at Buffalo, New York, August 1, 1849, reprinted in *North Star*, August 17, 1849; *Pennsylvania Freeman* editorial reprinted in *North Star*, March 10, 1848.

8. Douglass, speech at Canandaigua, New York, August 3, 1857, in *FDP*, ser. 1, 3: 189; Wilson quoted in Bowers, "*Strange* Speech," 72.

9. Speech at Canandaigua, New York, August 3, 1857, in *FDP*, ser. 1, 3:189–90, 194; speech at Poughkeepsie, New York, August 2, 1858, in *FDP*, ser 1 3:219; speech at Rochester, New York, August 1, 1848, in *FDP*, ser. 1, 2:134.

10. My research has corroborated this numerical estimate offered by William Gravely in his "Dialectic of Double-Consciousness," 304.

11. Bowers, "*Strange* Speech," 106. David Swift also emphasizes the "dramatic expansion of awareness" that resulted from the public speeches by black leaders as they "express[ed] their sense of moral outrage to hundreds of whites" who were usually impressed with the orators' abilities and who might be moved to support African Americans' cause; see *Black Prophets*, 65, 90–91

12. Cited in Quarles, *Black Abolitionists*, 124.

13. For example, see *Liberator*, August 12, 1842; August 11, 18, 25, 1843; August 9, 16, 23, 1844.

14. Banneker Institute broadside in American Negro Historical Society Papers, box 13G, folder 1, Historical Society of Pennsylvania, hereafter cited as ANHSP.

15. Quarles, *Black Abolitionists*, 124–26; Bowers, "*Strange* Speech," 3, 75, 84–85; broadside, ANHSP, box 13G, folder 1.

16. *Liberator*, September 1, 1843; August 19, 1853; Quarles, *Black Abolitionists*, 124–26; Bowers, "*Strange* Speech," 75, 84–85, 94–95, 103–5.

17. *Weekly Anglo-African*, August 13, 1859.

18. *Liberator*, August 11, 1843; Quarles, *Black Abolitionists*, 153.

19. Garnet, "Address to the Slaves of the United States of America," excerpted in Newman, Rael, and Lapsansky, eds., *Pamphlets of Protest*, 156–64, quotations on 162, 156.

20. *Liberator*, August 20, 1852.

21. Ibid., August 19, 1853; July 27, 1855; August 15, 1856.

22. William S. McFeely, *Frederick Douglass* (New York, 1991), 77.

23. *Liberator*, September 1, 1843.

24. Ibid., August 9, 1844.

25. *Colored American* (New York), August 25, 1839; July 25, August 1, August 15, 1840; July 17, August 14, August 21, September 25, 1841.

26. *Colored American* (New York), August 15, 1840; July 17, 1841.

27. Patrick Rael, "Besieged by Freedom's Army: Antislavery Celebrations and Black Activism in the Antebellum North," paper presented at the Organization of American Historians Annual Meeting, St. Louis, March 2000, and Rael, *Black Identity and Black Protest in the Antebellum North* (Chapel Hill, 2001). See also Cooper, "Elevating the Race," and Donald Yacovone, "The Transformation of the Black Temperance Movement, 1827–1854: An Interpretation," *Journal of the Early Republic* 8, no. 3 (1988): 281–97.

28. *Liberator*, August 20, 1858; Quarles, *Black Abolitionists*, 125; Bowers, "*Strange* Speech," 103–5; Jessie Carney Smith and Carrell Peterson Horton, comps. and eds., *Historical Statistics of Black America*, vol. 2 (Detroit, 1995), 1728.

29. Gravely, "Dialectic of Double-Consciousness," 304–5; editor's note in *FDP*, ser. 1, 3:214.

30. Broadsides, ANHSP, box 13G, folder 1.

31. Bowers, "*Strange* Speech," 79–81; *FDP*, ser. 1, 2:69.

32. Quarles, *Black Abolitionists*, 127; *Colored American* (New York), July 17, 1841.

33. S. Newman, *Parades and the Politics of the Street*, 1–10, 186–92, and passim. Newman's analysis concentrates on the popular political culture that took shape in the 1790s. This formed the foundation for the continued evolution of practices throughout the nineteenth century and beyond.

34. Bowers, "*Strange* Speech," 78.

35. Quarles, *Black Abolitionists*, 124–27; Bowers, "*Strange* Speech," 79; *FDP*, ser. 1, 2:69.

36. *FDP*, ser. 1, 3:198.

37. William Wiggins, *O Freedom! Afro-American Emancipation Celebrations* (Knoxville, 1987); Quarles, *Black Abolitionists,* 125; Leonard P. Curry, *The Free Black in Urban America, 1800–1850: The Shadow of the Dream* (Chicago, 1981), 250.

38. S. Newman, *Parades and the Politics of the Street,* 7–9; *Palladium of Liberty,* August 14, 1844.

39. *Liberator,* August 15, 1851; September 1, 1843; *North Star,* September 7, 1849.

40. White in *Weekly Anglo-African,* August 6, 1859; Gilson in *Frederick Douglass' Paper,* September 4, 1851; Francis's oration reprinted in *North Star,* August 17, 1849. Biographical information on Francis in Martin Delany, *The Condition, Elevation, Emigration, and Destiny of the Colored People of the United States* (Philadelphia, 1852), 139; August 1 address by J. H. Perkins, Cincinnati, Ohio, reprinted in *North Star,* September 7, 1849; Johnson in *North Star,* August 21, 1848.

41. August 1 address by J. H. Perkins, Cincinnati, Ohio, reprinted in *North Star,* September 7, 1849. On nationalism and the "invention of traditions" during the nineteenth century, see, for example, Eric Hobsbawm, *Nations and Nationalism since 1780: Programme, Myth, Reality* (Cambridge, 1993); Hobsbawm and Terence Ranger, eds., *The Invention of Tradition* (Cambridge, 1983); and Benedict Anderson, *Imagined Communities: Reflections on the Origin and the Spread of Nationalism* (New York, 1991).

42. Letter from "Observer," *Frederick Douglass' Paper,* September 4, 1851.

43. Rael, "Besieged by Freedom's Army"; *Weekly Anglo-African,* September 3, 1859; *North Star,* July 14, 1848.

44. Documentation of some of these functions is difficult. In terms of meeting spouses, for example, the only specific reference I have found is in the autobiography of blues pioneer W. C. Handy, who reports having met his wife at a postbellum Emancipation Day celebration. W. C. Handy, *Father of the Blues: An Autobiography* (New York, 1970 [1941]).

45. *Liberator,* August 15, 1851.

46. Quarles, *Black Abolitionists,* 124–27; Bowers, "*Strange* Speech," 79; *FDP,* ser. 1, 2:69; *Weekly Anglo-African,* September 3, 1859; *North Star,* August 10, 1849.

47. Quarles, *Black Abolitionists,* 127; Gravely, "Dialectic of Double-Consciousness," 305; broadside, ANHSP, box 13G, folder 1.

48. *Liberator,* August 15, 1851; Gravely, "Dialectic of Double-Consciousness," 304–5; *Douglass' Monthly,* August 1859.

49. *Liberator,* August 20, 1858.

50. Cited in *Liberator,* August 4, 1854.

51. *North Star,* June 29, 1849; Quarles, *Black Abolitionists,* 124–27; *FDP,* ser. 1, 3: 198–99; *Douglass' Monthly,* August 1859.

52. Paul C. Nagel, *This Sacred Trust: American Nationality, 1798–1898* (New York, 1971), 53.

53. Reporter's quote in editor's notes, *FDP*, ser. 1, 2:133; Raymond in *Liberator*, August 14, 1857.

54. S. Davis, *Parades and Power*, 40–46. Roy Rosenzweig has noted a similar class differentiation during the postbellum decades in his *Eight Hours for What We Will: Workers and Leisure in an Industrial City, 1870–1920* (Cambridge, 1989), 71–74.

55. *Liberator*, July 28, 1854.

56. Ibid., August 13, 1847.

57. On the role of the parade among antebellum blacks, see S. White, "'It Was a Proud Day.'" The Harrisburg parade is described in *Weekly Anglo-African*, August 6, 1859.

58. Kimberly S. Hanger, *Bounded Lives, Bounded Places: Free Black Society in Colonial New Orleans, 1769–1803* (Durham, 1997); Charles Isadore Nero, "'To Develop Our Manhood': Free Black Leadership and the Rhetoric of the New Orleans *Tribune*," Ph.D. diss., Indiana University, 1991, 43–49; Quarles, *Black Abolitionists*, 229–30; James Oliver Horton and Lois E. Horton, "Violence, Protest, and Identity: Black Manhood in Antebellum America," in James Oliver Horton, *Free People of Color: Inside the African American Community* (Washington, D.C., 1993), 91–93.

59. *Weekly Anglo-African*, August 6, 1859; June 30, 1860.

60. Wiggins, *O Freedom!*.

61. *Weekly Anglo-African*, June 30, 1860; *Provincial Freeman*, July 29, 1854; August 22, 1855; Quarles, *Black Abolitionists*, 125; Curry, *Free Black in Urban America*, 250.

62. Douglass's speaking itinerary between 1847 and 1854 is listed in *FDP*, ser. 1, 2:xvii–xxxvii; the 1848 Rochester quotation is on 134. Intensive research into local practices may well reveal more about what I expect are intricate patterns of social networking involved in the coordination of Freedom Day events within particular regions. See also the discussions of planning for the 1849 Buffalo celebration in *North Star*, July 27, August 10, 24, September 14, 1849.

63. *Frederick Douglass' Paper*, September 4, 1851; *Weekly Anglo-African*, July 23, 30, 1859; *National Era*, September 16, 1852; *North Star*, June 29, 1849.

64. *North Star*, May 11, April 20, 1849.

65. Ibid., August 10, 24, September 14, 1849.

66. Ibid., July 27, August 10, 1849.

67. Ibid., August 10, September 14, 1849.

68. Ibid., August 24, September 14, 1849.

69. Ibid.

70. *Weekly Anglo-African*, June 16, 1860.

71. On black literacy in the free states, see James O. Horton and Lois E. Horton, *Hard Road to Freedom: The Story of African America* (New Brunswick, 2001), 130. On the transformation of black oral culture and the significance of history related through the spoken word, see Lawrence W. Levine, *Black Culture and Black Con-*

sciousness: Afro-American Folk Thought from Slavery to Freedom (New York, 1977), esp. 155–58, 177.

72. Ruth Finnegan has stated quite succinctly the importance of recognizing the complexity and interrelatedness of oral and literate orientations: "'orality' and 'literacy' are not two separate and independent things; nor . . . are oral and written modes two mutually exclusive and opposed processes for representing and communicating information . . . insofar as they can be distinguished at all as separate modes rather than a continuum, they mutually interact and affect each other, and the relations between them are problematic rather than self-evident." Finnegan, *Literacy and Orality: Studies in the Technology of Communication* (New York, 1988), 175.

73. *Weekly Anglo-African,* August 20, 1859. Though my interest here is primarily with the flow of information and opinion from the educated class toward the masses, the current ran in the other direction as well. One excellent example occurred not at a Freedom Day celebration, but at a mass meeting called in Philadelphia in 1817 to discuss the program of the newly formed American Colonization Society. Black organizers James Forten and Richard Allen were initially sympathetic with the society's aims and attempted to relate the benefits of colonization to the several thousand blacks assembled in Allen's Bethel AME Church. But when a resolution supporting colonization was called to a vote, it went down to an almost unanimous defeat. In this case race "leaders" received a clear message from their ostensible followers, which spurred them to oppose colonization fairly consistently throughout the antebellum period. See Nash, *Forging Freedom,* 237–41.

74. *Weekly Anglo-African,* June 6, 1860; September 17, 1859.

75. *Colored American* (New York), August 25, 1839; *Liberator,* August 19, 1859; *Liberator,* August 20, 1847. On the role of pamphlets, see the thoughtful introduction in Newman, Rael, and Lapsansky, eds., *Pamphlets of Protest.*

76. *Liberator,* August 31 [*sic*], 1844 [actual date of publication was August 30]; *Weekly Anglo-African,* September 17, 1859.

77. Kenneth Cmiel, *Democratic Eloquence: The Fight over Popular Speech in Nineteenth-Century America* (Berkeley, 1990), 23–93.

78. *Weekly Anglo-African,* September 24, 1859; *Weekly Anglo-African,* September 3, 1859; *Weekly Anglo-African,* August 6, 1859; *North Star,* August 21, 1848.

79. *Weekly Anglo-African,* August 27, 1859; *North Star,* August 21, 1848; *Liberator,* August 19, 1853; *Weekly Anglo-African,* August 6, 1859.

80. Speech at Rochester, N.Y., August 1, 1848, in *FDP,* ser. 1, 2:134.

81. Watkins quoted in Gravely, "Dialectic of Double-Consciousness," 311; Douglass speech at Poughkeepsie, N.Y., August 2, 1858, in *FDP,* ser. 1, 3:223; Douglass devoted several pages of this particular address to the critique of specific July Fourth addresses by popular orators Rufus Choate, Edward Everett, and Caleb Cushing (ibid., 3:227–31).

82. *Douglass' Monthly*, September 1860.

83. Lorenzo Sears, *The Occasional Address: Its Composition and Literature* (New York, 1897), 251, 4, 9–10.

84. See, for example, Michael Kammen, *Mystic Chords of Memory: The Transformation of Tradition in American Culture* (New York, 1991); David Glassberg, *American Historical Pageantry: The Uses of Tradition in the Early Twentieth Century* (Chapel Hill, 1990); and John Bodnar, *Remaking America: Public Memory, Commemoration, and Patriotism in the Twentieth Century* (Princeton, 1991).

85. Bowers, "*Strange* Speech," 5.

86. Peter Williams, *An Oration on the Abolition of the Slave Trade*, in *Negro Orators*, ed. Woodson, 36; Walker, *David Walker's Appeal*, 61.

87. The works by Lewis, Easton, and Pennington are discussed in Bay, *The White Image in the Black Mind*, 44–55. See also Stephen G. Hall, "To Give a Faithful Account of the Race: History and Historical Consciousness in the African American Community, 1827–1915," Ph.D. diss., Ohio State University, 1999; J. Franklin, *From Slavery to Freedom*, 228–31, quotation on 230.

88. The movement, led by Daniel Payne, M. M. Clark, and a few others among the educated clergy, succeeded in founding the *Christian Recorder* in the 1850s. The paper remained an extremely influential black voice into the twentieth century. Efforts to impose stricter educational requirements for ministers met with considerable resistance throughout the nineteenth century. See Carol V. R. George, "Widening the Circle: The Black Church and the Abolitionist Crusade, 1830–1860," in *Antislavery Reconsidered: New Perspectives on the Abolitionists*, ed. Lewis Perry and Michael Fellman (Baton Rouge, 1979), 75–95.

89. R. J. M. Blackett, *Beating against the Barriers: The Lives of Six Nineteenth-Century Afro-Americans* (Ithaca, 1989), 16–17; Swift, *Black Prophets*, 204–43. Physical monuments in the form of statues, plaques, or obelisks in recognition of great African American individuals or events did not begin to grace the commemorative landscape for several decades. The monument to Richard Allen, founder of the African Methodist Episcopal Church, unveiled at the National Centennial Exhibition at Philadelphia in 1876, is thought to be the first such monument erected by American blacks. I discuss this at length in Mitchell Kachun, "'Before the Eyes of All Nations': African-American Identity and Historical Memory at the Centennial Exposition of 1876," *Pennsylvania History* 65, no. 3 (summer 1998), 300–323.

90. For example, Frederick Douglass, *The Narrative of the Life of Frederick Douglass* (Boston, 1845); Henry Highland Garnet, *The Past and the Present Condition, and the Destiny of the Colored Race* (Troy, 1848); William Wells Brown, *Clotel; or, the President's Daughter* (London, 1853); William Cooper Nell, *The Colored Patriots of the American Revolution* (Boston, 1855); Harriet E. Wilson, *Our Nig; or Sketches from the Life of a Free Black* (Boston, 1859); Martin Delany, *Blake; or, The Huts of America*, published serially in the *Anglo-African Magazine* and the *Weekly Anglo-*

African, 1859–1862. See also Dickson D. Bruce Jr., *The Origins of African American Literature, 1680–1865* (Charlottesville, 2001).

91. Speech at Canandaigua, New York, August 3, 1857, in *FDP*, ser. 1, 3:197.

92. Detine Bowers and William Wiggins concur with this assessment, though neither elaborates on the idea. See Bowers, *"Strange* Speech," 75, and Wiggins, *O Freedom!* 45.

93. Speech at Canandaigua, New York, August 2, 1847, in *FDP*, ser. 1, 2:73–83.

94. Jones, *A Thanksgiving Sermon . . . on Account of the Abolition of the Slave Trade* (1808) in Porter, *Early Negro Writing*, 340–41; Paul (1827) in Porter, *Early Negro Writing*, 64; Beman quoted in Gravely, "Dialectic of Double-Consciousness," 307.

95. *Weekly Anglo-African*, August 6, 1859.

96. *FDP*, ser., 1 3:200–201n. 29; Sweet, "Fourth of July and Black Americans," 270–71; Quarles, *Black Abolitionists*, 128–29.

97. *Weekly Anglo-African*, August 20, 1859.

98. Speech at Canandaigua, New York, August 3, 1857, in *FDP*, ser. 1, 3:201, 206–8; on Douglass's treatment of the *Creole* affair and his attitudes on violence as a tool of liberation, see Douglass, "The Heroic Slave," in *Violence in the Black Imagination: Essays and Documents*, ed. Ronald Takaki (New York, 1972), 17–77.

99. Speech at Canandaigua, New York, August 3, 1857, in *FDP*, ser. 1, 3:204–5; Quarles, *Black Abolitionists*, 203–7; Sweet, "Fourth of July and Black Americans," 269.

100. Speech at Canandaigua, New York, August 3, 1857, in *FDP*, ser. 1, 3:207.

101. Ibid., 203–4.

102. Ibid., 199. Many blacks and some whites interpreted West Indian emancipation as an indication that Britain adhered more closely to the ideals of the American Revolution than did the United States. See John R. McKivigan and Jason H. Silverman, "Monarchial Liberty and Republican Slavery: West Indies Emancipation Celebrations in Upstate New York and Canada West," *Afro-Americans in New York Life and History* 10, no. 1 (1986): 7–18.

103. Speech at Canandaigua, New York, August 3, 1857, in *FDP*, ser. 1, 3:199; ibid., August 1, 1847, in *FDP*, ser. 1, 2:70–71.

104. Speech at Rochester, New York, August 1, 1848, in *FDP*, ser. 1, 2:135.

105. Speech at Canandaigua, New York, August 3, 1857, in *FDP*, ser. 1, 3:194, 196–98.

106. *Douglass' Monthly*, September 1860; speech at Canandaigua, New York, August 3, 1857, in *FDP*, ser. 1, 3:199.

3. *"An American celebration"*

1. *Christian Recorder*, April 20, 1861.

2. Tanner diary, entries for November 7, 1860, reel 4, item 343, Benjamin Tucker Tanner Papers, Carter G. Woodson Collection.

3. Ibid., entry for December 24, 1860; January 4, 6, 18, 1861, reel 4, items 368, 374, 375, and 382.

4. Vincent Harding, *There Is a River: The Black Struggle for Freedom in America* (New York, 1981), 219–21; James M. McPherson, *The Struggle for Equality: Abolitionists and the Negro in the Civil War and Reconstruction* (Princeton, 1964), 29–64; Frederick Douglass quoted from *Douglass' Monthly*, May 1861, 62; *Christian Recorder*, January 18, 1862; for a sense of southern slaves' views of the war, see Litwack, *Been in the Storm So Long*, 15–27; on northern abolitionists' view that the war was a divinely inspired aid to their cause, see George M. Fredrickson, *The Inner Civil War: Northern Intellectuals and the Crisis of the Union* (New York, 1965), esp. 61, 73–74.

5. Speech at Canandaigua, New York, August 3, 1857, in *FDP*, ser. 1, 3:199. On the Thirteenth Amendment, see Michael Vorenberg, *Final Freedom : The Civil War, the Abolition of Slavery, and the Thirteenth Amendment* (Cambridge and New York, 2001).

6. *Douglass' Monthly*, August 1861, September 1862.

7. John Hope Franklin, *The Emancipation Proclamation* (Garden City, 1963), 16–17.

8. James M. McPherson, *Battle Cry of Freedom: The Civil War Era* (New York, 1988), 494–96; Fredrickson, *Inner Civil War*, 113–15; Joseph T. Wilson, *Emancipation: Its Course and Progress, from 1481 b.c. to a.d. 1875* (New York, 1969 [1882]), 44–53.

9. Unidentified letter writer and *Anglo-African* editorial, both cited in James M. McPherson, *The Negro's Civil War: How American Blacks Felt and Acted during the War for the Union* (New York, 1991), 45.

10. Constance McLaughlin Green, *The Secret City: A History of Race Relations in the Nation's Capital* (Princeton, 1967), 59–66; Willard B. Gatewood, *Aristocrats of Color: The Black Elite, 1880–1920* (Bloomington, 1990), 47, 51–52, 58; Litwack, *Been in the Storm So Long*, 513–14.

11. Daniel A. Payne, *Welcome to the Ransomed; or, Duties of the Inhabitants of the District of Columbia* (Baltimore, 1862), reprinted in Payne, *Sermons and Addresses, 1853–1891*, ed. Charles Killian (New York, 1972); J. Franklin, *The Emancipation Proclamation*, 19.

12. J. Wilson, *Emancipation*, 57–60; J. Franklin, *Emancipation Proclamation*, 17–21, 39–40.

13. Swift, *Black Prophets*, 323; *FDP*, ser. 1, vol. 3, xxxiv; *Douglass' Monthly*, August 1862; *Christian Recorder*, June 28, 1862. The *Recorder*'s appeal for a large turnout in

Philadelphia suggested the important fund-raising function of at least some Freedom Day events, as a collection to benefit the AME organ was to be included in the arrangements.

14. *Douglass' Monthly*, August 1862.

15. Speech at Canandaigua, New York, August 3, 1857, in *FDP*, ser. 1, 3:199.

16. J. Franklin, *Emancipation Proclamation*, 50.

17. Ibid., 58–89; Fredrickson, *Inner Civil War*, 113–29; *Douglass' Monthly*, January 1863.

18. Speech at Rochester, New York, December 28, 1862, *FDP*, ser. 1, 3:543.

19. J. Franklin, *Emancipation Proclamation*, 93, 106–18; Robert Francis Engs, *Freedom's First Generation: Black Hampton, Virginia, 1861–1890* (Philadelphia, 1979), 36.

20. *New York Herald*, January 7, 1863.

21. Ibid.; *Colored American* (Augusta), January 6, 1866.

22. *New York Herald*, February 11, 1863; Lewis G. Schmidt, *The Civil War in Florida*, vol. 3, *Florida's Keys and Fevers* (Allentown, 1992), 400; John Jacob Hornbeck, diary, January 24, 1863, Key West Library.

23. *New York Herald*, February 11, 1863.

24. Lewis G. Schmidt, "From Slavery to Freedom: Sandy Cornish and Lillah Cornish," MS in the author's possession; Hornbeck diary, January 24, 1863, Key West Library; additional information at

http://www.innercitynews.com/discovering_african_american_his.htm;
http://www.seekeywest.com/HTML/whitehead_simonton_tour.htm; and
http://www.keyshistory.org/keywest.html.

See also Schmidt, *Civil War in Florida*, 3:400.

25. *New York Herald*, February 11, 1863; Schmidt, "From Slavery to Freedom."

26. *New York Herald*, February 11, 1863; Schmidt, *Civil War in Florida*, 3:400.

27. *New York Herald*, February 11, 1863; Schmidt, *Civil War in Florida*, 3:400; U.S. War Department, *The War of the Rebellion: A Compilation of the Official Records of the Union and Confederate Armies*, ser. 1, vol. 18 (Washington, D.C., 1887), 501–2.

28. J. Franklin, *Emancipation Proclamation*, 109–14; *FDP*, ser. 1, 3:546–48.

29. J. Franklin, *Emancipation Proclamation*, 113–14; *Douglass' Monthly*, January 1863; Douglass speech at New York, February 6, 1863, *FDP*, ser. 1, 3:549.

30. *Christian Recorder*, March 28, 1863.

31. Representative written accounts of the role of African American troops from this period include William Wells Brown, *The Negro in the American Rebellion: His Heroism and His Fidelity* (Boston, 1867); George Washington Williams, *A History of the Negro Troops in the War of the Rebellion* (New York, 1888); Joseph T. Wilson, *The Black Phalanx* (Hartford, 1890); and Luis F. Emilio, *History of the Fifty-fourth Regiment of Massachusetts Volunteer Infantry, 1863–1865* (Boston, 1894). Black veterans, within the Grand Army of the Republic, in separate veterans' organizations,

and as individuals, attempted to perpetuate the memory of black efforts during the war by celebrating anniversaries, raising monuments, and sponsoring other commemorative and educative endeavors.

32. Letter to *Christian Recorder*, March 7, 1863. Virtually every issue of the *Recorder* between 1863 and the end of the war contained some statement to the effect that black soldiers had proved their manhood and their patriotism and would not accept less than the permanent end of slavery and full inclusion of African Americans as citizens as the result of a Union victory.

33. An early statement of this position can be seen in the account of a Buffalo, New York, celebration in January 1863; see *Christian Recorder*, February 14, 1863.

34. Letter from James H. Payne to *Christian Recorder*, December 26, 1863.

35. Letter from "A.R.G." to *Christian Recorder*, January 30, 1864; *Liberator*, August 19, 1859.

36. Letter from "A.R.G." to *Christian Recorder*, January 30, 1864.

37. Isaiah, 18:7; letter from Frisby J. Cooper to *Christian Recorder*, January 30, 1864.

38. Letter from George H. W. Stewart to *Christian Recorder*, January 23, 1864.

39. Letter from "Junius" (Cain's nom de plume) to *Christian Recorder*, January 16, 1864.

40. Letter from James Lynch to *Christian Recorder*, January 16, 1864; *New York Herald*, January 19, 1864.

41. Letter from Henry P. Jones to *Christian Recorder*, January 16, 1864.

42. Letter from Thomas H. C. Hinton (Washington, D.C.) to *Christian Recorder*, January 16, 1864.

43. New Bern's attendance was related by the orator of the day, the Reverend John J. Moore, in a speech four years after the fact; see *Elevator*, January 31, 1868.

44. "The Freeman's Anniversary," printed in *Christian Recorder*, January 16, 1864.

45. Commemorative broadside, ANHSP, box 10G, folder 15; Barbara Jeanne Fields, *Slavery and Freedom on the Middle Ground: Maryland during the Nineteenth Century* (New Haven, 1985), 131–35; *Elevator*, November 19, 1869.

46. The diffusion of Juneteenth celebrations is charted by William Wiggins Jr., from its Texas origin through human migrations that carried it to other parts of the country and to the passage of the 1980 legislation that made the day an official state holiday in Texas. See Wiggins, "From Galveston to Washington: Charting Juneteenth's Freedom Trail," in *Jubilation!* 61–67.

47. Letter from W. H. Haines to the *Age*, April 19, 1890; broadside number 1866: 13, dated April 2, 1866, Virginia Historical Society, advertising a Richmond celebration on April 9, 1866, cited in Elsa Barkley Brown and Gregg D. Kimball, "Mapping the Terrain of Black Richmond," *Journal of Urban History* 21, no. 3 (March 1995): 309, 340n. 22; Kathleen Clark, "Celebrating Freedom: Emancipation Day Celebrations and African American Memory in the Early Reconstruction South," in *Where*

These Memories Grow, 111; Litwack, *Been in the Storm So Long,* 177. Ellen Litwicki discusses important aspects of Richmond blacks' "Emancipation Days" in chap. 2 of *America's Public Holidays.*

48. *South Carolina Leader,* December 16, 1865.

49. *Colored American* (Augusta), January 6, 1866.

50. McPherson, *Battle Cry of Freedom,* 839–40; *Christian Recorder,* January 6, 1866.

51. Interestingly, the establishment of February 1 as National Freedom Day in June 1948 by the proclamation of President Harry S Truman was based on the date of the Thirteenth Amendment's passage in the House. Richard R. Wright Sr., the driving force behind the National Freedom Day movement, designated February 1, rather than January 31, as the appropriate date, perhaps to fit the official holiday into the same month as Negro History Week. Wright identified February 1 as the date Lincoln actually signed the joint resolution. Freedom Day advocates in the mid-twentieth century echoed their nineteenth-century predecessors in contending "that this day should be recognized as a historical day—a day which all people could commemorate as a national holiday . . . for the white as well as for the black people of this nation." Wright's mission to establish a single National Freedom Day holiday was motivated in part by his awareness of the "confusion among the colored people as to what they should celebrate for their Emancipation. . . . Many dates have been and are celebrated; some celebrate August; some in September; some January 1, and others think that they should celebrate March 5, the so-called Attucks Day; and some even think they should celebrate February 12, the birthday of Abraham Lincoln. Hence until the National Freedom Day bill passed there was no definite date recognized by the colored people of this country." See materials in ANHSP, box 2, folder 10.

52. Letters from "J.B.T." in Charleston and "A.B." in Memphis to *Christian Recorder,* August 26, 1865. On the May 1, 1866, Memphis riot see, for example, Eric Foner, *Reconstruction: America's Unfinished Revolution, 1863–1877* (New York, 1988), 261–62, and Litwack, *Been in the Storm So Long,* 280–82.

53. See, for example, Eugene D. Genovese, *Roll, Jordan, Roll: The World the Slaves Made* (New York, 1974), 573–76.

54. Turner, "On the Anniversary of Emancipation (1866)" in *Respect Black: The Writings and Speeches of Henry McNeal Turner,* ed. Edwin S. Redkey (New York, 1971), 5–6.

55. Letter from "Clericus" to *Christian Recorder,* August 26, 1865, italics added.

56. *Elevator,* September 27, 1867.

57. Letters from Samuel Hollensworth to *Christian Recorder,* July 22, August 26, 1865.

58. Letter from William H. Lester to *New Era,* August 18, 1870.

59. Bell founded New York City's *Colored American* (née *Weekly Advocate*) in the

1830s and edited San Francisco's *Pacific Appeal,* in the early 1860s, and the *Elevator,* from its inception in 1865 until his death in 1889. *Elevator,* July 24, August 7, 1868; Douglas Henry Daniels, *Pioneer Urbanites: A Social and Cultural History of Black San Francisco* (Philadelphia, 1980), 12–24, 114–15.

60. *Elevator,* August 7, 1868.

61. Ibid., August 9, 1873.

62. Ibid., June 10, 1870.

63. Ibid., January 11, 1867.

64. Ibid., December 20, 1867.

65. Ibid., January 3, 17, 1868; Daniels, *Pioneer Urbanites,* 133.

66. *Elevator,* January 3, 17, 1868.

67. Ibid., December 20, 1867; January 31, 1868.

68. Letter from "Semper Fidelis," *Elevator,* January 17, 1868.

69. *Weekly Anglo-African,* January 7, March 17, 1860. After the 1850s gold rush hundreds of black miners worked around Placerville, Marysville, Mariposa, and other towns in the California mountains. Many settled in the small towns and cities of the region. In 1865 the vicinity surrounding Marysville reported more than 200 black residents, including 25 farmers, 12 miners, and 18 barbers. San Francisco had about 1,600, Sacramento County more than 600, and Santa Clara County about 175 in the same year. Other reporting counties within 200 miles of San Francisco reported black populations well under 100. In 1860 steamers charged a deck rate of only fifty cents from San Francisco to Sacramento, but the trip from Sacramento to Marysville cost four dollars. *Proceedings of the California State Convention of Colored Citizens* (San Francisco, 1865), reprinted in California State Convention of Colored Citizens, *Proceedings of the First State Convention of the Colored Citizens of the State of California: 1855, 1856, 1865,* ed. Alan Eterovich (Saratoga, Calif.: R & E Associates, 1969), 84–86. See also Delilah L. Beasley, *The Negro Trail Blazers of California* (Los Angeles, 1919), esp. 98–106.

70. "The Way I Celebrate," *Elevator,* January 15, 1869.

71. Ibid.

72. *Elevator,* December 11, 1868; January 22, 1869; Elizabeth McLagan, *A Peculiar Paradise: A History of Blacks in Oregon, 1788–1940* (Portland, 1980), 91; population statistics, and their questionable accuracy, are discussed in McLagan, 185, 193n 18.

73. *Elevator,* September 17, 1869; Leroy Graham, *Baltimore: The Nineteenth-Century Black Capital* (Washington, D.C., 1982), 276. A single page of Bell's *Elevator,* June 3, 1870, further documents both Masons' and Odd Fellows' participation in numerous celebrations of the Fifteenth Amendment in New York, Baltimore, and New Bedford, Mass. See also Salvatore, *We All Got History,* 185, for Odd Fellows' participation, and *New Era,* April 28, 1870, for various fraternal organizations' participation in Richmond, Va. Other examples abound.

74. *Elevator,* October 15, 29, November 19, 26, December 31, 1869; Daniels, *Pioneer Urbanites,* 121, 203n. 56.

75. "On the Proclamation of the Fifteenth Amendment," poem by "W.J.H."; editorial comment; and Grant's message to Congress all in *New Era,* April 7, 1870. On the dissolution of the American Anti-Slavery Society, see McPherson, *The Struggle for Equality,* 427–29.

76. Accounts of most of these celebrations can be found in the *Elevator,* and *New Era* between April and June 1870. The *New Era* was edited by the Reverend J. Sella Martin and backed by a nine-member consortium of black leaders among whom Douglass appears to have had the most hands-on connection. More detail on the celebrations and the papers' coverage can be found in Mitchell Kachun, " 'This Golden Burden of Affranchisement': Themes in African-American Celebrations of the Fifteenth Amendment," MS in the possession of the author.

77. Kachun, " 'This Golden Burden,' " 4, 31n. 9. On the debate over women's suffrage and the Fifteenth Amendment, see Ellen Carol DuBois, *Feminism and Suffrage: The Emergence of an Independent Women's Movement in America, 1848–1869* (Ithaca, 1978), 162–202. On black women's public and private social and organizational activities in the late nineteenth century, see Evelyn Brooks Higginbotham, *Righteous Discontent: The Women's Movement in the Black Baptist Church, 1880–1920* (Cambridge, Mass., 1993); Kathleen C. Berkeley, " 'Colored Ladies Also Contributed': Black Women's Activities from Benevolence to Social Welfare, 1866–1896," in *The Web of Southern Social Relations: Women, Family, and Education,* ed. Walter J. Fraser Jr., R. Frank Saunders Jr., and Jon L. Wakelyn (Athens, 1985), 181–203; and Kathleen Clark, "Celebrating Freedom," 120–24.

78. *Elevator,* April 22, May 6, March 25, 1870.

79. Ibid., February 25, 1870.

80. Ibid.; "Letter from Cincinnati," *New National Era,* January 25, 1872.

81. *Elevator,* February 25, 1870.

82. Ibid., March 11, 1870.

83. Ibid., March 11, 18, 25, 1870.

84. Ibid., April 15, May 6, 1870.

85. Ibid., March 11, 18, 1870.

86. Ibid., March 18, 1870.

87. Graham, *Baltimore,* 286.

88. *Elevator,* June 3, 1870; *New Era,* May 26, 1870.

89. *New Era,* May 26, 1870.

90. Ibid., April 28, 1870.

91. Louisville transparency described in *Elevator,* June 10, 1870. I treat the general themes of Fifteenth Amendment celebrations in considerable detail in Kachun, " 'This Golden Burden.' "

92. *Elevator,* December 2, 1870.

93. *Christian Recorder,* August 20, 1870.

94. Broadside, ANHSP, box 13G, folder 1.

95. *Elevator,* October 18, 1867; "Celebration in West Virginia," *Globe,* October 6, 1883.

96. *Christian Recorder,* August 20, 1870; Wiggins, *O Freedom!* 72–73; Wiggins, "From Galveston to Washington," in *Jubilation!* 61.

97. *New Era,* August 18, 25, 1870; William Gillette, *The Right to Vote: Politics and the Passage of the Fifteenth Amendment* (Baltimore, 1969), 83–84.

98. *Elevator,* April 22, 1870; *New Era,* April 7, 1870.

99. *Christian Recorder,* August 18, 1866. The celebration in Cleveland the same year elicited "opposition" from "persons who were . . . averse to celebrating the 1st of August." See *Christian Recorder,* August 25, 1866.

100. *Louisianian,* August 20, 1871.

101. *New Orleans Tribune,* June 29, July 4, July 6, July 8, 1865; *Louisianian,* July 16, 1871.

102. *Christian Recorder,* July 3, 1869, August 14, 1869; *New Orleans Tribune,* March 3, 1865.

103. *Christian Recorder,* August 17, 1872.

104. From a speech at the April 16, 1872, celebration of District emancipation in Washington, D.C., in the *Elevator,* May 25, 1872; *Elevator,* April 5, 1873.

105. Roger Lane, *William Dorsey's Philadelphia and Ours: On the Past and Future of the Black City in America* (New York, 1991), 203.

4. "Let children's children never forget"

1. Greener's speech reprinted in *New Era,* May 5, 1870.

2. *New Era,* May 5, 1870. On the reunion of white North and white South, see Blight, *Race and Reunion;* Nina Silber, *The Romance of Reunion: Northerners and the South, 1865–1900* (Chapel Hill, 1993); and Paul Buck, *The Road to Reunion* (Boston, 1937).

3. Foner, *Reconstruction,* 421–24, 587–601, quotation on 598. See also Leon F. Litwack, *Trouble in Mind: Black Southerners in the Age of Jim Crow* (New York, 1998).

4. "From Our Regular Correspondent," *Elevator,* January 25, 1873.

5. Floyd's 1909 Emancipation Day speech at Augusta, Ga., quoted in Blight, *Race and Reunion,* 336–37; *American Citizen* (Kansas City), October 19, 1894.

6. See David Blight's insightful discussion of blacks' multidimensional ideas about history and memory during the half century after emancipation in *Race and Reunion,* 300–337, quotation on 312. On blacks as a "redeemer race," see Bay, *The White Image in the Black Mind.*

7. "'Jubilee' Singers," *Christian Recorder,* January 15, 1874. For interesting dis-

cussions of minstrelsy, slave spirituals, and white perceptions, see Eric Lott, "'The Seeming Counterfeit': Racial Politics and Early Blackface Minstrelsy," *American Quarterly* 43, no. 2 (June 1991): 223–54, and Robert C. Toll, *Blacking Up: The Minstrel Show in Nineteenth-Century America* (New York, 1974), esp. 235–44. Nina Silber also discusses postbellum white constructions of slavery and the former slaves in *Romance of Reunion.*

8. "Colored Society," installment 5, *Christian Recorder,* December 14, 1876; *American Citizen* (Kansas City), October 19, 1894.

9. "Colored Society," *Christian Recorder,* December 14, 1876; William Seraile, *Voice of Dissent: Theophilus Gould Steward (1843–1924) and Black America* (Brooklyn, 1991), 59–64; *Elevator,* January 8, 15, 1869. On black Americans' views of Africa, see, for example, Tunde Adeleke, *UnAfrican Americans: Nineteenth-Century Black Nationalists and the Civilizing Mission* (Lexington, 1998); Wilson Jeremiah Moses, *Alexander Crummell: A Study of Civilization and Discontent* (Amherst, 1992); Blight, *Race and Reunion,* 320–34; and Lawrence S. Little, *Disciples of Liberty: The African Methodist Episcopal Church in the Age of Imperialism, 1884–1916* (Knoxville, 2000).

10. *Elevator,* January 8, 15, 1869.

11. *Christian Recorder,* September 21, 1872; "Our Heroic Age," *Christian Recorder,* September 10, 1874.

12. "The First Decade after Jubilee," same title of two separate columns, *Christian Recorder,* December 10, 1874. On the theme of "race progress," see Blight, *Race and Reunion,* 319–37, and Kevin Kelly Gaines, *Uplifting the Race: Black Leadership, Politics, and Culture since the Turn of the Century* (Chapel Hill, 1996).

13. "A Loud Call" (reprinted from the *Elevator*), *Christian Recorder,* August 17, 1876. Bell's activities and career, and his attention to history and commemorations, are briefly summarized in chap. 3. The works Bell referred to were William C. Nell, *The Colored Patriots of the American Revolution* (Boston, 1855), and William Wells Brown, *The Rising Son: or, The Antecedents and Advancement of the Colored Race* (Boston, 1874); he could have added Brown's *The Black Man: His Antecedents, His Genius, and His Achievements* (New York, 1863) and *The Negro in the American Rebellion: His Heroism and His Fidelity* (Boston, 1867), and William Still, *The Underground Railroad* (Philadelphia, 1872).

14. David Blight, *Frederick Douglass' Civil War: Keeping Faith in Jubilee* (Baton Rouge, 1989); *Christian Recorder,* August 25, 1866; Salvatore, *We All Got History,* 280–85. See also Blight, *Race and Reunion,* 192–96.

15. "The Negro in Line at the GAR Encampment," unidentified clipping, ANHSP, box 9G, folder 10. Fortune's New York *Freeman* provided extensive coverage of the 1887 reunion of black veterans in Boston. It is perhaps significant that the event was held on August 1 and 2. *Freeman* (New York), June 18, July 23, August 6, 1887. Fortune's papers had a regular column entitled "Grand Army Notes" that focused on the activities of black GAR chapters, especially around Decoration Day.

See particularly the *Freeman* (New York), August 20, 1887, and the *Bee*, September 3, 1892, for poignant statements of the importance of acknowledging blacks' military role and the role of black veterans in perpetuating the "real" history. On the Grand Army, see Stuart McConnell, *Glorious Contentment: The Grand Army of the Republic, 1865–1900* (Chapel Hill, 1992), and Mary R. Dearing, *Veterans in Politics: The Story of the GAR* (Baton Rouge, 1952). Barbara A. Gannon argues that the GAR was far more supportive of black veterans and of black rights generally, than has previously been acknowledged by historians. See Gannon, "Sites of Memory, Sites of Glory: African-American Grand Army of the Republic Posts in Pennsylvania," in *Making and Remaking Pennsylvania's Civil War,* ed. William Blair and William Pencak (University Park, 2001), 165–87.

16. Report from the *Cleveland Gazette* reprinted in the *Freeman* (New York), April 17, 1886; *Freeman* (New York), March 12, 1887.

17. *Age,* July 17, 1913.

18. Flyer from archives of the Massachusetts National Guard, July 18, 1913; *Chicago Defender,* July 19, 1913.

19. *Age,* August 2, 1917.

20. ANHSP, box 13G, folder 1; John Hope Franklin, *George Washington Williams: A Biography* (Chicago, 1985), 55; editorial, *Freeman* (New York), June 5, 1886; "A Brooklyn Monument Scheme," *Age,* September 20, 1890; July 18, 1891; Graham, *Baltimore,* 283; *Huntsville Gazette,* November 24, 1888.

21. "The Colored Union Soldier," *Bee,* April 28, 1883.

22. *Bee,* December 6, 20, 1884; May 16, 1885; December 18, 1886; April 20, 1887; *Age,* August 6, 1887. On Hoar's work for black rights and his abiding interest in historical memory, see Kammen, *Mystic Chords of Memory,* 184, 212, 226; and Salvatore, *We All Got History,* 210, 216–17, 248. In 1998, after repeated delays and budget shortfalls, an eleven-foot, $2.6 million monument honoring black Civil War veterans, entitled "Spirit of Freedom," was erected in Washington, D.C.

23. "Monument Wanted," *Bee,* January 1, 1887; "Another Monument Scheme," *Age,* April 6, 1889. On black support for the Lincoln and Shaw monuments, among others, see Kirk Savage, *Standing Soldiers, Kneeling Slaves: Race, War, and Monument in Nineteenth-Century America* (Princeton, 1997).

24. *Huntsville Gazette,* November 24, 1888. A perusal of the May editions of T. Thomas Fortune's New York papers during the 1880s suggests the attention given to Decoration Day observances by blacks in the North, though they do appear to have been largely segregated affairs. See also Blight, *Race and Reunion,* chap. 3.

25. "The Garnet Memorial" and "Bergen Star Concert" (advertisement), *Freeman* (New York), December 26, 1885.

26. "The Garnet Memorial," *Freeman* (New York), January 30, 1886; "A Lack of Public Spirit," *Age,* June 16, 1888.

27. "A Lack of Public Spirit," *Age,* June 16, 1888; Kammen, *Mystic Chords of*

Memory, 115; Eric Hobsbawm, "Mass-Producing Traditions: Europe, 1870–1914," in *The Invention of Tradition*, ed. Hobsbawm and Terence Ranger (Cambridge, 1983), 263–307, quotation on 263, 271; Savage, *Standing Soldiers, Kneeling Slaves*, 164, 182. On 115–19 of *Mystic Chords of Memory* Kammen describes a number of specific monuments erected during this period.

28. "An Incident of the Lee Monument Unveiling," *Age*, June 7, 1890; *Huntsville Gazette*, May 31, 1890; Savage, *Standing Soldiers, Kneeling Slaves*, 129–61, quotation on 155.

29. *State Capital*, January 16, 1892; *Chicago Defender*, May 30, 1914; June 12, 1915. On efforts by the United Daughters of the Confederacy to create a "mammy monument," see Blight, *Race and Reunion*, 288, 459n. 57.

30. "Boston's Monument Fever," *Age*, March 23, 1889. On specific monument proposals: Nell, *Age*, February 27, April 27, 1886; Attucks, *Age*, November 17, 1888; Turner (the monument was not placed at the time, and the proposal by T. Thomas Fortune generated criticism from Frederick Douglass Jr., who suggested that John Brown was more deserving), *Age*, January 12, 26, February 16, 1889; Douglass, "The Douglass Monument," *Age*, January 4, 1900; Tubman (a monument raised through the efforts of a women's organization, which generated discussion over its placement in a cemetery; one critic complained that monuments to great leaders should be placed conspicuously in public places in order to inspire all blacks, especially black children), *Age*, February 11, March 25, July 15, 1915; Langston, *Richmond Planet*, January 28, 1899; *Bee*, various articles between 1904 and 1906.

31. Following is a summary of my research into the Allen monument, which is discussed in more detail in Kachun, "'Before the Eyes of All Nations,'" 300–323.

32. *Christian Recorder*, January 22, 1874.

33. "Remove the Debris," *Christian Recorder*, November 19, 1874.

34. *Press*, June 13, 1876.

35. Ibid.

36. Ibid.

37. *Christian Recorder*, December 3, 1874.

38. Ibid., November 9, 1876; *Press*, November 3, 1876. Another account held that the unveiling took place "in October, in the presence of 30,000 colored citizens, and many others," but I believe that the *Press* figures are more realistic. See *Southern Workman*, January 1877. Langston's speech, "Richard Allen," is reprinted in John Mercer Langston, *Freedom and Citizenship: Selected Lectures and Addresses* (Miami, 1969 [1883]). I have found no evidence to dispute Langston's claim for the primacy of the Allen monument.

39. "First Blood for American Liberty," *Globe*, January 20, 1883.

40. *Freeman* (New York), April 16, May 28, 1887; "Attucks and His Comrades," *Age*, November 17, 1888; *Huntsville Gazette*, May 26, November 24, 1888; Elizabeth

Rauh Bethel, *The Roots of African-American Identity: Memory and History in Antebellum Free Communities* (New York, 1997), 11–15; Kammen, *Mystic Chords of Memory,* 122.

41. "Our Hub Letter," *Globe,* October 4, 1884; "Prince Hall's Grave," *Freeman* (New York), October 17, 1885.

42. *Age,* November 5, 19, 26, 1887; *Christian Recorder,* February 17, 1887; Mitchell Kachun, "The Shaping of a Public Biography: Richard Allen and the African Methodist Episcopal Church," in *Black Lives: Essays in African American Biography,* ed. James L. Conyers (Armonk, 1999), 44–63.

43. This interconnectedness of purpose between the adulation of heroes and the construction of a larger historical interpretation contrasts with the pattern Michael Kammen has identified for partisans of the white South, for whom "it became the challenge of the 1880s to move forward from individual hero worship to more comprehensive control of the past." For black Americans the comprehensive view and the adulation of heroes worked together more seamlessly, without any real tension between the two. See Kammen, *Mystic Chords of Memory,* 111.

A sampling of specifically historical and biographical works from the 1880s includes J. Wilson, *Emancipation;* J. Wilson, *Black Phalanx;* George Washington Williams, *History of the Negro Race in America from 1619 to 1880,* 2 vols. (New York, 1883); Williams, *History of the Negro Troops;* William T. Alexander, *History of the Colored Race in America.* (Kansas City, 1887); William J. Simmons, *Men of Mark: Eminent, Progressive, and Rising* (New York, 1968 [1887]); and Daniel Payne, *Recollections of Seventy Years* (New York, 1968 [1888]). The publication of similar works, and of historically conscious novels, expanded even more after 1890. See, for example, J. Franklin, *From Slavery to Freedom,* 404–12; August Meier, *Negro Thought in America, 1880–1915* (Ann Arbor, 1969), 51–53, 260–64; and Hall, "To Give a Faithful Account of the Race."

44. *Age,* February 28, 1891.

45. "Race Literature, Past and Present—Fate of Colored Authors," *Age,* February 20, 1886.

46. *American Citizen* (Kansas City), October 26, 1894.

47. A sampling of citations will suffice: advertisement for Still, *Globe,* November 24, 1883; advertisement for Williams and Fortune (packaged together at a discount), *Freeman* (New York), October 10, 1885; positive review of Wilson (whose book "has done the race a valuable service"), *Age,* March 10, 1888; offer of copies of *Black Phalanx* with subscriptions, *Age,* August 24, 1889; praise for *Black Phalanx* in *Huntsville Gazette,* November 24, 1888; praise for Rowe's volume of poetry, which contained tributes to Attucks, Toussaint L'Ouverture, Daniel Payne, F. E. W. Harper, Robert Smalls, and others, in "Some Race Books of the Day," by W. H. A. Moore, *Age,* August 16, 1891; large advertisement for Johnson's *School History* in *Richmond Planet,* April 13, 1895; advertisement for various engravings, portraits, books, and

other "race literature, old and new" that offered more than thirty items, *Age*, January 4, 1900.

48. *Globe*, September 27, 1884; "No Race Pride in His," letter from J. M. Carroll, of Newport, R.I., *Freeman* (New York), November 20, 1886; *Richmond Planet*, June 8, 1895; *Chicago Defender*, January 20, 1912.

49. See, for example, *Age*, May 18, 1889; *Christian Recorder*, May 10, 1862; March 28, 1863; February 17, 1887; February 13, 1890.

50. *Bee*, December 12, 1885; *Freeman* (Indianapolis), July 5, September 20, 1890; "Souvenir Historical Chart," ANHSP, box 4G, folder 24.

51. Quoted in *Huntsville Gazette*, September 17, 1887.

52. "Literary Notes," *Globe*, July 5, 1884.

53. "Race Literature, Past and Present—Fate of Colored Authors," *Age*, February 20, 1886; *Huntsville Gazette*, September 17, 1887.

54. William Andrews, introduction to *The African-American Novel in the Age of Reaction: Three Classics*, ed. Andrews (New York, 1992), x. For a thorough analysis of Harper's career, see Frances Smith Foster, ed., *Minnie's Sacrifice; Sowing and Reaping; Trial and Triumph: Three Rediscovered Novels by Frances E. W. Harper* (Boston, 1994), and Melba Joyce Boyd, *Discarded Legacy: Politics and Poetics in the Life of Frances E. W. Harper, 1825–1911* (Detroit, 1994).

55. Frances Ellen Watkins Harper, *Iola Leroy, or Shadows Uplifted* (1892) as reprinted in *The African-American Novel in the Age of Reaction: Three Classics*, ed. William Andrews (New York, 1992), 244, 322–23, 343, 366, 435. On Harper's participation in Freedom Day events, it is particularly interesting that, at an 1898 celebration sponsored by Philadelphia's American Negro Historical Society, she was "introduced as a living historical Relic." Harper promptly "attempted to discuss the admission of women to the Society, but the president . . . did not make an answer to her overtures" (note-sheet from the *Weekly Astonisher*, ANHSP, box 10G, folder 1). A 1904 membership list for the ANHS lists four women, including Harper and Gertrude Mossell, among the thirty-seven members (ANHSP, box 10G, folder 4).

56. "Literary Societies," *Christian Recorder*, February 15, 1877; *American Citizen* (Kansas City), October 26, 1894; *Pittsburgh Courier*, September 13, 1912.

57. John W. Cromwell, *History of the Bethel Literary and Historical Association* (Washington, D.C., 1896); Meier, *Negro Thought in America*, 51–53, 260–64.

58. Letter to *Globe*, June 16, 1883; "Two Notable Collections, of Matter Relating to Race History," *Freeman* (New York), June 4, 1887.

59. "Our Race History," *Freeman* (New York), June 11, 1887; "That Historical Society," *Freeman* (New York), July 16, 1887.

60. The William Henry Dorsey Collection, containing various books, manuscripts, scrapbooks, biographical files, and ephemeral materials, is housed at Cheyney University of Pennsylvania in Philadelphia. See Lane, *William Dorsey's Philadelphia*.

61. "An Historical Society," *Age*, November 8, 1890.

62. "Historical Society Project," *Age*, September 19, 1891.

63. "Is Such a Society Needed?" *Age*, July 12, 1890. On the increasing interest in American folklife after the late 1880s, see Silber, *Romance of Reunion*, chap. 5; and Kammen, *Mystic Chords of Memory*, 156, 287, 426.

64. "To Preserve Our Folk Lore," *Age*, March 8, 1890; *Age*, November 8, 1890.

65. "Address on the Accomplishments of the NHS," author unknown, ANHSP, box 10G, folder 6, 3–6, 12–13.

66. Henry MacFarland to Woodson, reel 3, item 473, Carter G. Woodson Collection.

67. Meier, *Negro Thought in America*, 262–64; Meier and Elliott Rudwick, *Black History and the Historical Profession, 1915–1980* (Urbana, 1986), 1–4, 11–16; John Hope Franklin, "On the Evolution of Scholarship in Afro-American History," in *The State of Afro-American History: Past, Present, and Future*, ed. Darlene Clark Hine (Baton Rouge, 1986), 13–16.

68. David Levering Lewis, *W. E. B. Du Bois: Biography of a Race, 1868–1919* (New York, 1993), 379–80, 459–63; Robert L. Harris Jr., "Daniel Murray and *The Encyclopedia of the Colored Race*," *Phylon* 37, no. 3 (September 1976): 270–82.

5. *"Lessons of Emancipation for a New Generation"*

1. Lane, *William Dorsey's Philadelphia*, 203.

2. "Twenty-Fifth Anniversary," broadside advertising the 1889 celebration, which actually represented the twenty-*sixth* anniversary of Lincoln's Emancipation Proclamation, ANHSP, box 13G, folder 2; letters to William Still from Cable, Washington, Armstrong, and Douglass in ANHSP, box 9G, folder 16. Other Philadelphia celebrations in the 1890s can be verified for 1892, 1893, and 1898. See ANHSP, box 4G, folder 22; box 13G, folder 2; box 10G, folder 1.

3. "Emancipation Celebrations," *Age*, January 12, 1889.

4. *Globe*, April 14, 1883; *Freeman* (New York), April 9, 1887.

5. Mary C. Ames's commentary for the *Independent* is reprinted in *Addresses and Ceremonies at the New Year's Festival to the Freedmen, of Arlington Heights; and Statistics and Statements of the Educational Condition of the Colored People in the Southern States, and Other Facts* (Washington, D.C.: McGill and Witherow, Printers and Stereotypers, 1867), Murray Pamphlet Collection. See also Litwicki, *America's Public Holidays*. In limiting her study of emancipation celebrations to Richmond, Litwicki tends to overgeneralize regarding the degree of "official" white control, but her observations have considerable legitimacy for the early postemancipation years in the most occupied parts of the South.

6. *Emancipation Celebration, January 1st 1891 at Alexandria, Virginia*, Murray Pamphlet Collection.

7. Joshua A. Brockett, "The Emancipation Proclamation," speech given at the Metropolitan Hall, Raleigh, North Carolina, January 1, 1892, reprinted in *African Methodist Episcopal Church Review* 8, no. 4 (April 1892). Ellen Litwicki also emphasizes white Republicans' abandonment of black emancipation celebrations in Richmond during this period. See *America's Public Holidays,* chap. 2.

8. For example, *Richmond Planet,* July 12, 1890; December 25, 1897; *Huntsville Gazette,* June 30, July 14, 1883; January 4, 1890. See also Stewart E. Tolnay and E. M. Beck, *A Festival of Violence: An Analysis of Southern Lynchings, 1882–1930* (Urbana, 1995), and Litwack, *Trouble in Mind.*

9. Broadside, Virginia Historical Society, Richmond, as reproduced in Kammen, *Mystic Chords of Memory,* 122; *Emancipation Oration! Delivered by Rev. E. K. Love, D.D., Savannah, Ga., at the emancipation celebration, at Augusta, Georgia, January 1st, 1891; Oration Delivered on Emancipation Day January 2nd 1888, by Rev. E. K. Love,* both pamphlets in the Murray Pamphlet Collection.

10. *Emancipation Address: Our duties and how to discharge them, delivered in the town hall of Salem, Va., January 2, 1893, under the auspices of the Emancipation Club of Salem, with which was joined the Emancipation Club of Roanoke, Va., by Prof. Daniel B. Williams; A Glance at the Past and Present of the Negro: An Address, by Robert H. Terrell, delivered at Church's auditorium before the Citizen's industrial league of Memphis, Tennessee, September 22, 1903;* both pamphlets in the Murray Pamphlet Collection; Louis R. Harlan, *Booker T. Washington: The Wizard of Tuskegee, 1901–1915* (New York, 1983), 17.

11. *Gazette* (Raleigh), January 29, 1898; Glenda Elizabeth Gilmore, *Gender and Jim Crow: Women and the Politics of White Supremacy in North Carolina, 1896–1920* (Chapel Hill, 1996).

12. *Gazette* (Raleigh), January 8, 1898.

13. Ibid., January 15, 22, 29, 1898.

14. *Huntsville Gazette,* June 30, July 14, 1883; July 4, 1885; Clark, "Celebrating Freedom," 125.

15. *Age,* April 19, 1890; *Bee,* April 19, 1890; Brown and Kimball, "Mapping the Terrain of Black Richmond," 308–9; Litwicki, *America's Public Holidays,* chap. 2.

16. "The American Negro and His Emancipation," oration by W. Calvin Chase, reprinted in *Bee,* August 21, 1897. T. Thomas Fortune reported on Norfolk celebrations in his New York papers in the late 1880s. See *Freeman* (New York), December 6, 13, 1884; quotation in *Freeman,* January 9, 1886; *Age,* January 7, December 29, 1888; January 19, 1889; see also the hundred-page account of the 1885 celebration, T. F. Paige, *Twenty-two Years of Freedom: An Account of the Emancipation Celebration by the Freedmen of Norfolk, Virginia, and Vicinity on the First Day of January, Including the Literary Exercises, Oration, Poem, Review* (Norfolk, 1885).

17. Engs, *Freedom's First Generation,* 186; *Southern Workman,* February 1886.

18. "Emancipation Association," *Afro-American Ledger,* November 30, 1901.

19. *Afro-American Ledger,* August 17, September 21, November 30, 1901; August 30, 1902; October 24, 1903; January 3, 1914; January 9, 1915.

20. Reduced rates for trains to Frederick's 1893 celebration, for example, were advertised from Baltimore and Washington, each about forty-five miles away. See *Bee,* August 5, 1893. Trains often offered such rates for a variety of functions, including camp meetings, GAR encampments, regional fairs and expositions, chautauquas, tourist excursions, and bicycle meets. All the above events are advertised on a single page of the *Bee,* August 7, 1897.

21. "Negroes Ignored, Maryland Republicans Dissatisfied," *Bee,* August 14, 1897; "Emancipation at Frederick," *Bee,* August 21, 1897.

22. "The American Negro and His Emancipation," oration reprinted in *Bee,* August 21, 1897.

23. *Bee,* December 1890; September 26, 1891; September 21, 1901; quotation of the 1890 committee in "The Day for Celebration," *Age,* November 8, 1890.

24. *Huntsville Gazette,* June 18, 25, 1881; June 23, 1883; June 13, 1885; *Age,* July 12, 1890; *Chicago Defender,* May 15, 1915. On Covert, Mich., see Anna-Lisa Grace Cox, "The Open Door: Community, Race, and Identity in Nineteenth-Century Rural Michigan," Ph.D. diss., University of Illinois at Urbana-Champaign, 2000.

25. *Globe,* June 28, July 5, 1884.

26. *Freeman* (New York), June 27, July 25, 1885.

27. *Age,* October 5, 1889.

28. "Celebration at Parkersburg," *Globe,* October 6, 1883; *Bee,* August 22, 1891.

29. "Emancipation Day," *Bee,* October 1, 1904. Celebrations in the other areas are documented in *Age,* October 5, 1911 (Jackson City, Mo.); *Press,* September 23, 1876 (Philadelphia); *Freeman* (Indianapolis), October 5, 1889 (St. Louis); *Afro-American Ledger,* September 28, 1901 (Quincy, Ill.).

30. *Christian Recorder,* March 5, 1874; Kachun, "'Before the Eyes of All Nations,'" 300–323.

31. See Mitchell Kachun, "The Faith That the Dark Past Has Taught Us: African-American Commemorations in the North and West and the Construction of a Usable Past, 1808–1915," Ph.D. diss., Cornell University, 1997, 406–14; "The Negroe's Emancipation Day," *Bee,* September 21, 1901.

32. *Freeman* (Indianapolis), September 1, 15, 1888; *FDP,* ser. 1, 4:xxv, 5:xxiv, xviii.

33. *American Citizen* (Topeka), August 3, 1888. On the turn to local issues, see, for example, Salvatore, *We All Got History,* 232–33, 238. For a thorough account of Fortune's life and views, see Emma Lou Thornbrough, *T. Thomas Fortune: Militant Journalist* (Chicago, 1972). On blacks' relations with the two major parties and their respective presidential administrations during the 1880s, see Rayford Logan, *The Betrayal of the Negro: From Rutherford B. Hayes to Woodrow Wilson* (New York: Collier Books, 1965), 48–66.

34. Richard White, "Civil Rights Agitation: Emancipation Days in Central New

York in the 1880s," *Journal of Negro History* 78 (winter 1993): 16–24, quotation on 18.

35. "Mr. Fortune's Address—How the Day Was Observed at Owego," *Freeman* (New York), August 14, 1886.

36. Those offices, American minister to Haiti and Washington, D.C., recorder of deeds, were hardly as prestigious as Fortune suggested. They were, however, no less so than previous Republican appointments.

37. "Mr. Fortune's Address—How the Day Was Observed at Owego," *Freeman* (New York), August 14, 1886.

38. "The Emancipation Celebration," *Owego Times,* August 12, 1886, quoted in R. White, "Civil Rights Agitation," 19.

39. "Mr. Fortune's Address—How the Day Was Observed at Owego," *Freeman* (New York), August 14, 1886.

40. Ibid.

41. "Emancipation Celebrations," *Age,* August 3, 1889. On biracial working-class cooperation, see William H. Harris, *The Harder We Run: Black Workers since the Civil War* (New York, 1982), 26–36, and Edward L. Ayers, *The Promise of the New South: Life after Reconstruction* (New York, 1992), 234–48.

42. "Emancipation Celebrations," *Age,* August 3, 1889.

43. "Celebration at Corning—A Great Day for Central New York," *Age,* August 10, 1889.

44. Following is a partial but representative sample of reports in Fortune's New York papers that attest to these practices at celebrations in the 1880s and 1890s: Elmira, *Globe,* August 16, 1884; Waverly, *Age,* August 11, 1888; Watkins Glen, *Age,* August 23, 1890; Williamsport, Pa., *Age,* August 15, 1891.

45. The rough circle of towns that hosted celebrations during this period in what I have called the Finger Lakes sphere of interaction includes Syracuse, Auburn, and Geneva in the north; Penn Yan in the west; Corning, Elmira, Waverly, Owego, and Binghamton in the south; Norwich in the east; and Cortland, Ithaca, and Watkins Glen across the center. The communities around the periphery of this zone, of course, did not see themselves as peripheral. The local black community in each case remained the most fundamental source of identity and organization. Geneva, for example, was no closer to Ithaca or Syracuse than it was to Rochester. Indeed it was far closer to the latter city than it was to Binghamton or Norwich, at the far southeastern end of what I have designated as an interaction sphere. Each community surely saw itself at the center of its own network of regional interaction, with the overlapping of these local circles suggesting the arrangements of regional networks. My designation of a particular zone is not, however, completely arbitrary. It might best be considered as the Ithaca/Cortland sphere of interaction, since those two communities occupy the most central location in this Finger Lakes zone. More research on these regional communication networks would greatly advance our

understanding of African American community life during the nineteenth century. Some work has appeared that suggests the workings of local and regional black networks, including Salvatore, *We All Got History,* a cultural biography of a black community activist in Worcester, Mass., and Kathryn Grover, *Make a Way Somehow: African-American Life in a Northern Community, 1790–1965* (Syracuse, 1994), a community study of Geneva, N.Y.

46. "Emancipation Day," *Age,* August 25, 1888. Biographical information in "A Prominent Visitor," *Age,* September 21, 1911.

47. *Huntsville Gazette,* September 17, 1881; January 21, 1888.

48. *New Age,* January 5, 1907; *Richmond Planet,* January 7, 1899; *American Citizen* (Kansas City), July 24, 1891; *American Citizen* (Topeka), August 10, 1888. On the exoduster movement, see Nell Irvin Painter, *Exodusters: Black Migration to Kansas after Reconstruction* (Lawrence, 1976).

49. *Huntsville Gazette,* September 17, 1881; B. W. Arnett Jr., *The Centennial Jubilee of Freedom at Columbus, Ohio, Saturday, September 22, 1888* (Xenia, Ohio: Aldine Printing House, 1888), Murray Pamphlet Collection.

50. *Richmond Planet,* January 5, 26, 1895; *Cleveland Gazette,* December 1, 1888; *American Citizen* (Kansas City), September 23, 1898. The Richmond convention is discussed in Litwicki, *America's Public Holidays,* 58–66.

51. *American Citizen* (Kansas City), September 23, 30, 1898.

52. *American Citizen* (Topeka), August 3, 1888; *Cleveland Gazette,* April 26, 1890.

53. "African Emancipation," *Age,* September 15, 1883.

54. My interpretation of the maturation of the Freedom Day commemorative tradition can be found in chap. 2.

55. "African Emancipation," *Age,* September 15, 1883.

56. Arnett, *Centennial Jubilee of Freedom,* Murray Pamphlet Collection.

57. "The Lessons of Emancipation to the New Generation: An Address Delivered in Elmira, New York, on 3 August 1880," reprinted from account in the *Elmira Advertiser* (N.Y.) August 3, 1880, in *FDP,* ser. 1, 4:562–81.

58. Ibid., 565–66. Douglass's position on the post-Reconstruction black migration to the West is discussed in Painter, *Exodusters,* 213, 247–50; and McFeely, *Frederick Douglass,* 299–302.

59. *FDP,* ser. 1, 4:575, 578–79.

60. Blight, *Frederick Douglass' Civil War.* See also Blight, *Race and Reunion.*

61. "Emancipation Day at Greenville, S.C.," *Christian Recorder,* January 25, 1894.

6. *"A great occasion for display"*

1. On Washington's sporadic January 1 celebrations, see, for example, *Bee,* January 6, 1883.

2. Green, *The Secret City,* 59–66; Gatewood, *Aristocrats of Color,* 47, 51–52, 58,

and chap. 3; Jacqueline M. Moore, *Leading the Race: The Transformation of the Black Elite in the Nation's Capital, 1880–1920* (Charlottesville and London, 1999), 13, 14; "Washington, D.C.: Civic, Literary, and Mutual Aid Associations," in *Organizing Black America: An Encyclopedia of African American Associations,* ed. Nina Mjagkij (New York and London, 2001), 691–94.

3. "Fifth Anniversary of Emancipation—The Celebration Yesterday," *Daily National Intelligencer,* April 17, 1867.

4. "Emancipation Day—The Grand Parade of the Colored Population," *Daily National Intelligencer,* April 17, 1868; "The Emancipation Celebration," *Elevator,* May 15, 1868.

5. "Seventh Anniversary of Emancipation," *Daily National Intelligencer,* April 17, 1869.

6. Report from the *Washington Republican,* reprinted in the *New National Era,* April 25, 1872.

7. *New Era,* April 25, 1872. On Washington's "black aristocracy," see Gatewood, *Aristocrats of Color,* 39–68, and Moore, *Leading the Race.*

8. Moore, *Leading the Race,* 3.

9. "The Emancipation Celebration," *Bee,* April 21, 1883.

10. Holland's address reprinted in "The Emancipation Celebration," *Bee,* April 21, 1883; "Our Destiny Is Largely in Our Hands," reprinted in *FDP,* ser. 1, 5:59–80, quotations on 60.

11. "Our Destiny," *FDP,* ser. 1, 5:76, 66, 73, 80.

12. "The Emancipation Celebration," *Bee,* April 21, 1883. On the Washington black elite's desire to assimilate, see Moore, *Leading the Race,* 3, 5.

13. "The Emancipation Celebration," *Bee,* April 21, 1883.

14. Report from the *Boston Leader,* reprinted in *Bee,* April 28, 1883.

15. "The Emancipation Celebration," *Bee,* April 21, 1883; "The Emancipation," *Bee,* April 14, 1883. On the connections of these families, see Gatewood, *Aristocrats of Color,* 39–68.

16. "Mrs. Kail in Tuscarowas, Ohio—Washington Letter," *Bee,* May 5, 1883. On the very select group attending the Bruce dinner, see "Washington Letter," *Globe,* April 21, 1883.

17. "Washington, D.C." in *Organizing Black America,* 91; Moore, *Leading the Race,* 3, 5, 32.

18. "The Emancipation Celebration," *Bee,* April 21, 1883.

19. "Perry Carson's Removal," *Bee,* May 12, 1883; "The Emancipation Celebration," *Bee,* March 24, 1883.

20. "Arranging for Emancipation Day," *Bee,* March 15, 1884; "The Emancipation Celebration," *Bee,* March 15, 1884.

21. "Is It Opposition?" *Bee,* March 15, 1884; "Baltimore Topics," *Bee,* April 12, 1884. Hawkins, a Virginia native and a prominent Methodist Episcopal layman, was

a member of Baltimore's black upper class. He went on to a stellar career as a civil rights attorney and belonged to such exclusive organizations as the American Negro Academy and Boule, referred to by Willard Gatewood as "probably the most exclusive social organization of black men in America." See Gatewood, *Aristocrats of Color,* 264.

22. *Cleveland Gazette,* April 19, 26, 1884.

23. Biographical information taken from Simmons, *Men of Mark,* and *Cleveland Gazette,* April 12, 1884.

24. "Washington's Emancipation Celebration," *Cleveland Gazette,* April 26, 1884.

25. *Cleveland Gazette,* April 12, 1884; "The Emancipation Celebration," *Bee,* February 14, 1885.

26. *Cleveland Gazette,* April 12, 1884.

27. "The Emancipation Celebration," *Bee,* February 14, 1885; "From the Capital," *Richmond Planet,* February 21, 1885.

28. "The Emancipation Convention," *Bee,* March 7, 1885.

29. Ibid.; "The Emancipation Celebration," *Bee,* March 21, 1885; "To the Colored Citizens" and "Clara to Louise," *Bee,* April 11, 1885.

30. "The Emancipation Celebration," *Bee,* March 21, 1885; "The Emancipation Convention," *Bee,* March 7, 1885.

31. "The Emancipation Celebration," *Bee,* April 11, 1885; "Emancipation Day," *Bee,* April 18, 1885; *Cleveland Gazette,* April 18, 1885; *Huntsville Gazette,* April 18, 1885.

32. "Emancipation Celebration," *Freeman* (New York), April 25, 1885.

33. *Bee,* February 6, 1886; "Our Weekly Review," *Bee,* February 20, 1886; "The Emancipation," *Bee,* March 27, 1886; "Progress of the Colored People," *Bee,* April 10, 1886.

34. "The Emancipation," *Bee,* March 27, 1886; "Louise to Clara," *Bee,* February 20, 1886.

35. "The Emancipation Celebration," *Bee,* April 10, 1886; "Our Weekly Review," *Bee,* April 17, 1886; editor's note, *FDP,* ser. 1, 5:212–13.

36. "The Dual Celebration," "Our Weekly Review," "The Emancipation Celebration," *Bee,* April 24, 1886; editor's note, *FDP,* ser. 1, 5:212–13.

37. "The Dual Celebration," *Bee,* April 24, 1886.

38. "Strong to Suffer, and Yet Strong to Strive," an address delivered in Washington, D.C., on April 16, 1886, in *FDP,* ser. 1, 5:219, 223, 231–32.

39. Ibid., 215–17, 231. On the life of the alley dwellers criticized by Douglass and Chase, see James Borchert, *Alley Life in Washington: Family, Community, Religion, and Folklife in the City, 1850–1970* (Urbana, 1980), 208–9.

40. "Emancipation Day Committees Appointed," *Bee,* February 20, 1887; "The Emancipation Day Celebration," "Emancipation Day Parade," *Bee,* April 23, 1887; "Our Weekly Review," *Bee,* April 30, 1887; "Colored People of the District of Co-

lumbia's Recent Emancipation Celebration," *Cleveland Gazette,* April 30, 1887. Quotations in text: "a big procession," *Bee,* February 20, 1887; all others, *Cleveland Gazette,* April 30, 1887.

41. "Colored People of the District of Columbia's Recent Emancipation Celebration," *Cleveland Gazette,* April 30, 1887.

42. "District Emancipation and the President," *Freeman* (New York), April 23, 1887; "Col. Williams's Reply," *Freeman* (New York), May 21, 1887.

43. "District Emancipation and the President," *Freeman* (New York), April 23, 1887.

44. "Wait and See," "That Letter," *Bee,* April 14, 1888; *Cleveland Gazette,* March 24, 1888; McFeely, *Frederick Douglass,* 363–64.

45. "Expensive Parades," "The Emancipation Day," *Bee,* March 24, 1888; "Emancipation Day," *Bee,* March 31, 1888.

46. "Expensive Parades," "The Emancipation Day," *Bee,* March 24, 1888; "Emancipation Day," *Bee,* March 31, 1888.

47. "The Disgrace," *Bee,* April 21, 1888; editor's note, *FDP,* ser. 1, 5:357.

48. "Emancipation Day Parade," *Age,* April 28, 1888; Daniel Smith Lamb, *Howard University Medical Department, Washington, D.C.: A Historical, Biographical, and Statistical Souvenir* (Washington, D.C., 1900), 192–93.

49. "Emancipation Day Parade," *Age,* April 28, 1888.

50. "The Celebration," *Bee,* April 18, 1891. On Allen Day, see Kachun, "The Shaping of a Public Biography," 44–63.

51. Representative coverage of these affairs can be found in the *Bee,* April 20, 1889; February 22, March 1, 15, April 19, 1890; March 7, April 18, 25, 1891; April 23, 1892; April 15, 22, 1893; March 7, 1896; April 24, 1897; *Richmond Planet,* April 22, 1899.

52. "The Day We Celebrate," *Bee,* April 7, 1906.

53. "Emancipation Celebration," *Bee,* April 21, 1906.

54. "Celebrating Emancipation Day," *Washington, D.C., Tribune,* April 24, 1931, in Tuskegee Institute News Clipping File, microfilm reel 240, frame 933, hereafter referred to as TCF.

7. *"The faith that the dark past has taught us"*

1. Benjamin C. Wilson, *The Rural Black Heritage between Chicago and Detroit, 1850–1929: A Photograph Album and Random Thoughts* (Kalamazoo, 1985), 130–33; *Pittsburgh Courier,* January 6, 1912.

2. Sharyn Kane and Richard Keeton, *In Those Days: African-American Life near the Savannah River* (Harpers Ferry, 1994).

3. On the impact of the generational transition as it related to the life of one aging community activist in Worcester, Mass., see Salvatore, *We All Got History,*

295–300. "Afro-American Cullings," copied from *Southern Life Magazine*, *Pittsburgh Courier*, April 27, 1912; *Appendix to the Souvenir Presented to James M. Ashley on Emancipation Day, September 22, 1893*, Murray Pamphlet Collection.

4. McFeely, *Frederick Douglass*, 364.

5. *Minutes of the Fourth Annual Convention . . . of the Free People of Colour* (New York, 1834), 14–16, reprinted in Bell, *Minutes of the National Negro Conventions, 1830–1864*.

6. Handy quoted in Graham, *Baltimore*, 282. The series of columns by "Solonite" detailing the damaging effects of excursions appears in the *Huntsville Gazette*, June 12, 19, 26, July 3, 10, 17, 1886. See also the *Huntsville Gazette*, August 14, 1886.

7. Levine, *Black Culture and Black Consciousness*, 150.

8. *Louisville American Baptist* quoted in *Age*, September 14, 1911; *Age*, January 23, 1913. See also *Age*, December 27, 1913, for a report of another huge funeral procession.

9. "Conduct in Public Places," *Age*, September 28, 1911.

10. "Negro Excursions," *Afro-American Ledger*, July 12, 1902. Another representative example can be found in "A Plea against Excursions," *Voice of the Negro* 2, no. 8 (August 1905): 530–31.

11. On the workings of this moral code and its relation to personal standards of conduct and to public behavior, see Salvatore, *We All Got History*, esp. 65, 177, 286–87.

12. Michael Kammen, *A Season of Youth: The American Revolution and the Historical Imagination* (New York, 1978), 26–28, 43–49; Travers, *Celebrating the Fourth*; Waldstreicher, *In the Midst of Perpetual Fetes*; S. Newman, *Parades and the Politics of the Street*; Nagel, *This Sacred Trust*. I discuss white July Fourth celebrations from this period in chap. 1.

13. Kammen, *Mystic Chords of Memory*, 35, 49.

14. Ibid., 53–54; John T. Jenifer, speech at the dedication of the Richard Allen monument at the 1876 Centennial Exposition, reprinted in *Press*, June 13, 1876. See also, for example, the 1858 Freedom Day address by Frederick Douglass, reprinted in *FDP*, ser. 1, 3:224; the 1870 speech by Richard Greener cited above in n. 1, chap. 4; and the Emancipation/Decoration Day oration by the Reverend Ernest Lyon, delivered at Brownsville, Pa., May 30, 1913, reprinted in Alice Moore Dunbar, *Masterpieces of Negro Eloquence: The Best Speeches Delivered by the Negro from the Days of Slavery to the Present Time* (New York, 1914), 461–74. See also my analysis of slave trade orations from the early nineteenth century in chap. 1.

15. Kammen, *Mystic Chords of Memory*, 59.

16. Ibid., 94; Litwicki, *America's Public Holidays, 1865–1920*, 1–8, and passim.

17. Kammen, *Mystic Chords of Memory*, 132, 137.

18. McGerr, *Decline of Popular Politics*, esp. 3–106; quotations on 76, 70, 78, 85–86, 146; Jean H. Baker, "The Ceremonies of Politics: Nineteenth-Century Rituals of

National Affirmation," in *A Master's Due: Essays in Honor of David Herbert Donald*, ed. William J. Cooper Jr., Michael F. Holt, and John McCardell (Baton Rouge, 1985), 161–78. Some scholars have recently challenged the conventional characterization of antebellum political culture as inclusive and vital to the personal identities of individual Americans. See Glenn C. Altschuler and Stuart M. Blumin, *Rude Republic: Americans and Their Politics in the Nineteenth Century* (Princeton, 2000).

19. *American Citizen* (Kansas City), July 16, August 6, 1897; *Chicago Defender*, June 15, July 13, August 17, 31, 1912; *Cleveland Advocate*, July 28, 1917.

20. John F. Kasson, *Amusing the Million: Coney Island at the Turn of the Century* (New York, 1978), 6–7, 55–56. Several works that attest to blacks' influence in this emerging popular culture include Reid Badger, *A Life in Ragtime: A Biography of James Reese Europe* (New York, 1995); Lewis A. Erenberg, *Steppin' Out: New York Nightlife and the Transformation of American Culture, 1890–1930* (Westport, 1981); James Weldon Johnson, *Along This Way; the Autobiography of James Weldon Johnson* (New York, 1968 [1933]); Thomas Cripps, *Slow Fade to Black: The Negro in American Film, 1900–1942* (New York, 1977); and Handy, *Father of the Blues;* Kevin Kelly Gaines, "Assimilationist Minstrelsy as Racial Uplift Ideology: James D. Corrothers's Literary Quest for Black Leadership," *American Quarterly* 45, no. 3 (September 1993): 341–68.

21. *Pittsburgh Courier*, January 13, 1912; David Nasaw, *Going Out: The Rise and Fall of Public Amusements* (Cambridge, Mass., 1993), 31–32, 48–51, 91–92, 242–44.

22. McGerr, *Decline of Popular Politics*, 148–50; "Conduct in Public Places," *Age*, September 28, 1911; Daniel T. Rodgers, *The Work Ethic in Industrial America, 1850–1920* (Chicago, 1978), esp. 90–114.

23. "Midnight's Musings," *Afro-American Ledger*, September 28, 1901; July 19, 1902.

24. "Conduct at Public Entertainments," *Age*, February 29, 1912. For a class-centered description of this black critique of urban leisure see Gaines, "Assimilationist Minstrelsy as Racial Uplift Ideology." McGerr, *Decline of Popular Politics*, 149; Rosenzweig, *Eight Hours for What We Will*, 172, 181–83; Cohn, "A National Celebration: The Fourth of July in American History," *Cultures* 3 (1976): 153.

25. Kasson, *Amusing the Million*, 101–2.

26. Hampton University Newspaper Clipping File, microfiche 273, no. 1, frames 91–94; microfiche 274, frames 67–68, hereafter referred to as HCF.

27. "Exposition to Show Advance," *Afro-American Ledger*, July 12, 1913; *New York Press*, October 29, 1913, in HCF, microfiche 273, no. 1, frame 49.

28. "Keen Interest in Exposition," *Afro-American Ledger*, October 4, 1913. Quotation in "The Emancipation Commission," *Age*, July 3, 1913. See also *Age*, July 26, August 7, 1913; *Afro-American Ledger*, July 19, 1913; D. Lewis, *W. E. B. Du Bois*, 459–63, quotation on 459.

29. "'The Star of Ethiopia' Pleases," *Afro-American Ledger,* October 16, 1915; "Emancipation Pageant," *Age,* October 30, 1913.

30. Glassberg, *American Historical Pageantry,* 133. See also "Emancipation Pageant," *Age,* October 30, 1913.

31. Letter from Arthur P. Boyd to *Age,* January 15, 1914; "Race Is Dancing Itself to Death," *Age,* January 8, 1914.

32. *Age,* July 10, 19, November 6, 1913; HCF, microfiche 273, no. 1, frame 33, 34; "Commissioners Fuss as Exposition Closes," TCF, reel 240, frame 837.

33. *Chicago Defender,* March 9, 1912.

34. "The Emancipation Celebration," *Age,* July 24, 1913. On the various allegations of fiscal improprieties, see "The New Jersey Celebration," *Age,* August 21, 1913; "New Jersey Commission Is Now Seeking Funds," *Age,* July 10, 1913; "[New York] Commission Faces Big Deficit," *Age,* September 25, 1913; "[New York] Commissioners Fuss as Exposition Closes," *Age,* November 6, 1913; "[Philadelphia's] Bass Must Face Charges," *Afro-American Ledger,* September 20, 1913; "Richmond Exposition Gets Nice Coat of Whitewash" and "Secretary of Chicago Exposition Forced Out," *Afro-American Ledger,* September 11, 1915; "[New York] Fair Board's Plans Rapped by Negroes," HCF, microfiche 273, no. 1, frame 34; "[New York] Commissioners at Loggerheads," TCF, reel 240, frame 836; "Not Guilty Verdict in [Philadelphia] Harris-Bass Case" and "[New York] Commissioners Quarrel, Refuse to Sign Report," TCF, reel 240, frame 823.

35. "Exposition at 'Philly' a Dismal Failure," *Age,* October 9, 1913; "Negro Delegates Can Find No 'Exposition,'" HCF, microfiche 273, no. 1, frames 39, 50; "Emancipation Jubilee Opens in Quaker City," TCF, reel 240, frame 822.

36. HCF, microfiche 274, frames 40, 41, 49, 51, 52, 63, 69, 70.

37. Ibid., frames 40, 51, 78–81; TCF, reel 240, frame 854, 866; *American Review of Reviews* 52 (August 1915); *Richmond Planet,* June 15, 1889; Patricia Carter Ives, "Giles Beecher Jackson, Director-General of the Negro Development and Exposition Company of the United States for the Jamestown Tercentenary Exposition of 1907," *Negro History Bulletin* 38 (December 1975).

38. "Plan to Observe Negro Freedom," HCF, microfiche 273, no. 1, frame 66; "New Jersey Commission Is Now Seeking Funds," *Age,* July 10, 1913; "Commissioners Fuss as Exposition Closes," *Age,* November 6, 1913.

39. *Chicago Defender,* July 26, 1913.

40. Washington to Jesse Lawson, May 8, 1911, Louis R. Harlan et al., eds., *The Booker T. Washington Papers,* vol. 11, *1911–1912* (Urbana, 1981), 141.

41. Frank Lincoln Mather, *Who's Who of the Colored Race,* vol. 1, *1915* (Chicago, 1915); Washington to Lawson, May 8, 1911, Harlan et al., *Booker T. Washington Papers,* 11:141–43; Washington to Oswald Garrison Villard, August 29, 1912, Harlan et al., *Booker T. Washington Papers,* 11:587.

42. Coverage of these and several other celebrations in "Nation Celebrates 50th Anniversary of the Emancipation Proclamation," *Age,* January 9, 1913.

43. *Knoxville Sentinel* report in HCF, microfiche 273, no. 1, frame 64; Lima and Terre Haute reports in HCF, microfiche 273, no. 1, frames 34, 35. Newspaper articles describing scores of emancipation celebrations from the 1890s into the mid-twentieth century can be found in HCF, microfiche 273, nos. 1 and 2, and microfiche 274; and in TCF, reel 240.

44. *El Paso Herald,* June 19, 1918, in TCF, reel 240, frame 875.

45. *Dallas Express,* June 24, 1914, in TCF, reel 240, frame 846. Other Juneteenth accounts in TCF, reel 240, frames 852, 869, 871, 875, 879, 888, 915, 920; HCF, microfiche 273, no. 1, frames 36, 37, 74, 83.

46. "Emancipation Day Celebrated in Augusta," *Georgia Baptist* (Augusta), January 7, 1909, in HCF, microfiche 272.

47. *Afro-American Ledger,* November 14, 1914; December 25, 1915.

48. "Race History Discussed by Great Scholar," *Pittsburgh Courier,* January 13, 1912.

49. "The New Emancipation," *AME Church Review* 29, no. 3 (January 1913): 260–64.

50. TCF, reel 240, frame 889; Wilson, *The Rural Black Heritage between Chicago and Detroit.*

51. *Gary American* (Ind.), January 4, 1929, in TCF, reel 240, frame 925; unidentified 1922 editorial, TCF, reel 240, frame 887; *Atlanta Independent,* January 2, 1930, in TCF, reel 240, frame 930.

52. "Should Have Negro Histories," *Afro-American Ledger,* December 21, 1912. See also Arthur S. Schomburg, *Racial Integrity: A Plea for the Establishment of a Chair of Negro History in Our Schools and Colleges, etc.* (Yonkers, 1913). On blacks' attention to historical scholarship, writing, and teaching in this period, see Hall, "To Give a Faithful Account of the Race."

53. Wiggins, *O Freedom!* 1–24; Toni Morrison, *Jazz* (New York, 1992), 33.

BIBLIOGRAPHY

Primary Sources

ARCHIVES AND COLLECTIONS

American Negro Historical Society Papers (ANHSP). Historical Society of Pennsylvania, Philadelphia, Pa.
Black Abolitionist Archives. University of Detroit Mercy, Detroit, Mich.
W. E. B. Du Bois. Papers, 1877–1963. Microform.
Hampton University Newspaper Clipping File. Microform.
Key West Library. Key West, Fla.
Massachusetts National Guard Archives. Worcester, Mass.
Mother Bethel AME Church. Records, 1760–1972. Microform.
Daniel A. P. Murray. Pamphlet Collection. Library of Congress.
Tuskegee Institute News Clippings File. Microform.
Carter G. Woodson. Collection of Negro Papers and Related Documents, 1803–1936, 1830–1937. Microform.

NEWSPAPERS AND PERIODICALS

African Repository (Washington, D.C.), 1825–50.
African Sentinel (Albany, N.Y.), 1831.
Afro-American (Baltimore, Md.), 1892–1900s (succeeded by *Afro-American Ledger*).
Afro-American Ledger (Baltimore, Md.), 1900s–1915.

Age (New York), 1887–1915.

Alexander's Magazine, 1905–9.

American Citizen (Kansas City, Kans.), 1887–1909.

American Citizen (Topeka, Kans.), 1888–1909.

Bee (Washington, D.C.), 1882–1922.

Chicago Defender, 1905–15.

Christian Recorder (Philadelphia), 1856–1922.

Cleveland Gazette, 1883–92.

Colored American (Augusta, Ga.), 1865–66.

Colored American (New York), 1837–42.

Colored American Magazine, 1900–1909.

Crisis, 1910–20.

Daily National Intelligencer (Washington, D.C.), 1867–72.

Douglass' Monthly (Rochester, N.Y.), 1859–63.

Elevator (San Francisco), 1865–1904.

Frederick Douglass' Paper (Rochester, N.Y.), 1851–59.

Freedom's Journal (New York), 1827–29.

Freeman (Indianapolis), 1884–1915.

Freeman (New York), 1884–87.

Gazette (Raleigh, N.C.), 1883–1900.

Genius of Universal Emancipation (Baltimore, Md.), 1826–39.

Globe (New York), 1880–84.

Half-Century Magazine, 1916–25.

Huntsville Gazette (Ala.), 1881–94.

Liberator (Boston), 1831–65.

Louisianian (New Orleans), 1870–72.

National Era (Washington, D.C.), 1847–60.

New Age (Portland, Oreg.), 1905–7.

New Era (Washington, D.C.), Jan.–Sept. 1870 (succeeded by *New National Era*).

New National Era (Washington, D.C.), 1870–74.

New Orleans Tribune, 1864–70.

New York Herald, 1861–70.

North Star (Rochester, N.Y.), 1847–51.

Palladium of Liberty (Columbus, Ohio), 1843–44.

Pennsylvania Freeman (Philadelphia), 1838–54.

Pittsburgh Courier, 1910–20.

Press (Philadelphia), 1876.

Provincial Freeman (Toronto), 1853–57.

Richmond Planet, 1883–1920.

South Carolina Leader (Charleston), 1865–67.

Southern Workman (Hampton, Va.), 1872–92.

State Capital (Springfield, Ill.), 1892.

Voice of the Negro, 1904–7.

Weekly Anglo-African (New York), 1859–61.

PUBLISHED PRIMARY SOURCES

African Methodist Episcopal Church. *Journal of the Seventeenth General Conference of the African Methodist Episcopal Church.* Philadelphia: James C. Embry, 1884.

———. *Journal of the Twenty-fifth Quadrennial Session of the General Conference of the African Methodist Episcopal Church.* Nashville: AME Church Sunday School Union, 1916.

———. *Proceedings of the Thirteenth General Conference of the African ME Church.* Philadelphia: AME Book Concern, 1864.

Alexander, William T. *History of the Colored Race in America.* Kansas City, Mo.: Palmetto Publishing, 1887.

Allen, Richard. *The Life Experience and Gospel Labours of the Rt. Rev. Richard Allen.* Introduction by George A. Singleton. New York: Abingdon Press, 1960 [1833].

American Moral Reform Society. *The Minutes and Proceedings of the American Moral Reform Society.* Philadelphia: Merrihew and Gunn, 1837.

Aptheker, Herbert, ed. *A Documentary History of the Negro People in the United States.* New York: Citadel Press, 1969.

Arnett, Benjamin W., ed. *The Budget: Containing Biographical Sketches . . . of the General Officers of the African Methodist Church of the United States of America.* Dayton, Ohio: Christian Publishing House, 1884.

———. *Proceedings of the Quarto-Centennial Conference of the African ME Church of South Carolina.* Xenia, Ohio: Aldine Printing House, 1890.

Bell, Howard Holman, ed. *Minutes of the Proceedings of the National Negro Conventions, 1830–1864.* New York: Arno Press, 1969.

Blumin, Stuart M., ed. *New York by Gas-Light and Other Urban Sketches by George C. Foster.* Berkeley: University of California Press, 1990.

Bracey, John H., August Meier, and Elliott Rudwick, eds. *Black Nationalism in America.* Indianapolis: Bobbs-Merrill, 1970.

Brawley, Benjamin. *A Short History of the American Negro.* New York: MacMillan, 1913.

———, ed. *Early Negro American Writers.* New York: Dover Publications, 1970 [1935].

Brockett, Joshua A. "The Emancipation Proclamation." Speech, January 1, 1892, given at the Metropolitan Hall, Raleigh, North Carolina. Reprinted in *African Methodist Episcopal Church Review* 8, no. 4 (April 1892).

Brotz, Howard, ed. *African American Social and Political Thought, 1850–1920.* 2nd ed. New York: Basic Books, 1992.

Brown, William Wells. *The Black Man: His Antecedents, His Genius, and His Achievements.* New York: Thomas Hamilton, 1863.

———. *Clotel; or, the President's Daughter.* London: Partridge and Oakey, 1853.

———. *The Negro in the American Rebellion: His Heroism and His Fidelity.* Boston: A. G. Brown, 1867.

———. *The Rising Son; or, the Antecedents and Advancement of the Colored Race.* Boston: A. G. Brown, 1874.

Butt, Israel L. *History of African Methodism in Virginia; or Four Decades in the Old Dominion.* Norfolk: Hampton Institute Press, 1908.

California State Convention of Colored Citizens. *Proceedings of the First California State Convention of the Colored Citizens of the State of California, 1855, 1856, 1865.* Ed. Alan Eterovich. Saratoga, Calif.: R & E Associates, 1969.

Carter, Edmund Randolph. *The Black Side: A Partial History of the Business, Religious, and Educational Side of the Negro in Atlanta, Ga.* Atlanta: N.p., 1894.

Cashin, Herschel V. *Under Fire with the Tenth U.S. Cavalry.* New York: F. T. Neely, 1899.

Chesnutt, Charles. *The Marrow of Tradition* [1901]. Reprinted in *The African-American Novel in the Age of Reaction: Three Classics,* ed. William Andrews. New York: Mentor, 1992.

Crogman, William H. *The Progress of a Race.* New York: Negro Universities Press, 1969 [1897].

Cromwell, John W. *History of the Bethel Literary and Historical Association.* Washington, D.C.: R. L. Pendleton, 1896.

———. *The Negro in American History.* New York: J. F. Tapley, 1914.

Daniels, John. *In Freedom's Birthplace: A Study of Boston's Negroes.* New York: Johnson Reprint, 1969 [1914].

Dann, Martin E., ed. *The Black Press, 1827–1890: The Quest for National Identity.* New York: G. P. Putnam's Sons, 1971.

Delany, Martin. *The Condition, Elevation, Emigration, and Destiny of the Colored People of the United States.* Philadelphia: King and Baird, 1852.

Douglass, Frederick. *The Frederick Douglass Papers.* Ed. John Blassingame et al. Series 1, *Speeches, Debates, and Interviews.* 5 vols. New Haven: Yale University Press, 1979–92.

———. "The Heroic Slave" [1851]. Reprinted in *Violence in the Black Imagination: Essays and Documents,* ed. Ronald T. Takaki. New York: Putnam, 1972.

———. *The Narrative of the Life of Frederick Douglass.* Boston: Anti-Slavery Office, 1845.

Du Bois, W. E. B. "A History of the Negro Race in America." *Southern Workman* 28 (April 1899): 149–51.

———. *The Negro.* Millwood, N.Y.: Kraus-Thomson, 1975 [1915].

————. *The Philadelphia Negro: A Social Study*. New York: Schocken Books, 1967 [1899].

————. *The Souls of Black Folk*. New York: Penguin Books, 1989 [1903].

Dunbar, Alice Moore, ed. *Masterpieces of Negro Eloquence: The Best Speeches Delivered by the Negro from the Days of Slavery to the Present Time*. New York: Bookery Publishing, 1914.

Durham, John S. *To Teach the Negro History: A Suggestion*. Philadelphia: D. McKay, 1897.

Dyson, J. F. *Richard Allen's Place in History: A Commentary on the Life and Deeds of the Chief Founder and First Bishop of the African Methodist Episcopal Church*. Nashville: Cumberland Presbyterian Publishing House, 1887.

Emilio, Luis F. *History of the Fifty-fourth Regiment of Massachusetts Volunteer Infantry, 1863–1865*. Boston: Boston Book, 1894.

Ferris, William H. *The African Abroad; or, His Evolution in Western Civilization*. New Haven: Tuttle, Morehouse and Taylor, 1913.

Fishel, Leslie H., Jr., and Benjamin Quarles, eds. *The Black American: A Documentary History*. Glenview, Ill.: Scott, Foresman, 1970.

Foner, Philip S., and Robert James Burnham, eds. *Lift Every Voice: African American Oratory, 1787–1900*. Tuscaloosa and London: University of Alabama Press, 1998.

Fortune, Timothy Thomas. *Black and White: Land, Labor, and Politics in the South*. New York: Arno Press, 1969 [1884].

Freedom: A Documentary History of Emancipation, 1861–1867. Cambridge: Cambridge University Press, 1982.

Garnet, Henry Highland. *A Memorial Discourse by Reverend Henry Highland Garnet, with an Introduction by James McCune Smith, M.D*. Philadelphia: Joseph M. Wilson, 1865.

Handy, W. C. *Father of the Blues: An Autobiography*. New York: Collier Books, 1970 [1941].

Harlan, Louis R., et al., eds. *The Booker T. Washington Papers*. Vol. 11, *1911–12*. Urbana: University of Illinois Press, 1981.

Harper, Frances Ellen Watkins. *Iola Leroy; or, Shadows Uplifted* [1892]. Reprinted in *The African-American Novel in the Age of Reaction: Three Classics*, ed. William Andrews. New York: Mentor, 1992.

Hartshorn, W. N., ed. *An Era of Progress and Promise, 1863–1910: The Religious, Moral, and Educational Development of the American Negro since His Emancipation*. Boston: Priscilla Publishing, 1910.

Heard, William Henry. *From Slavery to the Bishopric in the A.M.E. Church*. New York: Arno Press, 1969 [1924].

Johnson, Edward A. *A School History of the Negro Race in America*. Raleigh, N.C.: Edwards and Broughton, Printers, 1890.

Johnson, James Weldon. *Along This Way: The Autobiography of James Weldon Johnson.* New York: Viking Press, 1968 [1933].

Langston, John Mercer. *Freedom and Citizenship: Selected Lectures and Addresses.* Miami: Mnemosyne Publishing, 1969 [1883].

Libby, Jean, ed. *From Slavery to Salvation: The Autobiography of Rev. Thomas N. Henry of the A.M.E. Church.* Jackson: University Press of Mississippi, 1994 [1872].

Mather, Frank Lincoln. *Who's Who of the Colored Race.* Vol, 1, 1915. Chicago, 1915.

Miller, William. *A Sermon on the Abolition of the Slave Trade: Delivered in the African Church, New York, on the First of January, 1810.* Philadelphia: Rhistoric Publications, 1969 [1810].

The Negro Element in American Life: An Oration Delivered by the Rev. A. L. DeMond, in the Dexter Avenue Baptist Church, Montgomery, Alabama, Jan. 1, 1900. Montgomery: Alabama Printing Co., 1900.

Nell, William C. *The Colored Patriots of the American Revolution.* Boston: R. F. Wallcut, 1855.

Newman, Richard, Patrick Rael, and Philip Lapsansky, eds. *Pamphlets of Protest: An Anthology of Early African American Protest Literature, 1790–1860.* New York: Routledge, 2000.

Paige, T. F. *Twenty-two Years of Freedom: An Account of the Emancipation Celebration by the Freedmen of Norfolk, Va., and Vicinity on the First Day of January, Including the Literary Exercises, Oration, Poem, Review.* Norfolk: T. F. Paige, 1885.

Parrott, Russell. *Two Orations on the Abolition of the Slave Trade Delivered in Philadelphia in 1812 and 1816.* Introd. Maxwell Whiteman. Philadelphia: Rhistoric Publications, 1969.

Payne, Daniel A. *History of the African Methodist Episcopal Church.* Ed. Rev. C. S. Smith. Nashville: Publishing House of the AME Sunday School Union, 1891.

———. *Recollections of Seventy Years.* New York: Arno Press, 1968 [1888].

———. *The Semi-Centenary and the Retrospection of the African Methodist Episcopal Church.* Baltimore: Sherwood and Co., 1866.

———. *Sermons and Addresses, 1853–1891.* Ed. Charles Killian. New York: Arno Press, 1972.

Pennington, James W. C. *A Text Book of the Origin and History of the Colored People.* Hartford: L. Skinner, Printer, 1841.

Porter, Dorothy, ed. *Early Negro Writing, 1760–1837.* Boston: Beacon Press, 1971.

Proceedings of the Black National and State Conventions, 1865–1900. Ed. Philip S. Foner and George E. Walker. Philadelphia: Temple University Press, 1986.

Redkey, Edwin S., ed. *A Grand Army of Black Men: Letters from African-American Soldiers in the Union Army, 1861–1865.* Cambridge: Cambridge University Press, 1992.

————. *Respect Black: The Writings and Speeches of Henry McNeal Turner*. New York: Arno Press, 1971.

Ripley, C. Peter, Roy E. Finkenbine, Michael F. Hembree, and Donald Yacovone, eds. *Witness for Freedom: African American Voices on Race, Slavery, and Emancipation*. Chapel Hill: University of North Carolina Press, 1993.

Saunders, Frederick, ed. *Our National Centennial Jubilee*. New York: E. B. Trout, 1877.

Schomburg, Arthur A. *Racial Integrity: A Plea for the Establishment of a Chair of Negro History in Our Schools and Colleges, etc.* Yonkers, N.Y.: Negro Society for Historical Research, 1913.

Sears, Lorenzo. *The Occasional Address: Its Composition and Literature*. New York: Putnam's, 1897.

Simmons, William J. *Men of Mark: Eminent, Progressive, and Rising*. New York: Arno, 1968 [1887].

Smith, Charles Spencer. *A History of the African Methodist Episcopal Church*. New York: Johnson Reprint, 1968 [1922].

Smith, David. *The Biography of Rev. David Smith of the A.M.E. Church*. Xenia, Ohio: Xenia Gazette, 1881.

Still, William. *The Underground Railroad*. Philadelphia: William Still, 1872.

Stuckey, Sterling, ed. *The Ideological Origins of Black Nationalism*. Boston: Beacon Press, 1972.

U.S. War Department. *The War of the Rebellion: A Compilation of the Official Records of the Union and Confederate Armies*. Ser. 1, vol. 18. Washington, D.C.: Government Printing Office, 1887.

Walker, David. *David Walker's Appeal to the Coloured Citizens of the World*. Ed. Peter P. Hinks. University Park: Pennsylvania State University Press, 2000.

Wayman, Alexander. *Cyclopedia of African Methodism*. Baltimore: Methodist Episcopal Book Depository, 1882.

————. *My Recollections of African M.E. Ministers*. Philadelphia: AME Book Rooms, 1881.

Williams, George Washington. *History of the Negro Race in America from 1619 to 1880*. 2 vols. New York: G. P. Putnam's Sons, 1883.

————. *A History of the Negro Troops in the War of the Rebellion, 1861–1865*. New York: Harper and Brothers, 1887.

Wilson, Harriet E. *Our Nig; or Sketches from the Life of a Free Black*. Boston: G. C. Rand and Avery, 1859.

Wilson, Joseph T. *The Black Phalanx*. Hartford: American Publishing, 1890.

————. *Emancipation: Its Course and Progress, from 1481 B.C. to A.D. 1875*. New York: Negro Universities Press, 1969 [1882].

Woodson, Carter G. "Negro History Week." *Journal of Negro History* 11, no. 2 (April 1926): 238–42.

————, ed. *Negro Orators and Their Orations.* New York: Russell and Russell, 1969 [1925].

Wright, Richard R., Jr., ed. *Centennial Encyclopedia of the African Methodist Episcopal Church.* Philadelphia: Book Concern of the AME Church, 1916.

Secondary Sources

Adeleke, Tunde. *UnAfrican Americans: Nineteenth-Century Black Nationalists and the Civilizing Mission.* Lexington: University of Kentucky Press, 1998.

Agulhon, Maurice. *Marianne into Battle: Republican Imagery and Symbolism in France, 1789–1880.* Trans. Janet Lloyd. Cambridge: Cambridge University Press, 1981.

Alexander, E. Curtis [Mwalimu Imara Mwadilifu]. *Richard Allen: First Exemplar of African American Education.* New York: ECA Associates, 1985.

Altink, Henrice. "Slavery by Another Name: Apprenticed Women in Jamaica, 1834–1838." *Social History* 26, no. 1 (2001): 40–59.

Altschuler, Glenn C., and Stuart M. Blumin. *Rude Republic: Americans and Their Politics in the Nineteenth Century.* Princeton: Princeton University Press, 2000.

Anderson, Benedict. *Imagined Communities: Reflections on the Origin and Spread of Nationalism.* New York: Verso, 1991.

Andrews, William, ed. *The African-American Novel in the Age of Reaction: Three Classics.* New York: Mentor, 1992.

Aptheker, Herbert, ed. *Annotated Bibliography of the Published Writings of W. E. B. Du Bois.* Millwood, N.Y.: Kraus-Thomson, 1973.

Ashe, Arthur R., Jr. *A Hard Road to Glory: A History of the African-American Athlete.* 3 vols. New York: Amistad, 1993.

Ayers, Edward L. *The Promise of the New South: Life after Reconstruction.* New York: Oxford University Press, 1992.

Badger, Reid. *A Life in Ragtime: A Biography of James Reese Europe.* New York: Oxford University Press, 1995.

Baker, Bruce E. "Under the Rope: Lynching and Memory in Laurens County, South Carolina." In *Where These Memories Grow: History, Memory, and Southern Identity,* ed. W. Fitzhugh Brundage, 319–45. Chapel Hill: University of North Carolina Press, 2000.

Baker, Jean H. "The Ceremonies of Politics: Nineteenth-Century Rituals of National Affirmation." In *A Master's Due: Essays in Honor of David Herbert Donald,* ed. William J. Cooper Jr., Michael F. Holt, and John McCardell, 161–78. Baton Rouge: Louisiana State University Press, 1985.

Bay, Mia. *The White Image in the Black Mind: African-American Ideas about White People, 1830–1925.* New York: Oxford University Press, 2000.

Bearden, Romare, and Harry Henderson. *A History of African-American Artists from 1792 to the Present*. New York: Pantheon Books, 1993.

Beasley, Delilah L. *The Negro Trail Blazers of California*. Los Angeles: Times Mirror Printing and Binding House, 1919.

Bell, Howard Holman. *A Survey of the Negro Convention Movement, 1830–1861*. New York: Arno Press, 1969.

Bennett, Lerone, Jr. *Pioneers in Protest*. Chicago: Johnson Publishing, 1968.

———. "Remarks at the ASALH Sixtieth Anniversary Meeting." *Negro History Bulletin* 39, no. 2 (February 1976): 524–26.

Berkeley, Kathleen C. "'Colored Ladies Also Contributed': Black Women's Activities from Benevolence to Social Welfare, 1866–1896." In *The Web of Southern Social Relations: Women, Family, and Education,* ed. Walter J. Fraser, R. Frank Saunders Jr., and Jon L. Wakelyn, 181–203. Athens: University of Georgia Press, 1985.

Berlin, Ira. *Slaves without Masters: The Free Negro in the Antebellum South*. New York: Pantheon, 1974.

Berlin, Ira, and Richard Hoffman, eds. *Slavery and Freedom in the Age of the American Revolution*. Charlottesville: University Press of Virginia, 1983.

Berrett, Joshua. "The Golden Anniversary of the Emancipation Proclamation." *Black Perspective in Music* 16 (spring 1988): 63–80.

Bethel, Elizabeth Rauh. *The Roots of African-American Identity: Memory and History in Antebellum Free Communities*. New York: St. Martin's Press, 1997.

Blackett, R. J. M. *Beating against the Barriers: The Lives of Six Nineteenth-Century Afro-Americans*. Ithaca: Cornell University Press, 1989.

Blight, David. *Frederick Douglass' Civil War: Keeping Faith in Jubilee*. Baton Rouge: Louisiana State University Press, 1989.

———. *Race and Reunion: The Civil War in American Memory*. Cambridge, Mass.: Harvard University Press, Belknap Press, 2001.

Bodnar, John. *Remaking America: Public Memory, Commemoration, and Patriotism in the Twentieth Century*. Princeton: Princeton University Press, 1991.

Bolster, W. Jeffrey. *Black Jacks: African American Seamen in the Age of Sail*. Cambridge, Mass.: Harvard University Press, 1997.

Borchert, James. *Alley Life in Washington: Family, Community, Religion, and Folklife in the City, 1850–1970*. Urbana: University of Illinois Press, 1980.

Boveare, Walter. "The Idea of Progress in African-American Thought, 1890–1915." In *The Quest for Social Justice: The Morris Fromkin Lectures, 1970–1980,* ed. Ralph M. Aderman. Madison: University of Wisconsin Press, 1983.

Bowers, Detine L. "A *Strange* Speech of an Estranged People: Theory and Practice of Antebellum Freedom Day Orations." Ph.D. diss., Purdue University, 1992.

Boyd, Melba Joyce. *Discarded Legacy: Politics and Poetics in the Life of Frances E. W. Harper, 1825–1911*. Detroit: Wayne State University Press, 1994.

Braden, Waldo W., ed. *Building the Myth: Selected Speeches Memorializing Abraham Lincoln.* Urbana: University of Illinois Press, 1990.

Bragg, George F. *Men of Maryland.* Baltimore: Church Advocate Press, 1914.

Brooks, Van Wyck. "On Creating a Usable Past." *The Dial* 64 (April 11, 1918): 337–41.

Brown, Elsa Barkley, and Gregg D. Kimball. "Mapping the Terrain of Black Richmond." *Journal of Urban History* 21, no. 3 (March 1995).

Bruce, Dickson D., Jr. "Ancient Africa and the Early Black Historians, 1883–1915." *American Quarterly* 36, no. 5 (1984): 684–99.

———. *Black American Writing from the Nadir: The Evolution of a Literary Tradition, 1877–1915.* Baton Rouge: Louisiana State University Press, 1989.

———. *The Origins of African American Literature, 1680–1865.* Charlottesville: University Press of Virginia, 2001.

Brundage, W. Fitzhugh, ed. *Where These Memories Grow: History, Memory, and Southern Identity.* Chapel Hill: University of North Carolina Press, 2000.

Buck, Paul Herman. *The Road to Reunion.* Boston: Viking, 1937.

Carnes, Mark C. *Secret Ritual and Manhood in Victorian America.* New Haven: Yale University Press, 1989.

Cheek, Charles D., and Amy Friedlander. "Pottery and Pig's Feet: Space, Ethnicity, and Neighborhood in Washington, D.C., 1880–1940." *Historical Archaeology* 24, no. 1 (1990): 34–60.

Clark, Kathleen. "Celebrating Freedom: Emancipation Day Celebrations and African American Memory in the Early Reconstruction South." In *Where These Memories Grow: History, Memory, and Southern Identity,* ed. W. Fitzhugh Brundage. Chapel Hill: University of North Carolina Press, 2000.

Cmiel, Kenneth. *Democratic Eloquence: The Fight over Popular Speech in Nineteenth-Century America.* Berkeley: University of California Press, 1990.

Coates, James Roland. "Recreation and Sport in the African-American Community of Baltimore, 1890–1920." Ph.D. diss., University of Maryland, College Park, 1991.

Cohen, David Steven. *Folk Legacies Revisited.* New Brunswick, N.J.: Rutgers University Press, 1995.

Cohen, William. "Symbols of Power: Statues in Nineteenth-Century Provincial France." *Comparative Studies in Society and History* 31 (1989): 491–513.

Cohn, William H. "A National Celebration: The Fourth of July in American History." *Cultures* 3 (1976): 141–56.

Cooper, Frederick. "Elevating the Race: The Social Thought of Black Leaders, 1827–1850." *American Quarterly* 24 (1972): 604–25.

Cox, Anna-Lisa Grace. "The Open Door: Community, Race, and Identity in Nineteenth-Century Rural Michigan." Ph.D. diss., University of Illinois at Urbana-Champaign, 2000.

Cox, LaWanda. *Lincoln and Black Freedom: A Study in Presidential Leadership.* Columbia: University of South Carolina Press, 1981.

Creel, Margaret Washington. *"A Peculiar People": Slave Religion and Community Culture among the Gullahs.* New York: New York University Press, 1988.

Cripps, Thomas. *Slow Fade to Black: The Negro in American Film, 1900–1942.* New York: Oxford University Press, 1977.

Curry, Leonard P. *The Free Black in Urban America, 1800–1850: The Shadow of the Dream.* Chicago: University of Chicago Press, 1981.

Dain, Bruce. "Haiti and Egypt in Early Black Racial Discourse in the United States." *Slavery and Abolition* 14, no. 3 (1993): 139–61.

Daniel, Walter C. "W. E. B. Du Bois' First Efforts as a Playwright." *CLA Journal* 33, no. 4 (June 1990): 415–27.

Daniels, Douglas Henry. *Pioneer Urbanites: A Social and Cultural History of Black San Francisco.* Philadelphia: Temple University Press, 1980.

Davis, Michael. *The Image of Lincoln in the South.* Knoxville: University of Tennessee Press, 1971.

Davis, Susan G. *Parades and Power: Street Theatre in Nineteenth-Century Philadelphia.* Berkeley: University of California Press, 1988.

Davis, Thomas J. *A Rumor of Revolt: The "Great Negro Plot" in Colonial New York.* New York: Free Press, 1985; Amherst: University of Massachusetts Press, 1990.

Dearing, Mary R. *Veterans in Politics: The Story of the GAR.* Baton Rouge: Louisiana State University Press, 1952.

Dickerson, Dennis C. "William Fisher Dickerson: Northern Preacher, Southern Prelate." *Methodist History* 23, no. 3 (April 1985): 135–52.

Doyle, Ruby Wilkins. *A Richard Allen Celebration: Religious Plays and Pageants for All Age Groups.* Winona, Minn.: Apollo Books, 1985.

DuBois, Ellen Carol. *Feminism and Suffrage: The Emergence of an Independent Women's Movement in America, 1848–1869.* Ithaca: Cornell University Press, 1978.

Egerton, Douglas R. *Gabriel's Rebellion: The Virginia Slave Conspiracies of 1800 and 1802.* Chapel Hill: University of North Carolina Press, 1993.

Eliot, T. S. "Tradition and the Individual Talent." In *Selected Essays, 1917–1932,* 3–11. New York: Harcourt, Brace, 1932.

Ellison, Ralph. "Change the Joke and Slip the Yoke." In *Shadow and Act.* New York: Random House, 1964.

———. *Juneteenth: A Novel.* Ed. John F. Callahan. New York: Random House, 1999.

Engs, Robert Francis. *Freedom's First Generation: Black Hampton, Virginia, 1861–1890.* Philadelphia: University of Pennsylvania Press, 1979.

Erenberg, Lewis A. *Steppin' Out: New York Nightlife and the Transformation of American Culture, 1890–1930.* Westport, Conn.: Greenwood Press, 1981.

Fabre, Genevieve. "African-American Commemorative Celebrations in the Nineteenth Century." In *History and Memory in African-American Culture,* ed. Fabre and Robert O'Meally. New York: Oxford University Press, 1994.

Fabre, Genevieve, and Robert O'Meally, eds. *History and Memory in African American Culture.* New York: Oxford University Press, 1994.

Field, Phyllis F. *The Politics of Race in New York: The Struggle for Black Suffrage in the Civil War Era.* Ithaca: Cornell University Press, 1982.

Fields, Barbara Jeanne. *Slavery and Freedom on the Middle Ground: Maryland during the Nineteenth Century.* New Haven: Yale University Press, 1985.

Finkelman, Paul, ed. *His Soul Goes Marching On: Responses to John Brown and the Harpers Ferry Raid.* Charlottesville: University Press of Virginia, 1995.

Finnegan, Ruth. *Literacy and Orality: Studies in the Technology of Communication.* New York: Blackwell, 1988.

Foner, Eric. *Reconstruction: America's Unfinished Revolution, 1863–1877.* New York: Harper and Row, 1988.

Foner, Philip S. "Black Participation in the Centennial of 1876." *Negro History Bulletin* 39, no. 2 (February 1976): 533–38.

Foster, Frances Smith, ed. *Minnie's Sacrifice; Sowing and Reaping; Trial and Triumph: Three Rediscovered Novels by Frances E. W, Harper.* Boston: Beacon Press, 1994.

Franklin, John Hope. *The Emancipation Proclamation.* Garden City, N.Y.: Doubleday, 1963.

———. *From Slavery to Freedom: A History of Negro Americans.* 3rd ed. New York: Random House, 1967.

———. *George Washington Williams: A Biography.* Chicago: University of Chicago Press, 1985.

———. "On the Evolution of Scholarship in Afro-American History." In *The State of Afro-American History: Past, Present, and Future,* ed. Darlene Clark Hine. Baton Rouge: Louisiana State University Press, 1986.

Franklin, V. P. *Living Our Stories, Telling Our Truths: Autobiography and the Making of the African-American Intellectual Tradition.* New York: Scribner, 1995.

Fredrickson, George M. *The Inner Civil War: Northern Intellectuals and the Crisis of the Union.* New York: Harper, 1965.

Frey, Sylvia. *Water from the Rock: Black Resistance in a Revolutionary Age.* Princeton: Princeton University Press, 1991.

Gaines, Kevin Kelly. "Assimilationist Minstrelsy as Racial Uplift Ideology: James D. Corrothers's Literary Quest for Black Leadership." *American Quarterly* 45, no. 3 (September 1993): 341–68.

———. *Uplifting the Race: Black Leadership, Politics, and Culture since the Turn of the Century.* Chapel Hill: University of North Carolina Press, 1996.

———. "Uplifting the Race: Black Middle-Class Ideology in the Era of the New Negro, 1890–1935." Ph.D. diss., Brown University, 1991.

Gannon, Barbara A. "Sites of Memory, Sites of Glory: African-American Grand Army of the Republic Posts in Pennsylvania." In *Making and Remaking Pennsylvania's Civil War,* ed. William Blair and William Pencak, 165–87. University Park: Pennsylvania State University Press, 2001.

Gatewood, Willard B. *Aristocrats of Color: The Black Elite, 1880–1920.* Bloomington: Indiana University Press, 1990.

Genovese, Eugene D. *Roll, Jordan, Roll: The World the Slaves Made.* New York: Random House, 1974.

George, Carol V. R. *Segregated Sabbaths: Richard Allen and the Emergence of Independent Black Churches, 1760–1840.* New York: Oxford University Press, 1973.

———. "Widening the Circle: The Black Church and the Abolitionist Crusade, 1830–1860." In *Antislavery Reconsidered: New Perspectives on the Abolitionists,* ed. Lewis Perry and Michael Fellman. Baton Rouge: Louisiana State University Press, 1979.

Gilje, Paul. *The Road to Mobocracy: Popular Disorder in New York City, 1763–1834.* Chapel Hill: University of North Carolina Press, 1987.

Gillette, William. *The Right to Vote: Politics and the Passage of the Fifteenth Amendment.* Baltimore: Johns Hopkins University Press, 1969.

Gilmore, Glenda Elizabeth. *Gender and Jim Crow: Women and the Politics of White Supremacy in North Carolina, 1896–1920.* Chapel Hill: University of North Carolina Press, 1996.

Glassberg, David. *American Historical Pageantry: The Uses of Tradition in the Early Twentieth Century.* Chapel Hill: University of North Carolina Press, 1990.

Goldstein, Michael. "Preface to the Rise of Booker T. Washington: A View from New York City of the Demise of Independent Black Politics, 1889–1902." *Journal of Negro History* 62, no. 1 (1977): 81–99.

Graham, Leroy. *Baltimore: The Nineteenth-Century Black Capital.* Washington, D.C.: University Press of America, 1982.

Gravely, William B. "The Dialectic of Double-Consciousness in Black American Freedom Celebrations, 1808–1863." *Journal of Negro History* 67 (winter 1982): 302–17.

Green, Constance McLaughlin. *The Secret City: A History of Race Relations in the Nation's Capital.* Princeton: Princeton University Press, 1967.

Gregg, Robert. *Sparks from the Anvil of Oppression: Philadelphia's African Methodists and Southern Migrants, 1890–1940.* Philadelphia: Temple University Press, 1993.

Grover, Kathryn. *Make a Way Somehow: African-American Life in a Northern Community, 1790–1965.* Syracuse: Syracuse University Press, 1994.

Gupert, Betty Kaplan. *Early Black Bibliographies, 1863–1918.* New York: Garland Publishing, 1982.

Hall, Stephen G. "To Give a Faithful Account of the Race: History and Historical

Consciousness in the African American Community, 1827–1915." Ph.D. diss., Ohio State University, 1999.

Handelman, Don. *Models and Mirrors: Towards an Anthropology of Public Events.* Cambridge: Cambridge University Press, 1990.

Hanger, Kimberly S. *Bounded Lives, Bounded Places: Free Black Society in Colonial New Orleans, 1769–1803.* Durham, N.C.: Duke University Press, 1997.

Harding, Vincent. *There Is a River: The Black Struggle for Freedom in America.* New York: Random House, 1981.

Harlan, Louis R. *Booker T. Washington: The Wizard of Tuskegee, 1901–1915.* New York: Oxford University Press, 1983.

Harris, Neil, ed. *The Land of Contrasts, 1880–1901.* New York: George Braziller, 1970.

Harris, Robert L., Jr. "Daniel Murray and the *Encyclopedia of the Colored Race.*" *Phylon* 37, no. 3 (September 1976): 270–82.

Harris, William H. *The Harder We Run: Black Workers since the Civil War.* New York: Oxford University Press, 1982.

Halbwachs, Maurice. *The Collective Memory.* Trans. Francis J. Ditter and Vida Yazdi Ditter. New York: Harper and Row, 1980 [1950].

Hershberg, Theodore, ed. *Philadelphia: Space, Family, and Group Experience in the Nineteenth Century.* New York: Oxford University Press, 1981.

Higginbotham, Evelyn Brooks. *Righteous Discontent: The Women's Movement in the Black Baptist Church, 1880–1920.* Cambridge, Mass.: Harvard University Press, 1993.

Hildebrand, Reginald F. *The Times Were Strange and Stirring: Methodist Preachers and the Crisis of Emancipation.* Durham: Duke University Press, 1995.

Hine, Darlene Clark. *Hine Sight: Black Women and the Re-construction of American History.* Brooklyn: Carlson Publishing, 1994.

———, ed. *The State of Afro-American History: Past, Present, and Future.* Baton Rouge: Louisiana State University Press, 1986.

Hinks, Peter P. *To Awaken My Afflicted Brethren: David Walker and the Problem of Antebellum Slave Resistance.* University Park: Pennsylvania State University Press, 1997.

Hobsbawm, Eric. "Mass-Producing Traditions: Europe, 1870–1914." In *The Invention of Tradition,* ed. Hobsbawm and Terence Ranger, 263–307. Cambridge: Cambridge University Press, 1983.

———. *Nations and Nationalism since 1780: Programme, Myth, Reality.* Cambridge: Cambridge University Press, 1993.

Hobsbawm, Eric, and Terence Ranger, eds. *The Invention of Tradition.* Cambridge: Cambridge University Press, 1983.

Hodges, Graham Russell. *Root and Branch: African Americans in New York and East Jersey, 1613–1863.* Chapel Hill: University of North Carolina Press, 1999.

Holloway, Joseph E., ed. *Africanisms in American Culture*. Bloomington: Indiana University Press, 1990.

Horton, James Oliver. *Free People of Color: Inside the African American Community*. Washington, D.C.: Smithsonian Institution Press, 1993.

Horton, James Oliver, and Lois E. Horton. *Black Bostonians: Family Life and Community Struggle in the Antebellum North*. New York: Holmes and Meier, 1979.

———. *Hard Road to Freedom: The Story of African America*. New Brunswick, N.J.: Rutgers University Press, 2001.

———. *In Hope of Liberty: Culture, Community, and Protest among Northern Free Blacks, 1790–1860*. New York: Oxford University Press, 1997.

———. "Violence, Protest, and Identity: Black Manhood in Antebellum America." In James Oliver Horton, *Free People of Color: Inside the African American Community* (Washington, D.C., 1993), 80–97.

Howard-Pitney, David. "Calvin Chase's Washington *Bee* and Black Middle-Class Ideology, 1882–1900." *Journalism Quarterly* 63, no. 1 (1986): 89–97.

Hunt, Alfred N. *Haiti's Influence on Antebellum America: Slumbering Volcano in the Caribbean*. Baton Rouge: Louisiana State University Press, 1988.

Hutton, Patrick H. *History as an Art of Memory*. Hanover: University Press of New England, 1993.

Irwin-Zarecka, Iwona. *Frames of Remembrance: The Dynamics of Collective Memory*. New Brunswick, N.J.: Transaction Publishers, 1994.

Ives, Patricia Carter. "Giles Beecher Jackson, Director-General of the Negro Development and Exposition Company of the United States for the Jamestown Tercentenary Exposition of 1907." *Negro History Bulletin* 38 (December 1975).

Johnston, William M. *Celebrations: The Cult of Anniversaries in Europe and the United States Today*. New Brunswick, N.J.: Transaction Publishers, 1991.

Jones, Robert R. *The Afro-American Experience: A Cultural History through Emancipation*. New York: John Wiley and Sons, 1974.

Kachun, Mitch. "'Before the Eyes of All Nations': African-American Identity and Historical Memory at the Centennial Exposition of 1876." *Pennsylvania History* 65, no. 3 (summer 1998): 300–323.

———. "The Faith That the Dark Past Has Taught Us: African-American Commemorations in the North and West and the Construction of a Usable Past, 1808–1915." Ph.D. diss., Cornell University, 1997.

———. "The Shaping of a Public Biography: Richard Allen and the African Methodist Episcopal Church." In *Black Lives: Essays in African American Biography*, ed. James L. Conyers, 44–63. Armonk, N.Y.: M. E. Sharpe, 1999.

———. "'This Golden Burden of Affranchisement': Themes in African-American Celebrations of the Fifteenth Amendment." MS in the possession of the author.

Kammen, Michael. *Mystic Chords of Memory: The Transformation of Tradition in American Culture*. New York: Random House, 1991.

————. *A Season of Youth: The American Revolution and the Historical Imagination.* New York: Oxford University Press, 1978.

Kane, Sharyn, and Richard Keeton. *In Those Days: African-American Life near the Savannah River.* Harpers Ferry: National Park Service, 1994.

Kasson, John. *Amusing the Million: Coney Island at the Turn of the Century.* New York: Hill and Wang, 1978.

Kusmer, Kenneth. "Urban Black History at the Crossroads." *Journal of Urban History* 13, no. 4 (August 1987): 460–70.

Lamb, Daniel Smith. *Howard University Medical Department, Washington, D.C.: A Historical, Biographical, and Statistical Souvenir.* Washington, D.C.: Printed by R. Beresford, 1900.

Lane, Roger. *William Dorsey's Philadelphia and Ours: On the Past and Future of the Black City in America.* New York: Oxford University Press, 1991.

Lapp, Rudolph M. "Jeremiah B. Sanderson: Early California Negro Leader." *Journal of Negro History* 53, no. 3 (July 1968): 321–33.

Le Goff, Jacques. *History and Memory.* Trans. Steven Rendall and Elizabeth Claman. New York: Columbia University Press, 1992.

Levine, Lawrence W. *Black Culture and Black Consciousness: Afro-American Folk Thought from Slavery to Freedom.* New York: Oxford University Press, 1977.

————. "The New Negro and the Realities of Black Culture." In *The Unpredictable Past: Explorations in American Cultural History,* 86–106. New York: Oxford University Press, 1993.

Lewis, Bernard. *History: Remembered, Recovered, Invented.* Princeton: Princeton University Press, 1975.

Lewis, David Levering. *W. E. B. Du Bois: Biography of a Race, 1868–1919.* New York: Henry Holt, 1993.

Lipsitz, George. *Time Passages: Collective Memory and American Popular Culture.* Minneapolis: University of Minnesota Press, 1990.

Little, Lawrence S. *Disciples of Liberty: The African Methodist Episcopal Church in the Age of Imperialism, 1884–1916.* Knoxville: University of Tennessee Press, 2000.

Litwack, Leon F. *Been in the Storm So Long: The Aftermath of Slavery.* New York: Random House, 1979.

————. *North of Slavery: The Negro in the Free States, 1790–1860.* Chicago: University of Chicago Press, 1961.

————. *Trouble in Mind: Black Southerners in the Age of Jim Crow.* New York: Vintage Books, 1999.

Litwicki, Ellen M. *America's Public Holidays, 1865–1920.* Washington, D.C.: Smithsonian Institution Press, 2000.

Logan, Rayford W. *The Betrayal of the Negro: From Rutherford B. Hayes to Woodrow Wilson.* New York: Collier Books, 1965.

Lorini, Alessandra. "Public Rituals, Race Ideology, and the Transformation of Urban Culture: The Making of the New York African-American Community, 1825–1918." Ph.D. diss., Columbia University, 1991.

Lott, Eric. *Love and Theft: Blackface Minstrelsy and the American Working Class.* New York: Oxford University Press, 1993.

———. "Love and Theft: The Racial Unconscious of Blackface Minstrelsy." *Representations* 39 (summer 1992): 23–50.

———. "'The Seeming Counterfeit': Racial Politics and Early Blackface Minstrelsy." *American Quarterly* 43, no. 2 (June 1991): 223–54.

Lowenthal, David. *The Heritage Crusade and the Spoils of History.* Cambridge: Cambridge University Press, 1998.

———. *The Past Is a Foreign Country.* Cambridge: Cambridge University Press, 1985.

Lyman, Stanford. *Color, Culture, and Civilization: Race and Minority Issues in American Society.* Urbana: University of Illinois Press, 1994.

Mathews, Marcia M. *Richard Allen.* Baltimore: Helicon, 1963.

Matthews, Geraldine O. *Black American Writers, 1773–1949: A Bibliography and Union List.* Boston: G. K. Hall, 1975.

McConnell, Stuart. *Glorious Contentment: The Grand Army of the Republic, 1865–1900.* Chapel Hill: University of North Carolina Press, 1992.

McFeely, William S. *Frederick Douglass.* New York: Simon and Schuster, 1991.

McGerr, Michael E. *The Decline of Popular Politics: The American North, 1865–1928.* New York: Oxford University Press, 1986.

McKivigan, John R., and Jason H. Silverman. "Monarchial Liberty and Republican Slavery: West Indies Emancipation Celebrations in Upstate New York and Canada West." *Afro-Americans in New York Life and History* 10, no. 1 (1986): 7–18.

McLagan, Elizabeth. *A Peculiar Paradise: A History of Blacks in Oregon, 1788–1940.* Portland: Georgian Press, 1980.

McPherson, James M. *Battle Cry of Freedom: The Civil War Era.* New York: Oxford University Press, 1988.

———. "A House Divided: Historians Confront Disney's America." *OAH Newsletter* 22, no. 3 (August 1994).

———. *The Negro's Civil War: How American Blacks Felt and Acted during the War for the Union.* New York: Ballantine Books, 1991 [1965].

———. *The Struggle for Equality: Abolitionists and the Negro in the Civil War and Reconstruction.* Princeton: Princeton University Press, 1964.

Meier, August. *Negro Thought in America, 1880–1915.* Ann Arbor: University of Michigan Press, 1969.

Meier, August, and Elliott Rudwick. *Black History and the Historical Profession, 1915–1980.* Urbana: University of Illinois Press, 1986.

Melish, Joanne Pope. *Disowning Slavery: Gradual Emancipation and Race in New England, 1780–1860*. Ithaca: Cornell University Press, 1998.

Miller, Floyd J. *The Search for Black Nationality: Black Emigration and Colonization, 1787–1863*. Urbana.: University of Illinois Press, 1975.

Mitchell, Reid. *The Vacant Chair: The Northern Soldier Leaves Home*. New York: Oxford University Press, 1993.

Mjagkij, Nina, ed *Organizing Black America: An Encyclopedia of African American Associations*. New York and London: Garland, 2001.

Montgomery, William E. *Under Their Own Vine and Fig Tree: The African-American Church in the South, 1865–1900*. Baton Rouge: Louisiana State University Press, 1992.

Moore, Jacqueline M. *Leading the Race: The Transformation of the Black Elite in the Nation's Capital, 1880–1920*. Charlottesville and London: University Press of Virginia, 1999.

Morrison, Toni. *Jazz*. New York: Knopf, 1992.

Moses, Wilson Jeremiah. *Alexander Crummell: A Study of Civilization and Discontent*. Amherst: University of Massachusetts Press, 1992.

———. *The Golden Age of Black Nationalism, 1850–1925*. New York: Oxford University Press, 1978.

———. *The Wings of Ethiopia: Studies in African-American Life and Literature*. Ames: Iowa State University Press, 1990.

Moss, Alfred A., Jr. *The American Negro Academy: Voice of the Talented Tenth*. Baton Rouge: Louisiana State University Press, 1981.

Muraskin, William. *Middle-Class Blacks in a White Society: Prince Hall Freemasonry in America*. Berkeley: University of California Press, 1975.

Nagel, Paul C. *This Sacred Trust: American Nationality, 1798–1898*. New York: Oxford University Press, 1971.

Nasaw, David. *Going Out: The Rise and Fall of Public Amusements*. Cambridge, Mass.: Harvard University Press, 1993.

Nash, Gary B. *Forging Freedom: The Formation of Philadelphia's Black Community, 1720–1840*. Cambridge, Mass.: Harvard University Press, 1988.

———. *The Urban Crucible: Social Change, Political Consciousness, and the Origins of the American Revolution*. Cambridge, Mass.: Harvard University Press, 1979.

Nero, Charles Isadore. "'To Develop Our Manhood': Free Black Leadership and the Rhetoric of the New Orleans *Tribune*." Ph.D. diss., Indiana University, 1991.

"The New Emancipation." *AME Church Review* 29, no. 3 (January 1913): 260–64.

Newman, Simon P. *Parades and the Politics of the Street: Festive Culture in the Early American Republic*. Philadelphia: University of Pennsylvania Press, 1997.

Nora, Pierre. "Between History and Memory: *Les Lieux de Memoire*." *Representations* 26 (spring 1989): 7–25.

Ownby, Ted, ed. *Black and White Cultural Interaction in the Antebellum South.* Jackson: University of Mississippi Press, 1993.

Painter, Nell Irvin. *Exodusters: Black Migration to Kansas after Reconstruction.* Lawrence: University of Kansas Press, 1976.

Patterson, John S. "A Patriotic Landscape: Gettysburg, 1863–1913." *Prospects* 7 (1982): 315–33.

Patton, Adell, Jr. "The 'Back to Africa' Movement in Arkansas." *Arkansas Historical Quarterly* 51, no. 2 (summer 1992): 164–77.

Pease, Jane H., and William H. Pease. *They Who Would Be Free: Blacks' Search for Freedom, 1830–1861.* New York: Atheneum, 1974.

Peretti, Burton W. *The Creation of Jazz: Music, Race, and Culture in Urban America.* Urbana: University of Illinois Press, 1992.

Peterson, Merrill D. *Lincoln in American Memory.* New York: Oxford University Press, 1994.

Phillips, Christopher. *Freedom's Port: The African American Community of Baltimore, 1790–1860.* Urbana: University of Illinois Press, 1997.

Piersen, William D. *Black Legacy: America's Hidden Heritage.* Amherst: University of Massachusetts Press, 1993.

———. *Black Yankees: The Development of an Afro-American Subculture in Eighteenth-Century New England.* Amherst: University of Massachusetts Press, 1988.

Preston, Dickson J. *Young Frederick Douglass: The Maryland Years.* Baltimore: Johns Hopkins University Press, 1980.

Quarles, Benjamin. *Allies for Freedom: Blacks and John Brown.* New York: Oxford University Press, 1974.

———. "Antebellum Free Blacks and the 'Spirit of '76.'" *Journal of Negro History* 61 (July 1976): 229–42.

———. *Black Abolitionists.* New York: Oxford University Press, 1969.

———. *Blacks on John Brown.* Urbana: University of Illinois Press, 1972.

———. *The Negro in the American Revolution.* Chapel Hill: Institute of Early American History and Culture, Williamsburg, Va., by University of North Carolina Press, 1961.

Raboteau, Albert J. *A Fire in the Bones: Reflections on African-American Religious History.* Boston: Beacon Press, 1995.

Rael, Patrick ."Besieged by Freedom's Army: Antislavery Celebrations and Black Activism in the Antebellum North." Paper presented at the Organization of American Historians Annual Meeting, St. Louis, March 2000.

———. *Black Identity and Black Protest in the Antebellum North.* Chapel Hill: University of North Carolina Press, 2001.

Rearick, Charles. "Festivals and Politics: The Michelet Centennial of 1898." *Historians in Politics* 1 (1974): 59–78.

———. "Festivals in Modern France: The Experience of the Third Republic." *Journal of Contemporary History* 12 (1977): 435–60.

Redding, J. Saunders. *On Being Negro in America*. New York: Bobbs-Merrill, 1951.

———. *Troubled in Mind: J. Saunders Redding's Early Years in Wilmington, Delaware*. Wilmington: Delaware Heritage Press, 1991.

Reed, Harry. *Platform for Change: The Foundations of the Northern Free Black Community, 1775–1865*. East Lansing: Michigan State University Press, 1994.

Ritchie, Andrew. *Major Taylor: The Extraordinary Career of a Champion Bicycle Racer*. San Francisco: Bicycle Books, 1988.

Rodgers, Daniel T. *The Work Ethic in Industrial America, 1850–1920*. Chicago: University of Chicago Press, 1978.

Rosenzweig, Roy. *Eight Hours for What We Will: Workers and Leisure in an Industrial City, 1870–1920*. Cambridge: Cambridge University Press, 1983.

Rosenzweig, Roy, and David Thelen. *The Presence of the Past: Popular Uses of History in Everyday Life*. New York: Columbia University Press, 1998.

Ryan, Dennis P. "The Crispus Attucks Monument Controversy of 1887." *Negro History Bulletin* 40 (January 1977): 656–57.

Ryan, Mary. "The American Parade: Representations of Nineteenth-Century Social Order." In *The New Cultural History*, ed. Lynn Hunt, 131–53. Berkeley: University of California Press, 1989.

Rydell, Robert W. *All the World's a Fair: Visions of Empire at American International Expositions, 1876–1916*. Chicago: University of Chicago Press, 1984.

———. *The Books of the Fairs: Materials about World's Fairs, 1834–1916, in the Smithsonian Institution Libraries*. Chicago: American Library Association, 1992.

Salem, Dorothy C. *African American Women: A Biographical Dictionary*. New York: Garland Publishing, 1993.

Salvatore, Nick. *We All Got History: The Memory Books of Amos Webber*. New York: Times Books, 1996.

———. "Two Tales of a City: Nineteenth-Century Black Philadelphia." *Dissent* (spring 1991): 227–35.

Samuels, Raphael. *Theatres of Memory*. Vol. 1, *Past and Present in Contemporary Culture*. London: Verso, 1994.

Savage, Kirk. *Standing Soldiers, Kneeling Slaves: Race, War, and Monument in Nineteenth-Century America*. Princeton: Princeton University Press, 1997.

Schafer, William John, and Johannes Riedel. *The Art of Ragtime: Form and Meaning of an Original Black American Art*. Baton Rouge: Louisiana State University Press, 1973.

Schmidt, Lewis G. *The Civil War in Florida*. Vol. 3, *Florida's Keys and Fevers*. Allentown, Pa.: Lewis G. Schmidt, 1992.

———. "From Slavery to Freedom: Sandy Cornish and Lillah Cornish." MS in the author's possession.

Schwartz, Barry. "The Social Context of Commemoration: A Study in Collective Memory." *Social Forces* 61 (1982): 374–402.

Seraile, William. *Voice of Dissent: Theophilus Gould Steward (1843–1924) and Black America*. Brooklyn: Carlson Publishing, 1991.

Sernett, Milton C. *Black Religion and American Evangelism: White Protestants, Plantation Missions, and the Flowering of Negro Christianity, 1787–1865*. Metuchen, N.J.: Scarecrow Press, 1975.

Shaw, Arnold. *Black Popular Music in America: From the Spirituals, Minstrels, and Ragtime to Soul, Disco, and Hip-Hop*. New York: Schirmer Books, 1986.

Shaw, Harry B., ed. *Perspectives of Black Popular Culture*. Bowling Green: Bowling Green State University Popular Press, 1990.

Shelton, Robert S. "A Modified Crime: The Apprenticeship System in St. Kitts." *Slavery and Abolition* 16, no. 3 (1995): 331–45.

Sidbury, James. "Saint Domingue in Virginia: Ideology, Local Meanings, and Resistance to Slavery, 1790–1800." *Journal of Southern History* 63, no. 3 (1997): 531–52.

Silber, Nina. *The Romance of Reunion: Northerners and the South, 1865–1900*. Chapel Hill: University of North Carolina Press, 1993.

Sinnette, Elinor Des Verney. *Arthur Alfonso Schomburg: Black Bibliophile and Collector, a Biography*. Detroit: Wayne State University Press, 1989.

Smith, Jessie Carney, and Carrell Peterson Horton, eds. *Historical Statistics of Black America*. Vol. 2. Detroit: Gale Publishing, 1995.

Smith, John David. *An Old Creed for the New South: Proslavery Ideology and Historiography, 1865–1918*. Westport, Conn.: Greenwood Press, 1985.

———, ed. *Anti-Black Thought, 1863–1925*. New York: Garland Publishing, 1993.

Snyder, Robert W. *The Voice of the City: Vaudeville and Popular Culture in New York*. New York: Oxford University Press, 1989.

Sobel, Mechal. *Trabelin' On: The Slave Journey to an Afro-Baptist Faith*. Westport, Conn.: Greenwood Press, 1979.

———. *The World They Made Together: Black and White Values in Eighteenth-Century Virginia*. Princeton: Princeton University Press, 1987.

Spady, James. "The Afro-American Historical Society: The Nucleus of Black Bibliophiles, 1898–1923." *Negro History Bulletin* 37 (July 1974): 254–57.

Stansell, Christine. *City of Women: Sex and Class in New York, 1789–1860*. Urbana and Chicago: University of Illinois Press, 1986.

Stott, Richard B. *Workers in the Metropolis: Class, Ethnicity, and Youth in Antebellum New York City*. Ithaca and London: Cornell University Press, 1990.

Stuckey, Sterling. *Slave Culture: Nationalist Theory and the Foundations of Black America*. New York: Oxford University Press, 1987.

Suggs, Henry Lewis, ed. *The Black Press in the South, 1865–1979*. Westport, Conn.: Greenwood Press, 1983.

Sundquist, Eric J. *To Wake the Nations: Race in the Making of American Literature.* Cambridge, Mass.: Harvard University Press, Belknap Press, 1993.

Sweet, Leonard I. *Black Images of America, 1784–1870.* New York: Norton, 1976.

———. "The Fourth of July and Black Americans in the Nineteenth Century: Northern Leadership Opinion within the Context of the Black Experience." *Journal of Negro History* 61 (July 1976): 256–75.

Swift, David. *Black Prophets of Justice: Activist Clergy before the Civil War.* Baton Rouge: Louisiana State University Press, 1989.

Thomas, Lamont D. *Paul Cuffe: Black Entrepreneur and Activist.* Urbana: University of Illinois Press, 1988.

Thornbrough, Emma Lou. "American Negro Newspapers, 1880–1914." *Business History Review* 40, no. 4 (winter 1966): 467–90.

———. "The National Afro-American League, 1887–1908." *Journal of Southern History* 27, no. 4 (November 1961): 494–512.

———. *T. Thomas Fortune: Militant Journalist.* Chicago: University of Chicago Press, 1972.

Toll, Robert C. *Blacking Up: The Minstrel Show in Nineteenth-Century America.* New York: Oxford University Press, 1974.

Tolnay, Stewart E., and E. M. Beck, *A Festival of Violence: An Analysis of Southern Lynchings, 1882–1930.* Urbana: University of Illinois Press, 1995.

Travers, Len. *Celebrating the Fourth: Independence Day and the Rites of Nationalism in the Early Republic.* Amherst: University of Massachusetts Press, 1997.

Tripp, Bernell. *Origins of the Black Press, 1827–1847.* Northport, Ala.: Vision Press, 1992.

Trotter, Joe William. *The Great Migration in Historical Perspective: New Dimensions of Race, Class, and Gender.* Bloomington: Indiana University Press, 1991.

Turner, Victor, ed. *Celebration: Studies in Festivity and Ritual.* Washington, D.C.: Smithsonian Institution Press, 1982.

VanDeburg, William L. "The Battleground of Historical Memory: Creating Alternative Culture Heroes in Postbellum America." *Journal of Popular Culture* 20, no. 1 (1986): 49–62.

Vaz, Kim Marie, ed. *Black Women in America.* Thousand Oaks: Sage Publications, 1995.

Vorenberg, Michael. *Final Freedom: The Civil War, the Abolition of Slavery, and the Thirteenth Amendment.* Cambridge and New York: Cambridge University Press, 2001.

Wachtel, Nathan. "Memory and History: An Introduction." *History and Anthropology* 2 (1986): 210–11.

Waldstreicher, David. *In the Midst of Perpetual Fetes: The Making of American Nationalism, 1776–1820.* Chapel Hill: University of North Carolina Press, 1997.

Walker, Clarence E. *A Rock in a Weary Land: The African Methodist Episcopal Church during the Civil War and Reconstruction.* Baton Rouge: Louisiana State University Press, 1982.

Walker, Robbie Jean, ed. *The Rhetoric of Struggle: Public Address by African American Women.* New York: Garland Publishing, 1992.

"Washington, D.C.: Civic, Literary, and Mutual Aid Associations." In *Organizing Black America: An Encyclopedia of African American Associations,* ed. Nina Mjagkij, 691–94. New York and London, 2001.

Wesley, Charles H. "Creating and Maintaining an Historical Tradition." *Journal of Negro History* 49 (January 1964).

———. "Racial Historical Societies and the American Heritage." *Journal of Negro History* 37 (January 1952): 11–35.

———. *Richard Allen, Apostle of Freedom.* Washington, D.C.: Associated Publishers, 1935.

White, Richard. "Civil Rights Agitation: Emancipation Days in Central New York in the 1880s." *Journal of Negro History* 78 (winter 1993): 16–24.

White, Shane. "The Death of James Johnson." *American Quarterly* 51, no. 4 (December 1999): 753–95.

———. "'It Was a Proud Day': African Americans, Festivals, and Parades in the North, 1741–1834." *Journal of American History* 81, no. 1 (June 1994): 13–50.

———. "Pinkster: Afro-Dutch Syncretization in New York City and the Hudson Valley." *Journal of American Folklore* 102, no. 403 (January–March 1989): 68–75.

White, Shane, and Graham J. White. *Stylin': African American Expressive Culture, from Its Beginnings to the Zoot Suit.* Ithaca: Cornell University Press, 1998.

Wiggins, William, Jr. *O Freedom! Afro-American Emancipation Celebrations.* Knoxville: University of Tennessee Press, 1987.

———. "From Galveston to Washington: Charting Juneteenth's Freedom Trail." In *Jubilation! African American Celebrations in the Southeast,* ed. Wiggins and Douglas DeNatale, 61–67. Columbia: McKissick Museum, University of South Carolina, 1993.

Wiggins, William, Jr., and Douglas DeNatale, eds. *Jubilation! African American Celebrations in the Southeast.* Columbia: McKissick Museum, University of South Carolina, 1993.

Wilentz, Sean. "Artisan Republican Festivals and the Rise of Class Conflict in New York City, 1788–1837." In *Working Class America: Essays on Labor, Community, and American Society,* ed. Michael H. Frisch and Daniel J. Walkowitz. Urbana: University of Illinois Press, 1983.

Williams-Myers, A. J. "Pinkster Carnival: Africanisms in the Hudson River Valley." *Afro-Americans in New York Life and History* 9, no. 1 (January 1985): 7–17.

Wilson, Benjamin C. *The Rural Black Heritage between Chicago and Detroit, 1850–1929: A Photograph Album and Random Thoughts.* Kalamazoo: Western Michigan University Press, 1985.

Winch, Julie. *Philadelphia's Black Elite: Activism, Accommodation, and the Struggle for Autonomy, 1787–1848.* Philadelphia: Temple University Press, 1988.

Woll, Allen. *Black Musical Theatre: From Coontown to Dreamgirls.* Baton Rouge: Louisiana State University Press, 1989.

Wolseley, Roland E. *The Black Press, U.S.A.* 2nd ed. Ames: Iowa State University Press, 1990.

Wood, Gordon S. *The Radicalism of the American Revolution.* New York: Random House, 1992.

Yacovone, Donald. "The Transformation of the Black Temperance Movement, 1827–1854: An Interpretation." *Journal of the Early Republic* 8, no. 3 (1988): 281–97.

Zilversmit, Arthur. *The First Emancipation: The Abolition of Slavery in the North.* Chicago: University of Chicago Press, 1967.

INDEX

Abbott, Robert S., 160, 252
abolitionists: British, 32, 123; interactions between white and black, 61, 93–94; white American, 32, 45, 123
acculturation, 20–21, 36–37
Adams, John, 22, 24, 34
Aesop, 152
Africa: collective memory of, 30–33, 40, 49, 52–53, 69, 90–91, 113, 126, 151–52, 161–63, 167, 169, 172–74, 180, 249; cultural influence of, 17, 20, 22, 39, 54, 263n. 2, 264n. 13, 267n. 37, 268n. 43; negative associations of, 11, 54, 151, 180
African Abolition Society, 41
African Americans: class and cultural divisions among, 5, 10, 36–39, 43–53, 100–101, 177–78, 183–84, 210–11, 213–14, 218–21, 223–25, 227–31, 237–39, 244–48, 269n. 61; collective identity of, 5–8, 13–15, 27–28, 40, 44, 46, 49–50, 64–65, 88–91, 113, 141, 150–52, 161–63, 239–40, 255–57, 262n. 9; conflicts among, 3, 8, 34–39, 214–32,

248–52; historical consciousness of, 6–15, 20, 28, 30, 32, 34, 39–41, 69–70, 87–91, 151–55, 158–74, 255–60; leadership, 4–9, 12, 61–62, 64–65, 185, 216–17, 221, 225–26, 230–31, 235–36, 245–47, 253, 257, 276n. 73; military service of, 32, 69–70, 110–11, 119, 125, 154–58, 162, 169; nativism of, 188–89; organizations and institutions, 4–5, 19, 35–36, 38, 50–52, 68, 94, 115, 236; partisan affiliations of, 35, 181, 189–92, 137, 203–4, 211, 216–17, 266–67n. 35; patriotism of, 7, 32, 69–70, 110, 125, 155, 162–64, 187–89; public behavior of, 17–19, 34–36, 44–49, 64–65, 105–6, 111–12, 126, 185, 208–10, 216–31, 237–39, 244–47, fig. 7; race heroes, 7, 69–70, 89, 91–93, 113, 151–55, 158–59, 161–67, 171, 205, 289n. 43, figs. 12, 13, 14; racial destiny of, 113, 115; racist characterizations of, 6, 27, 75, 102, 172; transnational perspective of, 113–14, 125; and veterans' organizations, 154, 156–

ML   4/09